DIFFICULT CHOICES

DIFFICULT CHOICES

Taiwan's Quest for Security and the Good Life

Richard C. Bush

BROOKINGS INSTITUTION PRESS

Washington, D.C.

Library of Congress Control Number: 2021932506
ISBN 9780815738336 (pbk)
ISBN 9780815738343 (ebook)

9 8 7 6 5 4 3 2 1

Typeset in Garamond Premier Pro

Composition by Elliott Beard

To the memory of Alan Demuth Romberg (1938–2018)

Mentor, colleague, and friend

Senator John McCain's Last Senate Speech*

[Senate debates] are more partisan, more tribal more of the time than any other time I remember. Our deliberations can still be important and useful, but I think we'd all agree they haven't been overburdened by greatness lately. And right now they aren't producing much for the American people. . . .

I hope we can again rely on humility, on our need to cooperate, on our dependence on each other to learn how to trust each other again and by so doing better serve the people who elected us. Stop listening to the bombastic loudmouths on the radio and television and the Internet. To hell with them. They don't want anything done for the public good. Our incapacity is their livelihood.

Let's trust each other. Let's return to regular order. We've been spinning our wheels on too many important issues because we keep trying to find a way to win without help from across the aisle. That's an approach that's been employed by both sides, mandating legislation from the top down, without any support from the other side, with all the parliamentary maneuvers that requires. . . .

What have we to lose by trying to work together to find those solutions? We're not getting much done apart. I don't think any of us feels very proud of our incapacity. Merely preventing your political opponents from doing what they want isn't the most inspiring work. There's greater satisfaction in respecting our differences, but not letting them prevent agreements that don't require abandonment of core principles, agreements made in good faith that help improve lives and protect the American people.

American Health Care Act of 2017; *Congressional Record*, vol. 163, no. 125 (U.S. Senate, July 25, 2017), statement of Senator John McCain.

Contents

Acknowledgments

As with every author, I accumulated a number of debts in doing the research and writing of this book—debts that can never be paid. The least that I can do is express my gratitude to all the people who assisted me and hope that I do not leave too many people out or make invidious distinctions. Of course, any remaining errors and misinterpretations are my responsibility alone.

First of all, I deeply grateful to the Smith Richardson Foundation for its generous grant funding the project that produced this book. The confidence that Marin Strmecki and Allan Song have shown in me and my scholarly work over the years means a lot to me and to Brookings.

I have benefited greatly from the insights and friendship of scholar colleagues in the Center for East Asia Policy Studies and the John L. Thornton China Center: Mireya Solis, Cheng Li, Jung Pak, Jonathan Stromseth, Lindsey Ford, David Dollar, Ryan Hass, Rush Doshi, and Jamie Horsley (Rush and Jamie were particularly helpful). Stephen Tan, who heads Taiwan's Cross-Strait Policy Association, was a visiting scholar with the Center for East Asia Policy Studies during much of the time I worked on this book, and I learned a lot from him. Elisa Glaser, Miguel Viera, and Jennifer Mason ably managed the administrative side of the project. Through its duration, I was lucky to have three very able research assistants: Maeve Whelan-Wuest, Jasmine Zhao, and Adrien Chorn. Adrien had the tedious task of copyediting successive versions of the manuscript, but he performed the task well. Interns at the two centers kindly helped me on specific research tasks: Konstantin Burudshiew, Ethan Jewell, Huang Tianlei, Xu Qiansheng, and Zhang Xinyue.

The Foreign Policy Program at Brookings, of which the East Asia and China Centers are a part, provided a collegial environment for my research and writing. I am particularly grateful to Bruce Jones, who was program director when I began the project, and Suzanne Maloney, who was director at the end. Mike O'Hanlon, our director of research, has been a constant source of encouragement. My colleagues provided a number of useful suggestions at a session where I presented the ideas at the core of this book. Daniel Byman, Brian Reeves, Amanda Sloat, Constanze Stelzenmüller, and Tamara Wittes provided useful answers to specific questions. Samantha Gross kindly reviewed chapter 5 and made a number of suggestions for improvement. Although retired, Jeff Bader and Jonathan Pollack continue to be sources of guidance.

At Brookings more broadly, I am grateful to the staff of the library, and particularly to Sarah Chilton and Laura Mooney, who cheerfully tracked down my every research request. William Finan and his team at the Brookings Institution Press worked hard to turn my manuscript into a real book. In that process, two external, anonymous reviewers provided a wealth of valuable suggestions.

Beyond Brookings, there were a number of people who have offered stimulating insights and answers to specific questions. I have learned a lot over the years from the community of China and Taiwan specialists, from Taiwan's cadre of very talented political scientists, and from many other friends and colleagues. To name them all would create a very long list, but I would be remiss if I did not mention the following: Nathan Batto, Nelson Chang An-ping, Charles Chen I-hsin, Chen Fang-yu, Janice Chen, Brent Christensen, Chu Yun-han, Jacques deLisle, Larry Diamond, Lauren Dickey, Michael Fonte, Bonnie Glaser, Timothy Heath, James Heller, Ho Ming-sho, Ho Szu-yin, Hu Lingwei, Huang Kwei-bo, Huang Sheng-Feng, A. J. Huang, Huang Ching-lung, Tracy Huang, Alastair Iain Johnston, David Keegan, Lin Cheng-wei, Chris Lin, Lin Fei-fan, Jared Lin, June Lin, Syaru Shirley Lin, Lin Ying-yu, Lung Ying-tai, Ma Ying-jeou, James Moriarty, Kevin Nealer, John Norris, Peng Fu-jung, Shelley Rigger, Su Chi, Jonathan Sullivan, Gunter Schubert, Jonathan Sullivan, Kharis Templeman, Tien Hung-mao, Tsai Gwo-yu, Yu Ching-hsin, Yu Donghui, and Zhang Nianchi. In addition, I would like to express my appreciation to the staffs of the Asian Barometer Survey, the Election Study Center of National Chengchi University, the Taiwan's Election and Democratization Survey, the Taiwan National Security Survey, and the

Taiwan Social Change Survey for giving me access to their useful survey data. I dedicate *Difficult Choices* to my dear friend, Alan Romberg, from whom I learned a lot but who passed away in 2018.

Most of all, I wish to express my profound gratitude to my family for their sustained support during my professional career, and especially to my wife, Marty, for standing by me for more than five decades.

Notes on Terminology

When it comes to rendering proper names, Taiwan is something of a termi-nological jumble. When romanizing place names and the names of individu-als, the Kuomintang regime generally used Wade-Giles system for standard or Mandarin Chinese, which was developed by Westerners in the nineteenth century. Thus the romanization for the man who served as president from 1978 to 1988 is Chiang Ching-kuo. The system that was definitely not used was the pinyin system developed in the People's Republic of China ("Com-munist China"), which has been used worldwide since around 1980. But there were Taiwan exceptions to traditional use of Wade-Giles. The romanized name for Chiang Ching-kuo's father and predecessor as president is Chiang Kai-shek (Chiang Chieh-shih in Wade Giles and Jiang Jieshi in pinyin). The founder of the Kuomintang is usually written Sun Yat-sen (Sun I-hsien in Wade-Giles and Sun Yixian in pinyin).

The exceptions grew as time went on. Individuals chose to romanize their names according to their own preferences. For example, the names of the current and previous president are written Tsai Ing-wen and Ma Ying-jeou, which are variants of the Wade-Giles system. As Taiwanese consciousness grew in the 1990s and thereafter, many people romanized their names the way they sounded in the Taiwanese or Southern Fujianese dialect, and not in Mandarin. Street signs in cities were rendered more phonetically than the not-so-phonetic Wade-Giles system.

In this book, I take an eclectic approach when it comes to personal and place names. For Taiwan residents, I render their names as they romanize them (mainly the Wade-Giles form unless an individual does it differently). For place names, I use the forms used in Taiwan since the Kuomintang regime moved there in 1949. I use the pinyin form for the names of people and places in the PRC and for non-proper nouns, such as "nation" or "country." In footnotes, I use pinyin except for names of Taiwan individuals, where I use their preferred rendering.

The issue of terminology is more fraught when it comes to the names given to political entities. Substantive issues of international law are at play, and people use the same proper noun to mean different things (often without knowing it). As I note in chapter 10, the terminological confusion is even greater than in English.

The problem starts with the word "China." In normal usage, the word refers to the territory controlled by the government of the People's Republic of China (PRC). But there is also the Republic of China (ROC), which was founded in 1912 and remains to this day the formal name of the government on Taiwan. Similarly, the word "Chinese" sometimes refers to ethnic Chinese people, including those on Taiwan; at other times to citizens of the People's Republic of China; and at yet other times to the government of the PRC ("the Chinese position").

International law offers some clarification. The key components of the international system are states. They are the members of the global club, and, among other things, members of organizations like the United Nations. One of those states, as recognized by other states, is China. As explained in later chapters, there is no state known and recognized as Taiwan, even though some in Taiwan badly want there to be.

But the state "China" should be distinguished from the government that represents China, and indeed, two governments claimed to represent China internationally after 1949: the government of the ROC on Taiwan and the government of the PRC, which has jurisdiction over what is sometimes called mainland China. Their rivalry is similar to the conflicts in medieval and early-modern England over who was the rightful monarch (for example, between the House of Lancaster and the House of York before 1485). The point here is that England did not cease to exist internationally just because there was a fight over who was the sovereign domestically. Strictly speaking, therefore, the word "China" does not mean the same thing as the PRC or the ROC, and I avoid conflating the two.

Thus in the parts of this book that touch on political relations between the two sides of the Taiwan Strait (everything besides chapters 2 through 6), I refer to the entity on the mainland side of the Strait as the PRC or Beijing or mainland China and the island on the other side as Taiwan or Taipei. In chapters 2 through 6, which concern purely domestic matters in Taiwan, I simply refer to the PRC as China.

One reason to maintain this distinction is the complicated issue of territory, specifically whether the geographic entity of Taiwan is part of the sovereign territory of the state China. That question is debated on Taiwan, and some people answer the question by saying that the island has never been part of the PRC and believe that therefore Taiwan is not a part of China. It is true that Taiwan has never been under the jurisdiction of the PRC when it comes to government and administration. But that is not the same as saying that Taiwan is not a part of China.

Finally, there is the term "Taiwanese." The commonsense meaning is anyone who lives in Taiwan or comes from there. Yet the more precise usage would limit the description to those residents of the island whose families migrated from southeast China into the early twentieth century. They are often known as "native Taiwanese." The word "mainlander," with which "Taiwanese" is contrasted, is usually applied to those people whose families came to Taiwan after 1945, when the ROC government took control of Taiwan from the Japanese, who had ruled it since 1895. The deep political cleavage between mainlanders and Taiwanese that was formed in the late 1940s has been attenuated over time, but the distinction still exists. To use the word "Taiwanese" in its commonsense connotation thus incorporates mainlanders in the term even though it might not be appropriate. Therefore, when I use the word "Taiwanese," I am referring to the native Taiwanese. Otherwise, I substitute the word "Taiwan" as an adjective ("Taiwan people," "Taiwan companies") when the mainlander-Taiwanese cleavage is relevant.

DIFFICULT CHOICES

1

Introduction

Taiwan has never had it easy. It is a relatively small place with little in the way of natural resources. Its size is slightly more than that of Maryland and the District of Columbia combined, somewhat less than Switzerland's, and about the same as Hainan Island, one of the smaller provincial-level units of the People's Republic of China (PRC). Its population is about 23 million people, which is 2 million more than the state of Florida, 2 million less than Australia, and about the same as Shanghai Municipality. With these limitations, it has never had the option to build a robust military, for example.

In addition, Taiwan has some large and sometimes predatory neighbors. For more than three centuries, successive governments of China have believed that controlling or dominating Taiwan—which lies ninety miles across the Taiwan Strait at the narrowest points—contributes to the security of China. The first was the imperial Qing dynasty in the late seventeenth century. The most recent is the PRC in the twenty-first century. Japan took Taiwan as its first colony in 1895 and ruled it for fifty years. The principal reason the island[1] has been so sought after is its strategic value: it is a middle link in the Asia-Pacific's first island chain, which runs from Japan to Australia and defines the security geography of East Asia. Since World War II, many American strategists have also regarded the first island chain as the United States' optimal security perimeter in the Pacific, demonstrating their understanding of Taiwan's strategic geography.[2]

In the 1950s, Taiwan's leaders developed a grand strategy—or more pre-

1

cisely, a survival strategy—to cope with the twin problems of the island's small size and its dangerous neighborhood. To ensure security, they sought and received the protection of the United States. The relationship that developed was complicated and fraught with uncertainty for each party, but it has lasted for seventy years. To foster internal stability and encourage popular support for the regime, the government embarked on a program of export-led industrialization. That too succeeded beyond all expectations and over time fostered "the good life" for most of the island's residents. In the 1980s, there was a decision to move gradually from the authoritarian regime that had been in place since the late 1940s to a full and now lively democracy. That transition also had a strategic impact, if not a strategic motivation.

Economy and Society: Success and Its Effects

Socially and economically, Taiwan's strategy was a huge success, as figures from the CIA's *World Factbook* and other sources delineate:

- In 2016 GDP (at purchasing power parity) per capita was US$47,800, ranking thirtieth in the world. (Taiwan's nominal GDP per capita was US$22,497 for 2016, but its global ranking was probably similar).[3]

- In 2020 life expectancy at birth is 80.6 years (43rd).

- Only 1.5 percent of the population lived below the poverty line in 2012 (the last year for which data is available).

- The population growth rate in 2020 was only 0.1 percent (187th).

- The urban share of the population is 77.5 percent (45th).[4]

- The infant mortality rate is 4.3 deaths per 1,000 live births (187th).

- In 2016 agriculture contributed only 1.8 percent to GDP; industry accounted for 36.1 percent, and services 62.1 percent.

- Of the labor force, 59.2 percent works in the service sector, 35.9 percent in the industrial sector, and 4.9 percent in agriculture.

- Like other advanced economies, the rate of GDP growth has slowed to the range of 1–5 percent.[5] The unemployment rate has risen in the past decade to around 3–5 percent after being 1–3 percent in the 1990s.[6]

- Virtually the entire population—98.5 percent—is literate. Around 20 percent of the population are in school at any one time, and more than 5 percent of the population (95 percent of secondary school graduates) attend an institution of higher learning.[7] Around 44.5 percent of the population have attended tertiary educational institutions.[8]

- There are 124 mobile telephone subscriptions for every 100 persons (43rd).
- There are five television networks and 171 radio stations islandwide.
- Eighty-eight percent of the population are Internet users (33rd).
- Facebook's penetration of Taiwan is at the top of its presence in Asian markets.[9]

Yet like other advanced economies, Taiwan in recent years has had to cope with the consequences of its past success. Real GDP growth has gradually declined, from 9.0 percent in 1983 to 8.5 percent in 1993, 6.9 percent in 2003, 6.0 percent in 2013, and 5.5 percent in 2018.[10] The island's best companies continue to perform well, particularly those in the computer and information technology sector, but for others growth is sluggish. Moreover, not all residents of Taiwan are benefiting from Taiwan's growing prosperity and enjoy an upper-middle-class or upper-class lifestyle. Indeed, in recent decades, there has been a trend toward greater inequality. Regarding income, the highest quintile's average disposable household income in 1996 was 5.38 times that of the lowest. In 2010 it was 6.06 times. The Gini coefficient, a statistical measure of distribution often used to gauge economic inequality, was 0.317 in 1996 and 0.338 in 2015.[11]

The large number of high school graduates attending tertiary education institutions (seventy universities and eighty-seven technical colleges) may seem impressive, but it belies some problems. There is a growing consensus that Taiwan actually has too many universities. Some universities were built for political reasons, rather than for the needs of Taiwan's labor force. As a result, there is a mismatch between the number of school places and the number of students, as well as between the skills of college graduates and the availability of jobs. The unemployment rate for university graduates is 5.1 percent, which is higher than the average for the whole workforce (less than 4 percent).[12] Moreover, intense competition to get into the best universities fosters a contest to get into the best high schools, and so on. In this competition, the already well-off have a built-in advantage in passing opportunities along to their children.

Inequality is also serious in the availability of residential housing. The first fifteen years of the twenty-first century saw a rapid increase in the house price index, from 100 to more than 300, until the government took steps to stabilize prices. The problem was particularly acute in Taipei City, where the house price–to-income ratio doubled between 2004 and 2014.[13] Like other major metropolitan areas around the world, this run-up in property prices hits young adults the hardest and fosters the fear that they will not be able to achieve the same standard of living as their parents have. According to one estimate, the prospective buyer of an average-price apartment in Taipei would have to save more than fifteen years of income to make the purchase without leverage. In Taiwan as a whole, household indebtedness as a percentage of GDP has exceeded 80 percent since 2004.[14]

Demography creates its own kind of inequality in Taiwan, which has an aged society and a decreasing population growth rate. The population estimate for mid-2016 was 23.4 million people, which is about twice the figure in 1965 and 4 million more than that for 1985. And yet the population growth rate, which stood at 3.4 percent in 1965 and at 1.2 percent in 1985, has fallen to around 0.2 percent, which means that only a part of the older population is being replaced. The island's total population has thus peaked and will soon begin to decline. It is estimated that the current population will drop to 22.9 million people in 2035 and to 20.4 million in 2045.[15]

Consequently, the composition of the population will change. The share of people aged sixty-five and older was 8.3 percent in 1998 and an estimated 13.1 percent in 2016, but it is likely to rise to 27.4 percent in 2035 and 36.6 percent in 2050.[16] Taiwan's working population, on the other hand, is on the cusp of a fairly steep decline: from 74.0 percent in 2014 to 71.4 percent in 2020, to 62.5 percent in 2035, and to 59.0 percent in 2044.[17] An aging society creates a burden for a working-age population, whose size relative to the rest of the population is declining. In other words, there will be more children and elderly people depending on a shrinking number of people to support them.

Taiwan's social, economic, and political development has had environmental consequences. During Taiwan's period of rapid growth through industrialization, citizens had to tolerate the pollution of air, soil, and water. They either did not know the repercussions of environmental degradation or they were unable to complain about it because the political system was not yet open. However, after Taiwan's transition to democracy began, environmental advocacy became widespread and raised the salience of environmental protection in government policy. That task became easier as many industrial plants firms moved to mainland China and Southeast Asia to ensure business survival in the face of globalization. Yet pollution problems persist in a predominantly service economy, with polluting industries still fouling the air on parts of the island. Taiwan ranks forty-sixth in Yale University's global assessment of environmental protection, trailing behind countries in East Asia such as Singapore, Japan, and South Korea.[18]

In short, Taiwan's emergence as a modern, prosperous society has created serious competition among priorities, as well as dilemmas in how to address them. It must figure out how to make tough choices among a variety of matters: between rising energy demands and environmental protection, between economic growth and economic equity, and between the needs of the young and the needs of the elderly.

Domestic Transformation: External Political and Military Conflict

On the security front, Taiwan has reason to fear that the U.S. shield that has protected it for decades is losing strength. What has changed is not the PRC's goal of unification, which remains the same today as it was in 1949, but rather the ability of the People's Liberation Army (PLA) to achieve that goal. That has improved steadily since the late 1990s, both in terms of projecting power across the Taiwan Strait and in complicating any effort by the United States to come to Taiwan's defense. How Taiwan should address this new reality is a daunting challenge. Moreover, it is critical to understand that what is at play here is not simply the possibility of one state seizing the territory of another internationally recognized state, as Japan seized Manchuria in 1931 or Nazi Germany conquered countries in Western Europe in 1940. There is a special political dimension to this dispute that stems from decades of conflict on the Chinese mainland in the first half of the twentieth century, how Taiwan's legal character has been understood, and how its people define their identity. To clarify this very political dimension requires a short historical detour.

When the Qing or Manchu dynasty ended in 1911, a new government, which called itself the Republic of China (ROC), succeeded it. Yet it was soon a republic in name only, as contending military forces fought for territory and control of the façade that was the central government. Out of that conflict emerged two political and military forces that, in turn, established relative dominance. The first was the Nationalist Party, known conventionally as the Kuomintang (KMT). Under the leadership of Generalissimo Chiang Kai-shek, the KMT took over the ROC government in 1928 and sought to make it more effective. Its army eliminated some, though not all, of its remaining contenders for power. One that barely escaped elimination was the Chinese Communist Party (CCP) and its army, led by Mao Zedong.

Meanwhile, Japan embarked on aggression against the ROC. Six years after the seizure of Manchuria, full-scale war broke out in North and East China. Once the Japanese army had occupied those regions and penetrated into the center of the country, the ROC government moved inland. It survived through its own efforts and the aid first of the Soviet Union and then the United States. Meanwhile, Mao's CCP expanded from its main base area in the northwest into Japanese-held areas, building its military and administrative strength in the process. With the end of the war with Japan, and after two unsuccessful American attempts to mediate between the KMT and the CCP, civil war between the two armies began.

As the tide of fighting on the mainland increasingly went the way of the CCP, Taiwan became vital territory for the KMT. The island had been a frontier territory of the Qing dynasty since the seventeenth century, one that the imperial government began to develop only after other countries appeared to covet the island. In 1895 Taiwan became a colony of Japan, a prize that Tokyo took after defeating China in a war over Korea. During World War II, the allied powers decided that Taiwan should be returned to the ROC, and units of Chiang Kai-shek's armies accepted the Japanese surrender in the fall of 1945. With the civil war on the mainland lost, Chiang, the ROC government, and the ROC armies retreated to Taiwan, with Taipei as its new capital. On October 1, 1949, Mao Zedong declared the establishment of the PRC as the government of China, with its capital in Beijing, and the successor to the ROC. He also vowed to "liberate" Taiwan, an outcome that the Truman administration initially decided not to oppose.

Yet Taiwan did not fall to the PLA, primarily because the United States gradually resumed its support for the island's security. A military stalemate ensued, one that has persisted to this day. It was on a political battlefield that the two sides of the Strait then fought, hammer and tongs.

The first battle was over which government—the ROC or the PRC—was the legitimate representative of the state that the international community knew as China. At stake here was which would hold China's seat in the United Nations and other international organizations. A related issue was diplomatic relations with third countries. Should they recognize the PRC or the ROC? In which capital should their embassies be located? A very special case here was the United States, which not only continued to recognize the ROC as the government of China after 1949 but also concluded a mutual defense treaty with it in 1954, pledging to come to Taiwan's defense if attacked. But Taipei was fighting a losing political battle. It was forced to leave the UN in 1971, and by the early 1980s the PRC had effectively won the contest within the international system. Beijing represents China in international organizations, and Taiwan participates only under special circumstances. Only fourteen countries and the Vatican maintain diplomatic relations with the ROC. As for the United States, it terminated diplomatic relations with Taipei at the end of 1978 and established them with Beijing on New Year's Day, 1979. The mutual defense treaty ended a year later, having been terminated according to its provisions. The Taiwan Relations Act, passed by the U.S. Congress in March 1979, created a framework for unofficial yet substantive relations going forward.

The second issue between Beijing and Taipei began in 1979 and is still unresolved: that is, whether and under what terms the two sides might settle the political and legal dispute between them (the details of this are covered in later chapters). From 1949 into the early 1980s, Beijing and Taipei had agreed that unification should occur; they simply differed over which China would disappear as a result. In the late 1970s and early 1980s, however, Beijing changed the nature of the disagreement. It asserted that it wanted unification to occur peacefully, but it did not rule out the use of force. It also proposed a formula for unification of Taiwan, known as "one country, two systems." This was the same approach applied to Hong Kong, and, based on those arrangements, what this meant for Taiwan was that the ROC would disappear. Taiwan would subsequently become a "special administrative region" of the PRC, subordinate to the central government. Taiwan leaders would continue to manage internal affairs, but Beijing would control who led the island's government. Taipei rejected those terms at the time and has done so ever since.

New Directions

Beginning in the mid-1980s, the cross-Strait relationship changed in three significant ways that were relevant to the political dimension of this political-military dispute. The first was economic. Gradually, an array of Taiwanese companies, which had been losing global competitiveness by continuing to manufacture products on Taiwan itself, revived their businesses by relocating some of their operations to China. This shift was an immediate boon to the PRC because it put its people to work and led to the transfer of technology and management skills. But the government in Beijing, led as it was by Marxists, hoped that growing economic integration would lead ultimately to political unification. The process would take time, but it was enough at this time to put the one country, two systems formula on the table for future negotiations.

The second development was a decision in 1985 and 1986 by Taiwan's president, Chiang Ching-kuo, son of Chiang Kai-shek, to open up the political system. The elder Chiang had imposed a hard-authoritarian regime on the island. His son softened the system and then decided that it was in the interests of the KMT and Taiwan to move gradually to democracy.[19] From the late 1940s to the late 1980s, the public at large had no voice concerning who held power and what policies were best. From the early 1990s on, in contrast, they have been free to debate the dangers and opportunities posed by China, the pros and cons of dependence on the United States, and what kind of society Taiwan should be. In addition, they effectively gained a seat at the negotiating table if talks with Beijing ever began.

Democratization also introduced a new, third element into the long-running political disagreement between Beijing and Taipei. In addition to the issues of whether the ROC or the PRC would represent China in the world and how the dispute between them should be resolved, a new issue arose concerning the territory of Taiwan: whether it was a part of China at all. The constant view in Beijing, and the traditional view in Taipei, was that the island had legally been returned to China. (A small Taiwan independence movement had begun after the KMT takeover and was made up of overseas exiles who believed Taiwan should be its own country.)

Yet once people in Taiwan gained the right of free expression and free assembly, previously taboo ideas about the island's future became everyday topics of political discussion and advocacy. Only a small share of the population regarded themselves as exclusively Chinese, while an overwhelming majority saw themselves as Taiwanese or some undefined mixture of both. At the same time, some Taiwan people rejected the idea that Taiwan was part of a divided country (China). Instead, they said, it should become an independent country—a Republic of Taiwan—that had no legal connection with China. This was an outcome that Beijing and KMT traditionalists strongly opposed, and the PRC has warned repeatedly that independence would lead to war. These issues have created a mare's nest of complexity that the average Taiwan citizen or a member of the U.S. Congress does not understand. Yet these questions of political and legal identity are the fulcrum governing Taiwan's future and whether that future will be peaceful.

Before long, the KMT, which had remade itself to engage in democratic competition, and the Democratic Progressive Party (DPP), which was founded by opponents to authoritarian rule, established themselves as the main contenders for power and policy. By 2000, each major party led a coalition that included smaller splinter parties. These two camps became known as the Blues and the Greens, the respective colors of the KMT and DPP flags.

The Blues believed that Taiwan could reap the benefits of economic interactions with China without risking its political autonomy. The Greens perceived a greater risk that economic dependence would lead to political subordination to the PRC.

Both camps generally agree that they must rely on the United States to preserve Taiwan's autonomy, but the Blue camp has more confidence in its ability to manage the China risk. In addition, both camps have a spectrum of views that run from "deep" to "light." The Deep Blues tend to adhere to the ROC's early staunch anticommunist and anti-independence stance and favor unification of some sort, while the Light Blues are more comfortable with Taiwan's maintaining political distance from China, even as it secures benefits from economic relations. The Deep Greens favor a more radical approach to securing autonomy through measures that call for Taiwanese independence, while the Light Green are more concerned about the potential for conflict and are more comfortable maintaining some sort of status quo between the ROC and the PRC.

Political power in Taiwan has shifted back and forth between Blue and Green camps, as well as between light and deep within each camp. President Lee Teng-hui, who dominated the Taiwan political system during the 1990s, started out with a Blue stance and moved increasingly toward a Green one during his time in office. The DPP's Chen Shui-bian, who was president from 2000 to 2008, began as a Light Green leader and shifted to Deep Green after a couple of years.

In 2008 Ma Ying-jeou and the KMT swept the DPP from power. Ma believed that to preserve its prosperity, freedom, and security, Taiwan needed to maintain some degree of engagement with Beijing. That policy worked politically until around 2014, after which more and more people worried that Taiwan was becoming too dependent on China and that any benefits of that dependence were not broadly shared.

In 2016 Tsai Ing-wen and the DPP brought about the latest turn of this wheel. On January 16 of that year, Tsai won an easy victory in the presidential election and her party, the DPP, won an absolute majority in the island's Legislative Yuan (LY), a stunning reversal from only eight years earlier. Four years later, Tsai won reelection with a higher margin than in 2016, and the DPP maintained its legislative majority, but with fewer seats. Political competition is firmly institutionalized, and the voters have the final say.

The Dilemmas Posed by Taiwan's Democracy

Taiwan's democratization created dilemmas for both the PRC and the United States. For Beijing, achieving unification would be more difficult now that the public had a say in decisions concerning their fundamental future. Moreover, there was the danger that elements on the island who wanted de jure independence would exploit the more open system to achieve their goals, which in turn might lead the PRC to go to war to stop it. For Washington, cross-Strait conflict would require it to decide whether to come to Taiwan's defense. For Taipei, preserving security and the good life would be more difficult in a political system where contending forces all had a say.

For Beijing

Taiwan's democracy and open discussion of de jure independence have worked very much to the PRC's disadvantage. Once the island's people gained their political voice, it was no longer possible for Beijing to negotiate a deal with a small group of leaders in Taipei, as it no doubt had hoped. Most people identify to some degree with Taiwan and less with China, and a minority of people want a Republic of Taiwan. Support for unification is low. The people Taiwan voters have picked to be their presidents have not always been to Beijing's liking. Indeed, of the candidates elected since the first direct vote in 1996—Lee Teng-hui, Chen Shui-bian, Ma Ying-jeou, and Tsai Ing-wen—Ma was the one with whom Beijing was most comfortable, and his effort to stabilize cross-Strait relations and put the PRC and Taiwan on a mutually beneficial basis ultimately met strong opposition. That again called into question the PRC approach of working through Taiwan leaders to create circumstances conducive to unification. Then there is the reality that Taiwan is a constitutional democracy. That means, in my view, that if Beijing's approach to unification requires significant changes in Taiwan's political institutions and legal identity, as it would under one country, two systems, that would require amendments to the ROC Constitution. The hurdles involved in enacting those amendments are so high that passage is impossible unless the DPP and the KMT agree that the changes proffered are worth accepting.

Beijing has made its task more difficult by misperceiving the goals of the Taiwan leaders. It has branded Lee Teng-hui, Chen Shui-bian, and Tsai Ing-wen as proponents of Taiwan independence, who would use their power as president to bring about that goal. I argue that what Lee Teng-hui advocated was not de jure independence but PRC acceptance that Taiwan and its government were a sovereign entity both for purposes of Taiwan's international role and of any negotiations concerning unification. He did not oppose unification, just the terms that Beijing offered, which were contrary to the idea of a sovereign Taiwan. Chen Shui-bian was more complicated in his goals, strategy, and tactics, but he was constrained not only by Beijing but also by the KMT, the Taiwan public, and the United States. Given Tsai's moderate, cautious approach to the PRC, Beijing has been hard-pressed to make the case that her goal is what Beijing said it was. Ironically, Ma Ying-jeou was willing to accept the PRC precondition for productive relations, but he did so in a way that would have been a two-China policy, which Beijing opposes as much as Taiwan independence. Also, he deflected PRC pressure to begin political talks.

In short, the PRC faces a more serious problem than the unwelcome policies of this or that Taiwan president. Over a four-decade period, it has not been able to convince Taiwan's leaders and the island's people to accept unification or even to begin political talks that might lead to unification. Its formula for unification—one country, two systems—has never had a market on Taiwan, particularly after the democratic transition. The public may not support de jure independence, but their identification with Taiwan, where, by now, most of them were born and raised, is strong. Cross-Strait economic interdependence sustained Taiwan's prosperity, but it did not change political attitudes appreciably and instead created fears of overdependence. Beijing had hoped that successful application of the formula in Hong Kong would encourage Taiwan citizens and leaders to accept it. But growing political conflict in Hong Kong in the 2010s, capped by violent protests in the summer and fall of 2019, and Beijing's May 2020 decision to impose a national security law only strengthened Taiwan citizens' opposition to unification. This has left PRC leaders with a difficult choice. Do they accommodate to the Taiwan public's opposition to unification based on one country, two systems and try to make the best of the status quo? Do they formulate an approach to unification that is more compatible with the views of the DPP, the KMT, and the public at large? Do they roll the dice and go to war to achieve their objective, and then have to rule an unhappy populace?

For Washington

The United States had strongly supported Taiwan's democratization as evidence of the triumph of American values at the end of the Cold War. Washington was not so pleased when the policies of Taiwan's elected leaders ran contrary to its long-stated abiding interest in peace and security in the Taiwan area. In particular, U.S. officials worried that Presidents Lee Teng-hui and Chen Shui-bian were taking Taiwan in a direction that would provoke Beijing, destabilize cross-Strait relations, and increase the possibility of a conflict that was unnecessary in Washington's view. For this reason, Washington distanced itself from Lee's and Chen's destabilizing initiatives in an effort to restrain them.

On the other hand, the United States had a more positive assessment of Ma Ying-jeou, and it shifted its approach to Taiwan accordingly. Similarly, Tsai Ing-wen has maintained good relations with the United States. Once she became a candidate for the 2016 election, she worked hard to reassure the Obama administration that her cautious approach to mainland China was compatible with the U.S. interest in cross-Strait stability. After Tsai was elected, Washington disagreed with Beijing's argument that she was changing the status quo. In a speech at the Brookings Institution in October 2017, James Moriarty, chairman of the American Institute in Taiwan, offered this judgment: "My interactions with President Tsai have reaffirmed my conviction that she is a responsible, pragmatic leader. The United States appreciates her determination to maintain stable cross-Strait ties in the face of increasing pressure from the PRC on a number of fronts."[20] Tsai understood that it was in her administration's interest to maintain a close alignment with the United States. Moreover, Tsai had worked in both the Lee Teng-hui and Chen Shui-bian administrations and saw what happens when Taiwan's leaders followed policies that Washington viewed as challenging its interests and ignored the risks of getting on Washington's bad side. Consequently, through her first four-year term, Tsai did nothing to create credible suggestions that she would do the same.

For Taiwan

Under the island's democratic system and with the support of the United States, Taiwan's leaders and its public have rejected any consideration of Beijing's plan for unification, even as they enjoy, with some anxiety, the benefits of the economic relationship. But this success has only blocked what Taiwan wishes to avoid. It has not defined clearly how it is that Taiwan should seek to survive in a dangerous world and preserve the good life, and how to accomplish that. Vigorous debates on the very meaning of political and legal identity continue. Are there two Chinas, the PRC and the ROC, or just one? Is Taiwan a part of the sovereign territory of that China, whichever Chinese government represents China internationally? Is Taiwan its own state, legally distinct from China?

Taiwan could better achieve those objectives if leaders, institutions, and the public forged a domestic consensus on grand strategy that is based on a realistic assessment of the island's strategic environment. They must then iterate the ends and create the means to implement this grand strategy to its full potential. Yet democratic systems often have a particularly difficult time effecting internal consensus, since contending political forces can disagree about the dangers they face and how to adjust to them.

Taiwan has a vibrant democracy, albeit sometimes an unruly one. Civil and political rights are protected. At all levels of the political system, the chief executive and legislators are picked by well-run competitive elections. There is an independent judiciary, which frees the courts from improper influence. Civil society plays an increasingly important role in politics. However, democratic systems also institutionalize conflict. Politics in Taiwan is polarized between the Blue and Green camps, making differences of opinion common and compromise difficult to reach. Furthermore, it is easier for opponents of a policy initiative to block it than for its proponents to build sufficient support to enact it. The media in Taiwan prefer sensation and scandal to policy substance. None of Taiwan's political institutions work perfectly, and there is a serious debate about the value of representative versus direct democracy. The public has periodically disapproved of the performance of both the DPP and the KMT, leading to regular transfers of power. Perhaps most serious is that political leaders have a severe aversion to being straight with the public on the need to choose between competing priorities regarding both domestic policy and how to cope with China and to work in a more bipartisan way to make authoritative choices.

The two levels of Taiwan's policy dilemma—navigating postindustrial democratic development, on the one hand, and managing the challenge from an increasingly powerful and revisionist PRC, on the other—reinforce each other and make meeting them all the more complicated. Even if China, with its dreams of unification, were 9,000 miles away from Taiwan, instead of just 90 miles—and even if the PLA were not enhancing its military capabilities to prepare to fight a war over Taiwan, as it is—Taiwan would still face major policy questions, for which answers are not always obvious. But China is ninety miles away, and its military capabilities are growing, complicating Taiwan's ability to defend itself against Chinese attack and the ability of the United States to come to its aid. Generally speaking, Taiwan's democratic system may appear to perform well in comparison with others, including the

United States. However, the stakes involved and the high costs of failure require a proportionately higher level of performance on the part of the island's elected leaders. Taiwan has little margin for neglect and even less margin for error.

The Aim of this Book

The primary focus of this book is not simply Taiwan's relationship with China. It is, rather, the dilemmas that Taiwan faces as a society and the difficulties that the political system has in reconciling those dilemmas. Furthermore, it gives special emphasis to the public's views of the issues at play in these dilemmas. The following chapter sets a baseline for what is known about public opinion on the domestic issues in play. The next four chapters look at domestic policy issues and the debates surrounding them: the government budget, the economy, energy security, and transitional justice. The six chapters that follow look at various aspects of cross-Strait relations. Chapter 7 presents Beijing's policy toward Taiwan, why it has failed so far, and its options to address that failure. Chapter 8 presents the contending Taiwan approaches to its security problem, and chapter 9 examines its defense strategy. Chapters 10 and 11 examine competing views that Taiwan citizens have about the nation with which they identify and how they might define Taiwan's statehood, key points of contention with Beijing. Chapter 12 describes China's efforts to weaken the island through means that are coercive but not violent. Chapter 13 discusses Taiwan's political system, the obstacles to creating consensus on admittedly difficult issues, and the consequences of not doing so. Chapter 14 examines implications for U.S. policy toward Taiwan and China, and chapter 15 offers ideas on how Taiwan can preserve security and its "good life," in spite of the dual dilemmas it faces.

Taiwan's democracy is an issue of special interest to me, since the arc of my professional and intellectual career parallels Taiwan's recent political history. I first lived in Taipei in 1975 in the middle of research on my Ph.D. thesis, when the authoritarian system still maintained strong control. However, my main interest in the late 1970s and early 1980s was the establishment of diplomatic relations between the United States and the PRC, a development that was a bitter blow to Taiwan. But Taiwan became the center of my attention in the summer of 1983 when I became a staff person on the House Committee of Foreign Affairs. Representative Steve Solarz, for whom I worked for most of the next decade, wanted to promote democratization and human rights in Taiwan, and it became my job to help him. Not long into my tenure as a staff person, Taiwan's president Chiang Ching-kuo made the decision to start the process of democratization.

In my view, the contribution of outsiders such as Solarz to both the start and completion of that transition was relatively modest, less significant than that of the opposition forces inside Taiwan (the *Dangwai*, which became the DPP) and of reformers within the regime. But the American role was not trivial.[21] Most significant was the result: the Taiwan people gained a say in their own affairs after being denied that say for decades. Before this, the U.S. government made decisions affecting the interests of the people of Taiwan without consulting them. It is because Taiwan's democratic transition was the pivot point of its political history that I try as much as possible to include information on public attitudes about policy issues.

Washington was in for something of a surprise once Taiwan politicians began taking advantage of their new-found freedom to advocate for policies that had previously been taboo and offering novel views on Taiwan's legal status and its relationship with China. American officials struggled to understand what was behind Taipei's moves even as they focused on priorities in U.S.-PRC relations.

One example that highlights how Taiwan began to perturb the United States occurred in the summer of 1999, amid diplomatic complications between China and the United States. At that time, Washington was trying to close its bilateral negotiations with China regarding its entry into the World Trade Organization while dealing with a firestorm of Chinese criticism over the U.S. accidental bombing of the PRC embassy in Belgrade in May. Two months later, Lee Teng-hui suddenly announced his view that cross-Strait relations were a "special state-to-state relationship." The PRC feared that Lee was establishing a legal basis for independence, and PLA jets flew farther out into the Strait than normal. There was actually a substantive basis for Lee's viewpoint, but U.S. officials did not fully understand it at the time.[22] Looming on the horizon were the March 2000 presidential elections in Taiwan and the real possibility that Chen Shui-bian of the DPP, which was associated with the goal of independence, would become president. Chen did become president, and as time went on, he played up Taiwanese nationalism and announced proposals without consulting with the United States about his potentially provocative initiatives.

In short, from about 1994 through 2007, the United States continued to state its admiration for Taiwan's democracy but was frustrated by the actions of Taiwan's democratically elected leaders. That situation changed in 2008, when Ma Ying-jeou became president and undertook policies to engage China economically and bring some stability to cross-Strait relations. This was very much in line with how both the Bush and Obama administrations defined U.S. interests in these matters. However, Ma's push to create a free trade regime with China was increasingly unpopular in Taiwan, and the KMT's failure to find a successor to run in the 2016 elections led to the DPP's Tsai Ing-wen's winning the presidency. She not only won that contest handily but was able to credibly reassure the United States that she wanted to preserve the status quo. Tsai and the DPP suffered a serious setback in the November 2018 local elections, but she rebounded over the course of 2019 to win reelection in 2020. When it comes to picking a president, it seems, Taiwan voters usually have the last word.

Yet there are other signs that some political forces are unhappy with Taiwan's representative democracy. First of all, since 2008 young people have engaged in demonstrations and protests, some of which were quite large, owing to the multiplier effect of social media. The Sunflower student movement of early 2014 was a high tide of this type of political action and reflected in part a desire on the part of activists to have a greater say in the discussions of policy relative to the executive and legislative branches. Second, Deep Green elements had long pushed for greater use of initiatives and referendums in formulating public policy. After the DPP won control of the government in 2016, it pushed forward changes in the referendum law to make such direct-democracy mechanisms easier to employ. However, the KMT and its allies soon sponsored referendums that complicated DPP governance. Third, populist candidates emerged as possible contenders in the 2020 elections. Only one, Kaohsiung mayor Han Kuo-yu, ended up as a candidate for the KMT. But he soon found that running for mayor is easier than running for president, and against a sitting incumbent at that. More generally, policy initiatives were often obstructed in several ways. It was easier to stop proposed actions than carry them through.

Given my personal connection to Taiwan's democratization, I hope that the island's public and leaders will find ways to work together to address the dilemmas that the society faces. Yet it is hard to avoid the conclusion that Taiwan's democratic political system is performing at only a suboptimal level and is not meeting its original promise. That would be too bad, because if any people deserve to have an effective political system it is the people of Taiwan—because of the policy challenges the island faces and the incredibly high stakes of not meeting those challenges. If priorities are in conflict, it is through politics that differences will be mitigated. If the system is polarized, it is through politics that divisions will be muted. If active minorities exercise vetoes, it is through a different kind of politics than what exists now that majorities will form. And if China is an increasingly serious challenge, it is through democratic politics that a broadly supported consensus on securing the country will emerge.

2

Popular Attitudes in Taiwan: A Preliminary Baseline

An important feature of Taiwan society is constant polling, which creates an almost permanent plebiscite. Some of these polls are methodologically sophisticated, designed by individuals well trained in survey research. Others are fashioned in a way that generates the results that the sponsors desire. As a Taiwan friend of mine who knows this field has explained to me, even surveys that appear to meet high methodological standards can be manipulated to secure biased results.

Moreover, even the soundest polls focus on some issues and not on others. Understandably, they try to measure the balance of sentiment on issues on which society is divided. They ask questions such as, Do you approve of the president's performance? Which candidate do you prefer in the next election? Do you regard yourself as Chinese, Taiwanese, or both? What is the ultimate outcome you prefer for Taiwan? (Later chapters will review the results of these surveys in detail.) That polls focus on issues of *political* conflict is to be expected, and they can be useful in clarifying the boundaries of public disagreement. Serious disagreements do exist on important issues, most of all on how to cope with the People's Republic of China. The stakes involved are high.

However, to borrow from Abraham Lincoln, although some people in Taiwan may think about domestic politics and policy toward China[1] all the time, it is a safe guess that many citizens think about these issues only some of the time and that others ignore them completely. This suggests the need for a more comprehensive understanding of how Taiwan's people face their present and their future, a picture that is much broader than what we usually see. The concerns of Taiwanese go beyond how they feel about national identity and cross-Strait relations. Those are hardly trivial matters, but they are insufficient to fully understand the sentiments of Taiwan's people. This chapter attempts to provide that broader baseline, based on the survey and other evidence available. The inventory is not complete, but it does draw on a broader range of data than are usually discussed.

The need for a bigger picture was brought home to me by news that the World Happiness Report for 2018 ranked Taiwan twenty-sixth in the world, with a composite score of 6.441 on a zero-to-ten scale.[2] That contrasts with the negative and pessimistic attitudes of people I know, at least those with whom I discuss politics and cross-Strait policy. Of course, the results of such surveys are only as good as their methodological design and question phrasing. Moreover, within any population, there is a variation in how happy people are. Individuals can find happiness and optimism from some parts of their lives and sadness and pessimism from others.[3]

One intriguing aspect of Taiwan's happiness ranking was its position relative to other places. Worldwide, most of the countries that were "happier" than Taiwan were in Europe and had reached high levels of economic development. Overall, the worldwide leaders were Finland, Norway, Demark, and Iceland. Outside Europe, Canada, Israel, Costa Rica, the United States, the United Arab Emirates, and Chile were ranked higher than Taiwan, but all of them except the UAE were settled and shaped by Europeans. In East Asia, the only country that had a higher ranking than Taiwan was Australia, which was also settled by Europeans. Other countries in East Asia lagged behind Taiwan: Japan was fifty-fourth, South Korea fifty-seventh, Hong Kong seventy-sixth, and China eighty-sixth. What Taiwan appears to share with at least some happier countries is modernity, as the benchmarks cited in the previous chapter demonstrated, and the blessings that come with it. Taiwan is indeed a modern, cosmopolitan, and prosperous society. Relative to less developed countries, its people do have reasons to feel happy. So Taiwan's top happiness ranking in cultural East Asia should not be dismissed as an artifact of how this survey measures happiness.

Absence of Social Cleavages

Politics aside, there are many ways in which Taiwan is not divided. The society is remarkably homogeneous. By objective definitions of race and ethnicity, 98 percent of the population is ethnically Chinese. The small exceptions to this ethnic homogeneity include the approximately half million people whose Malayo-Polynesian ancestors lived on the island thousands of years before ethnic Chinese began settlement in the seventeenth century and the more recent additions of a growing number of workers from Southeast Asia. Thus Taiwan does not have the relative diversity of countries such as the United States, with its population of Caucasians, Native Americans, African Americans, Hispanics, and people from Africa and Asia, or Singapore, with its population of Chinese, Malays, and South Asians. Ethnic origin does not produce attitudinal differences.

Social class has not been a source of deep divisions. Taiwan has not shared the experience of many Western societies, with their large, concentrated industrial sectors and the politically conscious labor forces that factory life produced. Even during the industrial period of Taiwan's development, a large number of small and medium enterprises employed the bulk of the nonagricultural labor force, not a small number of large factories. Moreover, until the 1990s, the level of inequality was relatively low, so people with lower incomes were less inclined toward feelings of material grievance and more toward a sense of opportunity. Political parties were never successful in promoting class-based politics. This is reflected in how Taiwan people see themselves. The Taiwan Election and Democratization Survey (TEDS), based at National Chengchi University, has asked its survey samples to identify the socioeconomic class to which they belong. In the December 2017 iteration of the survey, only 0.7 percent of respondents said they were in the upper class, while 24.3 percent said they were upper-middle class and 33.2 percent lower-middle class (for a total of 57.5 percent for the entire middle class), 32.4 percent said they were working class, and only 4.4 percent said the lower class.[4]

Nor is religion a source of social cleavage, as it has been in other countries. In the TEDS survey, the breakdown of respondents who associated themselves with one specific religious group was 26.5 percent Buddhist, 21.8 percent Daoists, 17.8 percent folk religion, 5.3 percent Protestant, 1.2 percent Catholic, and 22 percent "none." Actually, this survey question poses a false choice based on a very Western approach to religion. When it comes to the indigenous faiths of Daoism, Buddhism, and folk religion, ethnic Chinese can be very pluralistic in their attachments. The idea of "belonging" to a religion on an exclusive basis is foreign to them. What makes individuals religious is more belief and practice rather than membership in a particular organization or adherence to a specific doctrine. Because religious faith is pluralistic and often nonexclusive, it cannot be the basis for serious social cleavage. As André Laliberté summarizes, "Overall, the interactions between religion and politics in Taiwan have not been a matter of deep contention in the early stages of the democratic transition."[5]

Although a supermajority of people on Taiwan are ethnic Chinese, history and politics created significant divisions within that dominant group. On one side of this divide are the native Taiwanese, whose ancestors migrated from southeastern China to the island from the seventeenth to the twentieth centuries. The native Taiwanese are, in turn, divided into the Minnan or Hoklo, whose ancestors came from two different prefectures in southern Fujian province, and the Hakka, who came mainly from southeastern Guangdong province. (Within the Minnan group, there are a relatively small number of Taiwanese politicians today who claim that the native Taiwanese, those whose ancestors arrived in Taiwan before the twentieth century, are an ethnicity other than Chinese, but that view is not generally accepted.) On the other side of the divide are people who came from mainland China between 1945 and 1949 or are descended from those people. Originally, most people in this group had connections to the Kuomintang (KMT) regime that was defeated by Mao Zedong's communist armies and then retreated to Taiwan.[6] By 1978, mainlanders made up 14 percent of the island's population, while the Taiwanese constituted almost all the rest.[7]

The mainlander-Taiwanese split was politically important up through the 1990s because of the oppressive way that the KMT regime treated the Taiwanese. However, this cleavage is less relevant today, owing to a variety of reinforcing factors: intermarriage between mainlanders and Taiwanese that muddled the boundary between the two groups, the ongoing passing of the people who came from China after 1945, the growing numbers of younger people who did not have to endure the authoritarian period and for whom Taiwan itself is the dominant reality, and the impact of China's policies on how citizens define their political identity.[8]

Finally, a potential, social source of political division became politically significant in the 2010s: generation. Young people had good reason to believe that their standard of living would not be as good as what their parents achieved. They also were more in favor of independence and less willing to work through the established political system to advance their interests.

Uniformity of Basic Values

Taiwan is also remarkably uniform when it comes to values on a number of basic issues. Indeed, as two different, nonpolitical surveys demonstrate, there is substantial convergence of attitudes. The most recent waves of the World Values Survey (WVS) in 2012 and the Taiwan Social Change Survey (TSCS) in 2013 found a clustering of answers on a number of questions.[9] According to the WVS, 98.6 percent of respondents thought that family was "important in their life" (either very important or rather important). This result is not only very high, but it also suggests that despite economic development, Taiwan remains a very Confucian society, in that the key relationships in social life are found in the family. It also looks to be both modern and Confucian: a similarly large majority (90.3 percent) also thought friends were important. Regarding their confidence in personal relationships, 67.5 percent tended to believe to some degree that others would be fair to them, while the rest thought that others would take advantage.

Work was important to 90.1 percent of those surveyed, a mentality shaped by decades of poverty, development, and family values. Yet 84.3 percent also thought that leisure was desirable, a reflection of the island's economic success and modernity. Substantial majorities believed that hard work would lead to a better life.

Both of these surveys addressed the issue of individual agency versus determinism. The WVS asked respondents to rate their agency on a scale of 1 to 10, with 1 defined as having no control over their destiny and 10 defined as having absolute free choice. The mean response was 7.48, and more than 79.6 percent of respondents put themselves on the free-choice end of the scale, with a rating of 6.0 or higher. The TSCS asked questions on whether diligence and "efforts" could counteract the impact of fate; most respondents clearly agreed that they could. When the issue was posed somewhat differently—whether one can "negotiate with fate and materialize your dreams through one's actions"—the responses were less categorical: 26.3 percent were in clear agreement, 39.9 percent were in clear disagreement, and 39.2 percent were in the middle. Overall, however, these answers demonstrate the significant impact of modernization on Taiwan, since traditional Chinese religion, Buddhist and otherwise, takes the alternate view, that individuals must accept their fate and not fight against it.

On the TSCS, Taiwanese people also reported a substantially positive perspective on life in general and their own situation in particular.

- Asked whether it was "true or not true that the future is filled with opportunities," only 15.98 percent were at the "not true" end of the scale.

- On the question of whether there was "plenty of time in life to make a new plan," only 18.49 percent clearly disagreed.

- On the question of personal happiness, 89.9 percent of respondents to the WVS said that on the whole they were either "very happy" or "rather happy."

- The survey got a somewhat lower response when it asked about satisfaction with "your life as a whole," but 80.93 percent still said they were "satisfied," and only 18.14 percent said "dissatisfied."

- As for health, 73.26 percent said they were "satisfied" with their current health status (26.45 "dissatisfied").

- With respect to social relationships, 92.92 percent said they were "satisfied" in their relationship with friends, while only 5.41 percent were "dissatisfied."

- Job satisfaction was not overwhelmingly positive: 56.54 percent said they were "satisfied" in their current main job, and 10.72 percent were not (32.65 percent said they were not employed).

The prospect of losing their job was a source of worry for 70.4 percent of those surveyed by the WVS. Even more (73.0 percent) were worried about not being able to give their children a good education, which suggests again a convergence of basic Confucian values and the imperatives of completion in a modern economy.

At the individual level at least, there is a good reason that Taiwan scored the highest happiness ranking in cultural East Asia. On a widespread basis, people are happy with their lives. They recognize the importance of family and friends. They accept that working hard is important for individual success, but they remain confident that through their own efforts they can shape their future, despite outside forces. When there are anxieties, such as losing one's job, they are reasonable. Moreover, when it comes to these basic values, Taiwan is a Chinese society that has successfully melded tradition and modernity.

Institutions and Issues

All modern societies depend on institutions to sustain social, economic, and political life. But citizens of those societies do not necessarily hold all their institutions in high regard. At the same time, they usually place a high priority on certain policy issues instead of others. Polling in Taiwan indicates that it is no exception to this rule.

Institutions

Taiwan people vary substantially in the confidence they feel concerning various domestic institutions, according to the WVS findings. The level of confidence stood between 70 and 80 percent for banks and environmental organizations; between 60 and 70 percent for the civil service, religious organizations, and the police; between 50 and 60 percent for the armed forces; between 40 and 50 percent for the courts; and between 20 and 30 percent for the press and the legislature. That is, the closer the institution was to competitive politics, the less confidence people felt.

Not everything about politics creates divisions. Survey respondents strongly associate themselves with democracy in the abstract. An Asian Barometer Survey poll conducted in Taiwan in the summer and fall of 2014 found that 88 percent of those surveyed overwhelmingly agreed with the idea that democracy is still the best form of government. When it comes to how Taiwan's democratic system operates in practice, the views are less positive (as chapter 13 will discuss in detail). Yet along with people's basic social attitudes, belief in democracy is one of the areas of broadest value consensus.

Issues

Polling also provides a good sense of which issues voters think are the most important, with the economy proving to be the clear leader. In late 2017, TEDS asked respondents which of seventeen different issues were the highest and second-highest priority for political leaders to address. Economic development was first for 46.5 percent of respondents and second for 22.4 percent. That is, more than two-thirds of the public agreed that "it's the economy, stupid." The next two most important issues polled were cross-Strait relations and education policy. Navigating relations with China was the first or second priority for 33.2 percent, and 31.5 percent thought education was most important. Of course, education policy and some aspects of cross-Strait relations affect economic development, so all three are intertwined.

The priority placed on the economy was not simply a vague sentiment but rather a reflection of people's anxieties about the future. The TSCS asked respondents whether they expected that their living standards would be better or worse in the next five years, and responses divided almost equally into three groups: 30.7 percent said that their standard of living would be better, 30 percent said it would be about the same, and 31 percent thought that it would be worse.

Linked to the economy imperative are several subsidiary yet still important questions. The first is whether globalization is good or bad for Taiwan's economy. The TSCS asked respondents to locate their view on whether the "mobility of people/goods/capital is good or bad for TW economy," on a scale of one to six. These types of mobility were thought to be clearly good by 55.3 percent of respondents; only 9.6 percent thought they were clearly bad; and 25.1 percent were in the middle. When the survey asked whether these types of mobility were good for job opportunities, 40.7 percent of respondents said they were clearly good, 31.6 percent were in the middle, and 19.4 percent thought they were clearly bad.

The second question has to do with the tension between promoting economic growth and fostering greater equality. The TSCS probed this by asking whether most people would work less hard if people's incomes were more equal. Among those surveyed, 37.3 percent agreed with that statement, while 56.4 percent disagreed. Increasing equality would not change the value of hard work, especially as growth slows.

The third issue, related to the second, is whether the government is currently providing enough social welfare benefits. In all advanced economies there is a trade-off between growth and welfare, and one result of Taiwan's transition to democracy was public pressure for more welfare benefits after four decades of growth.[10] The political system accommodated that pressure to a significant extent, but the TSCS found that a majority of those polled believed that it could do even more. Only 10.6 percent believed that current benefits were more than enough, 25.4 percent thought they were just enough, and 58.9 percent said that current policy was insufficient.

By way of confirmation, the WVS combined twelve different items and asked respondents where each item belonged on a scale from materialist to post-materialist. Only 19.1 percent of the items were rated as post-materialist side, 70 percent being rated on the more materialist side of the scale. But materialism did not necessarily come out on top when the question was posed as a choice between two conflicting priorities, as opposed to ranking them. Asked to choose between environmental protection and economic growth, 61 percent of respondents said that protecting the environment was more important. This more post-materialist result suggests that people are sometimes conflicted.

The TEDS found similar tension between materialism and post-materialism, though in a different way. Although the economy was the highest priority issue for the people surveyed, some voters placed a priority on the other matters. Pension reform was ranked number one or number two by 23.3 percent of respondents (probably because it was a hot political issue at the time), 17.0 percent saw judicial reform as most or second-most important, and 8.6 did so regarding transitional justice with respect to past human rights abuses (rendering some form of accountability for the oppression of the old KMT). In contrast, fewer than 1.0 percent of those surveyed ranked issues of energy policy, food safety, social welfare, and marriage equality as high priority. In terms of actual political activity, however, these priorities receive far more attention than more general polling would suggest they should. On these, a network of active and vocal civil society groups has successfully placed each of these post-materialist issues on the political agenda, regardless of what people generally appear to believe.

On the China issue, rather stark differences exist. But despite that, there are two points of strong consensus. First, most people in Taiwan identify with Taiwan. Consistently, around 90 percent say they are either Taiwanese or both Taiwanese and Chinese. Fewer than 10 percent identify themselves as only Chinese. Second, a substantial majority prefers to maintain the status quo, either forever or for a long period of time (which probably amounts to the same thing). That is, a solid majority opposes both independence and unification.

The Youth Factor

Early in this chapter, I raised the possibility that generation is the most potent factor in creating social and political divisions in Taiwan, to the extent that Taiwan has divisions. Such a supposition seems plausible. It was young people who mounted a variety of social movements after 2008, which reached a peak in the Sunflower movement of early 2014. These movements focused on a variety of issues: marriage equality, historic preservation, property rights, nuclear power, labor rights, indigenous rights, migrant spouses, treatment of military conscripts, casino gambling, ownership of media organizations, and relations with China. Many of these movements have nothing to do with relations across the Taiwan Strait, but the Sunflower movement, which was mounted to oppose a draft agreement on cross-Strait trade in services, definitely did. Protesters believed that economic integration with China was growing too close and that it would inexorably lead to Taiwan's political incorporation.[11]

These social movements not only tried to put new issues on the political agenda. They also reflected a decision on the part of activists to promote their goals outside of the established institutions of Taiwan's democracy, particularly political parties. Digital media facilitated mobilization on a large scale, and traditional media boosted the exposure of civic actions.[12] The Sunflower movement, with its occupation of Taiwan's Legislative Yuan, gave physical expression to a rejection of established institutions. Direct democracy, it seemed, was replacing representative democracy. As National Taiwan University sociologist Ho Ming-sho says, "Taiwan's highly educated, but economically insecure, young people have been at the forefront of this insurgent civil society."[13] This is not an either-or matter by any means. After the Sunflower movement ended, its leaders and participants threw themselves into party and electoral politics. But those dissatisfied with the status quo and the performance of political parties do have alternatives for political action besides established institutions.

In 2016 *CommonWealth Magazine*, Taiwan's leading business journal, used its annual survey on the state of the nation to argue for the existence of a generational split. In summarizing its findings, it stated that "the point of cleavage in Taiwan public opinion is 'thirty-nine years old.' Almost 70 percent of those 39 and under approve of marriage equality while less than 50 percent of those 40 and older do." It further stated that "on the question of unification or independence in cross-Strait relations, the proportion of 39-year-olds [favoring independence] was far higher than [those favoring] maintaining the status quo, which has long been the point of consensus." The only issue in the poll on which there was not division was the importance of economic growth.[14] Similarly, an increasingly common idea around the time of the 2016 election was that Taiwan's young people were *tianrandu* (naturally inclined toward independence). If that is true, it would be a matter of concern for Beijing, since a trend in this direction will increase the difficulties China will face in bringing about unification.

Political issues like China policy and same-sex marriage aside, Taiwan's younger generations have very material reasons to resent the status quo and the politicians who manage it. The average unemployment rate for twenty- to twenty-four-year-olds ranged between 12 and 14 percent from 2013 through 2018, while that for people ten years their senior was between 3 and 4 percent.[15] One side effect was a rising tendency for young people to leave Taiwan to continue their education or get a job. This brain drain represented a loss of talent for employers, but the flow of at least some Taiwan residents to China, where opportunities were better, fostered some fears of brainwashing. The generally low salaries of those who stayed created added problems: an inability to find convenient and affordable housing and a reluctance or inability to get married and have children. These concerns about quality of life, it seems, combined with more political concerns to drive social activism. As Ho states, "This youthful movement has been driven by a generational sense of relative deprivation among young activists, as the rapid economic growth and upward class mobility that their parents' generation enjoyed have been denied to them." These "deep societal roots," he believes, have had more impact than specific policy issues such as trade.[16]

But the *CommonWealth* survey is also interesting because a decade earlier, a seminal monograph by the Davidson College political scientist Shelley Rigger argued that younger Taiwanese generations were actually more moderate than their elders on issues independence and similar issues. Specifically, Taiwanese who became politically aware from around 1985 and after were more pragmatic about China than those who became politically aware in the Japanese colonial period and during the time of KMT rule. It was soon after 1985 that Taiwan companies were allowed for the first time to trade and invest on the mainland and also around the time the first steps to democracy were taken.[17] Does that mean that the *tianrandu* trend represents a negation of Rigger's finding of greater pragmatism? Rigger, in a later analysis, answers, "no, but." She finds that the political generation that came of political age during the Chen Shui-bian administration (2000–2008) naturally identify with their birthplace because they never felt they had to make a choice psychologically between Taiwan and China. But just as naturally, they are more inclined than their elders to engage China, because that is where good employment opportunities exist.[18]

More general polling about the attitudes of young people compared with their elders suggests that their sentiments are more complicated than age or "natural independence" explanations would suggest. On questions about basic values, as measured by the WVS, there was no difference at all in the importance that different age groups placed on family. Friends, work, and leisure time were also very important for all respondents, though people over the age of fifty did not feel as strongly about the last three—which is probably because they are at a different stage in their life cycle. There was also virtually no gap in attitudes regarding whether one has control over one's destiny. In the related questions in the TSCS regarding human agency, there was similarly no difference in responses according to age group. All believed that diligence and effort were more important than luck or fate, while there was more ambivalence on the ability to negotiate with fate.

The WVS did find some difference in age groups on whether respondents associate with materialist or post-materialist values:[19]

- Among people younger than thirty, 65.5 percent were on the materialist side of the scale, while 34.9 percent were more post-materialist.

- Among people aged thirty to forty-nine, 81.6 percent tended toward materialist values, while 15.9 percent were the opposite.

- Among people aged fifty and older, 74.2 percent stressed materialist values and 13.4 percent post-materialist ones.

Thus, a significant majority of all Taiwan people tend toward materialism, but a third of those under twenty-nine years of age have a more post-materialist bent. The least post-materialist respondents were people aged thirty to forty-nine.

The results of the December 2017 TEDS survey on current events by and large do not manifest significant generational differences—defined here to be a difference of more than 10 percent between age cohorts. Indeed, when there is a gap, it is often between those sixty years old and above and everyone else or between the thirty- to thirty-nine-year-old cohort and other age groups. About two-thirds of most respondent age groups were dissatisfied with Tsai Ing-wen's performance since she had taken office, except for those sixty years and older, who were more evenly split. By more than a two-to-one margin, they were dissatisfied with her performance on cross-Strait relations, except for the oldest cohort, which was still unhappy but less so. There was a similar result on economic development. When asked to evaluate Tsai's leadership on a scale of zero to 10, the centrist position (4 to 6) was the majority or plurality in each age group, but the size of the middle position declined incrementally from 60.2 percent in the twenty- to twenty-nine-year-old cohort to 41 percent in the fifty- to fifty-nine-year-old group (the oldest cohort was a bit more positive). Only 9.6 percent of the thirty- to thirty-nine-year-old cohort had a high rating for Tsai.

On some policy issues, however, there was basic uniformity. Between

50 and 60 percent of most age cohorts thought that economic development was Taiwan's top priority (around 45 percent of the oldest group). The three younger cohorts thought that education was most important, while the three oldest ones felt that about cross-Strait relations. But the differences between the highest and lowest were only 12 percent for the former and less than 10 percent for the latter.

Do other social cleavages have similar impacts on attitudes? One possible factor is education. But when it comes to basic values, there is no perceptible difference. For example, in response to the proposition that "your efforts can compensate for your fate," 36.8 percent of people who had at least some college education and 47.1 percent of those with at most a high school education were in agreement. In each group, the share that disagreed was less than 10 percent. There were greater differences when it came to political issues such as identity and how to resolve the dispute with China, which will be touched upon in chapters 8 through 10.

Conclusion

Taiwan as a society is more homogeneous than the intense conflicts within the political system would suggest. Ethnic, class, and religious differences have been muted or appear nonexistent. People see eye to eye on basic human values, and what they believe gives them reason to be satisfied with their lives. Their society is modern and Confucian simultaneously. Citizens understand that promoting a strong economy is of overwhelming importance for Taiwan. Some issues that receive a lot of attention from politicians have a low priority for the average individual. People have reason to be ambivalent about their political system, as chapter 13 will detail, but they have no doubts about the value of democracy in general. Young people are a breed apart in some ways, but far less so than the media has sometimes implied. And on the key question of Taiwan's relationship with China, there is a broad consensus: "We regard ourselves as Taiwanese, and we like the status quo just fine."

3

Taiwan's Government Budget

The government budget may seem to be an odd place to start a discussion of how the Taiwan political system addresses pressing issues. What could be more boring? Yet a government's budget reflects a ranking of policy priorities. As Jessica Tuchman Mathews, former president of the Carnegie Endowment for International Peace, writes, "The [government] budget embodies the country's core political choices: how much government its citizens want, what their priorities for it are, and how large a debt they choose to shoulder and to pass on."[1] In any given year, the political system will allocate more resources to some activities, less to others, and none at all to yet others. As policy priorities change over time, some budget categories are likely to receive more money while others may receive less.

Of course, how much a government spends is a function of the resources it has available in the first place, which, in turn, are a function of both administrative capacity and political choices. In developing economies, administrative capacity is often lacking, which can constrict the boundaries of policy choice. Advanced economies are usually governed by states with high extractive capacity, so the amount of their revenues reflects a deliberate choice. Advanced economies that are also democracies have politically articulate publics that assert conflicting views on how much in resources to extract and then how to use those resources. On both the revenue and spending sides of advanced economies, therefore, the budget process ranks the priorities that a government sets for itself.

Revenues are never sufficient to fund all the tasks that a government would like to accomplish and to meet the challenges it faces. But the type of regime will determine how revenue and spending priorities are set. In Taiwan, Chiang Kai-shek dominated the process during the two first decades of the hard authoritarian rule under the Kuomintang (KMT). He initially allocated the bulk of budgetary allocations to the military in service of his illusory objective of retaking the mainland. Although national security remained a significant priority thereafter, Chiang eventually placed a higher priority to building up Taiwan, particularly through economic development. His son, Chiang Ching-kuo, whom the senior Chiang had groomed to be his successor, sustained this development priority. Not only did budget allocations change, but the power of economic agencies also grew and took on a technocratic character. Still, budgetary politics occurred in a small decisionmaking circle.

With Taiwan's transition to democracy, the budget process and the policy priorities it supported changed. Members of the Legislative Yuan (LY) gained a louder voice in conveying the preferences of their constituents. The most obvious was an increase in spending on social welfare and a reduction in military spending, which is a fairly common shift in new democracies.[2] Members also pushed for the creation of more universities in their districts, which was often done by turning technical schools into universities. Corporations were not silent when it came to budget politics. They argued that lower taxes were necessary to maintain competitiveness in a global economy. None of this was surprising. One would expect that in a democratic system, the public would, to some degree, shape the level of resources available for government spending and the allocation of budgetary resources to various priorities. What is somewhat surprising is where in Taiwan's process politicians convey their preferences.

This chapter describes the structure of the Taiwan government budget, the trends in government spending and resource extraction, the process by which the budget is constructed, and the political implications of budgetary choices.

Budget Structure and Allocations

Taiwan's central government makes the bulk of public expenditures, around 70 percent. The remainder occur in a variety of subcentral jurisdictions: six large and directly administered cities, thirteen counties, three county-level cities, and around 200 subcounty municipalities and townships. But even at the local level, the center dominates by transferring resources through grants and other mechanisms.[3] In understanding the political choices that budgeting represents, it is therefore more instructive to consider total government expenditures than to distinguish which level of government does the spending.[4] The process of building the Taiwan's government budget reveals something about competing policy priorities.

Budgeted government expenditures are divided into nine major categories and thirty-three subcategories, as outlined in table 3-1. Most of the categories are straightforward, but some subcategories are more important than others. Education constitutes about two-thirds of the education, science, and culture category. Approximately two-thirds of the money for economic development goes for agriculture and transportation. Spending on social insurance programs, such as pensions, constitutes 70 percent of social welfare spending,

TABLE 3-1. **Taiwan Budget Expenditure Categories and Subcategories**

Category	Subcategory
General administration	State affairs, Executive Yuan, Legislative Yuan, Judicial Yuan, Examination Yuan, Control Yuan, civil affairs, police, foreign affairs, financial affairs, overseas Chinese affairs
Defense	Defense
Education, science, culture	Education, science, and culture
Economic development	Agriculture, industry, communications, and other
Social welfare	Social insurance (pensions, and so on), public assistance, senior citizens welfare assistance, employment service, public health
Community development, environmental protection	Environmental protection
Retirement, condolence	Retirement and condolence: payments and services
Debt service	Repayment of interest; principal repayment services
Subsidies and other	Subsidies for special cases, balancing the budget, other items, and secondary reserve fund

Source: "The General Budget Proposal of Central Government: Summary Table for Annual Expenditures by Functions, FY 2019," Directorate-General of Budget, Accounting, and Statistics, Republic of China, Taiwan.

while welfare services for those in need makes up the rest.[5] Environmental protection consumes all the money in the category of community development and environmental protection.

Table 3-2 presents the percentage share of each category relative to total expenditures for 2001 and then for the fourteen years from 2006 through 2019, along with the average share and the high and low percentage for each category. The table reveals a fairly stable division of the budget pie among various categories. Education, economic development, and social welfare consume almost half of the budget, all of which reflect core social priorities. In some categories, the shares changed relatively little over thirteen years. The most constant was defense spending, which averaged 11.2 percent of the total budget, with no more than half a percent deviation from the mean.

But three categories showed at least temporary increases, and informed speculation about the reasons behind these choices can be made. First of all, the increase for economic development between 2008 and 2010 was most certainly a temporary budgetary stimulus to boost the Taiwan economy in the wake of the global financial crisis. Once the crisis subsided, the percentage share dropped.

Second, social welfare spending sustained an increase trend. It rose from 14.6 percent in 2009 to 19.7 percent in 2014 and 20.7 percent in 2018, the highest share for that category over the fourteen years. The increase occurred almost completely in the subcategory of social insurance. Indeed, the amount spent in this category climbed from NT$135.7 billion in 2007 to NT$345.4 billion in 2017, almost tripling in ten years. This stems from the island's aging population: the number of people sixty-five years and older increased by 46.1 percent between 2007 and 2018, which increased the amount of money that Taiwan's various pension payments paid out.[6] Similar to pension programs in other countries, Taiwan's pension programs do not necessarily receive as much in contributions as they are likely to have to pay out.[7] The same goes for health insurance. Taiwan has a single-payer system that has gotten high marks for proving good care to the public, but it has been underfunded. The National Health Insurance systems expenditures in 2019 exceeded revenues by around NT$55 billion. In 2020 there were public warnings that the system could go bankrupt within a year.[8]

Third, there was the significant increase in the amount spent on education, science, and culture, a response to a specific and growing social need. Spending in the education category is already higher than in any other, in part because of a constitutional mandate that 15 percent of the central government budget and 35 percent of local government budgets should be spent on edu-

TABLE 3-2. **Relative Shares of Total Taiwan Government Budget, 2001–2019, Various Years (Percent)**

Year	General administration	Defense	Education, science, culture	Economic development	Social welfare	Environment	Retirement, condolences	Debt service	Miscellaneous
2001	14.7	11.0	19.2	17.1	17.7	4.9	7.8	7.6	1
2006	15.7	10.7	22.0	15.5	16.8	4.0	8.9	6.3	1
2007	15.1	11.2	21.7	16.8	16.4	3.8	8.8	6.1	1
2008	15.1	11.3	21.3	18.6	15.8	3.5	8.7	5.8	1
2009	13.5	11.2	21.9	22.7	14.6	3.5	7.7	4.9	1
2010	14.4	11.2	21.7	20.3	16.3	3.5	7.9	4.7	1
2011	14.5	11.1	22.7	18.2	17.2	3.4	8.2	4.7	1
2012	14.6	11.4	22.4	15.2	20.3	3.2	8.2	4.7	1
2013	14.4	11.1	22.6	14.9	20.3	4.0	7.9	4.9	1
2014	14.5	11.1	23.5	15.2	19.7	3.2	8.1	4.8	1
2015	14.6	11.6	24.2	13.4	20.2	3.1	8.3	4.6	1
2016	14.1	11.5	24.4	14.5	20.1	3.4	7.6	4.4	1
2017	13.8	11.1	25.1	14.0	20.5	4.5	7.2	3.9	1
2018	14.1	10.8	23.7	15.9	20.7	3.8	6.7	3.7	1
2019	14.3	11.0	24.1	16.0	20.3	3.6	6.6	3.6	0.5
Average	14.5	11.2	22.7	16.6	18.5	3.7	7.9	5.0	1.0
Low	13.5	10.7	19.2	13.4	14.6	3.1	7.2	3.9	1.0
High	15.7	11.6	25.1	22.7	20.7	4.5	8.9	7.6	1.0

Source: Statistical Yearbook of the Republic of China, Directorate-General Budget, Accounting and Statistics, Executive Yuan, Republic of China, September 2019, table 91, "Net Government Expenditures of All Levels" (https://eng.stat.gov.tw/public/data/dgbas03/bs2/yearbook_eng/Yearbook2019.pdf).

cation, science, and culture.[9] Together, these are the only budget categories so earmarked in the constitution. In practice, education, science, and culture had received less than 23 percent of total government spending before 2014, but after that year expenditures on these categories began to climb. Education was the subcategory that rose the most, caused by a deliberate decision by the Ma Ying-jeou administration to expand preschool education.[10] As a result, the number of preschools more than doubled in the 2012–2013 school year, and the number of preschool teachers tripled.[11] The likely rationale for this expansion of the government's role was the decline in the marriage and birth rates, as well as the rise in the cost of housing. It was hoped that the existence of a stronger preschool sector would create incentives for women to get married and then have children, giving them the option of returning to the workplace. Furthermore, it might also contribute to their children's education and to Taiwan's economic competitiveness over the long term.

On the other hand, the defense sector's unchanging budget share is a puzzle, since China was steadily acquiring military capabilities during this period. One reason may have been the growth of spending on preschool education and pensions, squeezing all other categories in the budget. Still, Taiwan's growing vulnerability over the years was also a serious policy concern. Moreover, low and stagnant defense spending has been a source of great frustration to U.S. defense officials, who have complained since the first decade of this century that the Taipei government spends too little to protect itself. Why, they ask, don't policymakers shift resources to respond to the growing danger? (We will return to this puzzle in chapter 9.)

Overall, the trend of government expenditures has been relatively modest. From 2007 to 2017, spending increased overall by NT$500.953 billion. That was an increase of 21.4 percent over twelve years, about 1.75 percent a year. Early in that period, the total amount actually declined, from NT$2.922 trillion in 2007 to NT$2.671 trillion in 2009, a response no doubt to the global financial crisis. Expenditures remained at that general level until 2016, when they increased by around NT$100 trillion and then rose to NT$2.912 trillion in 2019, mainly because of increases for social insurance and education.

Explaining Taiwan's Budget Choices

How do we explain this pattern of spending? In part, it is what the public wants. The December 2019 Taiwan Election and Democratization Study found that 38.7 percent of those polled thought that economic development should be President Tsai Ing-wen's top priority, and another 20.9 percent favored cross-Strait relations. The only other significant category was education (12.1 percent).[12] These three categories affect one another, since quality education strengthens competitiveness and the business relationship with China has affected growth. Social welfare spending has enjoyed strong support for more than two decades and is growing automatically as the population ages. So it is no surprise that education, the economy, and social welfare consume more than 50 percent of government spending. Hypothetically, if voters were dissatisfied with this allocation of resources, they could shift support to a party that proposed a different distribution of the budget pie. But radical reallocations have never been proposed in Taiwan election campaigns.

Public consensus aside, there are other factors at play in understanding Taiwan's budget politics. One is the budgetary process itself. Another is a social aversion to providing the government with greater resources.

The Budget-Making Process

Two agencies of the Executive Yuan govern the budget formulation process at the central government. The Ministry of Finance estimates the total revenues that will be available in the next fiscal year (which is also the calendar year). The Directorate-General for Budget, Accounting, and Statistics (DGBAS), which is analogous in function to the U.S. Office of Management and Budget, then sets expenditure caps for each of the ministry-level agencies at the central level. Each agency prepares a more detailed budget, usually by referencing prior-year spending, even though they are supposed to start with a zero base. Once all agency budget proposals are aggregated into the draft central budget, the premier (also called the president of the EY) convenes the annual meeting of its program and budget council to review the draft. If any agency wishes to breach its DGBAS cap, it must justify its request at this point. Once approved internally, and before the end of August, the EY transmits the draft aggregate budget proposal to the LY. Up until this point, therefore, the process has taken a technocratic and top-down approach, conducted within the EY. Taiwan's president can use public and private appeals to shape budget parameters, but even those interventions have only a limited impact on a well-established division of market shares among spending categories.[13]

Moreover, there is a long-standing bias in budget construction. As Tsai-tsu Su, a specialist on government budgeting at National Taiwan University, comments, "the DGBAS is occupied more with controlling the level of total spending and the budget deficit than with focusing on whether each ministry's budget allocation corresponds to the needs of the public and fulfills the principles of efficiency, effectiveness and fairness."[14] Encouraging this frugality bias are legal limits on how much expenditures can exceed revenues, and therefore be covered by deficit financing, as well as a ceiling on the debt-to-GDP ratio, which in 2017 was estimated to be a quite manageable 35.7 percent.[15]

Once the EY sends the draft budget to the LY, the process becomes more political, but only somewhat. Su notes that "legislators focus more on gaining publicity during the budget approval process than on exercising professionalism."[16] One reason is that LY members are actually quite constrained when it comes to using the budget to affect national priorities, because they do not have the authority to do so. Article 70 of the Republic of China Constitution states that "the Legislative Yuan shall not propose any increases of the expenditure in the budgetary bill submitted by the Executive Yuan."[17] It may only reduce specific items or eliminate them. Yet LY members rarely use the power to cut spending on programs that they do not like in order to send a message to the administration. A comparison of the size of the total central government budget submitted to the LY and the size of the budget enacted from 2007 through 2017 shows only a tiny difference, around one-tenth of 1 percent.[18] If LY members are going to influence the budget proposal that comes to them, it is by promoting their spending preferences in the regular oversight process, through their periodic interpellations of EY officials and individual lobbying of executive agencies.[19]

Mechanisms do exist to provide some degree of flexibility in the budget process. Within the same program, up to 20 percent of the funds in one budget account may be transferred to another account. The government also maintains reserve funds for contingencies, and the EY may propose supplemental or special budgets to meet unanticipated needs, equal to about 5 percent of the regular budget. The Budget Act specifies that a special budget is justified in dealing with major national economic events, calamities, or periodic political events or for national defense facilities and other security purposes in the event of a major war or other national defense emergency. For example, a special budget was passed to respond to a major typhoon that struck Taiwan in August 2009. Major arms purchases from the United States are usually covered through special budgets, such as the one passed in November 2019 for jet aircraft.[20] In July 2020, a special budget was proposed to assist the economic sectors hurt by the coronavirus pandemic.[21]

In short, how Taiwan government budgets are constructed constrains the impact of public preferences on the how resources are allocated. There is a built-in bias throughout the budget process against any significant reordering of spending beyond the resources available. The executive branch sets strict parameters that reduce the discretion of individual ministries and the LY to change them. Constitutionally, legislators lack the power to move money from one spending priority to another. A ministry official or LY member, or even the president, who wishes to change priorities would best succeed in doing so before the DGBAS sets its spending caps. Various actors in each branch of the government are more interested in preserving their "market share" than in expanding it.

Revenues

The fundamental reason that government spending grew at a modest rate is the relative decline in the resources available. From 2008 to 2018, Taiwan's GDP increased by about one-third, while tax revenues as a share of GDP remained stable at an average of 12.1 percent (see table 3-3). Expenditures as a

TABLE 3-3. **Government Tax Revenue as Share of GDP**

Year	GDP	Tax Revenue	Share (percent)
2006	12,640,803	1,556,652	12.3
2007	13,407,062	1,685,875	12.6
2008	13,150,950	1,710,617	13.0
2009	12,961,650	1,483,518	11.4
2010	14,119,213	1,565,827	11.1
2011	14,312,200	1,703,989	11.9
2012	14,686,917	1,733,359	11.8
2013	15,230,739	1,768,817	11.6
2014	16,111,867	1,917,609	11.9
2015	16,770,671	2,076,623	12.4
2016	17,176,300	2,165,797	12.6
2017	17,501,181	2,187,690	12.5
2018	17,793,139	2.229.208	12.5
2008–2018 average	15,066,360	2,378,581	12.1

Source: Taiwan Statistical Data Book, 2019 (Taipei: National Development Council, ROC [Taiwan], 2018), table 3-1, "Gross Domestic Product and Gross National Income," and table 9-2a, "Net Government Revenues of All Levels by Source." (https://eng.stat.gov.tw/public/data/dgbas03/bs2/yearbook_eng/Yearbook2019.pdf), pp. 51, 177.

share of GDP fell from 17.9 percent to 16.0.[22] That is, the key political choice regarding the budget is not about how to allocate money going out but how much money to take in. Here is where the public has its greatest impact.

On first glance, the low level of revenues is puzzling. Relatively speaking, Taiwan is a pretty rich country. The CIA's *World Factbook* estimates that Taiwan's GDP in purchasing power parity terms in 2017 was twenty-second in the world. Furthermore, its per capita GDP was ranked twenty-eighth, and its gross national savings was seventeenth.[23] According to statistics compiled by Taiwan's National Development Council, the top 20 percent of households in 2017 had 40.4 percent of personal income, and the second quintile had 23.2 percent. That is, almost 40 percent of households had almost two-thirds of personal income. The highest quintile share was six times that of the lowest. The 2018 *Global Wealth Databook,* published by Research Institute of Credit Suisse, reports that the top 10 percent of Taiwan adults held 59.8 percent of Taiwan's wealth, the top 20 percent had 74.2 percent, and the top 40 percent had 89 percent.[24]

But relative to other countries, Taiwan's level of total resources available to the government is remarkably low. Those resources, as measured by the CIA *World Factbook,* are higher than tax revenue, but taxes are the most significant component. The 2017 figure for Taiwan was 16 percent of GDP, which ranked 184th worldwide. For other advanced economies in East Asia and the Pacific, the percentage of resources as a share of GDP was 36.8 for New Zealand, 35.5 for Australia, 35.1 for Japan, and 23.2 for Hong Kong and South Korea. Only Singapore, at 15.7 percent, was similar to Taiwan's ratio (the United States was at 17 percent).[25] Such a low rate could contribute to the island's economic competitiveness and private consumption. However, the Ministry of Finance was frank to say that more revenue could be extracted. "Considering the present levels of our economic development and national income, the current level of the tax burden can be called reasonable, and there is a potential capacity for additional taxation in the future."[26]

There is, therefore, a contradiction between the wealth in Taiwan society and the portion of that wealth the government requires citizens and companies to provide to underwrite government services. If government resources are to increase, it will probably have to be through higher taxes, because taxes constitute 79.5 percent of total government revenues (most of the remainder comes from public enterprises' surpluses and various fees).[27] A 2018 study of the relationship between social welfare policy and taxation found that "the trajectory of Taiwan's welfare regime is, in fact determined by the state's taxation capacity. While democratic competition does create incentives to expand public provision of welfare, the design and realization of these policies inevitably depend on whether the state has the capability to raise the needed revenues through taxation policies."[28] Facing this revenue constraint, the Ma and Tsai administrations undertook to reform the tax system, including income, estate, and gift taxes (see table 3-4 for different types of taxes).[29]

Taiwan has two types of income tax. The first type is the tax on profit-seeking enterprises, which is assessed on income earned from directly operating a business. The second is the individual income tax, which is assessed on all other income, including earnings from professional activities and investment dividends. Each type contributes about half of the total income taxes collected.

The Ma and Tsai administrations made reforms on both types of income tax. During the Ma administration in 2010, the income threshold below which no profit-seeking enterprise was required to pay tax was raised from NT$50,000 to NT$120,000, and the tax rate was reduced from 25 percent to 17 percent (later raised to 20 percent). In addition, the amount of tax an enterprise paid on its total taxable income could not exceed "half the amount of the taxable income in excess of NT$120,000" (see table 3-5 for current rates).[30]

The Ma administration also reformed the individual income tax, which is similar in configuration to that in the United States, with a progressive set of tax brackets plus a number of ways for taxpayers to reduce their liability. Under the preceding administration of Chen Shui-bian, there were five tax brackets, with 6 percent being the rate for the lowest bracket and 40 percent for the highest. In 2014 the Ma administration undertook a major reform for the stated purpose of achieving fiscal sustainability and fairness.[31] The

TABLE 3-4. **Tax Revenue in Major Categories, 2013 and 2019**

	Millions of NT$	
Category	2013	2019
Customs	97,009	116,500
Income	743,290	948,000
Estate and gift	23,728	12,537
Business	327,971	239,829
Commodity	207,153	190,056

Source: Taiwan Statistical Data Book, 2019 (Taipei: National Development Council, R.O.C. [Taiwan], 2019), p. 182.

Notes: Actual figures for 2013, 2019 figures are estimates.

TABLE 3-5. **Taiwan Income Tax Brackets, 2020**

Bracket (NT$)	Value of top amount in US$	Tax rate (percent)
1–540,000	16,364	5
540,001–1,210,000	36,667	12
1,210,001–2,420,000	43,030	20
2,420,001–4,530,000	137,272	30
4,535,001–10,310,000	137,272	40
10,310,001 and above	45	

Source: "Taiwan, Individual: Taxes on Personal Income," *Worldwide Tax Summaries,* PwC (https://taxsummaries.pwc.com/taiwan/individual/taxes-on-personal-income).

reforms added a sixth bracket and set the bracket rates at 5, 12, 20, 30, 40, and 45 percent. That top rate was charged on any income over NT$10 million (about US$300,000), making the system more progressive. Income tax receipts as a share of revenue increased from around 30 percent in the first half of the 2010s to 36 percent in the second half.

However, in February 2018, the Tsai administration and the legislature—controlled at the time by the Democratic Progressive Party (DPP)—reversed some of the Ma reforms. The stated goal was to establish a competitive, fair, and reasonable system that met the trend of international taxation. The personal standard deduction was increased by 30 percent, and the special deduction for preschool-age children was raised from NT$25,000 to NT$120,000 per child (to encourage a higher birthrate, no doubt). The highest bracket in the Ma administration's system was eliminated, setting the highest marginal tax rate back at 40 percent. Based on tax brackets alone, the 2018 reforms made the system less progressive. Deductions aside, under Ma's system, a person with an income of NT$12,000,000 would owe a tax of NT$4,054,900. Under the DPP reforms, the same person would owe NT$3,970,400, or NT$84,500 less. As a result, according to one estimate, taking deductions into account, the effective tax bracket for high-income individuals is roughly 30 to 33 percent.[32]

Taiwan's estate and gift tax had remained essentially unchanged since the mid-1990s and had not kept up with globalization and a host of innovations in financial instruments. The Ma administration undertook a major overhaul of the estate and gift tax in 2009. The prior system of ten tax brackets with graduated rates, the highest of which was 50 percent, was changed to one with a single, flat tax of 10 percent, along with higher deductions and exemptions.

Then, in 2017, after the Tsai administration took office, a more progressive system was instituted. An estate valued under NT$50 million was taxed at a 10 percent rate, while an estate valued between NT$50 and 100 million was taxed at 15 percent and one valued at more than NT$100 million at 20 percent.

The long-term impact of the various revenue reforms of the Ma and Tsai administrations remains to be seen. Comparing the actual revenues in 2013 for several major categories with the estimates for 2019 is not wholly encouraging. The projected income tax receipts for 2019 were NT$104.7 billion more than the 2013 collections, though that was partly offset by an unexplained NT$88.1 million drop in returns for the business tax. Moreover, the very gradual increase in overall revenues (NT$2.25 trillion in 2017) is significantly short of expenditures (NT$2.77 trillion in the same year).[33]

Taiwan, therefore, is a good example of what might be called the Thomas Piketty problem—that is, the consequences of taxing different types of assets at different rates.[34] Taxing wages and salaries at a higher rate than income on investments of various kinds, a phenomenon in Taiwan and other advanced economies, causes inequality of wealth and income to increase (and is also unfair from a normative point of view). Privileging the wealthy concerning their tax obligations also limits the resources that the government has available to create public goods, such as education and infrastructure, to provide social services, which contribute to economic development and human welfare, and to enhance security against external threats. The Credit Suisse data about the wealth held in Taiwan suggests that increasing the estate tax, which typically contributes only 2.3 percent of total revenues, would be one way for the state to enlarge its resources. Otherwise, those who have benefited most from Taiwan's long-term growth will pass most of their wealth on to their descendants, rather than returning some of those benefits to society. Therefore, taxes on land, property tax, and capital gains, none of which have been the objects of recent reform, may also be candidates for revision.

To be sure, taxing wealth does create incentives for evasion, and increasing the land and capital gains tax may rattle property and equity markets. Politically, tax reform is one of the hardest projects to undertake. But those risks and difficulties do not negate the need to design a package of changes that are technocratically smart and politically doable. Inaction entails its own costs. Fundamentally, budget reform will require a broader consensus among political actors that it is necessary.

The Politics of Pension Reform

This sort of consensus building did not happen in regard to pension reform. This was not a new project for the Taiwan government, since it was clear that pension funds were moving toward insolvency. It was not until Tsai Ing-wen's first term that reform was enacted, and the process was complex and a bit ugly. Technocrats and political leaders were involved but also civil society organizations and affected pensioners. The latter engaged in aggressive protests, which failed to block enactment of the administration's proposal but introduced a "you win, I lose" dimension to the dispute.

Taiwan has a fragmented pension system with different programs for different occupational groups. During the authoritarian period, the KMT regime instituted pensions for members of the armed services, civil servants, and teachers, which were key sectors of the regime. The key feature of these programs was a system of savings accounts for which the government guaranteed annual interest of 18 percent. It was only after democratization that public pressure began to build to establish social insurance programs for other classes of workers and, if possible, to integrate the systems.[35] Peasants and laborers gained protections, but not on the same generous terms granted to soldiers, civil servants, and teachers. Politicians, civil society groups, and competing government agencies clashed, leading to least-common-denominator progress. Shih Jiunn Shi, of the Graduate Institute of National Development at National Taiwan University, sums up the situation in the early years of the Ma administration: "The incessant efforts of social welfare associations and scholars have heaved pertinent ideas of social justice and generational solidarity to [a] certain political height, and consensus has emerged with regard to the advantages as well as disadvantages of different institutional designs. Nonetheless . . . they have failed to gain enough political momentum to contend with other [rival] ideas and interests."[36]

One reason for failure was the increasingly entrenched interests of the beneficiaries of each of the programs. Another reason was the competition of the two major parties to win political benefits for championing pension programs. As Shi notes, "The DPP [attempted] to find an arena where it could rally more support, [but] this strategy backfired when the KMT joined the game and gradually took the lead in the planning and promulgating of national pension insurance schemes. In an attempt to overtrump its opponent, the DPP turned to the issue of old-age allowances for specific groups, only to trigger even more countermoves of the KMT."[37] Indeed, this race to the bottom has been a common thread that runs through the designs of all Taiwan's social welfare programs. Stephan Haggard and Robert Kaufman conclude that "the shifts in . . . Taiwan happened not because lower-class parties demanded more benefits, but because conservative parties preemptively promoted programs such as health care and pensions, which appealed to the middle class, instead of programs that would be attractive to workers."[38]

The Ma administration made a valiant effort to reform the pension programs for retired military personnel, civil servants, and teachers. After extensive public consultations, Premier Jiang Yi-huah proposed a plan that he said would keep the programs solvent for at least three decades, but it had to be abandoned because of intense opposition from public employees and labor groups.[39]

By the time Tsai Ing-wen took office, it was no longer possible to ignore the financial straits of the public sector pensions, despite the opposition of vested interests. In late 2015, it was estimated that the "hidden debt" for payments to retired public servants was NT$8.2 trillion (US$248 billion), while government revenues for 2018 were US$86.3 billion.[40] Financial sustainability aside, there was the question of equity. Retired soldiers, civil servants, and teachers were treated better than pensioners from the private sector, and they viewed their pensions as a binding obligation that the government owed them. But those who opposed the Tsai administration's reform went beyond the normal tools of political opposition. Although there were peaceful demonstrations, some of them escalated into violence between protesters and the police. On several occasions, the protesters tried to storm the LY building, as members of the Sunflower movement had in 2014. There were even credible allegations that some of the leaders of the protests were sympathetic to the People's Republic of China.[41]

In the end, the DPP-controlled legislature passed reforms for each of the three systems (civil servants and teachers in 2017 and military in 2018). Opponents filed suit with the constitutional court, but the justices upheld the basic design of the system and found fault with only a few provisions.[42] Yet the contentious process by which this outcome was reached aggravated the conflict over substance. This was true even when it was generally clear that the status quo was not viable and fairness mandated a rebalancing of intergenerational obligations and benefits. This, in turn, has fostered doubts that the Taiwan political system can properly address even tougher policy problems.

Conclusion

The choices that Taiwan's political leaders make about revenues and expenditures say a lot about their contending priorities. Spending for economic construction is steady, while spending for education and social welfare grows, partly because it makes good policy sense but also because citizens want their tax dollars spent in these ways. However, in spite of China's continual buildup of its capabilities, Taiwan's spending on defense has remained steady.

The Taiwan system has a bias against deficit spending and against passing too great a burden onto the next generation, which has enough hurdles to achieving a prosperous life. Thus if the government is to meet its obviously looming policy needs, it must extract more from society in the form of revenue, from the people who have the resources to pay. Yet even though Taiwan is a relatively wealthy society, citizens and corporations are averse to paying more in taxes, and they do not want tax policy to undermine property and equity markets. Politicians show some willingness to adjust the tax system, but the changes made seem more incremental than the situation requires. Finite resources and pressing demands dictate the need for more significant choices, but the political will to craft the compromises and sell them to the public is not strong. To defer choices is itself a choice, and not one that is in the broader public interest. Moreover, although trade-offs exist between growth and the level of taxation, they need not be zero-sum. As a contributor to the *Taipei Times* puts it, "One of [a responsible government's] tasks should be to make society understand that a fair taxation system does not hinder economic growth; it can provide the public with more adequate public services and better infrastructure, improve the environment and cut pollution."[43]

4

Taiwan's Economy

Before Taiwan became the poster child of democratization in East Asia, it was the poster child of export-led growth. Ever since the 1960s, when the Kuomintang (KMT) leadership figured out that improving the people's standard of living was the best way to ensure stability and the party's continued rule, the economy has been the ballast of Taiwan society. Industrialization in the takeoff phase brought rising incomes to Taiwan families, who sent their sons and daughters to work in factories, to set up commercial enterprises, and to earn advance degrees overseas. The result was a rising, spreading tide of economic prosperity that in only a few decades transformed the island from a poor, agricultural society to a vibrant, middle-class society.

Scholars debate whether it is government policies or private enterprise that deserves the credit for this early success. Some hold up Taiwan as an example of the East Asian developmental state, where governments played a key role in picking the most likely sectors for future economic growth, allocating capital accordingly, and ensuring adequate public infrastructure and human capital.[1] Others claim that despite government policies, it was private entrepreneurs who stimulated rapid growth. They listened to demand signals from major retailers in the United States and other advanced economies as to which products consumers in those countries wanted and then produced those products to the price and quality specifications of their buyers. Successful companies did not internally create the capacity to manufacture all the parts and components needed for a finished product but instead created networks of small- and medium-size companies that supplied what the lead company needed. When big retailers in the West signaled that demand for previously popular products was declining, Taiwan entrepreneurs and their networks nimbly abandoned those products and moved on to something else, always staying one step ahead of the competitiveness curve.[2]

By the 1980s, however, growth was slowing. Domestic wages were rising, and the Reagan administration demanded that Taiwan increase the value of its currency, which would make its exports to America more expensive. Fortunately for Taiwan, China's own shift to export-led growth gave the island's companies a new lease on life. China needed outsiders' capital, technology, and management skills to stimulate its own growth. Many Taiwan firms concluded that China, with its low-cost, skilled labor force, was the most economical place to do the final assembly of a wide range of their products, and thus it became the primary destination for outward Taiwan investment. Some of this investment was used to create platforms for the assembly and production of goods for export globally. Other parts of it produced goods for the domestic market that Chinese firms could not make at the same quality level.

Cross-Strait trade followed investment. The parts and components for products assembled in China often came from Taiwan, so China became Taiwan's largest export market. It accounted for 37 percent of Taiwan's total exports in 2018, only a modest reduction from the 42 percent in 2009.[3] About 70 percent of its outbound investment goes to China, around 100,000 Taiwan firms have operations there, and around 50 percent of Taiwan citizens working off the island in 2016 were working on the mainland.[4]

It was not just large companies that migrated to the mainland. Even in the 1990s and later, large Taiwan firms continued to organize production the way they always had, by relying on their vast networks of smaller suppliers and subcontractors. Contract manufacturing had worked for shoes and toys, and it would also work for laptop computers and mobile phones. To ensure that ventures in China would be profitable, both the large Taiwan companies and their networks moved there.

As the complexity of this mode of production grew, the core firm of any production cluster had to become skillful in managing global supply or value chains that linked the productive process together. That was necessary to make sure that each network worked efficiently and as a team for the group to make deliveries, meet payrolls, and make profits. Some of these supply chains ran from the United States through Taiwan, Hong Kong, South Korea, and Japan to China and back to the United States.

The archaic way that customs authorities designate a product's country of origin obscures the achievements of Taiwan companies. For U.S. Customs, a product's country of origin is deemed to be where the item underwent "substantial transformation" into its final form. A product whose supply chain is managed by a Taiwan company may be labeled "made in China" merely because the final assembly took place in a Taiwan-owned subsidiary in China. A laptop computer might be labeled a Chinese product, but its parts and components would have had many sources. Furthermore, the stages of production would have occurred in multiple countries, with China being the last.

As cross-Strait economic relations first opened and then deepened, scholars, politicians, and citizens in Taiwan increasingly debated whether such an extensive relationship with China was too much of a good thing. As a general rule, an economy that depends too much on one trading partner, especially a much larger one, risks constraining its own freedom of action, and China is no ordinary trading partner. Government policies during the Lee Teng-hui and Chen Shui-bian administrations sought with limited success to restrict mainland investment. The reason was not just economic. Chinese leaders, whose long-term objective is to incorporate Taiwan into the People's Republic of China, saw business interdependence as a steppingstone to political amalgamation. It was during the administration of Taiwan president Ma Ying-jeou that there was substantial progress in normalizing and institutionalizing cross-Strait economic relations.[5] Yet it was also during that time that some in Taiwan issued more strident warnings about the dangers of depending for prosperity on a China with such political ambitions.

Taiwan has long since moved beyond the takeoff phase of growth powered through low-wage labor. A once-young society is now aging. Maintaining competitiveness is much harder today than it was in the past. Enjoying the benefits that China has provided while simultaneously deflecting its political demands is becoming more difficult. Managing these competing priorities has become a daunting task for political leaders.

A Modern Economy

It was through good government policies, an army of opportunistic entrepreneurs, a lot of hard work, and the protection from the United States that Taiwan became a modern, prosperous, and productive society. A number of indicators of Taiwan's modernity have been examined, but the speed with which it arrived was just as impressive. In 1960, Taiwan's per capita national income in current dollars was equivalent to only US$156. It had climbed to

US$371 by 1970, US$2,139 by 1980, and US$7,672 by 1990. The mainland's opening up and the further growth it stimulated ensured that Taiwan would avoid the middle-income trap. By 2017 the per capita national income was US$21,310.[6] On the basis of purchasing power parity, which adjusts for the cost of living, the 2017 figure was US$50,500.[7] The United Nations Development Program's Human Development Index score in 2017 was 0.907; only twenty other countries possessed a higher score.[8]

Taiwan also receives high marks from the World Economic Forum (WEF) in its annual competitiveness rankings. The forum defines competitiveness as "the attributes and qualities of an economy that allow for a more efficient use of factors of production. . . . Productivity gains are the most important determinant of long-term economic growth." On this basis, it ranked Taiwan twelfth worldwide in the survey released in October 2019, one level higher than the previous assessment. Its composite score was 80.2 out of 100.[9] Eight of Taiwan's neighbors in the Asia-Pacific were among the top thirty economies. Three of these economies, two of them cities, scored higher than Taiwan: Singapore (first, 84.8), Hong Kong (third, 83.1), and Japan (sixth, 82.3). Five of them scored lower: South Korea (thirteenth, 79.6), Australia (sixteenth, 78.7), New Zealand (nineteenth, 76.7), Malaysia (twenty-seventh, 74.6), and China (twenty-eighth, 73.9).

The WEF uses twelve factors—or "pillars"—to measure competitiveness. Taiwan ranks first in the world when it comes to macroeconomic stability, fourth in innovation capacity, sixth in its financial system, eleventh in information and communications technology adoption, fourteenth in the product market, fifteenth in its labor market, nineteenth in market size, and twentieth in business dynamism. Taiwan's innovation ranking was particularly significant in the WEF's assessment. Its report states that "there is a lot of scope [worldwide] to do better in both adopting technology and boosting innovation. Only four economies score above 80 on the Innovation capability pillar—Germany, United States, Switzerland and Taiwan."[10] On the remaining pillars, Taiwan ranked between twenty-first and thirtieth.

Another measure of its economic success is the number of products made by Taiwan companies that constitute at least one-third of total global production. They are listed in table 4-1. Only four of the products listed are actually produced in Taiwan itself (onshore), and even for those, a share of the total produced is still done overseas. Mainland China is the biggest offshore site, but Taiwan companies are active in other markets as well. The onshore-offshore distinction highlights the regional and global reach of Taiwan companies and their mastery of supply-chain management in a globalized economy.

TABLE 4-1. **Taiwan Companies' Share of the Global Production of Certain Products, 2018 (Percent)**

Motherboards	84.8
Cable CPE[a]	83.2
Golf-club heads	81.5
Notebook computers	78.7
IC Foundries[b]	75.6
Wireless local area network	68.1
Digital CPE[a]	66.1
IC packaging and testing[b]	55.8
Desktop computers	51.1
Functional textiles	51.1
Personal navigation devices[b]	47.9
Mobile device optical lens	46.4
Copper-clad laminate	43.4
Servers	35.4
High-end bicycles[b]	33.4

Source: Taiwan Statistical Data Book, 2019 (Taipei: National Development Council, R.O.C. [Taiwan]), 2019, introductory "Abstract of Key Economic and Social Statistics," table 4-a, "Products of which Taiwan Was among the World's Three Largest Producers in 2018, Including Offshore Production," p. 12; and table 4-b, "Products of which Taiwan Was among the World's Three Largest Producers in 2018," p. 12; and "Excluding Offshore Production," p. 13.

a. Customer premise equipment.
b. Produced onshore, in Taiwan.

One can see clear evidence of Taiwan's material prosperity when walking the main streets of Taipei, the capital city. There are cars of various makes and models, including luxury vehicles from Japan, Western Europe, and the United States. Traffic is orderly, and dedicated bus lanes reduce congestion, unlike the mid-1970s, when I lived in Taiwan as a graduate student. Public transportation works well. High-rise buildings with luxury condos that reflect global architectural trends are common on major avenues, as are business enterprises of all kinds, including those that one would expect to find in a high-income consumer economy: five-star hotels with luxury stores, shops selling women's fashions, bridal ware, lingerie, jewelry, men's bespoke apparel, shoes, and so on. There are also all manner of service firms for banking and finance, real estate, trading, medical and dental offices, gyms, spas, photographers' studios, language schools, convenience stores, and, most prevalent of all, food services. Taipei is strewn with restaurants, coffee shops, and tea shops of all shapes and sizes, all catering to a culture that likes to organize social intercourse around food and drink.

Multiple Imbalances

Yet a stroll through downtown Taipei also reveals that not everyone is in the lap of luxury. Even on major streets, fleets of noisy motorcycles, the vehicle of the lower classes, coexist with quiet luxury cars. Not far off the major thoroughfares, the neighborhoods take on a different appearance. The architecture is a throwback to the mid-twentieth century and before. Buildings are only a few stories high and purely functional: shops at street level and relatively small apartments above, with the upper floors cantilevered so that they cover sidewalks, providing protection in rainy weather. Most shops cater to lower-class consumers and specialize in traditional trades: hardware, stationery and art products, printing, cheap glasses, tea, drugs, religious items used for temple worship, small hotels, small groceries, and betel nut stands. These concerns tend to be family enterprises, rather than franchises of international brands, and smaller than the upscale retail outlets on the main thoroughfares. Here and there, markets appear in the morning selling food—fresh fruits and vegetables, raw meat, and so on—plus other items for daily life. Nearby, perhaps, is a temple where people from the neighborhood propitiate the traditional gods, asking them to cure a relative's illness, to help a student score well on an upcoming exam, or to resolve a family problem.

A city like Taipei is not strictly segregated between upper- and lower-class areas. "Indie" restaurants and chic dress shops can be found in more traditional neighborhoods as well as in major commercial areas. The transition between high-end and low-end is more gradual, defined by real estate prices and the proximity of consumers and foreign tourists. Still, even a short walk shows that economic prosperity has not benefited all to the same degree, and as one moves away from the center of town, the sheen of twenty-first-century affluence fades.

Indeed, Taiwan is a society marked by several overlapping, interactive, and reinforcing imbalances. These imbalances are socioeconomic in nature. They both cause and are exacerbated by slowing economic growth. The rate of growth of national income has declined on an annual basis from 7.7 percent in 1997 to 3.8 percent in 2007 to 1.6 percent in 2017.[11] Since the global financial crisis, and excepting a brief rebound thereafter, Taiwan's rates of economic growth, domestic fixed capital formation, private consumption, and exports of goods and services have all been essentially flat.[12] Taiwan has imbalances in the demography of its population, its incomes and standards of living, its firm sizes, and in its industrial structure, where information technology reigns supreme.

Demographic Shift

In April 2018, Taiwan was no longer an aging society but an aged one, according to World Health Organization criteria. The share of its population that was sixty-five years or older exceeded 14 percent.[13] The island's total population, which was estimated at around 23.55 million people in 2018, has peaked and will begin to decline in the 2030s. At the same time, the number of children being born has declined. In 2020, the population growth rate was estimated at 0.11 percent and the birth rate at only eight births per thousand people.[14] As the size of the elderly cohort grows and the working population declines, the cost of caring for old people will grow and present a burden for younger cohorts.[15]

The shift in the population's composition will be quite radical. The share of people sixty-five years and older was 8.3 percent in 1998 and an estimated 13.1 in 2016, but it will most likely rise to 25.7 percent in 2035 and 34.1 percent in 2050.[16] Taiwan's working population is on the cusp of a fairly steep relative decline: from 74.1 percent of the total population in 2014 to 71.5 percent in 2020, 61.8 percent in 2035, and 57.3 percent in 2044.[17] As a result, there will be considerably more elderly people, as well as more children, who will depend on a shrinking number of working-age people to support them. The government will have to increase taxes on the younger employed to pay for the retirement and health care of the elderly or reduce benefits allotted for the elderly, or both. Neither step would be politically popular. Furthermore, the smaller the share of young adults in the population, the fewer qualified applicants there will be for jobs for which the demand for labor is high, and the fewer young men there will be to serve in the armed forces.

This is a structural problem that is quite immune from any short-term amelioration. There are steps that governments can take, such as funding more public day care facilities so mothers can return to the workforce. But those measures may be insufficient to create a large enough cohort of young people to cover the cost of social programs for the elderly. Increasing the number of births requires, of course, that young people get married at a higher rate than is currently the case. In 2017–2018, 4.4 million Taiwan citizens between the ages of twenty and forty were unmarried, representing 64.5 percent of the people in that age cohort.[18]

Income and Wealth

In recent decades there has been a trend toward greater economic inequality and higher costs of living. Taiwan's level does not look too bad when measured by its Gini coefficient, where zero indicates even distribution of income and one represents maximum inequality. In 1980 it stood at 0.278; in 2017 it was 0.337.[19] However, another measure, tracking how many times the income of the top 20 percent of households exceeds that of the bottom 20 percent, is more telling. In 1981 the disposable income of the top 20 percent of Taiwan households was 4.18 times that of the lowest 20 percent. The ratio later grew to 4.97 in 1991 and 6.07 in 2017.[20] These measures are subject to distortion, and in Taiwan's case they probably underestimate the precise degree of inequality. But the trend is clear.[21]

A society's distribution of wealth is notoriously difficult to measure, since there are myriad ways to hide and disguise wealth if there are reasons to do so, such as tax avoidance. The Taiwan government only provides statistics of national wealth in aggregate and per capita, which gives no indication of distribution. The Credit Suisse Research Institute's *Global Wealth Report* for 2017 reports that Taiwan had 381,000 individuals with a net worth of more than US$1 million (China had 1.9 million individuals). That placed Taiwan at thirteenth in the world and contributed to an increase of 58,000 millionaires in 2016. Credit Suisse has judged that "Taiwan has high average wealth and only moderate wealth inequality." The mean wealth per adult of US$188,080 is better than most economies in the Asia-Pacific region and more like the level in Western Europe, the report indicates. Of total assets, 66 percent were financial assets.[22] As of mid-October 2020, out of the top 500 billionaires worldwide, three were in Taiwan: Terry Gou of Foxconn, Tsai Eng-meng in the food products sector, and Barry Lam in the technology sector.[23]

However, other evidence that looks at specific types of wealth confirm inferentially that the gap is fairly wide. When the Directorate-General for Budget, Accounting and Statistics reported on national wealth in April 2017, it indicated that the increase from 2014 to 2015 was "due mainly to growing property value and financial assets."[24] That is similar to the Credit Suisse judgment, yet it targets only those who already possess wealth in the form of property and financial assets. People who have not accumulated those types of wealth in the first place do not benefit from a run-up in asset prices.

In 2018 the Ministry of Interior reported that, on average, Taiwan households spent 37.58 percent of their income on mortgages, which is above the 30 percent estimate of what is appropriate, but in Taipei that figure was 61.52 percent. A 2017 Mastercard survey found that 79 percent of Taiwan parents save for their children's education, and on average save 17.27 percent of their household income.[25] This signifies that Taiwan families have to spend a lot of their income to create wealth in property and to invest in their children's future, while lacking a stock of wealth on which to draw. Finally, a survey conducted by 1111 Job Bank in 2018 reveals that almost 53 percent of people in their thirties are deeply in debt and have to pay 41.8 percent of their typically low salaries on average for loan repayment, which means that they had negative net worth.[26] If the financial goal of middle-class young people is to own their own home, the prospects are fairly bleak. In 2016 the ratio of house price to income in Taipei was 15.5, and for Taiwan as a whole it was 9.3.[27]

Firm Size

Taiwan business is skewed when it comes to company size. The economy is dominated by the more than 1.4 million small- and medium-size enterprises, which account for more than 97 percent of all companies in Taiwan. The remaining 3 percent of companies are large conglomerates that have operations in a variety of manufacturing and service fields. They recruit these enterprises into clusters that do contract work for them.[28] Small and medium-size enterprises are divided into two categories, depending on the activity, amount of capital or sales, and the number of employees they have. Firms in the first category tend to be in manufacturing and are deemed small and medium if they have fewer than 100 employees. Companies in the second category are more commonly found in the service sector and are only considered large if they have more than 200 employees.[29] Yet there are also a lot of very small firms—often purely family operations—that employ only a few people.

Industries

Information technology (IT) manufacturing dominates Taiwan's economy. In the 1980s Taiwan companies produced a range of low-tech to high-tech products. But inevitably, other economies would catch up in low-end manufacturing, and Taiwan would have to lead in a more limited set of products. Indeed, today IT manufacturing generates half of Taiwan's growth.[30] The other half, both goods and services, makes up everything else. Information technology companies employ 22 percent of the island's manufacturing workforce, and their products account for around 35 percent of Taiwan's total exports when semiconductors and electronic components are included.[31] It is quite possible that the World Economic Forum's ranking of the Taiwan economy as the thirteenth most-competitive in the world and its ranking of fourth in innovation gives excessive weight to the IT industry and insufficient attention to the rest of the economy.

However, within Taiwan's IT sector, there is a long-standing and persistent emphasis on hardware over software. Early on, it made sense for Taiwan and every other economy that saw a future in electronics and information technology to start with hardware. But unlike other countries, Taiwan kept doing hardware well and was reluctant to move into software, with serious consequences. As Roan Kang, a Microsoft Taiwan executive, puts it, tech executives find it a "big and difficult shift to think that something you can't see or touch is actually worth more than this beautiful piece of designed hardware that you know has substantial value. . . . The high-tech industry here tends to take a very hardware-centric view, and as a result the government has adopted a rather hardware approach to technology." These executives therefore focus more on the financial risk involved in software and less on the potential rewards.[32]

Yet as the American IT industry has demonstrated, the rewards from software development and hardware-software integration can be substantial. Molly Reiner writes in *Taiwan Business Topics*, "A well-developed software and services sector generates greater economic growth and more white-collar jobs than IT manufacturing. It also brings higher margins. . . . Software investment enables hardware investment to be exploited to the greatest extent possible." Vincent Shih, another Microsoft Taiwan executive, notes other advantages: "Investment in software and services will generate much higher GDP impact than buying hardware. . . . If you buy software and services, you need people to do the services, and the money will stay here [in Taiwan, as opposed to China and elsewhere]. If you want to help your unemployment rate, you should put more investment into software and services." Nevertheless, the Taiwan government has a long history of providing resources to the hardware sector and not software.

This imbalance is beginning to change, through both government and private initiative. One of the seven sectoral initiatives of the Tsai administration's 5+2 Major Innovative Industries policy that was launched in 2017 is the Asia Silicon Valley Development Plan, whose purpose is to "launch Taiwan into the innovation value ecosystem" by linking the creation of startups with technology for the "internet of things," according to National Development Council deputy minister Kung Ming-hsin. There is a recognition that cultivation of startups will require funding, revision of outdated, growth-impeding laws and regulations, and an increase in the talent supply. Four funds, aggregating about NT$11 billion, are being considered to try to close the funding gap. To increase the talent, the rules concerning expatriate employees need to be liberalized. The 2020 edition of the "White Paper" of the Taipei American Chamber of Commerce states that, "One of the areas needing priority attention is how to cultivate a more internationalized workforce—welcoming more talent from other countries while helping Taiwanese develop a more internationalized mindset."[33]

At least rhetorically, there is a recognition that Taiwan should aim for the integration of hardware and software, analogous to the alliance forged between Apple and Microsoft in 1997. "What we're advocating for Taiwan industry is a transformation from hardware-only business to hardware-software integration," according to Stephen Su, general director of the Industrial Economics and Knowledge Center at the Industrial Technology Research Institute. "Taiwan cannot do software only." For example, the internet of things requires that advanced hardware devices, the software that supports them, and cloud services that hold the relevant data be close linked. Taiwan has the potential to make these changes, and hidden resources may already be available: software specialists are already working in purportedly hardware-focused companies. It would be regrettable if Asia Silicon Valley took the easy way out and emphasized hardware over software or the integration of the two.[34]

True progress on the software side seems to be coming from private sector initiatives. A leading example is the AppWorks accelerator, founded in 2010 by Jamie Lin, a Taiwanese educated in the United States. As of the summer of 2019, AppWorks had US$170 million in venture capital funds under management and annual revenues of US$3.86 billion. Unlike some investors in Taiwan, who wait until a concept is well proved before providing funds, AppWorks is more comfortable with risk and prepared to advance seed money and Series A (early-stage) resources. The four funds mentioned earlier were created once the success of organizations such as AppWorks became apparent.[35]

The most impressive example of software creativity came during the coronavirus crisis, during which Taiwan's response limited the number of cases and deaths. For example, when infected passengers from a cruise ship arrived in Taiwan, the digital ministry, entrepreneurs, and the gOv open-government movement created a platform to share and verify reports about symptoms from various media and combine that information with software applications created within the community to match the movements of many individuals with the geographic incidence of infected persons. Containment occurred virtually, not physically. Another software application facilitated the distribution of facemasks in ways that reduced hoarding.[36]

Still, when it comes to creating and building out profit-making platforms, a lack of venture-capital and private-equity funding remains a serious limitation, as is the size of the Taiwan market. Only software products that can be scaled up regionally or globally will be profitable, and China is probably ahead of Taiwan when it comes to startups.[37] The government was also slow to create incentives for Taiwan firms that had been keeping money overseas to repatriate those funds, which would have greatly increased the amount of capital available for investment in Taiwan startups. Finally, the government's business regulations have been slow to catch up to the digital age. As of 2017, the government form to apply for a business operation license offered no category for e-commerce. When startup applicants listed many products on the form, the bureaucrats objected. Fintech was slow to take off in spite of the 2015 passage of an electronic payments bill, because third-party payment companies had to have US$16.5 million in capital. The government agency charged with enforcing transportation laws judged that Uber had violated those laws and imposed a stiff fine on unregistered drivers. Finally, the rules for foreign talent working in Taiwan are archaic, which decreases the potential for a larger labor force and also impedes knowledge exchange and innovation.[38]

The low level of private-equity financing does not apply just to IT platforms but is a more generic constraint on growth. A report by the U.S.-Taiwan Business Council highlights the obstacles that international private-equity firms face: a lack of transparency and predictability in investment reviews; a "negative list" of those sectors that are barred or restricted from external investment; the lack of multilayered, deep capital markets; and taxation rules related to private equity–based acquisitions. The report advocates an increase in transparency for both international private-equity companies and local stakeholders, cultivating local talent to maximize private-equity benefits, and building out Taiwan's capital markets.[39] Tsai Ing-wen has recognized rhetorically the need to deregulate the financial services industry. She has vowed to "relax rules for international financial institutions to establish offshore banking units," which would stimulate investment in local firms, and to "establish ourselves as a wealth management center," which would "attract more international institutions and capital to Taiwan."[40]

Taiwan did get a welcome yet unexpected boost from the U.S.-China trade war launched by the Trump administration. As Washington increased tariffs on some Chinese goods and threatened to apply them to more, the costs for Taiwan companies of operating in China rose while the benefits of relocating to Taiwan also rose. And a number of them did so. As of June 2019, the Ministry of Economic Affairs had received requests from eighty-four companies that wanted to "reshore" their operations back to Taiwan. The value of the investments was approximately US$14 billion, and the estimated number of new jobs was more than 39,000. Information technology companies were the most active in responding to the changes that U.S.-China tensions made to their business calculus. The government moved quickly to facilitate the relocations.[41]

For the longer term, however, it is uncertain whether the relocation of supply chains will continue to benefit the Taiwan economy. Liu Shi-chung, a former official at the island's trade promotion authority, cautions that "there are more uncertainties when the world enters the post-COVID era. It is unclear when or how countries will regain economic momentum. The continued U.S.-China wrestling has cast a shadow on the global order. It's getting harder and harder for countries to pursue strategic autonomy amid potential economic 'decoupling' between Washington and Beijing."[42] In the meantime, counsels Michael Reilly, a retired British diplomat, there are steps that Taiwan policymakers can take to accelerate and sustain this trend: reduce the regulatory burden on simple things such as customs clearance; persuade Taiwan companies to move away from their high-volume, low-profits models by emphasizing branding more; use tax and other incentives to encourage more investment in automation; and urge Taiwan companies to pay higher salaries to induce talented staff to stay in Taiwan.[43]

In addition to the imbalances concerning generation, income and wealth, firm size, and industries, there are two other issues that deserve more intensive analysis. These are access to external markets and employment.

Markets

A small country can survive and thrive in a globalized world only if it has good access to the markets of other economies. It cannot rely on domestic demand alone, as can a continental economy. Indeed, in 2017 Taiwan's total trade was around 1.25 times its gross national product, calculated on the basis of the official exchange rate.[44] If a trading nation is going to get access to the markets of others, however, it must reciprocally open its own market. Historically, the United States allowed Taiwan to defer trade liberalization for political and strategic reasons, even as it gave Taiwan wide market access to achieve economic growth. For example, the island benefited from the U.S. Generalized System of Preferences that reduced tariffs on the products of developing countries. Taiwan was also fortunate that China shifted to a policy of export-led growth when it did. Still, Taiwan ultimately had to join the trend of gradual liberalization of international trade and submit to the reciprocity bargain that came with it. Moreover, the globalization of production—the allocation of the different steps of production of a specific product to different countries—almost required trade liberalization. A company that sourced parts and components from several countries and then assembled them in yet another country needed low tariffs and quick customs processing to do its cross-border business. Globalized companies pressed their governments to conclude binding agreements to make their business possible.[45]

From the late 1980s on, Taiwan faced two major challenges to coping with the imperative of trade liberalization. On the one hand, it had to respond to the demands of its other trading partners to open markets, at precisely the time democratization gave domestic economic constituencies more power to defend their interests and sometimes preserve protectionist policies. On the other hand, China had political reasons to try to block Taiwan's participation in the institutional expressions of trade liberalization, such as the World Trade Organization (WTO). China deemed that Taiwan's accession to these economic clubs would increase confidence on the island in its separate political status and reduce its business dependence on the Chinese economy. But excluding Taiwan's producers from new, more liberalized arrangements puts Taiwan producers at a competitive disadvantage.

Opening of Global and East Asia Markets

In the 1990s the liberalization wave was global in scope. This was achieved by the Uruguay Round of multilateral trade negotiations within the General Agreement on Tariffs and Trade, which led to the creation of the WTO. This agreement, which was concluded in 1993, reduced tariffs among the contracting partners and addressed some behind-the-border issues. Because it was a global accord, it did not distort flows of trade and investment contrary to market forces, as regional or bilateral arrangements did. Taiwan had a good chance of entering the WTO because the People's Republic of China was not yet a member and so could not use the WTO's consensus rules to block Taiwan's entry.

But Taiwan would not have entered the WTO without the decision of the Clinton administration in 1997 to accelerate Taiwan's entry as a way of pressuring China to negotiate seriously on its own accession. The assumption behind this leverage tactic was that if Taiwan had met the concerns of all of its major trading partners while China was not making good progress, Washington would push for Taiwan's entry ahead of Beijing's, something that it knew China would oppose. In the event, the tactic worked, and Taiwan—using the name Separate Customs Territory of Taiwan, Penghu, Jinmen, and Mazu—entered immediately after China.

The Uruguay Round promoted freer trade by reducing tariffs. The Doha Round, which began in 2001, proposed to liberalize them even more but was stalled by conflicts of interest among the major parties. But the globalization of production did not stand still, particularly in advanced manufacturing, nor did the imperative to reduce or eliminate tariffs and nontariff barriers to increase efficiencies. Liberalization was thus stimulated on a less-than-global basis. In December 1996, economies that specialized in information technology industries came together under the aegis of the WTO to conclude the plurilateral Information Technology Agreement that eliminated tariffs on a wide range of products.[46] Given the importance of the IT sector for Taiwan, it was essential that it sign the agreement, which happened in May 2001. Fortunately, China was not able to block Taiwan's entry, even though it had acceded to the agreement four months before.[47] The agreement was revised and expanded in 2015.

Within East Asia itself, the complexities of intraregional trade led countries to begin movement toward some level of free trade, even as the Uruguay Round played out. The countries of the Association of Southeast Asian Nations (ASEAN) began work on an FTA in 1992. Japan, China, and Korea decided in 2002 to pursue a tripartite FTA. Gradually, ASEAN and Japan, China, and Korea broadened and deepened their cooperation through the ASEAN Plus Three. Yet the most ambitious effort among countries of Asia, and a culmination of other FTA projects, has been the Regional Comprehensive Economic Partnership (RCEP). Launched in 2012, membership would be confined to the ten countries of ASEAN and countries that already had an FTA with ASEAN (that is, China, Japan, Korea, India, Australia, and New Zealand).[48]

In a world without politics, Taiwan would be a natural candidate for bilateral free trade agreements with neighboring economies, for an FTA with ASEAN, and for membership in RCEP. But Beijing put politics into play by asserting, in effect, its right to block Taiwan from membership in these regional groups and bilateral FTAs with any third country, on the grounds that the island was a part of China. Chinese diplomats pressured different countries to reject liberalization agreements with Taiwan. The only countries besides China with which Taiwan had FTAs or economic cooperation agreements were Panama, Guatemala, El Salvador, Honduras, Paraguay, Singapore, New Zealand, and Eswatini (formerly Swaziland).[49] Singapore and New Zealand stand out because, unlike the other countries mentioned, they had diplomatic relations with China at the time the FTAs with Taiwan were concluded. Ma Ying-jeou was probably able to secure Beijing's support or tolerance for these FTAs during his presidency because Beijing trusted his own commitment to closer cross-Strait relations, not because China had adopted a more relaxed approach to Taiwan's improving and formalizing its economic relations with others. In fact, Taipei made less progress with the Philippines and India, which were the Ma administration's other candidates for FTAs. Taiwan also signed a bilateral investment agreement with Japan in 2014, because Tokyo was willing to brook Beijing's ire.

Meanwhile, trade liberalization and ever freer trade continues, putting Taiwan companies that are not in the IT sector at an increasingly severe disadvantage. Singapore has twenty-four FTAs (including the one with Taiwan); Malaysia has twenty-four; South Korea, eighteen; Japan, seventeen; China has fifteen; Australia, thirteen; New Zealand and Vietnam, twelve; the Philippines, ten; and Indonesia, eight. Not all of these agreements encompass a large volume of trade. Nor do they necessarily remove sensitive barriers, particularly in agriculture. Furthermore, some of these economies are not competitors with Taiwan. However, some are. Korea, which does compete with Taiwan in a number of product areas, has significant FTAs with the United States, the European Union, China, Japan, India, Vietnam, Australia, and New Zealand.

It is worth noting that even if China is successful in blocking Taiwan from participating in bilateral and multilateral economic groupings beyond what it already does, this marginalization does not apply to Taiwan companies. Once RCEP becomes a reality, it will reduce tariffs for member countries but keep in place those for goods exported from Taiwan at the older, higher levels. One way the affected Taiwan companies could compensate would be to move their operations to one of those countries, behind the tariff walls. Indeed, Taiwan companies already have a strong presence in Vietnam, Cambodia, and elsewhere. That would solve the companies' problem but would most likely result in a net loss of jobs in Taiwan itself.

The Free Trade Agreement with China

In the context of RCEP and other market-opening efforts, there were growing calls in Taiwan to liberalize the economic relationship with China. The mainland was Taiwan's leading trade partner for exports and imports, so liberalizing economic relations made eminently good sense. The economic impact of freer trade with China would be much greater than with small economies such as Panama and Paraguay. Moreover, the fact that many Taiwan companies had moved some of their operations to the mainland meant that at least some share of cross-Strait trade was intra-industry or intrafirm trade. Moreover, trade liberalization agreements have two purposes. The first is to open the markets of each economy to the products and services of the other. The second is to stimulate structural adjustment in each economy—to wind down sectors that are no longer competitive and to boost sectors that are the wave of the future.

The first task in liberalizing cross-Strait economic relations was to remove a number of existing obstacles to doing cross-Strait business. For example, Taiwan had long ago imposed a ban on direct flights between Taiwan and China, which meant that Taiwan business executives moving back and forth had had to stop in Hong Kong or Macau on the way. That could turn what should have been a two-hour trip into an all-day affair. During the 2008 presidential campaign, Ma Ying-jeou ran on a platform of normalizing economic relations with China. Although he understood that Taiwan should not put all of its eggs in the China market and should also diversify its trading partners, during his first term the emphasis was on China.[50] Institutional channels of communication were reopened and expanded, and the two sides negotiated a number of agreements, including ones on mainland tourists, postal services, sea transport, air transport, food safety, financial cooperation, joint investment, and industrial standards.[51]

Yet these matters did not fundamentally change the relationship between the two economies. More ambitious was Ma's effort to create, in effect, an FTA with China. The result was the Economic Cooperation Framework Agreement (ECFA), which was concluded in June 2010. The first step in the ECFA process was an "early harvest" understanding, whereby mainland tariffs on specified Taiwan products were reduced quickly. The anticipated later steps were agreements to liberalize trade in goods and trade in services and to establish mechanisms to protect investments and settle disputes.

But the Ma administration ran into a political buzz saw when it signed an agreement on trade in services in June 2013 and sent it to the Legislative Yuan for approval. The Democratic Progressive Party (DPP) slowed down consideration of the pact, and in February 2014, young activists occupied the chamber. They did not leave until it was agreed that the Legislative Yuan would institute closer legislative and public supervision before the service agreement or any other similar cross-Strait agreements went forward. Ma's initiative to deepen cross-Strait interdependence foundered on the politics of trade liberalization. As of late 2020, the supervision legislation for cross-Strait agreement was still on hold.

As ECFA went forward and then stalled, Ma sought to balance his plans to normalize economic relations with China with the need to continue economic liberalization with other trading partners, particularly as they liberalized trade among themselves. For example, the FTA established between the United States and South Korea that entered into force in 2012 put Taiwan companies that were competing directly with Korean companies in the U.S. market on the same product lines at a disadvantage, since Taiwan firms still had to pay the existing tariffs and Korean firms did not. But beyond the toleration for Taiwan's FTAs with Singapore and New Zealand and its investment agreement with Japan, Beijing was in a blocking mode for a very political reason. It wished to leverage any additional greater access for Taiwan to bilateral and multilateral trade and investment arrangements to press the Taipei government to make more concessions on defining the island's legal and political relationship with the mainland and thus move one step closer to unification.[52]

The Lost Opportunity of the Trans-Pacific Partnership

As Taiwan's liberalization with China was slowing down and as the results of bilateral FTAs faced limits, a new opportunity presented itself. This was the multilateral Trans-Pacific Partnership (TPP). Twelve countries, including some advanced economies, had come together to create an economic architecture that would not only create free trade in goods and services but would also address behind-the-border issues that created an unbalanced playing field. As such, the TPP was to be a rival to RCEP. The issues to be addressed included state-owned enterprises, government subsidies, and product rules of origin. The TPP began as a 2005 agreement among Brunei, Chile, New Zealand, and Singapore. The United States joined the effort in 2008, and Japan agreed to do so in 2012. After arduous negotiations among countries at different levels of development and different economic systems, the agreement was signed in January 2016.

Dominated by the large Japanese and American economies, the TPP foreshadowed a revolution in the international economic system. It was more extensive than RCEP in what it required member countries to do, which could create powerful incentives for countries that were not party to the agreement to join and strong disincentives to remain outside. The likely inclusion of South Korea, whose FTA with the United States was essentially a bilateral version of what the TPP became, would only increase those incentives and disincentives. Furthermore, the parts of the TPP agreement that had nothing to do with tariffs could stimulate structural adjustment within economies.

Taiwan was not one of the twelve economies that signed the TPP in 2016, but it understood both the economic and political reasons for trying to enter in the second round and expressed strong interest in doing so. The TPP's rules regarding eligibility worked in Taiwan's favor: the agreement was open to any economy in the Asia-Pacific Economic Cooperation forum, of which Taiwan had been a member since 1990. This was in contrast to rules to join RCEP, by which Taiwan would first need to do an FTA with ASEAN—a nonstarter because of China's opposition. In addition, China was not one of the creators of the TPP and so would not be able to block a Taiwan membership bid from the inside. However, China could exert political and economic pressure on smaller members that were dependent on the Chinese economy for growth and prosperity. My own view was that Taiwan could only have joined the TPP under two conditions. The first was for the bloc to be so robust that China could not afford economically to remain outside, even if TPP rules required extensive domestic economic reforms. The second condition was that the United States and perhaps Japan would have to advance negotiations with Taiwan to exert pressure on China and also be prepared to lobby hard to convince other members to admit Taiwan despite Chinese resistance. In effect, this would be a replay of the scenario by which Taiwan got into the WTO.[53] There was no guarantee that, even if Taiwan had been approved for TPP membership, the Legislative Yuan and the public would have accepted the policy disciplines the agreement entailed. But forging consensus for the TPP would have been far less divisive than a bilateral trade liberalization agreement with China.

There was, of course, a third condition for Taiwan's entry, which was that the United States would have to actually approve the agreement itself. However, Donald Trump had campaigned on a promise of taking the United States out of the TPP, and he did so right after his inauguration in 2017.[54]

Taiwan thus became collateral damage to Trump's deep-seated opposition to multilateral trade agreements.

Other Options

Japan, to its credit, took the lead to keep the TPP alive without the United States, and thus the Comprehensive and Progressive Trans-Pacific Partnership (CPTPP) was signed in March 2018. Once all signatories have ratified, it will be the third-largest FTA, after NAFTA and the economies of the European Single Market. Of course, Taiwan could seek CPTPP membership at a later date, but that would require resolving some underlying bilateral issues with Japan. If it is not included, Taiwan as an economy will not be able to participate in writing the future rules for interregional trade and will face more pressure to rely on the Chinese economy alone. Taiwan companies that do not benefit from the Information Technology Agreement would have greater incentives to move operations inside the CPTPP's free trade walls and perhaps reduce employment opportunities at home.

As for RCEP, given its membership rules and China's political heft within the group, the chances of Taiwan's joining seem to be slim to none. It was to respond to this reality that the Tsai administration initiated its New Southbound Policy, which aimed at new engagements with more countries in its regional neighborhood. Its target countries were the ten member countries of ASEAN, six South Asia countries, and Australia and New Zealand. The policy did have an economic emphasis, encouraging Taiwan companies to include the economies of these countries in their business plans and to foster dialogues to enhance economic cooperation and address disputes. Just as important, though, was the expansion of interaction and connectivity in the areas of culture, medicine and health, education, people-to-people ties, and youth exchanges, as well as the creation of capabilities within Taiwan to carry out the program. Prashanth Parameswaran, senior Washington editor of *The Diplomat*, has given the program high marks for increasing tourism, education, trade, and investment between Taiwan and the target countries and highlighted the 2017 bilateral investment agreement concluded between Taiwan and the Philippines. But he notes that the program created some concerns within Taiwan about workers from the target countries taking jobs away from local residents and also required improvement in coordination and resourcing within the Taiwan government. Moreover, the governments of some target countries were reluctant to participate too much out of fear of alienating China.[55]

The Tsai administration looked north and east, as well as south and west, with hopes of beginning FTA talks with Japan and the United States, its two largest trading partners after China. However, domestic political obstacles have blocked the way forward. In the Japan case, the issue was food products from the prefectures in northern Honshu that were most affected by the Fukushima nuclear disaster of March 2011. Scientific evidence suggested that the food products were safe, but food safety groups in Taiwan argued for a no-risk policy. The KMT took advantage of the DPP-controlled legislature acted to relax the requirements for holding referendums on policy issues. They got approval for a referendum to be held in November 2018 that opposed importation of "foodstuffs from nuclear-contaminated areas" (not whether the food itself was contaminated but whether it came from an area affected by the nuclear disaster). The Tsai administration had been hoping to dispose of the Fukushima food issue in order to begin talks on an FTA, but under the terms of the referendum act, it would have to wait at least two years to do so. Again, politics blocked policy progress (on the United States, see chapter 14).

When it comes to having market access to other economies, therefore, Taiwan faces multiple constraints: the relentless removal of barriers between and among other economies, protectionist and other interests at home, China's politically motivated exclusion, the negotiating strategy of the United States, and so on. That Taiwan is a member of the Information Technology Agreement, with its free trade basis, is particularly fortunate, even as it reinforces the dominant position of the information technology industry. Without the Information Technology Agreement, Taiwan would face even more problems than it already does. However, even with it, questions remain. Should the government make the concessions necessary to start FTA negotiations with the United States and Japan, even though there is no certainty that agreements could pass the Legislative Yuan, given the probable resistance of domestic interests that benefit from protectionism? Should it make politically sensitive concessions to Beijing to increase its external economic freedom of action, even if it risks provoking new unrest like the Sunflower movement? Should it seek the passage of a bill governing trade negotiations with China and then return to the ECFA agenda, even though the future of cross-Strait relations is the most salient issue in Taiwan politics? Each option faces external obstacles and internal resistance.

Employment

When Bill Clinton stressed the need for good jobs at good wages during the 1992 presidential campaign, he pinpointed the key challenge facing all advanced economies in today's competitive, globalized world. Employing young people and paying them a good salary is a particular challenge. Parents want their children to achieve a better standard of living than they themselves have had, and children assume they will be at least as well off as their parents. But that is only possible if the economy creates the right kinds of jobs and opportunities for families to create wealth. Moreover, what is good for families is good for societies as a whole. Economists have demonstrated that the existence of a large middle class and the widespread prosperity that it enjoys is necessary for broad-based economic growth. A shrinking middle class increases inequality, suppresses demand, and slows growth.[56] The ultrarich will purchase only so many Lexus cars and Gucci bags. But globalization intensifies competition among economies: companies respond by slowing salary growth, and governments respond by reducing taxes on corporations and the wealthy. What governments do not do frequently enough is increase resources for skills enhancement, which is the best way to respond to technological changes and to sustain good jobs at good wages.

Taiwan is but one example of the plight in which many advanced economies find themselves, particularly when it comes to employment. One might think that the declining birth rate would guarantee a buyers' market for members of younger cohorts for both jobs and wages. But that is not the case. While the overall employment rate in 2017 was 3.8 percent, the unemployment rate for people between the ages of fifteen and nineteen was 8.8 percent, and 12.4 percent for those between the ages of twenty and twenty-four. It was worse for those with a university education than for those without. Salaries for new graduates in Taiwan come to less than NT$30,000 monthly (around US$1,050 in October 2020), whereas they are almost double that for Hong Kong and two-and-a-half times that for Singapore. Part of that difference is accounted for by the higher cost of living in those two cities, but there is still a gap. The more significant comparison is with China, where the average starting salary for new graduates, converted into Taiwan's currency, is NT$37,000. China's GDP per capita measured in terms of purchasing power parity, which takes cost of living into account, is one-third that of Taiwan. So salaries go a much longer way in China than they do in Taiwan. In a study of some 500 Taiwan companies, salary increases for employees were about half of what they had been twenty years earlier (3–4 percent versus 8 percent).[57] In China, salaries increase at a rate about double that of Taiwan.[58]

The main reason for the low salaries in Taiwan is its sluggish economy, whose rate of growth declined by 38 percent from 1997 to 2007 and by 63 percent from 2007 to 2017.[59] The level of investment has also declined, which means shrinking job opportunities. Total investment stood around 30 percent of GDP before 2007 but dropped to about 21 percent in 2017. Companies struggle to get profits of only 2–3 percent, which limits what they can pay employees.[60] Intense global competition breeds insecurity and conservatism among Taiwan's corporate leaders. They tend to reward employees with bonuses in good years rather than increase base salary levels.[61] Economists cite the failure of many Taiwan companies to upgrade their industries in the face of global competition and to find other ways, such as branding, to add value, which would, in turn, lift professional salaries. As Chiou Jiunn-rong, the deputy minister of the government's National Development Council, admits, "Simply speaking, we have no new industries."[62]

Other factors connected with slow growth that also affect salary levels. The first is an atrophy of the linkage between productivity and salary growth. A study by Chao Wen-heng, a research fellow at the Taiwan Institute of Economic Research, has found that between 1991 to 2001, gross profits generated per hour of work expanded 66 percent, and salaries on average rose 56 percent. Thereafter and through 2016, productivity grew at the same rate as before, but salaries rose only 16 percent. Owners allocated less of the companies' profits to workers. This was true across the board—in manufacturing, in services (where a majority of employees work), and in the exceptionally productive IT sector.[63]

A second reason for low salaries in Taiwan is that many Taiwan companies still rely on the production models that served Taiwan well in the era of more rapid growth, doing contract work for the Western and Japanese companies then market products under their own brands. Their models are original equipment manufacturing and original design manufacturing. But these approaches yield narrow profit margins and encourage entrepreneurs to cut costs wherever they can. The executives of these companies do not regard higher salaries as an investment in their employees that could bring enhanced productivity.[64] Reinforcing this reluctance is government policy that provides companies with incentives to invest in capital equipment but not in the development of their employees.[65]

A third reason has to do with an apparent inverse correlation between firm size and salary growth. The median monthly salary was less than NT$30,000 for companies with fewer than 10 workers (the great majority of companies) and more than NT$40,000 for those with more than 100 employees. Salaries for larger listed companies are 54 percent higher, on average, than for smaller, unlisted ones.[66] Corporate culture is at play here. Small companies are family firms whose leaders tend to choose relatives to succeed them and not use resources to train aspiring executives outside the family.[67]

A fourth reason is that employers are keeping salaries flat to offset increasing labor costs owing to government-required payments for labor insurance pensions and contributions to health insurance. As a result, companies rely more on part-time and temporary workers, who represented 7.11 percent of the workforce in 2018, according to the National Development Council.[68]

If these features of the economy tend to suppress salaries, so does the mismatch between the skills that job aspirants bring to the labor market and the talents that employers need. As of 2018, as Jane Rickards explains in *Taiwan Business Topics*, "employers frequently complain that they can't find the right person to fill a vacancy, while job-seekers complain they are not being offered enough after all their hard study."[69] The main culprit here is the tertiary education system and its emphasis on universities over vocational and technical education. Taiwan used to have strong vocational and technical schools whose graduates contributed to the success of the companies for which they worked. But many of those schools were converted into second- and third-tier universities so that elected politicians could demonstrate to voters that they were bringing benefits to their districts. Overall quality of education and training suffered, and the supply of university graduates exceeded demand. The National Development Council estimates that the number of graduates and postgraduates from the island's 126 universities is almost double that of twenty years ago.[70] Yet Oxford Economics estimates that of forty-six countries—some developed and others developing—Taiwan had the largest "talent deficit," a mismatch between the supply and demand for talent in 2021.[71] The one exception in which demand exceeds supply are the engineering fields, where global competition for talent is intense.[72]

The mismatch is more complicated than the differences between universities and technical schools in their curriculums, which technology-enabled learning through massive online open courses has begun to mitigate.[73] But the gap also stems from the evolution in the nature of work and the failure of educational institutions to adapt. By and large, Taiwan job seekers have no interest in doing labor-intensive jobs in factories and construction sites, for which they are overqualified anyway. The default, therefore, is office work, for which at least some degree of specialized training is required, whether the jobs have a scientific, economic, or people-related focus. Even for science and engineering placement, graduates are not always able to meet job requirements.[74]

Because even office jobs can be automated or relocated to cheaper labor markets, identifying the work of the future must be more granular. A 2013 MIT study analyzed five categories of work in terms of the type of skill required and whether the job was routine. The five types of tasks were routine manual, routine cognitive, nonroutine manual, nonroutine analytical, and nonroutine interpersonal. The study determined that in the United States between 1960 and 2009, job growth occurred only in the last two: nonroutine analytical and nonroutine interpersonal. A 2017 McKinsey study found that certain types of jobs—managing and developing people; planning, decisionmaking, and creative tasks; and interfacing with stakeholders—have the lowest probability of automation. Yet an annual business climate survey conducted by the Taipei American Chamber of Commerce found that these were the areas where Taiwan employees were deficient. As William Zyzo summarizes in *Taiwan Business Topics*, "Over many years, the survey has consistently shown that managers find Taiwan's human resources lacking in the competencies most needed for performing non-routine analytical and non-routine interpersonal tasks, including creativity and innovation, showing initiative, and being able to compete at an international level."[75]

Exit, Voice, or Loyalty?

Exit, voice, and loyalty are three analytic categories that the economist Albert Hirschman developed to study the responses of individuals or groups to an unsatisfactory situation, whether it was a substandard product, an unpopular political regime, or, in the case of Taiwan, the limited life chances that young people face because of a dearth of appealing, well-paying jobs.[76] Loyalty, in this case, equates to putting up with a job for which one is vastly overqualified and never making enough money to get married, have a family, and buy a home. It spells a future without happiness or self-fulfillment. Given the Taiwan peoples' propensity for Confucian values, a young person who is unmarried and therefore without children can face particularly problematic circumstances.

Exit, in this context, means moving elsewhere to take advantage of better job opportunities. Just as Taiwan companies can move their operations behind the tariff walls of other countries, job seekers can move to the places where more appealing jobs are available, such as China, Hong Kong, Singapore, Japan, or the United States. *Business Weekly,* surveying Taiwan people twenty to thirty-five years old concerning their job plans, found that 62 percent planned to seek employment abroad. Eighty-nine percent of that cohort cited low salaries as the main reason for working elsewhere. China's competitive job market bids up salaries for locals and outsiders alike, so job seekers from Taiwan can earn much more doing the same work they do at home. According to government statistics for 2015, around seven hundred thousand Taiwanese worked overseas, and about 60 percent of them in China. However, unofficial estimates have exceeded these official figures for years, estimating a range closer to 1 million to 2 million Taiwanese working overseas. It also appears that people are willing to work overseas at a younger age than they were a decade ago.[77]

This brain drain is having a significant effect on Taiwan's talent pool. A 2014 *CommonWealth* magazine survey found that most of the people working overseas were either working professionals (60.2 percent) or top executives and researchers (25.5 percent), meaning people at the highest skill levels. There seemed to be little resistance to leaving. Of professionals working in Taiwan, 76 percent were willing to accept an overseas appointment, depending, in part, on where the job was. Moreover, the relocations could well be permanent. Of Taiwanese professionals already overseas, 65 percent said they would not consider returning to Taiwan because of the low wage levels.[78] So Taiwan's shortage of good jobs at good wages means that the island has been losing its best and brightest.

The Chinese government has tried to enlarge the Taiwan exodus beyond what market forces would dictate and has done so for political purposes. In early 2018, it announced a 31 Measures policy to give members of various sectors of Taiwan society—business executives, entrepreneurs, professionals, cultural workers, young adults, and students—the same treatment that is applied to people on the mainland. For example, a Taiwan business executive who sets up a high-technology firm in China will be subject to only a 15 percent corporate income tax. Licensing for professionals was liberalized.[79] The initiative had apparently been under desultory development for several years but was eventually finalized two years after Tsai Ing-wen was elected Taiwan's president. In November 2019, Beijing supplemented these with twenty-six additional policy steps. Yet the measures related to business came long after rising labor costs and tighter enforcement of environmental protection measures had deteriorated the situation for Taiwan companies.[80] Whether the measures would get implemented depended on local governments in China, which might be reluctant to give Taiwanese special treatment at the expense of local interests.[81] But the immediate reaction in Taiwan at the outset of the 31 Measures in early 2018 was fairly positive. A March 2018 poll by the Taiwan Public Opinion Foundation revealed that 31 percent of those surveyed welcomed the measures. Young people between the ages of twenty and twenty-four and university graduates expressed even stronger approval, with approval at 40 percent and 38 percent, respectively.[82]

The political purpose of these economic incentives was to drive a political wedge between the Tsai administration and key constituencies in Taiwan politics. One was the business community, which has traditionally supported the KMT but which the DPP would like at least to keep politically neutral, if not win over. The other constituency was young people, who strongly supported Tsai and the DPP in the 2016 elections and was growing increasingly anti-China and anti-unification. To advance its unification goals, Beijing needed to encourage young people to take at least a neutral stand, if not a pro-China position. This maneuvering come straight out the Leninist "united front" playbook for coping with situations in which the Chinese Communist Party did not have the kind of control it desired over matters such as Taiwan. Distinctions were drawn between friends, neutrals, and enemies, and the goal of the policy was to maintain support of friends, turn neutrals into friends, and reduce and isolate the number of enemies. The 31 Measures policy was also consistent with China's policy shift from discouraging mainland people from leaving for Taiwan to inducing Taiwanese to move to China. The Tsai administration objected strongly to the political motivation behind these efforts, and its Mainland Affairs Council developed its own countermeasures and periodically presented evidence that the incentives were having little or no effect.[83]

Voice, in Hirschman's framework, signifies protest against the economic status quo. Unions can be agents of voice, but in Taiwan they are not. Union membership in Taiwan accounts for only 7.3 percent of employees, less than the rate in Singapore (19.7 percent), Japan (17.3 percent), or Korea (10.2 percent). Union membership has dropped as employers make greater use of temporary and part-time employees.[84]

Taiwan does have examples of voice, the most vivid being the Sunflower movement of March and April 2014. This movement was sparked by activists protesting the passing of the Cross-Strait Service Trade Agreement in the KMT-led legislature without proper clause-by-clause review. There were specific reasons for the DPP and activists to oppose the service-trade agreement: a nontransparent process, narrow distribution benefits, political slippery slope, and so on. However, drawing on interviews of Sunflower participants, André Beckershoff, of the University of Tubingen, highlights a deeper sense of disillusionment about the life chances of young people as motivation for joining the movement:

> The so-called "22,000 NT$ generation," referring to the monthly US$700 that a university student can expect after graduation, had been promised "10 Golden Years" by President Ma. Instead, rising housing prices compelled them to live with their parents, they experienced difficulties in finding a job after graduation and they became concerned by the urban and rural redevelopment that had taken place in their neighborhood and was often accompanied by the display of police force. Particularly in Taipei, the rising housing and living costs meant that young people ... deferred plans of marriage or parenthood. "Hard work," [as] a [survey] respondent summarized the students' disillusionment with the promised golden age, "does not guarantee rewards.[85]

The Sunflower movement was significant not just because it effectively ended the Ma Ying-jeou administration's policy of mainland engagement: it also reflected a transformation of the Taiwan politics of trade. To end the protest, it was agreed that legislation should be enacted governing the process for negotiating and approving cross-Strait trade. As of late 2020, that legislation had still not passed. Moreover, the delay suggests that it will never be passed and that, barring a pro-business shift in the new politics of trade, no economic agreements will ever be concluded with China, even if the original economic rationale was compelling.

A Dual Economy

Taiwan's economy brings to mind the comedy and tragedy masks used in ancient Greek drama. In general, there are reasons to smile. There are sectors in which the island's companies are profitable and have seized significant global market share. Rankings exercises such as the World Economic Forum's competitiveness index give Taiwan high ranks. Market fundamentals are good, and the entrepreneurial spirit is strong. The population is well educated. The standard of living is relatively low, so a New Taiwan dollar goes further than a Hong Kong dollar. The living environment is pleasant.

On the other hand, there are reasons to frown. Domestic growth, investment, wages, and the birth rate are all low or flat. The coronavirus pandemic, with its disruption of supply chains and contraction of global demand, slowed Taiwan's growth. In May 2020, the government reduced its estimate for GDP growth in 2020 to 1.67 percent, a sharp decline from its forecast of 2.37 percent three months earlier.[86] Despite the WEF's favorable ranking and the demonstrated ability of some companies to keep up with the competition, there is also the sense that Taiwan has rested on its laurels and failed to advance into strategic new fields. The failure to create a software sector to match Taiwan's world-class hardware manufacturing is probably the most serious missed opportunity. At the same time, the Taiwan economy has done much better on growth than on distribution. Inequality of income, wealth, and access to housing is growing. The talents of many well-trained young people are underutilized, to the point that many are choosing to find jobs in China and elsewhere. For those who remain, enduring a lower standard of living than that of their parents is problematic, both for the economy, in low domestic demand, and for the political system, in loss of legitimacy.

A case could be made that Taiwan has a dual economy.[87] On the one hand, there is the IT sector, which accounts for half of the economy and 35 percent of exports, is exceptionally productive, and pays relatively high salaries. It also benefits from Taiwan's participation in the Information Technology Agreement. The information technology sector is joined by certain other standout companies in advanced manufacturing that produce goods, such as specialty bicycles, and by firms that have established strong brands, such as the Uni-President Food Conglomerate and the Din Tai Fung restaurant chain. Then there is the rest of the economy, which suffers from stagnant growth and wages and, for companies that export their products, must cope with Taiwan's exclusion from regional trade liberalization and the absence of an FTA with the United States. The National Development Council measures changes in the index of labor productivity for various sectors. From 2008 to 2018, the indexes for IT products increased by around fifty points. For sectors such as wearing apparel, food, and rubber products, there were significant declines.[88] The Taipei American Chamber of Commerce has noted this gap by calling for wide-ranging and continuous innovation, not only in leading sectors such as green energy, biomedicine, and artificial intelligence but also in traditional manufacturing and the service sector, including government services.[89]

Even the IT sector will face headwinds in the future. In a major study on innovation in Taiwan's future economy, Evan Feigenbaum, a vice president at the Carnegie Endowment for International Peace, identified five "acute challenges." The first is the pressing need to ensure a strong talent pool in science, technology, engineering, and math. Second is the need to overcome the constraints to scaling up the products of innovations, given the island's relatively small economy. The third is to transform Taiwan's innovation ecosystem for

IT, with its emphasis on hardware, to one that stimulates the development of software and hardware-software integration. Fourth is the need to increase the value added to technology supply-chains in Taiwan itself, instead of those from China and other markets. Finally, the government needs to revise government technology and education policies to enhance competitiveness.[90]

Taiwan's marginalization from the international economic system aggravates the effect of these domestic issues, which are a function of Taiwan's stage of development. If the government cannot conclude FTAs or other market liberalization agreements with countries or regional groupings because of pressure from China, then Taiwan companies will suffer a built-in disadvantage in trying to compete with firms in other countries. These companies may have the option of moving production operations behind tariff walls, but that would result in hiring fewer Taiwan employees. The only sector that is spared from marginalization is the IT sector.

Although tariff and nontariff barriers protect some parts of the Taiwan economy (particularly agriculture), it is China that bears the principal responsibility for restricting Taiwan's ability to undertake economic liberalization with its trading partners. China's diplomats will most likely claim that concluding FTAs with Taiwan is a violation of the one-China principle, but that comes down to an issue of nomenclature. When the Ma administration was negotiating its FTAs with Singapore and New Zealand, it was willing to use terminology that did not imply a claim of statehood. What is really going on is a question of who has dispositive power. Even during the Ma administration, Beijing wanted to create the impression that Taipei sought its permission to do those agreements. Moreover, to restrict Taiwan's access to other markets in relative terms creates greater incentives for Taiwan companies to rely on China for their profitability. In Beijing's mind, making Taiwan more dependent economically on the mainland will advance the Beijing-advocated process of "development through integration."

China poses a much larger challenge than just its international obstructionism. In the WEF's competitiveness rankings and scores, it is only fifteen places and six points behind Taiwan. The island's companies have remained competitive, in part, because of the technological lead it has had over their Chinese counterparts. However, China is catching up technologically. Its companies have long desired to try to move up the technology ladder and even try to take over the place that Taiwan firms enjoyed in the relevant supply chains. The Chinese government signaled its general desire to increase the contribution of domestic firms to in-country production. This policy, known as Made in China 2025, has caused concern among Taiwan firms that they will be squeezed out. However, the Mainland Affairs Council stated in February 2019 that "the *Made in China 2025* plan has already led to international alertness and economic slowdown is reducing its attractiveness to Taiwanese companies, making it extremely difficult for mainland China to achieve its goal of absorbing Taiwan economically."[91]

This array of domestic and external constraints imposes a complicated set of dilemmas for Taiwan, where conflicting priorities mean that the possible or desirable solution to one problem makes it more difficult to resolve other problems, and creates some pertinent questions to contemplate:

- What can be done, in spite of existing constraints, to raise the anemic level of economic growth, particularly given that about half of those questioned in the TEDS say that economic development is the number-one problem that the government should address?[92]

- Can Taiwan's policymakers improve the distribution of economic benefits and subsequently enable the island's young people to attain the same standard of living that their parents' generation achieved?

- If it is essential to increase the birthrate, which requires, in turn, an expansion of child care, better access to quality housing, and higher wages for young people, would the attendant increases in government spending undermine prospects for growth and foster tax evasion?

- If some greater degree of economic integration on China is unavoidable, how can a politically polarized Taiwan insulate economics from politics and avoid unification? If it makes policy sense to resume the ECFA process and finish agreements on trade in services and goods, how can the government secure the political support to conclude and ratify them?

- If China sets political preconditions on a DPP government before it can consider liberalization measures, and Taiwan's future growth depends on enacting those measures, should it sacrifice the political stance it has taken so far in order to secure growth, or should it sacrifice growth and its electoral chances in order to maintain party unity?

- Similarly, would a DPP government be willing to accept those political preconditions in order to secure an FTA with ASEAN, and therefore enter RCEP?

- If Taiwan has to liberalize access to its economy to gain more favorable treatment for Taiwan goods and services in other markets, what should be done to compensate the domestic groups that suffer as a result, especially since the costs of liberalization will be fairly immediate while the benefits gained from structural adjustment for the Taiwan economy are only secured over time?

And so on.

Finding escapes from Taiwan's predicament is not easy. The Ma and Tsai administrations have tried different approaches to these conflicting questions. President Ma placed primary emphasis on improving and liberalizing economic relations with China, but he lost momentum midway when the project lost political support, at least from those who supported the Sunflower movement. Within Chinese constraints, Tsai Ing-wen has emphasized self-help at home and outreach to other major trading partners, with modest results. Yet neither Ma in his two terms nor Tsai in her first was able to close the gap between Taiwan's two economies. That will be a high priority for President Tsai in her second term.

5

Taiwan's Energy Policy

Energy policy is one of those issues to which each of Taiwan's options has a significant downside. As an advanced economy, the world's twenty-second largest, Taiwan uses a lot of energy: in 2016 it was the sixteenth largest consumer of electricity in the world, using about 237.4 billion kilowatt hours.[1] Business enterprises need a plentiful and steady supply of energy to operate. For the factories in the island's information technology sector, even a momentary loss of electric power to the sensitive machines that make semiconductors and switches will cost time and money. Taiwan's many cars, trucks, and motorcycles require fuel. Taiwan's residents now enjoy a middle-class lifestyle that includes a fondness for air-conditioned comfort, which is a big change from 1975, when my wife and I lived in the capital city of Taipei, and the Hilton Hotel was one of the few cool places we could go to escape the heat and humidity. They also oppose electricity prices that reflect costs of production. Finally, some energy sources are worse than others. Although people understand the need to address the danger of climate change, Taiwan still relies mostly on coal and oil, significant sources of greenhouse gases. Overall, Taiwan has added almost 30 billion metric tons of carbon equivalent a year to the atmosphere since 2004.[2] Nuclear power, it is feared, poses a safety risk. It is not clear that Taiwan leaders, companies, and consumers can formulate and agree on an energy policy that reconciles these conflicting goals.

Taiwan is not the only economy to face these sorts of dilemmas, but it uses more energy per capita than comparable countries, more than Germany,

France, Japan, Italy, and the United Kingdom, even though its own per capita gross domestic product is much less. One would expect that each person in a country such as Japan, which has a per capita GDP that is more than 50 percent greater than Taiwan's, would use more energy than each person in Taiwan. That is, the more active an economy is, the more energy it would use. But Taiwan's per capita energy consumption in Taiwan is equivalent to 4.7 metric tons of oil, while in Japan—with its robust conservation programs—is only 3.4 metric tons.[3]

How best to meet that demand for energy has long been a challenge. For starters, the island has no indigenous supplies of coal, oil, and natural gas, and so it has depended completely on external supply. Around 98 percent of its energy is imported: oil, from Saudi Arabia, Oman, Kuwait, Iraq, the United Arab Emirates, and Angola; liquefied natural gas (LNG), mainly from Qatar, Malaysia, the United States, and Indonesia; and coal, from Australia, Indonesia, Russia, Canada, and South Africa.[4] Much of these inputs must be shipped over long distances, and their price is subject to the vagaries of global markets. Because Taiwan is an island, it neither connects to a regional grid nor buys electricity from its neighbors, as Hong Kong does from China's Guangdong province, for example.[5] Moreover, each available source of energy—coal, oil, natural gas, nuclear power, hydropower, wind, and solar—has its advantages and disadvantages. For example, coal and oil are relatively efficient energy sources, but they produce greenhouse gases that foster climate change. Natural gas is a fossil fuel, and methane, its principal component, is a particularly potent greenhouse gas if it is released to the atmosphere before burning. Solar and wind have their own, different downsides.

Changes in Taiwan's political system have profoundly affected whether and how policy decisions on energy security are made. During Taiwan's authoritarian period, setting an optimal mix of energy sources was a decision made by the island's economic leadership, mainly comprising technical experts. Since Taiwan began its democratic transition in 1986, the arena for decisionmaking has expanded.[6] In addition to technocrats, different political constituencies evaluate relative costs and benefits differently. With all of these factors, the politics of energy can be intense.

Yet polling indicates that energy is not an issue on which the public places a high relative priority. In late 2017, the Taiwan Election and Democratization Survey asked respondents which of more than ten policy issues should be President Tsai Ing-wen's highest policy priority. Only one-tenth of 1 percent said energy.[7] (That finding is probably somewhat misleading, since the public might not be so passive if it had to pay more for electricity.)

Even more striking, the public appears to have had quite an inaccurate sense of Taiwan's energy mix. A survey conducted by the Risk Society and Policy Research Center in the fall of 2018 found that respondents believe nuclear power to be the source of 43.6 percent of the electricity supply, when in reality it was at most 8 percent. They believed that the share from coal was 32 percent and almost 3 percent from natural gas; the figure for coal was 14 percent too low and that for natural gas was one-fifth of the real share. Clearly, the antinuclear movement had done an excellent job in shaping—or misshaping—public opinion in favor of its cause.[8] In December 2018, asked how respondents felt about the Tsai administration's policy of replacing nuclear power with wind, solar, and thermal power, 44.8 percent agreed and 42.8 percent disagreed.[9]

Despite what polls say about the public's sense of priorities and its lack of basic information, energy is an issue that is important for political parties, civil society groups, the large industrial consumers of power, and government bureaucrats. Moreover, the interaction between the bureaucracy and "people power" has produced wide swings in policy and engendered a waste of resources. The politics of nuclear power have transformed a merely difficult policy problem into an almost insoluble one, marked by intense conflict. This is somewhat odd, since nuclear does not contribute that much to the mix for power generation. The conflict is a product of Taiwan's democratization and has intensified a babel of conflicting priorities and grinding frustrations. If there is to be an answer to the question of energy security, it will have to emerge from the political system. But so far, though political actors possess veto power over policies that they do not like, they lack a willingness to forge a compromise that is "good enough" to ensure the public good.

Basic Data

It was in the early 1970s that the Taiwan government decided to add civilian nuclear power to the energy mix, to reduce dependence on external energy sources. More recently, a campaign has begun to develop solar and wind power. Yet fossil fuels still dominate Taiwan's energy mix. From 2002 to 2018, oil hovered around 50 percent of the island's total energy sources, coal was steady around 30 percent, natural gas doubled from 7.0 to 15.2 percent, and nuclear dropped from 10.3 to 4.4 percent (see table 5-1). At the same time, energy consumption has remained stable, as table 5-2 indicates. Industry is by far the largest sectoral consumer. Transportation is about half of that, and the service and residential sectors are each half of transportation.

TABLE 5-1. **Sources of Energy Supply, 2002–2018, Various Years (Percent)**

	Coal	Oil	Natural gas	Biomass	Hydro	Nuclear	Solar and wind
2002	30.9	50.4	7.0	1.2	0.2	10.3	0.1
2007	30.1	52.4	7.8	1.2	0.3	8.2	0.1
2012	30.0	47.8	12.1	1.3	0.4	8.3	0.2
2018	29.4	48.3	15.2	1.1	0.3	5.4	0.3

Source: "Statistical Charts: Energy Supply (by Energy Form) and Total Domestic Consumption (by Sector)," *Energy Statistical Annual Reports,* Bureau of Energy, Ministry of Economic Affairs, Taiwan, July 29, 2020.

TABLE 5-2. **Sectoral Consumption Sources of Energy, 2007–2018, Various Years (Percent)**

	Energy	Industry	Transpor-tation	Agricul-ture	Service	Resi-dential	Non-energy use
2002	7.8	34.2	18.9	1.6	7.2	8.6	21.6
2007	7.2	33.6	16.3	0.8	7.3	7.9	27.6
2012	7.3	33.7	16.1	0.8	7.1	7.7	27.9
2018	8.4	31.0	15.4	0.8	6.8	7.5	29.7

Source: "Statistical Charts: Energy Supply (by Energy Form) and Total Domestic Consumption (by Sector)," *Energy Statistical Annual Reports*, Bureau of Energy, Ministry of Economic Affairs, Taiwan, July 29, 2020. "Nonenergy use" refers to use of commodities like oil as feedstock for plastics and other petrochemical products and natural gas for fertilizer.

Coal and LNG were the main fuels used by electricity generating plants in 2018: 47.6 percent for coal and 33.5 percent for LNG. Nuclear power accounted for 10.0 percent of electricity, while all renewables accounted for 4.6 percent. Of that 4.6 percent, hydropower provided just over one-third, solar 21.7 percent, and wind 13.3 percent.[10] The number of liters of oil equivalents of energy consumed on a per capita basis increased modestly during the 2003 to 2018 period, rising from 3,199 liters in 2003 to 3,495 in 2011 and 3,702 in 2018. The number of kilowatt hours of electricity consumed per person rose from 8,482 in 2002 to 11,097 in 2017.[11]

Each energy source has various pros and cons that need to be considered. First is the issue of price: How much does the consumer pay per kilowatt hour of each type of energy? Table 5-3 shows the significant divergence three months into the Tsai Ing-wen administration.

At first glance, solar is evidently the most expensive source of energy for electricity, at more than five times the cost of nuclear, the cheapest source. At a relatively low price, coal produces almost half of Taiwan's electricity. Liquefied natural gas, at a cost 42 percent higher than coal, covers another third. The cheapest source, nuclear, is responsible for less than 10 percent. Yet these values reflect both how the government sets prices for the market and the economics surrounding existing facilities. The underlying relative costs of electricity from any new generation capacity would not necessarily be the same as the current price structure. For example, for electricity from new facilities, the true price of solar would most likely be less than that of nuclear.[12]

The second factor to consider when differentiating energy sources is energy density, or the amount of energy available per unit of the source, which is measured by weight or volume and the land area needed to produce them. Coal and oil have been the workhorses of the modern energy economy because their densities are high and they are relatively easily transported. Natural gas has a relatively high energy density but must be liquefied to ship over long distances and then re-gasified on arrival. The density of wind and solar is relatively low, mainly because a large area is needed to tap those resources. Moreover, transmission grids must be built out to the generation sites. The capital investment required to exploit each renewable resource starts out high but declines as the cost of components such as solar panels falls.[13]

A third factor is the degree of intermittency. No method of generat-

TABLE 5-3. **Taipower Fuel Prices for Electricity, August 2016**

Energy type	Cost per kWh (NT$)
Nuclear	1.11
Coal	1.89
Hydro	1.55
Wind[a]	2.26
Liquefied natural gas	2.68
Solar	6.17

Source: Timothy Ferry, "Taiwan's 'Energiewende': Developing Renewable Energy," *Taiwan Business Topics*, October 2016, p. 18. The rates are based on data from Taipower.

a. The figure for wind is the cost for electricity purchased from wind power. Some units are "self-owned," and the average of the two is NT$1.76.

ing power can operate all the time. Even the most reliable generating plants must be shut down for regular maintenance. For reasons of faulty design and human error, accidents happen. In general, and assuming sufficient feed stock, generating plants that are fired by coal, oil, natural gas, and nuclear can operate at a high and predictable level. These four sources form Taiwan's base load. Its flow of power from hydro, solar, and wind are intermittent, because each ultimately depends on the weather, and a thoroughly effective way to store the electricity for use in unfavorable weather does not yet exist. Taiwan's small land mass also limits the number of wind and solar installations. Hydro and the two renewables are therefore not included in Taiwan's baseload. As of now, they are a useful surplus but not constantly reliable.

It is good energy policy to maintain a comfortable reserve above baseload supply. But in recent times, there have been occasions when Taiwan's available reserve has declined to very low levels. For example, electricity consumption came within less than 2 percent of operating reserves in the spring of 2016, and there was a similarly close call in April the following year.[14] Then on August 15, 2017, a widespread blackout affected more than 6 million businesses and households island-wide. The outage occurred because of operator error at a gas-fired power plant, but the low level of reserves exacerbated the outage.[15] These interruptions point to an underlying fact: Taiwan's available generating capacity has not kept pace with consumption. From 2007 to 2017, the total installed capacity of the power system grew by 8.4 percent while consumption climbed by 16.1 percent.[16]

As in other countries, Taiwan's energy policy is directed at ensuring an adequate energy supply for economic activity and the public's middle-class lifestyle. Few events will evoke more public ire than short-term shortages that result in blackouts or brownouts. At the same time, civil society groups spur the government to place higher priority on environmental protection. Taiwan does rank twenty-third on Yale University's environmental performance list and among East Asian countries trails only Japan, but it still has a significant industrial sector that has created harmful air pollution in some parts of the island, especially the large, central city of Taichung.[17] As just one small example of the conflict, in the summer of 2020, the Taichung city government and Taipower clashed over the latter's decision to restart a coal-powered generator. The utility's priority was to provide sufficient electricity during the high-demand summer months. The government wanted to limit air pollution and fined Taipower for its resumption of operations.[18]

Moreover, Taiwan has accepted its responsibility to slow down climate change, to which its long-term and heavy use of fossil fuels have contributed, in spite of its exclusion, as a result of China's diplomatic stonewall, from negotiations on the United Nations Framework Convention on Climate Change. The public understands clearly that climate change is occurring and that it is concerning. In a 2018 survey conducted by the Taiwan Institute for Sustainable Energy, 93 percent of respondents acknowledged climate change, and 70 percent were concerned.[19] In June 2015, Taiwan's legislature recognized the importance of combating climate change by approving the Greenhouse Gas Reduction and Management Act, which voluntarily and unilaterally set the goal of cutting its 2005 levels of greenhouse gas emissions in half by 2050.[20]

That will require a reduction in the use of coal and oil (natural gas, mainly composed of methane, is also a fossil fuel but once burned has a much smaller environmental impact). But that means other power sources must be increased. Wind, solar, and hydro do not produce greenhouse gases, but they are not available all the time. In a major study, scholars at Academia Sinica acknowledged that the 2015 legislation was a good start and should be fully implemented, but they pushed government and society to do much more: "The government must carefully assess the pros and cons of various power sources, including nuclear energy, when planning energy reforms while paying attention to potential socioeconomic problems. . . . It should work harder to promote energy preservation, boost energy efficiency and consider hiking electricity prices or levying a carbon tax."[21]

Then there is nuclear power. A nuclear power reactor does not produce greenhouse gases, but it does produce highly radioactive spent fuel that must be stored to prevent contamination. Nuclear plants also carry the risk of a major catastrophe, such as the Fukushima disaster in 2011. Like Japan, Taiwan sits at the intersection of tectonic plates and their attendant faults. Since the fall of 1999, Taiwan has experienced three earthquakes of a magnitude above 7.0 and seven between 6.0 and 7.0. The islandwide September 1999 quake took the lives of 2,415 people. There has never been a major accident at a nuclear plant, but, not surprisingly, the wisdom of relying on nuclear power has still been a subject of prolonged debate and a political obstacle to crafting an energy policy that enjoys broad public support.

Taiwan's Antinuclear Movement

Politics is the reason nuclear power provides so little of Taiwan's electricity. In a nuclear reactor, the controlled burning of fissile material produces heat, which, in turn, creates massive amounts of steam that turn power generators to produce electricity. Looked at solely from the perspective of energy security, it made good sense for Taiwan in the late 1960s to reduce reliance on imported fossil fuels and radically expand nuclear power's share of the energy mix. The oil crises in the 1970s added more justification to do so. At the time the switch was made, Taiwan still had an authoritarian political system, so technocrats dominated the policymaking process, especially on technically complex matters like energy. The public was not allowed a say in the matter.

What opposition there was at the time to Taiwan's nuclear option was external, namely, from the United States. Washington feared and later confirmed that the Kuomintang (KMT) regime had decided to undertake a nuclear weapons program around the same time that it decided on the civilian nuclear power program. The trigger for the weapons program was China's detonation of its first nuclear device in 1964. The link between the two programs was the spent fuel that civilian nuclear reactors produced. Once civilian power was generated, the spent fuel by-product could be reprocessed to acquire plutonium, which is what powers the chain reaction in one kind of nuclear weapon. Separating the plutonium from the rest of the radioactive waste requires reprocessing technology, but Taiwan had acquired it. The United States tried to shut down Taiwan's nuclear weapons program in 1978, but it continued surreptitiously. Washington discovered the deceit and forced termination of the program for good in 1986.[22]

Coincidentally, the liberalization of Taiwan's political system also began in 1986. Citizens began to voice opinions and organize groups on issues that had hitherto been in the purview of technocrats and security commissars. Environmental degradation was an obvious target because Taiwan's rapid economic development had indeed polluted the land, water, and air. It would also prove to damage public health, as had already become evident in Japan, Taiwan's economic forerunner. Siding with defenseless common people, those brave enough to organize and demonstrate against environmental degradation had morality on their side. The first major protest occurred in 1986 and 1987 in the traditional coastal town of Lukang, whose residents opposed the construction of a titanium dioxide plant by the Dupont Corporation.[23]

Taiwan's antinuclear movement was born around the same time and also around the time of the Chernobyl disaster in the Soviet Union.[24] By the mid-1980s, three plants were already in operation: Chinshan and Kuosheng at the north end of the island and Maanshan in the south. Each plant had two reactors. The movement focused primarily on stopping the construction of a fourth plant, called NPP-4, which was to be located in the village of Kongliao, in what is now New Taipei City, in northern Taiwan. A proposal to dispose of nuclear waste on Orchid Island off the east coast was a related issue. The pioneers of the antinuclear movement were professors and intellectuals who had the scientific knowledge to mount a challenge to the government's policies. With the lifting of martial law in July 1987, their political activism entailed less danger, and in the fall of that year the Taiwan Environmental Protection Union was formed. It engaged in a variety of public activities against the expansion of nuclear power.

But the biggest early boost to the antinuclear movement was the emergence of the Democratic Progressive Party (DPP) as Taiwan's leading opposition party and its adoption of a "green" agenda (the same color as the party's flag). The Taiwan Environmental Protection Union allied itself with DPP legislators, KMT Legislative Yuan members who shared their views, and the residents of Kongliao. Of course, the DPP could not act on this policy proposal until it gained governmental power, but the antinuclear movement's alliance with the party definitely increased the chances of achieving that goal. When Chen Shui-bian, who emerged as the DPP's leader in the late 1990s, won the 2000 presidential election, people believed this would be the death knell for the construction of NPP-4.

The obituaries were premature. The Chen administration drafted an order to terminate NPP-4 in October 2000 but then bungled the rollout. That gave the pronuclear KMT, which still had a majority in the Legislative Yuan, the opportunity to put the DPP on the political defensive. The issue was ultimately referred to the Council of Grand Justices, which in February 2001 ruled against the administration and allowed the construction of NPP-4 to resume. Economic interests that relied on a sufficient, steady energy supply were pleased, and some in the DPP hoped that this outcome might lead the business community to revise its perception that the party was antibusiness.[25] Conversely, antinuclear activists felt betrayed, and their movement was divided. The Taiwan Environmental Protection Union continued to cooperate with the DPP and the Chen administration, despite the latter's reversal on NPP-4. The Green Citizens Action Alliance was founded in 2000 and soon assumed the leading position in the antinuclear movement. It opposed both the DPP and KMT and did so through protests.

The Chen administration had to consider another factor in handling the nuclear issue: DPP party elder Lin Yi-hsiung. Lin is a saintly figure in the DPP because in early 1980, while he was unjustly incarcerated as a political prisoner, his wife and two daughters were brutally murdered under circumstances that still have not been explained, though agents of the KMT regime at the time were probably the perpetrators. Given Lin's immense personal sacrifices for his political beliefs, he commanded respect from within the party and public. It just so happened that the policy issue he adopted once he regained his freedom was ending Taiwan's reliance on nuclear power, and he cared little about how it would impact the economy. For the DPP, which did have to strike a balance between the antinuclear and business community interests, Lin's moral authority—and even the possibility that he might lead a public, antinuclear campaign—kept DPP leaders anxious.

If the Chen administration had reduced the salience of the nuclear issue in Taiwan politics and alienated the DPP's former activist allies, a countertrend began with the return of the KMT to power in 2008. First of all, the relative conservatism of the Ma Ying-jeou administration invigorated social movements that, across an array of issues, engaged in more media-grabbing activism and increasingly employed social media to mobilize followers. Second, the Fukushima nuclear disaster in March 2011 strengthened the hand of those who argued that living near nuclear reactors sited in an earthquake zone was dangerous (even though Fukushima was the result of a unique design flaw, not its presence in an earthquake zone per se). That it may have been the blackest of black swans really did not matter. Third, the success of the Sunflower movement in March 2014 in forcing the withdrawal of the Service Trade Agreement with China demonstrated that social movements had the ability to defeat technocrats and elect politicians on major policy issues.

Leaders of both the KMT and the DPP soon realized that they now had to be more responsive to the antinuclear movement. Gradually, the groups around the island that could be mobilized for rallies and demonstrations—more than a hundred by 2019—would become better networked, with a National Nuclear Abolition Action Platform serving as the central node of the network.[26] Local mayors and magistrates in jurisdictions with nuclear plants had to worry about resistance from residents, on whose votes they depended for their election. As the DPP's candidate for president in 2012, Tsai Ing-wen tried to restore her party's alliance with the antinuclear movement by opposing the operation of NPP-4 after its construction was completed and rejecting any delay in decommissioning the three other plants when the nominal deadline for doing so arrived. But the nuclear activists were unimpressed.

Then, the KMT tried to outflank the DPP. In February 2013, Premier Jiang Yi-huah proposed holding a referendum to settle the fate of NPP-4. That was something of a surprise because the DPP traditionally was the party that wished to give greater weight to public policy decisionmaking through referendums than through legislative action. Conceivably, the DPP could have joined the KMT in taking this issue to the public. But the legislative caucuses of the two parties engaged in endless arguments about the thresholds for authorizing and approving referendums for voter consideration, with the KMT sticking with the restrictive limits already in the referendum law and the DPP seeking to relax them. In the end, the proposal died.

Not long after the Sunflower movement came to an end, Lin Yi-hsiung sought to capitalize on the resurgence of public protests by undertaking a hunger strike against the construction of the NPP-4. This quickly stimulated islandwide protests, and on April 27 the Ma administration announced that once the first NPP-4 reactor passed its safety tests, it would be sealed. Construction on the second reactor would cease unless a referendum authorized resumption.

External events and domestic political dynamics appear to have placed nuclear power on the road to termination, but if that happens, it will severely constrain the options available to the government and to the public for ensuring adequate energy supply. How can policymakers close the gap between the competing priorities of the increasing demand for power and interest in maintaining economic growth with the commitment to reducing the use of fossil fuels that exacerbate climate change, while renewable sources of energy continue to be underdeveloped?

Tsai Ing-wen's Energy Policy

After Tsai Ing-wen took office in May 2016, she announced her administration's ambitious intention to radically reorder Taiwan's overall energy mix in line with her party's antinuclear agenda. By 2025, she said, 50 percent of Taiwan's energy sources should come from natural gas; 20 percent should come from renewables, mainly wind and solar; and coal and oil should drop from 80 percent to 30 percent. Nuclear power would disappear from the mix altogether. The three existing nuclear plants would be decommissioned at the earliest required time, the fourth one would be terminated without ever operating, and Taiwan would move toward becoming a nuclear-free island.[27] Politically, the proposal appealed to the antinuclear and pro-renewable movement but not to those sectors of society that worried that the gap between supply and demand for energy was getting too narrow. The big question, however, was whether the proposal could be carried out in spite of the technical and political obstacles involved.

President Tsai was not the first leader to try to increase the use of renewables. In 2009 the Ma Ying-jeou administration had promoted the passage of the Renewable Energy Development Act to provide funding for energy research and development. In 2012 it set the goal of installing a million photovoltaic (PV) cells on rooftops and erecting 1,000 wind turbines. The Bureau of Energy of the Ministry of Economic Affairs reported that between 2008 and 2014, the renewable energy sector grew in value by 195 percent, the annual revenue increased to NT$488.4 billion (more than US$15 billion), and nearly 70,000 job opportunities were created.[28] Moreover, the public were showing support for renewables. The Taiwan Institute for Sustainable Energy poll showed that 49 percent of respondents strongly supported renewable energy and 37 percent supported it.[29] Buoyed by this momentum, President Tsai sought to advance her party's antinuclear objective.

Solar Power

Taiwan would seem to be an ideal candidate for increasing its solar power sector. Crossed by the Tropic of Cancer, it has a tropical climate. The average temperature at Taiwan Taoyuan International Airport on the north part of the island is 65 degrees in January, 77 in April, 92 in July, and 87 in October.[30] Taiwan is also able to rely on its own factories to produce the solar-cells, solar wafers, and solar modules needed to produce electricity. Moreover, investors recognize the opportunity to profit from a boom in solar in Taiwan and are prepared to deploy money accordingly.[31] In the fall of 2016, President Tsai set a target for the expansion of PV infrastructure in Taiwan to 20 gigawatts of installed capacity by 2025, an increase by over twenty times the 962 megawatts of installed solar PV capacity at the time.[32]

Yet achieving that ambitious goal would require surmounting several imposing obstacles. First of all, the weather in Taiwan is not as favorable for solar power as it might seem. *Taiwan Business Topics*, the magazine of the American Chamber of Commerce in Taipei, reports that "due to the frequent rainy and cloudy days in Taiwan, solar-energy facilities on the island operate on average at only 14% of capacity, compared to nearly 30% in the United States, where extensive areas of the southwest enjoy exceptional sunlight."[33] Taiwan's less sunny weather thus reduces the amount of electricity that is actually available. Renewables in Taiwan constituted 8 percent of installed capacity in 2016 but provided only 3 percent of consumed power. Because the generation of solar power is intermittent, it cannot be part of the energy "base load," sources on which consumers can rely all the time.

Second, when it comes to solar, Taiwan has already picked the low-hanging fruit. As of 2016, most of the installed PV cells across the island were on farm structures, factories, and government buildings. In Taiwan's rural south, all of the installed PV cells are on barn rooftops. These units are relatively small and often under 500 kilowatts in capacity each. Small units have two advantages over larger, ground-based structures. Their owners face fewer regulations than they would for a bigger unit, and they earn relatively more money. The "feed-in tariff" (FiT) paid to owners of small units in 2017 was NT$6.02 per kilowatt-hour, while owners of large units were paid NT$4.35 per kilowatt-hour.[34]

Third, a shortage of land on the island impedes the expansion of solar energy. Only one-third of the island's land mass of 12,456 square miles is even theoretically available, because the rest is steep mountains that are prone to landslides caused by earthquakes and typhoons. But it is on that one-third that most of Taiwan's 23 million people live, work, and farm. Taiwan has the sixteenth-highest population density in the world, so larger installations tend to focus on rural areas. Creating an installed solar capacity of 20 gigawatts would quite likely require 20,000 to 25,000 hectares of land—nearly 3 percent of Taiwan's total 800,000 hectares of arable land.[35]

As the potential for the instillation of more small solar power units on roofs in rural areas declines, finding new ways of radically expanding installed capacity becomes crucial for solar power if targets are to be met. One option is to expand that program to nonrural areas. Frank Hiroshi Ling, an energy and climate policy analyst at Cypress River Advisors and former adviser to governments concerning green technology, has advocated establishing a community-scale "microgrid" in each urban area in Taiwan that "generates, transmits, and distributes power independently of the national grid" by using the roofs of residential, industrial, educational, and other structures. Ling cites the estimate of a scholar at the Metal Industries Research and Development Center in Kaohsiung that one-third of urban residential requirements could be met by installing rooftop solar units.[36] However, for this to be possible, the government would have to update building codes and upgrade nonresidential structures to facilitate generation of solar power.

Another option is to install ground-mounted systems on unused land. Unfortunately, the shortage of land and government regulations can discourage larger-scale ground-mounted solar installations, even though they can produce power at low costs. Ground-mounted solar already exists in Taiwan, but nearly all of it is relatively small scale, beneath 500 kilowatts in capacity. This is owing to rules that define power projects of 500 kilowatts and above as power plants, which are subject to stricter regulations.[37] For developers who wish to install larger units, government red tape and the need to coordinate with a wide array of stakeholders creates a large number of hurdles to clear before even getting a permit. The agencies that developers must go through include the Bureau of Energy, the Council of Agriculture (COA), and the Environmental Protection Administration and its Environmental Impact Assessment committee (EIAC). In addition, the state-owned enterprise Taipower must give permission for connection to the grid.[38]

The agricultural sector is particularly problematic. The COA has allocated 803 hectares of agricultural land that is considered no longer arable for solar-power development and is considering opening up another 1,200 more hectares. But the government does not own this land. Instead, it is the property of hundreds of small land holders, with whom developers must negotiate for the rights to use their lands. The firm Sinogreenergy estimates that 700 landlords stand in the way of getting enough leases to produce roughly 100 megawatts of solar power. The local village heads and agricultural associations, which are important political actors in rural Taiwan and have links to the COA, must also be convinced. Many of the associations are opposed to solar power. In areas with a lot of indigenous people, developers must also negotiate with the aboriginal council, which is not always responsive. There is therefore a great deal of obstruction to the expansion of solar energy, even though individual farmers could reasonably expect to receive NT$350,000 annually by leasing a hectare of land for solar energy.[39] It does not require too much cynicism to conclude that local interests are taking advantage of the priority that the central government has placed on developing renewable energy to engage in rent seeking on a significant scale.

Council of Agriculture regulations governing farm land are another problem. The regulations begin with a statement of principle: "Agricultural use is the core value of agricultural land use."[40] The agency insists that farming land must be used for farming, and land use to generate renewable energy is secondary. Solar panels thus can cover no more than 70 percent of an agricultural plot and then for only twenty years. Thereafter, the land must revert to farming. Moreover, the COA regulates what farmers grow. An agency representative stated that farmers "are required to have a plan to describe the agricultural production" and that farmers who deviate from the plan risk revocation of their permit to farm by the local agriculture bureau. The Council on Agriculture has canceled the permissions to produce solar power to more than 100 farms because they stopped agricultural production altogether or because they did not follow their submitted plans.[41] The council tightened restrictions even more in July 2020, when it prohibited solar farms on designated agricultural or aquicultural areas and narrowed rules for all solar farms built on farmland in general. It required that solar farms whose area exceeded two hectares be approved by the COA, not local governments. These moves sparked howls of protest from industry representatives, who charged, with some justification, that the agency was undercutting the Tsai administration's policy of increasing reliance on renewables.[42]

Creative entrepreneurs are trying to find a way to square the circle. Big Sun Energy, a solar-cell manufacturer, developed a five-meter-high solar tracker that pivots throughout the day to harvest more sunshine by following the sun's path across the sky. The company also grows coffee in Yunlin County, and so the solar panels can also provide the shade that coffee plants favor.[43] Yet new COA rules may constrain Big Sun's innovation. To get an agriculture plan approved, farmers need to show a track record of success for the crops they wish to grow. Summer Luo, Big Sun's founder and CEO, notes the catch-22: "Integrating solar PV and farm crops will likely require experimenting with different crops, however, and this rule will potentially prevent farmers from making such experiments."[44]

Finally, there is the role of environmental groups in impeding development. Some of the land that COA made available for solar power was too contaminated by salt to farm. But environmentalists oppose the use of that land to develop solar power, arguing that these areas are salt marshes that are ideal habitats for rare migratory birds, including the black-faced spoonbill.[45]

Thus ramping up solar power's share of Taiwan's energy mix—a presidential priority—faces an array of obstacles. Some stem from the island's size, geography, and climate. But others are the result of the political system: government rules regulating different-sized solar installations, the parochialism and regulations of the COA, the resistance (or greed) of local stakeholders, and the opposition of environmental groups. Relatively narrow political interests supersede the broad, public interest in ensuring energy security.

Wind Power

Building large wind farms off the west coast of Taiwan is a significant part of the Tsai administration's policy plan to ensure energy security without reliance on nuclear power. The administration hopes to erect windmills up and down Taiwan's coasts with huge turbines on masts that rise 150 meters above the water and stand on a base 50 meters below. Each turbine can generate up to 9 megawatts of power.[46] The administration set the goal of building 3 gigawatts of offshore wind power by 2027 and a total of 4 gigawatts by 2030.

This may be an achievable goal, though not necessarily in the stated time frame. The government's overall goal and the funding it is providing for green-energy projects creates a positive climate. European countries, which have already proven the technology, will be a source of turbines and other components to construct these windmills. Taiwan itself has the capability to fulfill some ancillary requirements: steel, carbon fiber for the blades, electronics, ships, and so on.[47] Although local financial institutions remain reserved about investing in such large projects, foreign investors are enthusiastic, in part because Taiwan's current FiT for offshore wind power are high by world standards (US\$0.23 per kilowatt-hour for the first ten years). Also, the area off the west coast of Taiwan is a windy place, ideal for harvesting wind energy. Indeed, some Western observers believe that Taiwan is not being ambitious enough. They believe that there is potential for 10 gigawatts of power and that Taiwan should set its initial targets higher than it has.[48]

However, ramping up a significant wind-power sector in Taiwan faces a number of hurdles:

- The capital costs are high and are front loaded for the building and installation of the equipment (hence the incentive of a high FiT).

- Basic information about wind patterns in the Taiwan Strait, along with the regulations governing wind farms, are only now being developed. Typhoons with strong winds and high waves are the greatest threat to the viability of the structures, and so the wind patterns must be better understood before wind energy can be successfully harvested.

- Anchoring the steel monopiles into the seabed to provide support for the windmills above water is sometimes difficult. Moreover, some of the offshore areas that would be ideal for windfarms have undersea depths greater than the current maximum of fifty meters.

- The electricity that is produced must be connected to the grid, but normally the narrowest tentacles of an island's electrical grid end up at the coast, which is precisely where wind farms are producing large amounts of electricity.

- Environmental groups assert that the noise from driving the undersea piles damages the hearing of the Taiwanese humpbacked dolphin, a critically endangered species.[49]

In 2020, Taiwan's Civil Aeronautics Administration opposed the plan of wpd Taiwan Energy Co., a subsidiary of the German firm, and wpd AG in the waters off the Taoyuan area of northern Taiwan. The agency warned that the wind farm could affect the safety of commercial aircraft flying in and out of Taoyuan International Airport, which had nearly 50 million "passenger visits" a year before the onset of the coronavirus depressed traffic. It did permit the company to do a safety assessment, but as of September 2020, the issue had not been resolved to the satisfaction of the two parties, and the ultimate decision was up to the Bureau of Energy.[50]

In the second half of 2018, the Tsai administration faced a political challenge to its wind-power objectives. It originated from the KMT and focused on the level of FiTs that developers would receive in the future.

The struggle began in July 2018 when a group of legislators filed complaints with the Control Yuan against the minister of economic affairs, Shen Jongchin, who had primary responsibility for the development of wind power. Under the constitution, the Control Yuan serves a watchdog or ombudsman function and is institutionally equal to the Executive Yuan, of which the Ministry of Economic Affairs is a constituent agency. Although the mission of the Control Yuan is perfectly legitimate, it also provides an opening for opposition politicians to criticize and hamstring government policy.

The KMT legislators charged Minister Shen with squandering public funds in the implementation of the wind-power program. On December 7, 2018, the Control Yuan issued a report that found that ministry's planning was inadequate, that the FiT was too high and risked creating a public financial burden in the future, and that the time frame for creating new wind-power capacity was too short. It called on the ministry to review its decisions.[51]

Meanwhile, and perhaps in anticipation of the Control Yuan's report, the ministry announced plans on November 29 to reduce by 12.7 percent the FiT that developers would receive over the next twenty years. That led the developers temporarily to question whether the long-term return on their projected investment would be sufficient and to hold protracted discussions with the ministry on the rate it had set. The announcement forced developers to try to secure approval from the Changhua County government for six projects offshore, yet another hurdle that they had to clear before the new FiT kicked in. That effort was to no avail, because local elections on November 29 unseated the DPP magistrate, and the new KMT magistrate was not inclined to do a favor for the Tsai administration. On the FiT rate itself, the Ministry of Economic Affairs, in the end, agreed to reduce the cut to only 5.71 percent. As one local observer wrote, "For foreign companies seeking to make an investment, a stable political environment and a stable energy policy are essential. In contrast, the offshore wind power project shows a lack of political determination on energy policy. Even worse, ugly political conflicts between the KMT and the Democratic Progressive Party take place before the eyes of foreign businesses."[52]

A question that is not raised, much less answered, in Taiwan is whether the FiT system that sets costs is the best mechanism for attracting investment for the renewable industry. Evan Feigenbaum, of the Carnegie Endowment for International Peace, observes that "Taiwan's twenty-year FiT simply locks in costs that will have to be paid either by the government or by Taiwan's electricity consumers. . . . These costs will substantially affect economic performance as Taiwan adds ever greater baseloads of renewable power to the grid."[53] The alternative, to which a number of countries have shifted, is a market-based mechanism, such as auctions. Allowing the price to float would quite likely reduce costs and make solar a more attractive target for investment.

Natural Gas

As an alternative to oil, coal, and nuclear power, natural gas is a good option for Taiwan. Global supply is plentiful, and the price is reasonable. There are, however, several factors to take into account. Methane is a potent greenhouse gas before it is burned, so if its transmission lines have leaks, the escaped gas can make natural gas facilities no better for the climate than coal or oil. Nor is it certain that global prices for natural gas will remain at their current low levels, a key policy assumption. In addition, the plan to expand the use of natural gas on Taiwan has fostered political resistance over environmental protection.[54]

All the same, the Tsai administration sees expanding natural gas in Taiwan's energy mix as necessary to achieve their goal of energy security without reliance on nuclear power. The China Power Company, the state enterprise that is the sole importer of natural gas, must expand the capacity of gas-fired power plants to reach that goal. It hopes to increase Taiwan's natural gas power capacity to 24.0 gigawatts by 2025. Taking into consideration the plants that will be retired during that period, it must therefore build 13.5 gigawatts of capacity by then.

The snag in this ambitious program is ensuring that Taiwan has sufficient storing capacity for re-gasified liquid natural gas from Qatar, Australia, the United States, and other suppliers. It currently has the capacity to store about 10 million tons annually, split between facilities in Kaohsiung, in southern Taiwan, and Taichung, in central Taiwan. To meet the Tsai administration's goals, CPC Corporation, Taiwan, would have to increase this capacity by 8 to 10 million tons annually. To increase storage, it plans to build an LNG receiving terminal at Guantang, Taoyuan, in northern Taiwan, which would provide a much more reliable supply for the Datan gas-fired power plant, Taiwan's largest.[55]

But Guantang happens to be the site of an endemic species of coral and algae that have formed a reef that is around 7,500 years old and is the habitat for a number of ocean species, some of which supply the island's fishing sector. The long-term industrialization of the Taoyuan area and the pollutants it created has already damaged the reef. The possibility that construction of the Guantang receiving station might further damage the reef triggered a research study by the COA and extensive deliberation by the EIAC of Taiwan's Environmental Protection Administration. According to an informed observer, committee members "were facing a lot of pressure from the government [because of the need to expand LNG imports] but didn't know how to deal with the environmental groups. Their way out was to find something that is a legal concern and that was the reefs."[56] In October 2017, the EIAC ruled that the Guantang project be delayed for further study.

A year later, however, the EIAC reversed its ruling and gave approval for the construction of the terminal site. The government members of the committee all voted in favor, while other members either abstained or did not show up for the vote. One critic charged that "the vote was clearly pushed through by the government representatives and could hardly be regarded as a resounding endorsement." He further asserted that the "Democratic Progressive Party has abandoned its environmentally friendly image and can kiss goodbye . . . the idea of a green homeland."[57] The government's effort to assuage opponents of the decision by simultaneously canceling plans to restart a coal-fired plant in New Taipei City was unsuccessful.[58] Civil society activists were unable to stop the government's plan, which it regarded as essential to its overall policy, but they did manage to slow down the policy process and impose a reputational cost on the administration.

Overall during President Tsai's first term, steady progress occurred toward achievement of her goals.[59] Difficulties still remained in each sector, and the DPP's policy on nuclear power was attacked during the 2020 presidential election.[60] However, Tsai's reelection will allow her administration to keep moving away from nuclear and toward renewables. Whether the envisaged mix will ensure adequate supplies remains to be seen.

Supply- and Demand-Side Adjustments

There is a consensus across parties that one way to reduce the gap between energy supply and demand is greater efficiencies. Ma Ying-jeou, for example, instituted a Framework for Sustainable Energy Policy when he came into office in 2008. This included such measures as subsidies for industrial upgrades, energy audits, public education, and mandatory regulations and standards. As a result, energy intensity—the measure of how much energy is required to generate a certain amount of GDP—decreased by 2.46 percent a year over the next six years. The DPP has continued such efforts, and Taiwan's long-term shift from manufacturing to services has also reduced energy intensity.[61]

Yet the impact of these supply-side measures, which are more technocratic in nature, is far less than what could be achieved on the demand side by letting the market set the price that Taipower is allowed to charge for energy. But such a reform is highly political. Taiwan consumers may not know that what they pay on average per kilowatt-hour of electricity is quite low for developed nations. As of 2015, according to Taipower, the average price for power in Taiwan was US$0.09 per kilowatt-hour. In the United States, which is rich in energy, the price runs from almost US$0.20 in New England to US$0.11 in the South. In Japan, the average cost is US$0.22. The average price in South Korea is about US$0.06, but that is because nuclear energy occupies a much greater share of the energy mix in Korea than in Taiwan. Cheap, subsidized energy does help make Taiwan more competitive economically, but it is also a form of welfare. A consequence of this is that Taipower always operates at a loss, a condition that high FiTs for renewables will only aggravate, but those losses are ultimately covered by the taxpayers.[62]

In April 2012, three months after Ma Ying-jeou had won reelection, his administration announced that it would raise household electricity rates by an average of 16.9 percent, commercial rates by 30 percent, and industrial rates by 35 percent. Similar increases were also planned for fuel. This may have been good public policy, by better aligning the selling price of electricity to the cost of its production. However, the political impact was quite negative. Amid general public anger, there were public protests by the opposition political parties and civic groups. Ma soon backed off by phasing in the increases gradually and reducing their aggregate amount to only 6.8 percent for household and commensurate drops for other consumers.[63] It would be another two years before prices were raised again, and then only by 3 percent, and the projected price per kilowatt hour for 2025 was still a low US$0.11.[64]

Direct Democracy and the Nuclear-Free Policy

Less than three years after President Tsai's inauguration and after declaring her goal of a nuclear-free Taiwan, Taiwan's pronuclear forces hoisted the DPP on its own petard regarding energy policy. On the day of local elections,

November 24, 2018, there were three referendums on the ballot concerning energy policy. Two of these sought to reduce the reliance on coal and oil, one seeking to reduce electricity production in thermal power plants by 1 percent a year and the other advocating an end to the construction of coal-fired thermal power plants or generator units. The first of these was passed by 79.0 percent and the second by 76.4 percent. Although reducing the use of fossil fuels would help the climate, doing so could indirectly increase Taiwan's need for nuclear in the energy mix.

The direct attack on the administration's policy came in the third energy-related referendum: "Do you agree to repeal Article 95 Paragraph 1 of the Electricity Act, 'Nuclear-energy based power generating facilities shall wholly stop running by 2025?'" This proposal secured a majority of 60 percent, and its passage had a more immediate and profound effect than the other two measures.[65] This one repealed a provision of law almost immediately, though the other two certainly reflected opinion on policy. The referendum law specified that "the same law cannot be enacted by the legislative agencies within two years after implementation," which meant that a new referendum could not be proposed on the same issue for two years.[66] Those restrictions notwithstanding, the law is not clear exactly on the degree to which the administration must act on the results, and there is no enforcement body to determine compliance.[67]

There was a double irony in these results. First of all, it had been leaders of the DPP who pushed for the use of referendums in Taiwan's democracy and secured passage of a referendum law in 2003 (see chapter 13). Then, in December 2017, the DPP-controlled legislature liberalized the law's provisions on putting a referendum on the ballot and then getting it passed. The number of signatures needed to authorize a referendum was reduced from 5.0 percent of the electorate to 1.5 percent. For passage, the number voting in favor originally had to be 50 percent of eligible voters, but the approval share was dropped to 25 percent of the total electorate, a threshold cleared in the 2018 votes. Second, it was the DPP's signature, nonnuclear issue that the KMT used a referendum to frustrate.

The Ministry of Economic Affairs pledged to revamp energy policies in line with the referendum's results, even as the administration retained the broad goal of a nuclear-free Taiwan. On December 6, 2018, the ministry approved a proposal to abolish Article 95, with the intention of transmitting it to the Legislative Yuan for action.[68] But two months later, the ministry made public an "updated" energy policy that proposed abolition of nuclear power by 2025 and a migration to its previously designated energy mix (50 percent natural gas, 30 percent renewables, and 20 percent oil and coal). Kuomintang legislators cried foul, noting that the ministry's announcement came one day after its decision on new FiTs for wind power.[69]

In the meantime, activist groups developed new and competing referendum proposals that technically were different from the three that had passed in November 2018 but substantively sustained the fossil-fuel versus nuclear debate in new ways. One, promoted by the organization Nuclear Myth Busters, proposed resuming the completion of the fourth nuclear power plant and putting it into commercial operation. Another, proposed by a professor at National Taiwan University, called for the abolition of the project and use of the site for one of several alternative purposes. A third, put forward by the National Nuclear Abolition Action Platform, would forbid building, expanding, and constructing nuclear plants and bar any extension of the prescribed lifespan of existing plants until a repository for high-level radioactive waste was built and operating.[70]

A week after the 2018 referendums, American political scientist Nathan Batto, an associate research fellow at the Institute of Political Science at Academia Sinica, wrote this properly acerbic comment about the use of referendums to make public policy:

> So what the hell is Taiwan's energy policy supposed to be now? . . . To summarize, the voters don't want . . . coal. They definitely don't want nuclear, or maybe they do. They don't want any power plants in their neighborhood, and they definitely don't want electricity generated in their neighborhood to be sent elsewhere. They want low prices, and they absolutely demand a stable supply of electricity. It should be easy to satisfy all those demands simultaneously. I'm glad we used referenda to clear up this entire matter."[71]

Conclusion

Taiwan's energy policy does not lack for ambitious targets to increase the reliance on renewables, eliminate nuclear power completely, and reduce dependence on coal and oil. Plans to meet those targets have been formulated.[72] Yet the results of the 2018 referendums on nuclear power demonstrate once again the chronic yet shifting political stalemate over energy policy that has bedeviled Taiwan for years. What Taiwan needs, therefore, is a political system that can choose an energy mix informed by a clear and objective sense of the costs and benefits of competing options and then stick with that choice and implement it well. Whatever the bias that such a choice might reflect (for or against nuclear power, for example), government and society would know the downside risks that choice entailed and what steps might be taken to mitigate them. Yet that sort of rational choice is probably not possible, since the various contenders in the policy and politics debate each have their own, self-serving cost-benefit analysis, and the rotation of power probably makes final decisions impossible.

Yet to eschew a final decision is to make a decision. The factors producing the decision to not decide are clear. Restoring nuclear power to its former level is not possible, something that even the KMT seems to have accepted. It remains to be seen whether imported natural gas can become 50 percent of the island's power supply, as the Tsai administration intends. A significant rise in global prices could frustrate achievement of that objective. It will be some time before the benefits of renewables is known, and even then, they cannot be part of the base load for electricity in Taiwan. It seems clear that political leaders do not wish to risk the public's wrath by aligning consumers' price of energy at its true value. As long as all of these realities persist, by default the only way to ensure sufficient supply is to do what the government and public say they prefer not to do, and that is to continue burning large amounts of coal and oil, to the neglect of the environment.

6

The Politics of Taiwan's Past

In the former Soviet Union there was a joke that ran, "The future is secure; it's only the past that's uncertain."[1] Political debate about the past and about the very facts of history itself is common around the world, regardless of the political system. In the United States, for example, citizens to this day debate the legacies of slavery, and American politicians argue over where in the pantheon of U.S. presidents Ronald Reagan should stand. Verdicts regarding the past can change the balance of legitimacy and, therefore, power among today's political forces. This contention is particularly fraught in political systems that have made the transition from totalitarian or authoritarian rule to democracy. In Latin America, South Africa, Eastern Europe, and Asia, the victims of past repression seek to hold accountable the former power holders, while the abusers themselves usually prefer to set that past aside and move on.

Taiwan is one case of this phenomenon, and it has its own arguments over political history. Was the rule of the Nationalist Party, the Kuomintang (KMT), before the beginning of democratization relatively positive overall, especially in growing the economy, but simply marred by some unfortunate abuses? Or was it by its nature a harsh authoritarian regime that engaged in systematic repression of the Taiwanese majority, denying it a say over its destiny at key junctures? Viewed through the first lens, the KMT has abandoned its authoritarian past and become a credible contender for power in a democratic polity. The latter lens legitimizes the opposition Democratic Progressive

Party (DPP), which claims to represent the victims of KMT repression. Or was Taiwan, as some scholars contend, the object of several episodes of colonial rule by outside powers, including the Qing dynasty, Japanese imperialists, and the Republic of China? If viewed through this third lens, then an act of national self-determination is called for.[2]

Taiwan's political camps go beyond arguing about the facts of the past. They also disagree over how much today's KMT should be held accountable for its actions when it monopolized political power. Defining the historical record and the degrees of accountability are both part of the issue of transitional justice. Kuomintang leaders have not necessarily rejected the need to account and atone, but they disagree with the DPP over the different ways in which it should be done. Finally, there is the question of what this issue means for the political system as a whole. Will contention over the past ultimately result in a shared judgment that strengthens society by promoting future reconciliation? Or will the division and the political weakness it produces only strengthen the hand of China, which some in Taiwan regard as their greatest danger?

Transitional Justice Defined

In 2004 the United Nations Secretariat issued a report titled *The Rule of Law and Transitional Justice in Conflict and Post Conflict Societies*. It defined transitional justice as "the full range of processes and mechanisms associated with a society's attempt to come to terms with a legacy of large-scale past abuses, in order to ensure accountability, serve justice and achieve reconciliation."[3] Hwang Jau-Yuan, a professor at the School of Law at National Taiwan University, has developed a useful inventory of the "full range of processes and mechanisms" involved in successful transitional justice. He groups them in the categories of truth finding, victim reparations, wrongdoers' liabilities, and institutional reform.[4] Yet these activities are not necessarily mutually reinforcing. Wu Naiteh, of the Institute of Sociology at Taiwan's Academia Sinica, stresses the conflicts inherent in the steps chosen by democratic governments and societies to ensure transitional justice: "The thorny problem of transitional justice is further complicated by the frequent conflict of ethical principles and moral values, on the one hand, and political goals, such as democratic consolidation and ethnic harmony, on the other."[5] Similarly, Neil Kritz, who led a major project on transitional justice for the U.S. Institute of Peace, stresses the tension between "demonstrating a clear break" with the ancien régime, on the one hand, and adherence to the principles of democracy and the rule of law, on the other.[6]

Taiwan presents an exceptional case in the study of transitional justice in two respects. First, the change from an authoritarian to a democratic system was a negotiated transition in which the ruling KMT kept its seat at the table and led the new democracy for some years after the process was complete. For a while, at least, it could therefore govern the pace and scope of transitional justice. Indeed, it took the relatively easy step of providing reparations to victims while eschewing much truth finding or imposing liabilities on wrongdoers. Those issues would return to the political agenda in the DPP administrations of Chen Shui-bian (2000–2008) and Tsai Ing-wen (2016–the present). Second, unlike many new democracies, Taiwan has had to face a serious adversary in China. If national unity is an important resource in Taiwan's management of the impending threat from across the Strait, then the manner in which transitional justice is implemented in Taiwan is an important aspect to consider, owing to its ability to either foster unity or exacerbate division. That being the case, perhaps the scope of transitional justice should be a function not only of the abuses of the past but also of the future's looming danger.

Justice and Democracy Denied

The KMT's takeover of Taiwan was brutal and the system it imposed thereafter was a one-party state that placed severe limits on the exercise of civil and political rights and subverted the rule of law to ensure its control. Elections were held at the local level, but they served more to facilitate KMT control than to reflect the popular will. At higher levels of the political system, there were no popular elections, except for a limited number of supplemental seats in the Legislative Yuan (LY) after 1969.

The Republic of China (ROC) officials and soldiers who took over the island from the Japanese in late 1945 brought many of mainland China's problems with them, including economic mismanagement, corruption, disease, and predation. Before long, their abuse of longtime residents of the island (native Taiwanese) triggered an islandwide rebellion. It began as a hostile encounter on February 27, 1947, between the tax police of the tobacco agency and a local woman selling bootlegged cigarettes. One person died in the encounter, and violent protests fueled by pent-up rage erupted the next day. The resulting conflict has been known ever since as the February 28 incident (or 2-28/er-er-ba). While KMT officials played for time by negotiating with local Taiwanese, Generalissimo Chiang Kai-shek secretly sent troops from the mainland to suppress the rebellion and regain control. The rebellion was quashed quickly and brutally with indiscriminate violence. Many Taiwanese families lost relatives or good friends in the turmoil, leaving a searing effect on Taiwan society and politics. To this day, some Taiwanese regard it as blood debt that has yet to be paid.[7]

At the time of the incident, civil war was underway on the mainland between Chiang's armies and those of communist leader Mao Zedong. Gradually, the ROC forces lost ground to the communists, and by the end of 1948 it became clear that the end was near for KMT rule on the mainland. In this context, the regime acted to demobilize political activity in the areas that it controlled. In April 1948, the National Assembly added the Temporary Provisions Effective during the Period of Communist Rebellion to the ROC Constitution. This measure suspended sections of the constitution that, if implemented, would have guaranteed a democratic system in China, including Taiwan. For example, chapter 2 of the constitution had an exhaustive list of political rights and freedoms. Chapters 3 and 6 promised a national assembly and legislature constituted by elections. Chapter 12 established the mechanisms of election, recall, initiative, and referendum. The Temporary Provisions set all of that aside, and these rights were not restored until 1991. In addition, the regime imposed martial law (*jieyanfa*, also translated as "emergency rule") on most of the mainland in December 1948 and on Taiwan on May 20, 1949. Individuals deemed a threat to national security were subject to trial by military courts, thus criminalizing political dissent.[8]

After the defeated Nationalist government and armies moved to Taiwan at the end of 1949, the various security agencies of the KMT party-state proceeded to root out threats to their regime, whether they were communists, advocates of Taiwan independence, or other opponents of the regime. This was the White Terror, in which the instruments of a police state were employed to make arrests without probable cause, torture prisoners to extract confessions and accusations against others, conduct trials without due process, and impose cruel punishment against convicted offenders.[9] In the early 1950s, not all victims of the arrests and executions were Taiwanese. Indeed, during this period, 40 percent of the victims were mainlanders, though mainlanders made up only 15 percent of the population.[10]

The rationale for this repression was that the ROC was still at war with Mao's "communist bandits" and that opponents of the KMT regime were his witting or unwitting allies. Therefore, Chiang Kai-shek's illusory goal of mainland recovery took precedence over the protection of civil and political rights. The ROC claimed to be the government of all of China, and members of the LY and the National Assembly therefore represented districts all over China. Since the mainland was under communist control, elections had to be suspended.

The regime's arbitrary exercise of state power moderated as time went on. Wu Naiteh reports that most of the known White Terror cases occurred in the first decade: 76.4 percent from 1949 to 1960, 13.3 percent in the 1960s, and 9.1 percent in the 1970s.[11] Sheena Greitens, an associate professor of political science at the University of Texas at Austin, explores the state violence in Taiwan, South Korea, and the Philippines at different periods in her *Dictators and Their Secret Police* and seeks to explain the variation in each. For Taiwan, her measures of state violence are the number of individuals sentenced for political crimes and the number of executions for political crimes. In each category, the numbers are high from 1949 into the mid-1950s and then fall off fairly sharply. More than 600 were sentenced for political crimes from 1949 to 1950, slightly more than 300 from 1951 to 1960 (about 30 a year), and then fewer than ten a year from 1981 to 1987, after which martial law was ended. For executions, the numbers were between 150 and 200 in 1950, around 150 in 1951, more than 200 in 1952, then around 100 in 1954 and 1955, around 50 in 1956, and ten or fewer from 1958 to 1972 (and zero in some of those latter years).[12]

Greitens attributes these reductions to two factors. One was the consolidation of the regime's various security organizations, which facilitated better coordination of their activities and a reduction in the competition among them. The other was a systematic effort to better penetrate Taiwan society, partly by co-opting native Taiwanese into military and security agencies and partly by greatly stepping up surveillance of citizens' activities. The latter tactic provided early warning of dissident activities, allowing an opportunity to nip them in the bud, and also deterred such activities in the first place.[13]

Writing about the political system as a whole in the early 1980s, Edwin Winckler argues that Taiwan had begun a transition from "hard authoritarianism" to "soft authoritarianism."[14] Politically, this shift began around 1970, as the regime began to co-opt Taiwanese into what had been a mainlander-dominated system (one of those individuals was future president Lee Teng-hui). A few senior and loyal Taiwanese were made members of the KMT's central standing committee. The number of seats representing Taiwan in the LY and the National Assembly increased to take account of the island's growing population, and campaigns for those seats became venues for guarded debates about sensitive political issues. The government tolerated a series of demonstrations in late 1971 concerning the Diaoyu/Senkaku Islands until the focus shifted to the need for political reform.[15] The central headquarters of the KMT used county-level elections as a barometer for regime performance.

Nevertheless, when it came to civil liberties and political rights, Taiwan was still a rough place. After the United States terminated diplomatic relations with Taiwan on New Year's Day 1979 to establish them with the People's Republic of China (PRC), the *dangwai* (outside the party [KMT]) opposition politicians mounted a new round of antiregime political activity. This was tolerated until a major demonstration in the southern port city of Kaohsiung became violent after being manipulated by government agents provocateurs. This gave the security agencies the excuse they needed to jail opposition leaders, some of whom the agencies had planned on executing until the U.S. government stepped in.

A few of the targets of KMT repression had experiences more horrific than being confined to prison. Chapter 5 described the case of Lin Yi-hsiung, whose mother and two daughters were slain on February 28, 1980 (note the date), most likely by gangsters acting at the direction of security establishment. There was another extrajudicial killing in early July 1981. Chen Wenchen, a Carnegie Mellon University statistics professor who had returned to see family, was found dead on the grounds of National Taiwan University. Soon afterward, it became known that the Taiwan Garrison Command had called him in for questioning, that he had died after falling several stories, and that KMT regime spies in the United States had surveilled his attendance at Taiwanese community meetings. Both the Lin and Chen cases remain unresolved. In October 1984, Chinese-American author Henry Liu was murdered at his home in Daly City, California. It soon emerged that perpetrators were agents of a Taiwan security service, whose leaders wanted to stop Liu's critical writings about senior KMT political figures. The revelations caused great embarrassment for the Taipei government: enforcing political orthodoxy on Taiwan was one thing; doing so on U.S. soil was quite another.[16] As late as early 1987, when hopes for a democratic transition were growing, the Taiwan section of the U.S. State Department's annual human report began with this blunt statement: "Taiwan's polity is dominated by the Nationalist Party . . . in an essentially one-party, authoritarian system." Although the worst abuses of earlier days were over, and the promise of political liberalization was in the air, the institutions that prioritized national security over ensuring due process to constrain dissent remained in place.[17]

Transitional Justice in Taiwan's Democratic System

From the party-state's response to the February 28 incident and its actions through the decades of the White Terror up to the death of Chen Wen-chen, there was plenty of grist for a transitional justice mill. How finely that mill would grind was another question. An early, negative sign was Article 9 of the National Security Act. This law was passed to replace martial law, which President Chiang Ching-kuo had terminated on July 1, 1987, for all territory under ROC jurisdiction except the islands off the Chinese coast that it controlled (there, martial law was lifted in 1992). Article 9 unconditionally affirmed judgments made by military courts during the martial law era and prohibited any right of appeal. That ruled out full rehabilitation of those whom the military courts had convicted.[18]

Taiwan's democratization also did not guarantee that the issue of transitional justice would have high salience. The KMT strengthened its ability to compete successfully in elections, where it emphasized issues such as its success in creating economic prosperity, while continuing to avoid fully accepting responsibility for past abuses. The administration of Lee Teng-hui, who succeeded Chiang on the latter's death in 1988, made a start on the transitional justice project but confined itself to paying compensation to victims, establishing museums and memorials, and making official apologies. Later, the DPP administration of Chen Shui-bian named some of the officials responsible for the February 28 incident. The victims of these abuses were starting to receive recognition and legal rehabilitation, but the perpetrators remained untouchable.

Moreover, as Hwang Jau-Yuan makes clear, as of the mid-2010s, many measures usually associated with transitional justice had not been started:

- No truth commission was established.
- Although Lee Teng-hui authorized a formal report on the February 28 incident, no such report was ordered on the White Terror.
- Access to government files remained limited.
- Legal appeals for retrials were denied.
- Private memoirs and documents were destroyed.
- Confiscated property was not returned (a verdict of subversion always entailed seizure of property).[19]
- Perpetrators of abuses were protected from legal accountability by the National Security Law's statute of limitations, and damage claims against them were denied.

- There was no lustration law, which would have authorized the removal of current officials who had served under the authoritarian regime.[20]

Another transitional justice measure that Hwang could have mentioned, since it would figure heavily in Taiwan's transitional justice effort beginning in 2015, was "disgorgement"— that is, the seizure from the perpetrators of injustice of the alleged fruits of their actions.[21]

When Tsai Ing-wen was campaigning for the 2016 presidential elections, she made transitional justice a key issue. In a debate on December 2, 2015, she said, "I want to achieve transitional justice. I want to organize and reveal historical archives to unveil the truths and soothe the pain of victims." She then raised the issue of the assets owned by the KMT, which the DPP claim were "ill-gotten," and advocated for disgorgement.[22] After 1945, the party-state and individuals associated with it had acquired ownership of a wide array of existing properties in Taiwan, such as properties owned by Japanese entities during the colonial period. The KMT regime had later seized assets owned by individuals it had convicted of subversion under martial law. With these accumulated resources it later established new enterprises, such as television stations. It created investment companies to manage the assets.

As a result, the KMT had long been the richest political party in the world. But under pressure from the DPP, the KMT realized that its assets had become a political liability, and so it began shedding them, returning some properties to the government and liquidating some of its businesses. According to its own statements, the value of its assets had shrunk from more than NT$60 billion (about US$1.89 billion) in 2000 to NT$16.6 billion (about US$52 million) in late 2015, a drop of 75 percent.[23] In addition, the KMT had significant liabilities, such as the generous retirement pensions that it had promised to its employees.[24] Still, the DPP argued that this wealth and the income that flowed from it to the KMT gave it a structural advantage during election campaigns. In the campaign debate, Tsai promised, "We will also go after inappropriately obtained party assets. We shall stipulate the need to declare sources of party income and forbid political parties from investing in profit-seeking enterprises to deepen democracy and fair competition."[25]

Tsai's 2016 victory and the DPP's success in winning a majority in the LY created an unprecedented opportunity to right old wrongs and to level the political playing field. Some in the party were chomping at the bit. One of their priorities was to remove symbols of the authoritarian regime and its abuses, particularly statues and busts of Chiang Kai-shek. But in Tsai's inaugural address, the emphasis was on reconciliation: "For the new democratic system to move forward, we must first find a way to face the past together. . . . The goal of transitional justice is to pursue true social reconciliation, so that all Taiwanese can take to heart the mistakes of that era." She promised to establish a truth and reconciliation commission inside the presidential office, which would operate "in the most sincere and cautious manner." Within three years, after establishing the factual records, an investigative report would be issued and "follow-up work" would be carried out. Tsai continued, "We will discover the truth, heal wounds, and clarify responsibilities. From here on out, history will no longer divide Taiwan. Instead, it will propel Taiwan forward."[26] To that end, the Legislative Yuan's Judiciary and Law Committee reported out a comprehensive transitional justice bill in late June 2016.

However, the DPP caucus in the LY wanted to place priority on the KMT's assets.[27] In July 2016 it pushed through a bill establishing an Ill-Gotten Party Assets Settlement Committee.[28] The act applied to both political parties and their affiliates and defined *ill-gotten assets* as "those obtained by a political party in a manner that runs counter to the nature of a political party or the principles of democracy and rule of law."[29] The KMT was not implacably opposed to the bill, as it was willing to donate most of its assets to charity. However, it would be reluctant to return "legally acquired office space and funds to cover personnel costs." It also sought an interpretation from the Council of Grand Justices as to whether the act was constitutional (the court did not issue its ruling until August 2020).[30]

It became clear that the settlement committee, under the leadership of lawyer and DPP stalwart Wellington Koo, would not accept the KMT's partial accommodation. The committee's approach was to return to the government any assets the KMT allegedly seized. On September 21, 2016, it ordered a freeze on the KMT's directly held assets, which forced the party to get committee permission to pay salaries and pensions. Moreover, the committee focused a lot of its attention on KMT affiliates: the Central Investment Company, the Hsinyutai Company (also an investment company), the China Youth Corps, and the National Women's League. Each had been spawned by the party-state during the authoritarian period, but by 2016 they had a more distant relationship with the KMT. Still, they came under scrutiny, and evidence of their KMT origins was used as a basis for freezing their assets. The KMT struck back by filing lawsuits with the administrative court seeking injunctions to unfreeze the assets.

The court usually ruled in the KMT's favor after each lawsuit, but it appeared that the settlement committee simply ignored the court's orders and declined to inform banks to unfreeze the assets.[31] The committee also seized seventeen other properties, including the National Policy Foundation, the KMT's think tank. It did so not because of any evidence that the assets had been "ill-gotten" but to create a NT$865 million fund to compensate the government for the assets it had originally seized from the Japanese in the late 1940s and then transferred to the KMT between 1957 to 1961 through allegedly inappropriate arrangements, though the original properties were now in private hands.[32] Again the KMT sued, and the administrative court issued an injunction. As of March 2020, most of the settlement committee's seizures (worth NT$76 billion, according to one report) were still tied up in the courts.[33]

Understandably, the KMT regarded the settlement committee's efforts to deplete its assets as a not-so-subtle effort to destroy it, based on a premise that it was the DPP's sworn enemy. Over the course of these events, KMT supporters argued that the committee had placed the rule of law in jeopardy. An editorial in the *United Daily News* asserted that "since [the Ill-Gotten Party Assets Settlement Committee] began operations, it has assumed that it is above the law. It has acted in complete disregard of due process and justice. . . . Even more astonishing is the attitude of [the committee regarding] the burden of proof, the presumption of guilt, and the right to remain silent, allowing itself to ignore due process and to do whatever it pleases."[34] Former president Ma Ying-jeou charged that the committee "is unconstitutional, as it encompasses the powers of the executive, legislative and judicial branches of the government. [Its] statutes also violates [sic] the basic tenets of law such as the 'presumption of innocence,' 'no retroactive legislation,' 'no legislation involving a singular case' and 'no double jeopardy.'"[35]

From the Green camp, journalist Chin Heng-wei asserted in the *Taipei Times* in November 2016 that it could have been predicted in advance that the courts would rule in the KMT's favor:

> After the committee froze the KMT's bank accounts, the party applied to the Taipei High Administrative Court to lift the injunction. The court ruled in favor of the KMT, as many had predicted without even knowing the details of the legal dispute. The committee will most likely appeal the ruling, but its chance of winning is slim, for this is the way things are in Taiwan's judicial system: The KMT virtually owns the courts. . . . The KMT has bullied Taiwan for almost 70 years. During that time, the party—devoid of all virtue and rabid as a power-hungry monster—tried its very best to devour all in its path to make them its own. It absorbed military personnel, public servants,

public-school teachers and intelligence agents, and gained control of the courts and many civic groups."[36]

For Chin, power over institutions was the decisive factor, not the rule of law. Kuan Bi-ling, a DPP legislator, agreed. He charged that it was "unacceptable that the courts have ignored the public benefit" by postponing judgments on the accumulated cases. He suggested that the settlement committee take a "more hardline stance" against the Council of Grand Justices.[37]

But Chin and Kuan were proven wrong. In August 2020, the Council of Grand Justices ruled in favor of the settlement committee on the key provisions of the law that established it. Among other things, the ruling asserted that the law's enactment did not violate the constitution, and that the measure neither violated the "division of government power" under the constitution nor deprived parties of the funds they rely on for their legitimate operation. Now it was the KMT that asserted that the judiciary was politically biased: "The KMT is not surprised that the grand justices, who have been approved by the Democratic Progressive Party, would reach such a constitutional interpretation." The statement added that the council has become an "affiliate organization of the DPP."[38]

The committee's campaign to capture the KMT's assets exhibited a few ironies. The first is that the KMT was a relatively easy target, but it was able to use the regular legal system to protect itself, up to a point. If in the end the settlement committee is unable to deprive the KMT of much less than it sought, it will be partly because the committee acted in an extrajudicial fashion. Perhaps cooperation with prosecutors would have yielded better results. The second irony is that the government will benefit from the confiscations that stand, but the private citizens who were the victims of the KMT's abuse of their property rights will not get their assets back. Only in cases where the government owns or occupies a piece of property that can be traced to the original owner will restitution be possible. In most cases, too much time has passed, and documentation is sparse.[39] The third irony is that the KMT actually won a major victory in the November 2018 local elections. For all the concern from the KMT side that it would no longer be competitive, and for the expectations on the DPP side that they could play on a level field, the KMT overcame the loss of revenue from its seized properties. The principal reason for their victory in these elections was public dissatisfaction with the Tsai administration for its failure to tackle tough issues, including transitional justice. The KMT itself successfully undertook its first fundraising in some time, with good effect.[40]

Back to Justice: Problems of Scope and Legality

Having prioritized the issue of KMT assets, the Tsai administration did not return to the core matter of transitional justice until the middle of 2017. But it had not ignored that task completely. In June 2016 the National Records Administration, under the National Development Council, had requested that government agencies sort their files and transfer the relevant ones to it, and by February 2017 the Executive Yuan had approved a request for the documents.[41] Later that month, facing protests from civic groups demanding action, President Tsai announced the declassification of all documents related to the February 28 incident and said that almost 1 million documents would be transferred to the National Records Administration.[42] In her public address, she reaffirmed the goal of exposing the abuses of the authoritarian period and promised prudence on the question of who should be held responsible.[43] But activists were dissatisfied with this stance, and by May they were lobbying Su Chia-chyuan, speaker of the Legislative Yuan, to revive negotiations of the stalled transitional justice bill and pass the legislation.[44]

The bill finally passed on December 5, 2017. It authorized the creation of a nine-member Transitional Justice Commission with four missions: make political archives more available, remove authoritarian symbols, redress judicial injustice, and produce a report on the history of the authoritarian period. The period to be covered would be from August 15, 1945, when Japanese colonial rule nominally ended, to November 6, 1992, when martial law was lifted for the islands off the shore of the Chinese mainland that the Taiwan government controls. The commission was constituted in early April 2018 under the chairmanship of Huang Huang-hsiung, a respected *dangwai* and DPP elder. But only days after the passage of the legislation, its supporters began arguing over the relative priority of the first three of the mandated tasks.[45]

For Tsai Kuan-yu, the eighty-four-year-old honorary director of the Taiwan Association for the Care of the Victims of Political Persecution during the Martial Law Period, the top priority was uncovering the history of repression "still kept in the dark. . . . Most importantly we political victims very much hope to see guilty verdicts overturned in our late years."[46]

For *Taipei Times* commentator Chin Heng-wei, the priority was removing "authoritarian symbols," particularly the politically loaded street names, as well as the statues and monuments to Chiang Kai-shek, of which there were 1,083 on Taiwan and its associated islands. He pushed back against what he perceived to be the government's weak commitment to this task. He challenged the excuses for inaction he was hearing—that the task was too expensive or that the people did not want street names they had grown up with to be altered, and so on. Instead, he said, the issue was "whether the DPP will flinch, say one thing and do another, or if it has the courage to follow through. . . . The authoritarian party-state has ceased to exist and the only thing remaining are its symbols. If the nation cannot rid itself of these symbols, how can it rid itself of the authoritarianism they represent?"[47]

On the task of holding perpetrators accountable, supporters of transitional justice were immediately on the defensive, having to explain that vengeance was not the motivation driving the effort.[48] A December 14th *Liberty Times* editorial offered both reassurance and a warning: "Taiwan has not chosen a path of vengeful struggle, but rather one of truth and reconciliation. Having made that choice, Taiwanese need to bring as much of the truth to light as possible. Only when the subordinates of the former party-state face the sunlight and turn into democratic citizens will Taiwan's reconciliation process speed up—only then will flowers bloom from the gashes left by history."[49] Chang Kuo-tsai, a professor retired from National Hsinchu University, argued that the minimum requirement in dealing with perpetrators was to demand an admission of guilt. He wrote,

> Transitional justice in Germany has worked because it is underpinned with an admission of wrongdoing and an acknowledgement of guilt among the people. That is, the German national character understands the concepts of shame and disgrace. In a nation lacking this trait [that is, Taiwan], an oppressed and enslaved people do not know how to fight back, and choose to remain silent, even when having been dashed to the ground.[50]

The principal obstacle to holding perpetrators to account, as noted earlier, was the Article 9 provision of the National Security Law, which upheld the judgments made by military courts under martial law and barred any right of appeal, except under extraordinary circumstances.[51] The authors of the bill that established the Transitional Justice Commission sought to circumvent that provision by giving the commission the power to hear appeals from those who believed they had been unjustly convicted, to investigate those verdicts, and to revoke them if there were good reason to do so. The commission also had the power to convict perpetrators of human rights abuses and impose sentences on them if they could be identified. But that only raised questions as to whether the definition of *crime* (performance of an action that "contravene[s] the values of freedom and democracy or the constitutional order") was too vague, whether the process that the commission would follow in carrying out its investigatory and judicial functions was fully developed, whether a statute of limitations applied to the crimes it would investigate, and what sort of punishments it could impose.[52] Former president Ma Ying-jeou again weighed in, arguing along the same lines that this legislation violated fundamental principles of the rule of law, such as presumption of innocence and prohibition of ex post facto legislation.[53]

Not surprisingly, the KMT declined the commission's invitation to attend its proceedings. Party spokesperson Hung Meng-kai stated, "The commission is set to become this giant monster that views itself as above the Constitution. We are doing everything we can to seek a constitutional interpretation from the Council of Grand Justices on its legitimacy. Before the council issues any ruling, the party will not endorse any actions from the commission."[54]

A Pragmatic Approach and a Serious Mistake

Once the justice commission began work, on May 21, 2018, it chose not to tackle difficult tasks such as dealing with perpetrators. Instead, it focused on less controversial ones. First, it handled assembling the collection of documents relevant to the transitional justice project. Most agencies cooperated to declassify them, including the Ministry of Justice Investigation Bureau and the military organization that held the files of the Taiwan Garrison Command. The result of this effort was the creation of an online database of court files of almost 10,000 victims of the authoritarian period. This searchable database was remarkable not only in the number of individuals but also in the inclusion of the names of the military officers involved in the victims' trials.[55] But there were holdouts that resisted declassification. The KMT itself objected to an order from the justice commission in August 2018 to account for its political archives concerning the February 28 incident and the White Terror within one month, on the grounds that this order gave too little time for them to do the job with the limited personnel resources available.[56]

More serious was the commission's difficulty in getting access to the files on twenty-one relatively recent political cases, including the Kaohsiung incident of December 1979 and the arrests that followed, the murders of Lin Yi-hsiung's mother and daughters, and the death of Chen Wen-chen. The National Security Bureau, the Ministry of National Defense, the Ministry of Justice Investigation Bureau, and the National Police Agency, which each held files relevant to these cases, claimed that they had been "permanently classified." In the end, files concerning the Lin murders were turned over, and the government-funded history academy announced that it would publish materials related to the Chen Wen-chen case. In December 2019, some intelligence reports relevant to the Kaohsiung incident were declassified but not released to the public. In May 2020, reports of wiretaps of Chen Wen-chen were released to the public, but more remains to be revealed.[57]

The justice commission used its authority to revoke the convictions of a number of people jailed during the White Terror period. The first round of about 1,270 cases occurred in October 2018; there were another 1,505 in December 2018, and 2,006 in May 2019. Among the individuals cleared in the final round were Lei Chen, a liberal KMT figure and publisher who in 1960 had exceeded the regime's tolerance of press criticism, and those associated with *Formosa* magazine who were jailed after the Kaohsiung incident: Lu Hsiu-lien, Chen Chu, Yao Chia-wen, Huang Hsin-chieh, and Shih Ming-te. These 4,781 cases represent just over one-third of the approximately 13,000 White Terror prisoners who had already received monetary compensation from the government but not exoneration.[58]

But even before the first round of exonerations could be announced, the legitimacy of the transitional justice project was dealt a serious blow by the action of its vice chairman, Chang Tien-chin, a lawyer who had previously been working at the Mainland Affairs Council.[59] The incident concerned a man named Hou You-yi. Hou had spent most of his career in the police but had more recently served as vice mayor of New Taipei City and in 2018 was the KMT's candidate for mayor in the November local elections. In late August of that year, in an internal meeting of the Transitional Justice Commission, Vice Chairman Chang said that Hou was "the worst example of transitional justice" and that it was a pity his case had not been used to manipulate public opinion against him. Specifically, he asked attendees to think of ways to use the commission's draft lustration law against Hou for political mileage. Chang also compared the commission to the Ming dynasty's "eastern bureau" (*dongchang*), a secret police and spy agency. Unfortunately for Chang, a commission researcher leaked a recording of his remarks to the media, and the matter became a public issue. If critics of the Tsai administration needed evidence that the transitional justice project was tantamount to a political vendetta, Chang had provided it.[60]

After multiple official apologies, the commission's chairman, Huang Huang-hsiung, resigned soon after Chang Tien-chin's resignation. Late in 2018, KMT legislators proposed to repeal the act establishing the commission. When that failed because of the DPP majority in the Legislative Yuan, the KMT tried in early January to cut the commission's funding. That also failed, but the efforts telegraphed what the party might do if it had regained a majority in the 2020 legislative elections.[61]

In February 2020, at the time that the seventy-third anniversary of the February 28 incident was marked, the commission passed a major milestone by unveiling an online collection of records from cases in the White Terror era. It included the names of government officials who were involved in the cases.[62] However, this was only partial progress. At a ceremony marking the February 28 incident, Tsai Ing-wen announced that she had ordered the National Security Bureau to declassify within one month the political files that the commission had requested.[63]

Evaluation

In principle, conducting a transitional justice project, if properly conceived, could strengthen Taiwan society and its democracy. A large number of people in Taiwan, Taiwanese and mainlanders alike, had suffered from the arbitrary exercise of state power. They were wrongfully accused, convicted, jailed, deprived of property, and sometimes unjustly killed. Lives were ruined. In theory, for the state to authoritatively right these wrongs based on objective investigation, to apologize for the abuses, to open the case files, and to provide some degree of compensation seems proper. Moral rehabilitation of wronged individuals can promote social and political reconciliation.

In broad concept, the DPP's approach to transitional justice adopted many elements of the transitional-justice agenda pursued in formerly authoritarian countries in Latin America and Eastern Europe. But many of these cases were ones of broad regime change, one element of which was the elimination of former ruling parties. Taiwan's situation was different, in that it was one of regime transformation. There, the ruling party that was responsible for past injustices, the KMT, was also the party that was willing, under pressure, to initiate the transition to democracy, the restoration of civil and political rights, the restoration of the rule of law, and some modest transitional-justice measures.[64] The party still existed and still enjoyed popular support, as reflected in periodic electoral victories.

That basic difference—between regime change and regime transformation—might have led the DPP to carefully calibrate how to undertake transitional justice in a way that was appropriate to Taiwan's situation. Yet buoyed by the 2016 electoral victory, those in the party who took charge of the project forged ahead, discounting the potential obstacles.

Their first mistake was to overestimate the strength of public support for transitional justice. In the late 2017 Taiwan Election and Democratization Survey, only 1.9 percent of those polled said transitional justice was the highest priority that Tsai should address. Only 3.5 percent thought it was the second-highest priority. There was a small variation in responses according to age and a bit more in terms of education. But the bottom line is that fewer than 6 percent of the population thought it was a high priority. Of the respondents who ranked it as the first or second most important issue,

- 6.2 percent were twenty- to twenty-nine years old,
- 4.0 percent were thirty- to thirty-nine years old,
- 3.7 percent were forty- to forty-nine years old,
- 6.9 percent were fifty- to fifty-nine years old, and
- 6.7 percent were sixty years old or older.

Hence a modestly larger group in the youngest generation and the two oldest generations were more inclined to assess transitional justice as a top priority issue than other age cohorts. Controlling for educational level, fewer than 3.2 percent of those with a primary or technical college education thought that transitional justice was the first or second most important issue, while between 5.4 and 6.9 percent of those with a junior high, high school, or university education believed so.

What are the reasons for this only modest support? One is that other issues have a much higher priority among the general public: economic growth, relations with China, and education are considered the most important. Another is that most of the abuses occurred a long time ago, before many of today's Taiwan people were even born, and this passage of time has likely mitigated the drive for transitional justice. Third, the KMT of today is not the harsh party-state of the 1950s and 1960s, and it receives popular credit for having built a prosperous society.

These historical realities handicap DPP members who try to carry out transitional justice and, at the same time, use the past as a weapon in contemporary political combat. The better time window for them would have been the 1990s, when memories of the past were stronger and personified in a larger number of victims. But the KMT was in power during that entire decade and could control the pace and scope of transitional justice—all the more reason activists wished to use the 2016 victory to advance the cause, particularly at a time when the KMT was at its weakest. Still, this was a case in which an active minority pursued a cause that the broad majority did not see as a priority. Active minorities often drive politics, but on an issue such as transitional justice in Taiwan, perhaps it would have been a good thing to have broad and active majority support.

Second, there were differences within the DPP over priorities. President Tsai Ing-wen, who was DPP party chairwoman as well as president, appeared to adopt a more limited approach that emphasized social reconciliation and truth seeking as the means to achieving transitional justice (on that matter, she proclaimed, "We will discover the truth, heal wounds, and clarify responsibilities"[65]). But the DPP caucus in the LY was more ambitious. It forged ahead, starting with the assets of the KMT and the organizations linked to it. It did not pass legislation on a comprehensive transitional-justice measure until the end of 2017, legislation that included a mandate on the fraught political issue of authoritarian symbols.[66] The conflict over priorities was at the heart of the judgment that the Deep Green *Liberty Times* rendered on Tsai's first term when it said that "from the point of view of victims' relatives, out of the three stages of procedural justice that they call for—truth, justice and reconciliation—the process is still stuck at the stage of clarifying the truth."[67]

Third, those promoting transitional justice could have worked to better sequence its actions in the effort to convince the public and the KMT that the DPP's true objective was political reconciliation and not a witch hunt. President Tsai appeared to lean in that direction, but the desire in her party to first target KMT assets was strong. Strictly speaking, this issue is less about transitional justice that about ensuring a level playing field for political competition. Given the weak position of the KMT after its devastating electoral defeat, its members could be forgiven for thinking that the DPP's goal really was the destruction of their party. Moreover, the charge given to the Ill-Gotten Party Assets Settlement Commission was to address not just the KMT, which competed in elections, but also its affiliated organizations that did not. Indeed, the DPP's belief that KMT assets created an unlevel playing field in recent elections has been more asserted than proved.

The DPP should also have anticipated the KMT's pushback in response to the DPP's campaign to take away its property after evoking fears in the KMT that its very existence was at stake. It was inevitable that the KMT would mount legal challenges to the actions of the settlement commission, given the investigatory and judicial authority the LY had given it outside the existing system. The August 2020 ruling of the Council of Grand Justices may have given the commission a new lease on life, but a lot of time had been lost in the process.

Many of these deficiencies in the way the DPP conducted transitional justice were in the realm of tactics. Yet there was a strategic mistake as well: it conducted its campaign in a way that divided the polity even further. Reconciliation, one of the core objectives of transitional justice, should bridge the gaps that divide a society, not deepen them. This is all the more the case when the costs of division are high, as they are in Taiwan. China's ambitions regarding Taiwan's future are an existential challenge, and meeting that challenge requires broad unity within the public and among political parties. To achieve that unity, the KMT and the DPP would have had to meet each other half way: the KMT would have had to more clearly acknowledge that China was a threat (a subject addressed in more detail in later chapters), and the DPP would have had to recognize that the KMT feared the way transitional justice was being carried out.

To say that China poses no threat at all ignores the ways in which Beijing seeks to shape and constrain Taiwan's future. To put the KMT in the historical dock and argue that it is an instrument of China's unification strategy today, as some in the Green camp do, is excessive. Unintentionally or not, sowing these deep divisions within Taiwan only serves Beijing's interests. As Hu Wen-chi, a former KMT official, has recently written, "Regardless of whether people support or detest the DPP, all 23.5 million Taiwanese are in the same boat: They make up a shared community, and they will only be able to deal with external threats if they first can stop fighting domestically."[68] A divided Taiwan is a vulnerable Taiwan.

7

Beijing's Taiwan Ambition

Taiwan, with its aging society, maturing economy with few natural resources, and fraught political history, faces some serious domestic policy dilemmas. Other countries with these same characteristics would also find it difficult to reconcile competing priorities. But Taiwan is an almost unique case: the government of the People's Republic of China (PRC) in Beijing has ambitions for the island and its people that, if achieved, would fundamentally change Taiwan's legal character and much of its way of life.[1] Taiwan would go from being a political entity that claimed to be a sovereign state to an administrative unit of the PRC, and with a less democratic system than it has now. The China factor thus creates a whole new level of complexity that further exacerbates Taiwan's policy challenges. True, the PRC has been a place of opportunity for Taiwan companies since the 1980s. On the other hand, the People's Liberation Army (PLA) has been acquiring more advanced military equipment since the late 1990s, and in the 2010s has undertaken programs of institutional reform. If the reforms are successful, Beijing will have an enhanced ability to fight and win a war for Taiwan. The PLA's expanding developing capabilities may never be used, but their existence changes the way Taiwan's leaders and the public address the PRC's political ambitions.

Why Unification

When the Chinese Communist Party (CCP) founded the PRC regime in October 1949, it declared the objective of liberating Taiwan. One motivation was to restore to the new regime the boundaries of China that existed during the Qing dynasty (1644–1911), an objective that affected Tibet and Xinjiang, as well. Beijing also wished to defeat the rival Republic of China regime (ROC) that it had fought for most of the prior two decades and that had retreated to Taiwan. The PRC wanted both the people of Taiwan and the international community to accept Taiwan as a part of China's sovereign territory, and it sought to incorporate the island within the PRC's political and administrative system.[2] Finally, there was a strategic logic behind this ambition, a logic that was almost three centuries old.[3] In the mid-seventeenth century, Manchu forces defeated the Ming dynasty, founded the Qing dynasty, and, over time, gained control of the core provinces of what is now regarded as mainland China. They then turned their attention to Taiwan, which until then had not been treated as Chinese territory and to which defeated Ming loyalists had retreated. In 1683 Qing forces ended that holdout regime and took control of key points on the island.

There ensued a debate at the Qing court over what to do with the new possession. Some officials argued that maintaining control of this frontier area would be more trouble than it was worth. Others, led by Admiral Shi Lang, offered a strategic argument for retaining what people in the West then called Formosa (originally the Portuguese name). Controlling Taiwan, they argued, could allow them to use the territory as a protective screen for the mainland of China. Furthermore, occupying Taiwan could help them more easily prevent foreigners from seizing the island, thereby posing a potential threat to China. Shi's logic convinced the emperor, and Taiwan became a prefecture of Fujian province across the Taiwan Strait. Thereafter, the trickle of Han Chinese from Fujian and Guangdong became more of a flood, and the indigenous peoples were either assimilated or contained in the mountains. What began as a campaign to end internal rebellion in Taiwan eventually turned into an expansion of the Chinese empire. In 1887, after Japan and France had threatened to seize Taiwan, the island became a full-fledged Chinese province. Then, in 1895, Japan defeated China militarily and demanded Taiwan as a prize of victory. The Qing court ceded the island to Japan and Shi Liang's nightmare came true.

Fast forward to the early 1940s, during the middle of World War II. Up until then, the ROC government that succeeded the Qing dynasty after it fell in 1911 had accepted that Taiwan was a Japanese colony. Yet after the United States entered the war against Japan, hopes grew for a Chinese victory and the recovery of lost territory. Generalissimo Chiang Kai-shek, the leader of the ROC since 1928, revived Shi Lang's strategic concept and argued for the return of Taiwan and the three Manchurian provinces so they could serve as China's outer fortresses. Franklin Roosevelt had other, equally strategic reasons of his own for returning Taiwan to the ROC, and accordingly he decided around the end of 1942 to support Taiwan's return to Chinese sovereignty, a decision that was ratified a year later at the Cairo Conference.[4] In the fall of 1945, after the end of World War II, ROC civilian and military personnel took control over Taiwan from the Japanese. Internationally, the working assumption was that the Allied powers would negotiate a peace treaty with Japan, in which, among other things, Tokyo would renounce sovereignty over Taiwan and its associated islands and transfer them to a unified China.

But the civil war between the ROC government led by Chiang Kai-shek and the CCP armies led by Mao Zedong negated that assumption. The communists won military control of the Chinese mainland and established the PRC government, while the ROC government and its defeated forces retreated to Taiwan. There were now two parties claiming to be the government of China. If Mao was going to defeat his civil war rival Chiang, terminate the ROC regime, and be recognized as the leader of the sole government of China internationally, he would either have to get the Kuomintang (KMT) regime to surrender peacefully or direct the PLA to defeat it by force. By 1950, preparations for a military campaign against the island had begun, but Kim Il-sung's invasion of South Korea and the U.S. intervention in that conflict compelled Beijing to put off the military campaign against Taiwan.

The Korean conflict had another important consequence. On June 27, 1950, two days after Kim Il-sung's invasion, the Truman administration made an announcement that ordered U.S. air and naval forces to defend against the PRC invasion. It declared that "the determination of the future status of Formosa [Taiwan] must await the restoration of security in the Pacific, a peace settlement with Japan, or consideration by the United Nations."[5] Previously, the United States had taken the position that Taiwan was a part of China. By saying that Taiwan's legal status was undecided, Truman was, in effect, stating that U.S. intervention was not an interference in China's internal affair but a matter of international peace and security.[6] The governments in both Beijing and Taipei stoutly rejected this position. Indeed, one of the few things they agreed on was that Taiwan had been returned to China.

The Korean War had another impact that constrained China. It reinforced American support for a national security strategy of containment of communism. In practical terms, this led to increased U.S. military support for Taiwan and culminated in the U.S.-ROC Mutual Defense Treaty of 1954, in which the United States pledged to come to Taiwan's defense if it were attacked.[7] Early on, therefore, the PRC had three reasons to pursue unification: defeating the KMT regime; enforcing its claim that Taiwan was within the sovereign territory of China, over which it was the legitimate government; and ending what it regarded as U.S. interference in the PRC's internal affairs.

Over time, Beijing asserted two more justifications for unification. The first was that Taiwan's continued separateness constrained the PRC's ambition to restore China as a great power. Chinese president Xi Jinping spoke to this theme in the authoritative speech on Taiwan policy that he gave on January 2, 2019. "The Taiwan issue," he said, "is an outcome of a weak China and a country in turmoil."[8] In Xi's words, to resolve the Taiwan issue and complete unification was "an unshakable historical task. . . . The major historical trend is that our country is becoming strong, that we are heading toward the rejuvenation of the nation, and that we are moving in the direction of cross-Strait reunification. No one and no external forces [i.e. the United States] can stop that."[9] The association between unification and Xi's signature policy of achieving the great rejuvenation of the Chinese nation has increased the salience of the Taiwan issue.

The second justification arose from an increasing discussion of Taiwan's geographic importance for China's larger grand strategy. Hu Bo, a PRC scholar at the Pangoal Institution in Beijing, argues that any rising power needs first to establish superiority in its home region. For the PRC, that means dominating the near seas—more or less the waters inside the first island chain that runs from Japan through the Ryukyus, Taiwan, and the Philippines and all the way to Australia. In Hu's view, unification of Taiwan in the PRC is essential to the latter's aspiration to become a maritime power. "If China still has no way to decide Taiwan's future, then at the end of the day our grand ambition for maritime rights is just one huge soap bubble."

More immediately, Hu sees defensive reasons for controlling Taiwan. Echoing the views of Shi Lang and Chiang Kai-shek, he asserts, "In China's view, Taiwan is still a natural protective screen [*pingzhang*] for the coast of the Mainland. It is an ideal point for protecting sea lanes of communication. It is a key to the Navy's breaking out of the island-chain blockade and extending its reach into the Pacific and Indian Oceans. Its strategic importance is extremely important." Yet it is external threats that Hu believes pose the greatest danger to the PRC and justifies its goal of establishing firm control objective: "Once

Taiwan falls into the hands of an adversary, it will render the prospect of China's building a strong navy increasingly gloomy." The adversary to which Hu alludes is the United States, of course. The spirit of Shi Lang lives on.[10]

How to Unify: One Country, Two Systems

Having first established and then persisted in the declaratory goal of unification, the next question for the Beijing government is how to achieve it. Should it use military force or peaceful persuasion? If force is the chosen option, does the PLA actually have the capabilities it needs, particularly given the possibility—or certainty—that the United States would come to Taiwan's defense? If persuasion is preferred, is there any basis for a mutually acceptable agreement? What incentives can China offer Taiwan to make consensus more likely? How urgently must Beijing resolve the cross-Strait dispute, and does delay entail unacceptable risks? China's answers to these questions would subsequently shape Taiwan's calculus of survival.

Focused as it was on domestic transformation, the Mao regime had to be flexible and patient when it came to the pursuit of the PRC's unification objective. After 1949, it lacked the military capabilities needed to take the island, particularly after it became clear that the United States would protect the ROC regime. Into the 1970s, a cold war between the ROC and the PRC prevailed, so a peaceful resolution of their dispute through negotiations was a nonissue. Beijing did periodically send feelers to Taipei proposing "peaceful liberation," but these went nowhere. A likely reason is that this term has been applied in the PRC to the takeover of Beijing in February 1949, which entailed cutting off the city and starving it into submission until the authorities surrendered.[11] Hardly an attractive precedent for Taiwan.

Important developments in the 1970s transformed the cross-Strait dispute. First of all, the PRC gradually degraded the ROC's international position. Beijing had replaced Taipei as the government representing China in the United Nations in 1971. It then proceeded to establish diplomatic relations with most of the world's countries, some of which previously had official ties with the ROC. The most important country was the United States, which in 1979 switched diplomatic relations from Taipei to Beijing and then terminated the U.S.-ROC Mutual Defense Treaty. A vague U.S. commitment to come to Taiwan's defense remained, but it was political rather than legal in character. Finally, the PRC gradually displaced the ROC in many international organizations, such as the World Bank, the International Monetary

Fund, and the specialized agencies of the UN. By the early 1980s, Taiwan was a marginal player in the international community.

Second, in late 1978 the PRC made a fundamental change in its economic policies, opening up to external investment and shifting to a strategy of export-led growth. Taiwan companies were soon deeply involved in facilitating mainland growth through transfers of capital, technology, and management as well as the employment of a large number of people. Some of those companies came to manage global supply chains for companies such as Apple and Dell. For the first time since the CCP came to power, Taiwan and China had overlapping interests that might become a basis for convergence. Chinese leaders hoped that economic interdependence would lead to political unification, in part by creating a constituency within Taiwan for positive ties.

Third, having closed many of Taiwan's doors to the international community and having opened doors to Taiwan businesses, Chinese leaders now directly targeted the island's leaders to lobby for their unification goal. In a significant change in formulation, Beijing no longer used the terms *liberation* (with its connotation of violence) or *peaceful liberation* to describe how unification would occur. Instead, they adopted a new one: "peaceful unification." Embedded in this idea was growing confidence on the part of PRC leaders that they might be able to persuade Taiwan's leaders to accept an end to cross-Strait division on Beijing's terms.

To this end, the PRC defined what those terms would be. It gradually elaborated a blueprint for the post-unification relationship between the central government, on one hand, and Taiwan, Hong Kong, and Macau, on the other.[12] This was the basis of "one country, two systems" (*yiguo liangzhi*). The "two systems" were not political but economic: socialism and capitalism.

It was the 1990 Basic Law for Hong Kong that provided the most detailed blueprint for one country, two systems (1C2S). Although the legal status of Hong Kong and the ROC in Taiwan were different, because Hong Kong was a British colony and the ROC was a rival Chinese government, the PRC still applied the 1C2S to both territories. Supplemented by some reasonable speculation, the Hong Kong case reveals a lot about how 1C2S would be applied to Taiwan:

- Taiwan would become a special administrative region of the PRC. Consequently, the ROC would cease to exist, and the PRC flag would fly over the island.

- Politically and administratively, the Taiwan special administrative region would be subordinate to the central government in Beijing.

- The claim of some of the island's people that Taiwan and the associated Penghu Islands were not part of China's sovereign territory would be negated.

- The PRC government in Beijing would control Taipei's foreign and defense affairs. Among other things, it would dictate the scope and character of Taiwan's relationship with the United States. In particular, Beijing would ensure that Taiwan was no longer a platform for the projection of U.S. power against China.

- Despite all of these changes, Beijing claimed, economic and social life in Taiwan would continue as before.

- The PRC government in Beijing would entrust individuals in Taiwan with the power to administer the island's internal affairs, based on the principle of a "high degree of autonomy."

- Under this original template, it can be surmised, Taiwan would enjoy significant protections of civil and political rights, the rule of law, and an independent legal system. Even then, however, Taiwan political leaders and political forces would not be allowed to advocate de jure independence for Taiwan, and Beijing would reserve the right to determine what constituted such advocacy. Moreover, Taiwan's electoral system would be designed in such a way that an advocate of Taiwan independence could not secure the top executive position, and a political party that opposed 1C2S would be unable to secure a majority in the legislature.

To be clear, these are a set of inferences based on how Beijing has applied the 1C2S formula to Hong Kong and on Beijing's official but general statements about the meaning of 1C2S for Taiwan. Officials of the PRC have signaled from time to time that 1C2S for Taiwan would be more favorable for Taiwan than it has been for Hong Kong, but they have never spelled out how. Particularly uncertain is whether the Taiwan armed forces would continue to exist and what their mission would be. Also uncertain is whether Beijing would station PLA troops on the island.[13] However, Beijing's response to the Hong Kong protests in 2019 by tightening its control over political action in the name of protecting national security suggests that whatever civil and political rights Beijing would grant to Taiwan under 1C2S would be less generous than those that were in place at the time Hong Kong reverted to China in 1997.

At the time it was formulated, this model of "home rule with CCP characteristics" seemed to PRC leaders like a plausible yet optimal formula for

ending their fundamental dispute with Taiwan. They believed that the benefits of economic interdependence, which began in the 1980s, combined with
the fact that the grand majority of the residents of the island were ethnic
Chinese would create sufficient material and psychological incentives to get
Taiwan to give up the claim that it was a rival government. They hoped that
the success they expected in their application of 1C2S to Hong Kong would
have a positive demonstration effect across the Taiwan Strait. Also, CCP leaders hoped that their KMT counterparts could be brought around to grudg-
ingly but voluntarily accepting unification.

True, KMT leaders resisted 1C2S-style unification for reasons of ideology, history, and pride. But Beijing could take confidence from the fact that
those leaders were from mainland China and had a strong Chinese national
identity. The KMT's stated goal into the 1990s was also unification, albeit
under a very different formula from 1C2S. Moreover, at the time 1C2S was
formulated, the KMT maintained tough, authoritarian control over the island's population, and its leaders would have the freedom to cut a deal, if they
chose to do so, and then the power to implement the new arrangements. In
short, Beijing leaders understood that implementation of this strategy would
take time and that they might have to exert a certain amount of pressure on
Taipei to get what they wanted. But they assumed that as the power balance
continued to shift in their favor, persuasion would work, and Taiwan's leaders
would recognize the turning tides and settle. As the Chinese saying puts it,
"Once ripe, the melon drops from its stem" (*guashu diluo*).

But the melon did not drop for the PRC. For most of the past forty years,
David has outplayed Goliath. A number of international factors worked in
Taiwan's favor. One significant factor was revitalized American support for
Taiwan's security under the Reagan administration and its successors. The
end of the Soviet Union diminished China's global strategic significance,
so Washington did not have to tread as lightly as before on issues that Beijing claimed were sensitive, such as Taiwan. The end of the Soviet Union
also created a buyers' market for advanced weaponry, which Taiwan tried
to exploit.

But the most important reason that China made little or no progress
toward its unification goal is that from the late 1980s into the early 1990s,
Taiwan made the transition from a tough authoritarian system to a full democracy. This opened the door for new players and new ideas—regarding what
Taiwan was, as well as the circumstances of its relationship to China and the
international system. It effectively gave the Taiwan people a seat at the table
for any negotiations between Beijing and Taipei over Taiwan's future. The de-

bates within Taiwan over its relationship with the PRC have been intense, and the China issue has long been the most salient in Taiwan politics.[14] Yet people agree in their opposition to unification on Beijing's terms. A March 2019 poll by the Election Study Center of National Chengchi University found that 79.0 percent of those polled rejected the 1C2S formula and only 10.4 percent accepted it.[15] The PRC's chances of achieving its goal through persuasion and negotiations fell to a low level and stayed there.

From Beijing's perspective, Taiwan's democratization had another consequence. For more than a decade starting around 1994, China also feared first that President Lee Teng-hui and later President Chen Shui-bian intended to create an independent Taiwan. Whether or not these fears were justified, Beijing believed that its interests and its unification goal were under challenge. As a result, in its terminology it temporarily set aside promoting unification through persuasion and undertook opposing independence.[16] It has also taken the same stance toward President Tsai Ing-wen.

China's Fears

Beijing actually has a broader set of fears than a simple scenario in which some Taiwan leaders engineer a July 4, 1776, moment for Taiwan by formally declaring de jure independence. It has long believed that those leaders will be cleverer than to take that single, fundamentally provocative act.

There is actually some historical basis for Beijing's fear of Taiwan independence. After 1949, there was a small Taiwanese group in Japan that advocated a Republic of Taiwan, and a similar effort in the United States began in the 1960s.[17] More serious from Beijing's point of view was an attempt by democracy and Taiwan independence activist Peng Ming-min to publish a Taiwan independence declaration in Taipei in 1964. Though Peng was imprisoned and later put under house arrest for his acts, he later escaped from Taiwan and made it to the United States, where he published a memoir, *A Taste of Freedom,* and then tried to promote the independence cause.[18] Then, as Taiwan was making its transition to democracy, the opposition Democratic Progressive Party (DPP) set the establishment of a Republic of Taiwan as an objective. (This goal met with little public approval and was gradually muted.)

How serious of a threat does Beijing believe Taiwan independence poses? At first glance, its assessment appears overly alarmist. As the next chapter will detail, public opinion surveys indicate that support for that option in Taiwan is relatively low. Moreover, even if the public supported it, the constitutional process for making it happen is difficult. Yet there are a few semi-plausible explanations for Beijing's fear of a move to independence.

First, China's leaders view the results of Taiwan's elections not as more or less accurate expressions of the popular will but rather as evidence of the skill of demagogic politicians to create public support for policies where it does not really exist. They might successfully play on popular emotions and whip up enthusiasm for an independence project, overriding what the polls say and the long-standing public preference for the status quo.

Second, the PRC system tends to define very broadly what behaviors constitute a quest for independence. Lee Teng-hui's campaign to expand Taiwan's international space in the mid-1990s were attributed to independence intentions on his part, when, in fact, he continued to associate himself formally with the goal of unification (though on terms that conflicted with those of Beijing).

Third, in terms of process, Beijing has believed that the strategy that Lee Teng-hui, Chen Shui-bian, and Tsai Ing-wen have employed is to achieve independence by moving incrementally and covertly, to create a fait accompli, to which Beijing would find harder to respond. Based on this assessment, PRC policymakers identified an inventory of Taiwan steps that constituted evidence of a stealth movement to de jure independence. These include increasing Taiwan-specific content in textbooks, promoting Taiwan culture and diminishing Chinese culture, and changing the use of the word "China" to "Taiwan" in the name of some institutions. Lee, Chen, and Tsai have all used the formulation that Taiwan does not need to declare independence because it is already an independent sovereign state. This is legally complicated, as chapter 11 will explain, but it also serves a domestic political purpose of justifying adherence to the status quo. In Beijing, no doubt, the formulation is viewed as a rhetorical sleight of hand used to advance a separatist goal. The most disturbing step for Beijing was Chen Shui-bian's effort to conduct a referendum at the time of the 2008 presidential election that asked voters whether they wished to pursue United Nations membership under the name "Taiwan." The referendum failed, but if it had passed, the PRC could have interpreted it as a formal assertion that Taiwan was a separate state. More recently, there has been increasing PRC concern that the Tsai administration would edge closer to changes in the ROC Constitution that would cumulatively amount to de jure independence.[19]

There is a mismatch between Beijing's stated fears and the political reality within the Democratic Progressive Party (DPP). To be sure, the Deep Green camp of the party is where some of the loudest voices for Taiwan independence are heard. But when it comes to actions, the party itself has been more restrained in recent years. For example, in the 2018 political season in Taiwan, the pro-independence faction in the DPP was able to get a referendum on the ballot that called for Taiwan to participate in the Olympics under the name "Taiwan," as opposed to "Chinese-Taipei," as internationally agreed. Tsai did not support the referendum, and she greatly annoyed its proponents by not attending their rally a few days before the vote, which failed. Moreover, the political success of DPP magistrates and mayors depends in part on their ability to sustain their jurisdiction's economic ties with the mainland.

My own view is that PRC leaders cannot afford to accept the reality that the mainstream of the DPP recognizes that independence is not an option. To do so would be to legitimize the DPP and require Beijing to creatively find a way to coexist with it, which, in turn, would reduce even further the chances for unification and produce an outcome of permanent de facto separation. Beijing must therefore demonize the DPP and deliberately set the bar for coexistence higher than the DPP is willing to go. Moreover, in situations such as Taiwan, where the CCP exercises less control than it would like, the PRC seeks to ally with internal forces that share its goals in order to obstruct, constrain, and isolate adversaries that defy the CCP's interests. Having an enemy to demonize and oppose is an essential element of this Leninist, united-front strategy.

Those in the PRC who worry about changes to the ROC Constitution that might move Taiwan on the road to independence should recognize that the amendment procedure is a built-in obstacle to de jure independence. Passing any amendment on any subject, including the territory of the Republic of China, requires a three-fourths majority in the Legislative Yuan, with at least three-fourths of the membership voting, and a majority of eligible voters voting yes in a referendum. In effect, constitutional change in Taiwan requires a broad public consensus that the proposed change is worthwhile. Taiwan's constitution thus blocks what the China's leaders fear; at the same time, it also makes impossible what they most want: unification on their terms.

As much as the PRC government inveighs against Taiwan independence, it also opposes two Chinas: the PRC and the ROC. After all, reducing the ROC's presence in the international system has been a goal of Beijing's since 1949. Again, Beijing has some reason for concern about two Chinas, or *permanent separation*. Taipei fought to stay in the international system through the 1970s and has tried since the 1990s to expand its international space. PRC officials recall that the United States promoted a two-China policy in the late 1950s and early 1960s.[20] To this day, moreover, the Republic of China remains an article of faith in the KMT, especially among its mainlander members.[21]

The Ma Ying-jeou Opportunity

For China, the prospects for unification through persuasion improved with the 2008 victory of Ma Ying-jeou.[22] After all its frustrations with Lee Teng-hui and Chen Shui-bian and the perceived need to oppose independence, this seemed to be the magic moment for Beijing to return to its policy of promoting unification and resume progress toward its ultimate objective. Ma is a mainlander by birth and a Chinese nationalist by temperament. As an official in Taiwan's Mainland Affairs Council in the early 1990s, he had participated in the initial effort to facilitate cross-Strait relations. Although he affirmed Taiwan's success, he would not rule out unification. In 2005 his party had come to a consensus with the CCP on a way forward for developing cross-Strait relations incrementally and deferring final-status issues through a concept they termed "peaceful development." To the PRC, Ma's victory meant that its resistance to the DPP administration had worked and had confined the party to political oblivion.

Once he became president, Ma accepted the 1992 Consensus, an ambiguous formula stating the commitment for the two sides to one China, and pushed the process of normalizing, expanding, and institutionalizing cross-Strait relations. However, Ma redefined this formula to allow him to say that for him, one China meant the Republic of China, which Beijing asserts ceased to exist in 1949. Still, he worked to reassure Beijing that his intentions did not challenge its fundamental interests. His grand strategy was to increase Beijing's stakes in a positive relationship that would deter resolution of the Taiwan issue through force. For its part, Beijing had reason to believe that, by working with Taipei, the two governments could move from easy issues to hard ones and progress from the economic arena to the political one. In response to Taiwan's desire for greater international space, the PRC did not block Taiwan's participation at meetings of selected international governmental organizations such as the World Health Organization, nor did it obstruct Taiwan from negotiating a bilateral economic arrangement with New Zealand and Singapore. But Beijing's accommodation in this sphere was still limited, and its bottom line was still tough: In essence, the message was, "If you want us to be more generous on your international space, you need to agree to political talks to better define Taiwan's legal identity."[23]

But Ma had no choice but to respect domestic opinion, and opinion opposed moving toward political talks. There were also conceptual obstacles—namely, Ma's strong belief in the ROC, which Beijing insists is defunct. With a sovereign ROC as Ma's starting point, there was no way that the two sides could get even partway to Beijing's preferred end point of 1C2S, in which Taiwan was a subordinate part of the PRC. Under those circumstances, to try to undertake government-to-government political talks was premature. At least twice, Beijing pressed Ma on this point, and twice he turned them down. This and Ma's clear definition of China as the ROC furthered the PRC's concerns about permanent separation and a two-China outcome. If even the Ma administration refused to move down a path toward unification, what hope was there of achieving that objective?

To make matters worse for Beijing, Taiwan's political system was changing. Politics was no longer confined to the competition and interaction of political parties. New social and political forces emerged to promote a variety of causes, mobilized by postmodern sentiments and social media. The Sunflower movement was the most consequential of these, and it brought Ma's cross-Strait engagement to a halt. It also helped sweep Tsai Ing-wen and the DPP to power at the local and central levels of government in the 2016 elections, making it appear as if the KMT had permanently become a minority party. More than a decade of patient work by Beijing was down the drain, it seemed.

Xi Jinping's Vision of Unification through Persuasion

On January 2, 2019, Xi Jinping gave a major speech on Taiwan policy, the most important one since he had taken power in the fall of 2012.[24] The occasion was the fortieth anniversary of a message that the standing committee of the National People's Congress (the PRC's legislature) had sent to its "Taiwan compatriots" announcing the shift from the policy of liberation to one of peaceful unification. This occurred on the same day that the United States terminated diplomatic relations with the ROC and established them with the PRC in 1979. What was striking about the speech, at least to some observers, was that Xi reaffirmed the persuasion approach, despite the fact that a DPP government was still in power.

Xi speech's, which ran over 3,600 words in the English translation, purported to make the case to Taiwan that unification was in its interests and presented a doctrinal presentation statement of PRC views of the Taiwan issue. It set forth basic principles, framed the policy problem, and stated the ends and means for solving it. The text was most likely the product of a bureaucratic coordination process, but it still bore Xi's imprint. It was an authoritative statement, in part, because Xi Jinping—the PRC's paramount leader—delivered it but also because, in March 2018, Xi had engineered the repeal of term limits for the president of the PRC, so his words could remain policy dogma for a long time.

The first part of the speech was a review of the past. Xi folded Taiwan's history into Beijing's broader narrative of the foreign victimization of China after the Opium War. He defined the division of the two sides of the Strait after 1949 as a "long-term political confrontation" caused by the "continuation of the Chinese civil war and the interference of external forces" (that is, the United States). He then outlined the subsequent successes of PRC policy, both internationally and toward Taiwan. He stressed that Beijing had "resolutely thwarted various attempts to create 'two Chinas,' 'one China, one Taiwan,' and 'Taiwan independence.'" He reiterated the principle that "Taiwan was a part of China and the two sides of the Strait belong to one China." As noted, he also tied the rejuvenation of China to unification with Taiwan.

Of course, Beijing's narrative about the past and its optimism about the future glossed over certain inconvenient facts, including the dilemma over identity. Xi asserted that "the compatriots on both sides of the Strait are Chinese. Blood is thicker than water. . . . There is a natural feeling for helping each other. There is national identification between the people on the two sides of the Strait. No one and no external forces can change that." Yet polling on Taiwan consistently reveals that just a small fraction of the public regards itself as Chinese only (see chapter 10). Looking to the future, Xi Jinping identified a single goal: reunification. As is common with communist rhetoric, he insisted that this outcome ("the major historical trend") was a matter of historical necessity. All that was necessary was for "Taiwan compatriots" to accept the inevitable and work with Beijing to bring about unification.

To this end, Xi laid out a five-part agenda. The first part restated the link between China's national rejuvenation and Taiwan unification, as well as the contribution that a post-unification Taiwan could make to that grand goal. The Taiwan issue, therefore, was enclosed in the frame of Chinese nationalism. National unification was the premise for a "prosperous and beautiful life" on both sides of the Strait. Yet Xi counseled people on Taiwan to reflect on the implications of his national mission: "Taiwan compatriots are all members of the Chinese nation. They should be proud to be Chinese. They should seriously think about the status and role of Taiwan in the rejuvenation of the nation." Of course, a number of people on Taiwan would take issue with Xi's view of how they should define their national identity. Taiwanese nationalism has evolved since the 1990s, but it is still a political force.

Having enunciated the broad context of the Taiwan issue, Xi turned to the second and most important part of his action plan: how to bring about unification. For him, "the best way" (read: "the only way") was 1C2S. He re-iterated that this approach fully took into account Taiwan's realities and con-cerns and called for a "Taiwan plan" for 1C2S. He may have been alluding to the fact that Taiwan was a democracy when he asserted that "differences in systems do not constitute an obstacle to reunification, let alone a pretext for separatism." That may be true, but Xi ignored a fundamental implication: if Beijing and Taipei ever reached a detailed agreement on unification, it would have to be approved by the institutions of Taiwan's democracy, and probably through constitutional amendments, which require a broad majority in sup-port. Taiwan's system may not be an obstacle to unification in Xi's theory, but it certainly is in Taiwan's practice.

There is another catch in Xi's reassurance that 1C2S sufficiently takes Taiwan "interests and feelings" into account. He said, "Under the premise of ensuring national sovereignty, security, and development interests, the social system and life styles of Taiwan compatriots will be fully respected after the peaceful unification, and the private property, religious beliefs, and legitimate rights and interests of Taiwan compatriots will be fully guaranteed."[25] But this position is actually a retreat from previous PRC commitments, which included the preservation of Taiwan's political institutions and its military. Their omission here was certainly no accident. Also, the precondition of "en-suring national sovereignty" could be used to limit Taiwan people's rights and interests, and Beijing would reserve to itself the authority to make a judgment of whether the precondition has been violated. Moreover, the adjective "legiti-mate" in reference to the rights and interests of Taiwan compatriots was prob-ably a poison pill, since Beijing would decide what is legitimate. Then there is the inconvenient truth that even when 1C2S worked relatively well in Hong Kong, up to 2014, Beijing had designed the political system so that it was only partly democratic, denying significant political power to those politicians and parties that it feared.[26] If these are the elements of a Taiwan plan for 1C2S, they are certainly contrary to Taiwan opinion.

Xi provided an extensive discussion of how the two sides should seek con-sensus on unification. He repeated once again his metaphor that "the compa-triots on both sides of the Strait are members of the same family." He said that "family affairs . . . should be discussed among family members" (assuming, of course, that this is a harmonious family.) He promised equal consultations and joint discussions, a long-standing formula that actually refers to the format of discussions—each delegation sitting across the table from the other—rather than the status of the parties to the negotiations. But he set conditions on who in Taiwan might participate in discussions. To say that "there is no obstacle for any political parties or groups in Taiwan to engage in exchanges with us" but to then insist on upholding the "one-China principle" as the basis of these exchanges is to exclude the DPP and any groups associated with it. To propose that there be "extensive and in-depth democratic consultations on cross-Strait relations" with "representative individuals" who are "recommended by various political parties and various circles" on both sides, but only on "the common political basis of adhering to the '1992 Consensus' and opposing 'Taiwan independence,'" has the same consequence.

Hence the process that Xi proposed was probably a nonstarter from Taiwan's point of view. Nowhere did he suggest that the officials of the PRC and ROC governments would, sooner or later, be the parties trying to resolve cross-Strait differences, which negated the ROC's view of itself as a government on a par with that of the PRC. That fewer elements of the existing Taiwan system would be preserved after unification than previously promised implied that Beijing would seek to exercise control over those institutions that were not mentioned.

This provides a segue to Xi's third point, which is the need to "adhere to the one-China principle and safeguard the prospect of peaceful unification." In this regard, Xi revived the policy principle of "placing hopes on the Taiwan people," by whom he probably means Taiwan people who will be more pliant than the DPP.[27] But this section was really a warning against any perceived manifestations of Taiwan independence. He stated that "'Taiwan independence' is an adverse current of history and is the road to ruin." He warned that all Taiwan residents, whatever their political, social, and occupational background, "must understand clearly that 'Taiwan independence' will only bring immense catastrophes to Taiwan, and must therefore resolutely oppose a split by the 'Taiwan independence' force and jointly seek the bright prospect of peaceful reunification. . . . We shall never leave any room for any form of 'Taiwan independence' separatist activities." Since Beijing associates the DPP with the goal of de jure independence, Xi in effect was asking Taiwan citizens to oppose the Tsai government and the DPP to serve PRC goals. Xi also warned that the existence and activities of an "extremely small number of 'Taiwan independence' separatists would justify the PRC's use of force against Taiwan," despite its stated principle that "Chinese will not fight Chinese."

Xi's fourth point called for deepening what he called "integrated cross-Strait development" and consolidation of the foundation for unification. This represented an evolution of the concept of "peaceful development," which was developed during the time that Hu Jintao was the PRC's top leader. That term refers to the gradual improvement of cross-Strait relations prior to any discussion of unification. For Beijing, Ma Ying-jeou's presidency was a time of peaceful development, with an emphasis on economic and social issues. The concept of "integrated development" was introduced in 2017, as a response to the election of Tsai Ing-wen. The Chinese version of the term is *zonghe fazhan*, which can also be translated as "development through integration" or "development through fusion." The idea is that despite the DPP's control of the political system, the people of Taiwan and the mainland can grow closer together through social and economic interaction. Specifically, Xi called for creation of a common market and greater cooperation concerning infrastructure, energy, industrial standards, education, healthcare, and so on.

Xi's fifth point was similar and stressed the importance of culture in fostering what he called "closer bonds of heart and mind." He argued that because people on the two sides of the Strait share the same origin, language, race, "between loved ones, there is no knot of perception that cannot be untied. With perseverance, we are sure to forge closer bonds of heart and mind between people on both sides."

Whether sharing origin, language, and the like is a sufficient basis for a political union is a germane question here. The histories of the United States, Canada, Australia, and New Zealand certainly suggest otherwise. More significant is Xi's ethno-racial basis for defining the contours of the Chinese political union, which is a strong trend in Chinese Communist Party political discourse. The Chinese he is talking about are Han Chinese. This ethno-racial basis glosses over the reality that the PRC is actually a multiethnic state and ignores the fact that human beings usually have multiple political identities at the same time. Of specific significance for Beijing's Taiwan policy, the sense of political identity of Taiwan people is, for the most part, not ethno-racial but grounded more in the island's political system and values.[28] As James Millward, a Georgetown University specialist on PRC policy toward Xinjiang Autonomous Region, writes: "Today, rather than celebrating the uniqueness of individual cultures, the C.C.P. increasingly promotes a unitary category called *zhonghua*, a kind of pan-Chinese identity. Though supposedly all-inclusive, the customs and characteristics of *zhonghua* are practically identical to those of the Han."[29]

Overall, Xi Jinping's speech is puzzling. For all his optimism about unification, his stated vigilance vis-à-vis Taiwan independence, his appeals to Han Chinese nationalism, and his apparent intention to go around the DPP government when discussing 1C2S, indicates that his remarks do not really speak to the situation in Taiwan today. The question he has not answered is, How did Tsai and the DPP win both the presidential and legislative elections in 2016? By extension, how did they win again in 2020 if China's policy, especially its opposition to Taiwan independence, has been working so well?

Also puzzling are the scant details that Xi and his government offer about what a post-unification Taiwan would look like. The list of items has changed over time. Their content is minimal and formulaic (for example, "the legitimate rights and interests of Taiwan compatriots"). If there is a more detailed blueprint for the Taiwan version of 1C2S, the point of reference has to be the system that was established for post-reversion Hong Kong, which, when it comes to the political system, would mean a retreat from the existing fully democratic system. It's all well and good for PRC officials to say that the Taiwan version would be different, but it is incumbent on them to explain how and in great detail. It is they who wish to change Taiwan's status quo, so it is they who must make the case to the Taiwan people—and to do so in a way that will yield sufficiently broad support for the constitutional amendments that would be required. Of course, Beijing's imposition of the anti-democratic national security law on Hong Kong and the implications it has for civil and political rights raises the bar of persuasion that it must clear for Taiwan.

Moreover, if Beijing is ever going to get to discussions of unification, what is its plan for getting out of the current stalemate and resuming forward movement on more day-to-day issues? Beijing has so far unjustly pinned the blame for the stalemate on Tsai Ing-wen, as if it began on the day she was sworn in as president in May 2016. But the difficulties actually began during Ma Ying-jeou's presidency. It was he who rejected Beijing's request for preliminary political talks. It was during his time in office that the DPP caucus in the legislature and the Sunflower movement were able to block the agreement on cross-Strait services. No doubt, Xi and his colleagues were putting their hopes on the election of a non-DPP president and legislature, but that would not negate the persistent division in the Taiwan polity. The politics of Ma Ying-jeou's second term demonstrated that if a new KMT administration attempts to resume significant movement on cross-Strait relations, there will have to be some buy-in from the DPP.

In addition, events in Hong Kong, where 1C2S had been most widely applied, undercut Xi's message that the formula was the best option for Taiwan. First, an effort from 2013 to 2015 to reform Hong Kong's electoral system and make it more democratic failed. Leaders of the PRC were not exclusively to blame; pro-democracy actors in Hong Kong undermined their own cause. The Umbrella movement that occurred in the middle of the process, in which activists occupied three major thoroughfares in the city for weeks, raised fears in Beijing that it was losing political control. Once electoral reform was set aside, Beijing began to nibble away at some of the political freedoms that it had originally granted.[30]

If the purpose of Xi's 2019 speech was to weaken Tsai Ing-wen, the alleged leader of the Taiwan independence forces, it had the opposite effect. Tsai skillfully conflated the 1992 Consensus, 1C2S, and unification, even though the 1992 Consensus really governed relations well before any discussion of 1C2S.[31] Aided by the Taiwan media, which was spooked by the emphasis that Xi placed on 1C2S, she warned repeatedly about the dangers that she believed Beijing posed to Taiwan. She also put her political opponents on the defensive, and the KMT had no choice but to reiterate its opposition to 1C2S to assure the public that it had Taiwan's interests at heart, not the PRC's. As a result of this episode, Tsai began to move up in the polls and strengthened her position in the 2020 election race.

Then came the massive, and sometimes violent, protests in Hong Kong in the second half of 2019 against a draft extradition law proposed by the city's government. This provided Tsai with another way of mobilizing electoral support by making the case that 1C2S had clearly not worked in Hong Kong and so was not applicable to Taiwan, though there was already a broad public consensus on that latter point. By late summer 2019, the presidential race was essentially over. Hong Kong's negative-demonstration effect regarding 1C2S, the opposite of what Beijing had originally planned, was even more strongly pronounced by the national security law that the PRC's National People's Congress imposed on Hong Kong in June 2020, which limited political freedoms even more.[32] Hong Kong's political system had become starkly different from Taiwan's.

The most plausible explanation for Xi's puzzling exposition of the Taiwan issue is that his address was intended mostly, if not entirely, for the domestic audience on the mainland. There is evidence that elements of the CCP regime are unhappy with trends on Taiwan, including the mere fact that Tsai was elected in the first place and that she has been able to improve relations with the United States. Luo Yuan, a retired PLA general, periodically warns that the trends in Taiwan and in Taiwan-U.S. relations are creating dangers for China's interests. "All these influences have seriously touched the one-China bottom line," he writes, "and therefore the Chinese People's Liberation Army must use powerful methods to maintain law and order and to deter the 'Taiwan independence' forces."[33]

Facing such opposition, the object of Xi's persuasion was not so much the people on Taiwan but critics in his own regime. He gave them a rousing, nationalistic defense of past policy, with reassurance that he was vigilant about Taiwan independence and had plans for how to bring about unification. It was still a cover for the reality that long-standing policy had not succeeded, or even had failed, a reality that Tsai's 2020 reelection likely reinforced.

Beijing's Strategic Patience: Is There a Deadline?

Xi Jinping's repeated association of Taiwan unification with the "great rejuvenation of the Chinese nation" has led some to infer that the 2049 target for the latter is also the deadline for the former. As a younger Chinese scholar suggested to me, "There's a deadline within a non-deadline." Some Chinese leaders may in fact believe that 2049 is the unification deadline, but my reading of Xi's speeches is that he is, in fact, careful not to make explicit what may seem to be implicit. This makes perfect sense. To merely suggest that there is an unstated, working deadline does exert a degree of pressure on Taiwan leaders and introduces uncertainty in their decisionmaking. To *not* set a specific, public target date for unification avoids the risk of having to act on the implied threat, should the designated time arrive with Taiwan still outside "the embrace of the Motherland."

Looking to the longer term, Xi's speech did revive the idea that "the long-standing political differences between the two sides of the Strait are the major causes that prevent cross-Strait relations from proceeding steadily. This should not be passed down generation after generation." One implication of that statement is that the longer the issue is unresolved, the more likely another outcome unacceptable to the PRC will occur: peaceful separation. From its point of view, the more time that passes without significant movement toward unification will both increase doubts that it will ever achieve its goal and engender fear that de facto peaceful separation will become more likely. The closer Hong Kong gets to 2047 and the end of its fifty-year period under 1C2S, the more policymakers in Beijing will feel the need to rely on more than strategic patience with Taiwan characteristics.

Rather than think in terms of a deadline, it makes more sense to try to determine, at any given time, whether PRC leaders perceive that the door to achieving their goal is opening, closing, or standing still. Clearly, a judgment that the door is closing—for example, in the form of an active program by Taiwan leaders to move toward what looks like de jure independence—would demand action in response. If Beijing believes that the long-term trends are favorable for unification, that the door is remaining open, and that the melon will finally fall from the stem, then patience is justified. Yet the level of PRC confidence about the prospects for unification shifts with each Taiwan presidential and legislative election and the attendant reshuffling of the political deck. It declined during the administrations of Lee Teng-hui and Chen Shui-bian, rose with the election of Ma Ying-jeou, and then declined again with the DPP's return to power in 2016.[34]

Having survived two terms of Chen Shui-bian, the PRC probably believed it could survive at least one term of Tsai. Xi's five points in his January 2019 speech suggest that Beijing believes that the door to unification may not be closing and that patience is justified and necessary. Although the unification goal and 1C2S formula remain clear, Xi's remarks do not suggest a sense of danger looming or urgency to resolve the issue.

Conclusion

In terms of implementation, China's Taiwan policy since 1979 has possessed essential characteristics:

- Remarkable patience concerning the time frame for persuading Taiwan to accept China's ultimate goal;
- an almost naïve optimism that the benefits to Taiwan of cross-Strait relations—mainly, economic benefits—would be enough to induce its accommodation to China's terms;
- a firmness in enforcing the boundaries that Taiwan may not cross, regarding both its international role and the definition of its legal identity (for example, Taiwan independence);
- deep suspicions of U.S. motives in supporting Taiwan while exaggerating Washington's impact on Taiwan's China policy; and
- a persistent rigidity regarding the terms and conditions of a negotiated resolution of the fundamental dispute (1C2S), even as sentiment on Taiwan was shifting.

But since the PRC unveiled the 1C2S approach to unification in the early 1980s, there has been an unreconciled conflict between its ambitions, on the one hand, and the opposition of the Taiwan government and public to China's terms for resolving the fundamental cross-Strait dispute, on the other. In the 1980s, the KMT regime's anticommunist ideology was the reason for the stalemate. But since Taiwan's democratization in the early 1990s, the obstacle has been public opposition to 1C2S, including its likely consequences for Taiwan's competitive democratic system and the natural reluctance to trade the known status quo for an unknowable future.

One might think that the PRC government would consider changing its proposal to make it more accommodating to Taiwan sensibilities, seeing that much has changed in Taiwan since the formulation of 1C2S and that the island's citizens have long had a strong say in cross-Strait policy after having had no say during the decades of authoritarianism. Muthiah Alagappa, a distinguished scholar-in-residence at American University, goes so far as to argue that under current circumstances, Beijing must radically alter its approach: "If Beijing is to resolve the Taiwan conflict in a peaceful manner, it must rethink its ideas about nation and state making as well as sovereignty. It has to accept that there can be more than one Chinese nation and state. This will allow Beijing to accept Taiwan as a separate nation and sovereign state with which it shares cultural affinities that may facilitate closer interaction."[35]

Yet adjusting to changing circumstances, particularly Taiwan's democratization, is the one thing that Beijing has been unwilling to do. Indeed, President Xi Jinping has doubled down on the original proposal, at least for purposes of domestic politics. Yet this adherence to an out-of-date concept is not born of sheer stubbornness, although some stubbornness is at play. In part, it stems from a mentality about power and its exercise. That is, Beijing believes that the simple change in the relative balance of power between the mainland and Taiwan, and between the United States and China, will create the circumstances for Beijing to fulfill its ambitions without making the concessions needed to persuade Taiwan's political leaders and its people that 1C2S is in their interests. As a PRC specialist on Taiwan told me, "Because China is becoming more powerful, it will set the rules for the development of cross-Strait relations."[36] The implication of this shift in Beijing's assessment of its power is that persuasion need not be the dominant mode for achieving its Taiwan objective, which, in turn, complicates Taipei's task of ensuring the island's security.

But this new perspective raises the question of how the PRC might convert its increased power into sufficient influence to end Taiwan's opposition to 1C2S. In the past, PRC leaders thought in terms of a binary choice: peaceful unification or going to war. They spoke of having a "two-handed" Taiwan policy. In a May 2000 speech, for example, Vice Premier Qian Qichen said, "Comrade Deng Xiaoping used to say that we should use 'two hands' in settling the Taiwan issue and not rule out any of the two ways: Doing as much as we can without the right hand to settle the issue peacefully [but] in case this does not work, we will also use the left hand, namely military force." [37] But given the costs that Beijing perceives from going to war, on the one hand, and accommodating the Taiwan public, on the other, does the current environment create the possibility of a "third hand," an option between persuasion and war? I return to this question in chapter 12.

8

Taiwan's Search for Security

Rhetorically, Beijing has adopted a dual approach toward Taiwan (Deng Xiaoping's "two hands"). In his January 2019 address, Xi Jinping presented for Taiwan people all the things that the mainland and Taiwan had in common and all the reasons he believed that unification was their best outcome. He reminded Taiwan listeners that the island's companies had been able to "share the opportunities of [economic] development in the mainland." But Xi also took a hard line against independence and did not rule out the use of force. He did not set a deadline for settling the cross-Strait dispute but made clear that Beijing's patience was not infinite. Yet this policy duality was absent when it came to Beijing's ultimate objective of unification, along with the basic terms on which it should occur: one country, two systems (1C2S).[1] Those were fundamental and unchanging.

This combination of rigidity of ends and some flexibility of means creates a profound dilemma for Taiwan. How can it benefit from the soft hand and avoid the harm of the hard hand of Beijing's approach? How should it calculate and manage the risks of both conciliating and confronting the People's Republic of China (PRC)? In short, how can it maximize its security when, clearly, one purpose of the PRC's two-handed policy is to place Taiwan's leaders and citizens in a state of permanent insecurity?

Security as a Concept

This chapter addresses Taiwan's security, its available response options, and the views of the public. But security encompasses more than whether it has the capabilities to deter an attack by the People's Liberation Army (PLA) and to mount an effective defense if deterrence fails. Taiwan's security also rests on maintaining the backing of the United States and its at least implied commitment to intervene in the event of a PRC attack. It has at times relied on diplomacy to reduce tensions and increase cooperation. Taiwan must also cope with the PRC's employment of coercion through nonviolent tools in such domains as economics, diplomacy, the military, and information (a.k.a. propaganda). But accommodation and conciliation can also enhance security.

As important as the idea of security is to the study of international relations, it is a remarkably undefined concept. The idea of a "security dilemma" is at the heart of the school of defensive realism, but scholars who use it (this one included) are much more interested in the dilemma itself than in the security about which the dilemma exists.[2]

There are exceptions. The MIT political scientist Barry Posen has offered one definition: "Security has traditionally encompassed the preservation of sovereignty, safety, territorial integrity, and power position—the last being the necessary means to the first three."[3] Much earlier, in the early 1950s, Arnold Wolfers defined security in a different, more abstract way, as "the absence of threats to acquired values."[4] Based on that essentialist definition, the question then is, what does a particular state and its people regard as so valuable that its loss—or the possibility of its loss—would constitute serious danger? There are many possibilities: absence of military threat, preservation of political and social self-determination, an optimal level of economic welfare, protection against natural disasters, freedom from fear, and so on.[5]

Hence security and its components depend very much on context. What constitutes security for Canada is very different from what it is for Pakistan. For Taiwan, the main source of insecurity is the PRC and the threat it poses that stems from their unique, shared history. The PRC government claims that Taiwan is part of the sovereign territory of China, which it represents in the international system. It has set its terms for ending the cross-Strait dispute through "peaceful unification" based on the formula of 1C2S. If Beijing had its way, Taiwan would fundamentally change from the reality to which its people are currently accustomed. At the end of the day, its insecurity is existential.

From Wolfer's essentialist definition of security, another fundamental point can be inferred: the way states decide what is valuable enough to make secure and the steps it would take to do so can often be a highly contested and political process. That is certainly true on Taiwan today, with several different approaches in play. It was different during the authoritarian period, when first Chiang Kai-shek and then Chiang Ching-kuo made their key national security decisions for Taiwan. The only serious opposition to Chiang's approach was not an opposition party, as there were none at the time, but the United States. Once Taiwan democratized, however, the debate over what Taiwan should hold dear and how to secure it was wide open.

Moreover, for leaders and citizens of an insecure state to assess the intentions of the adversary is a highly subjective enterprise. In the end, how do they know how much security is sufficient? There is no guarantee of a realistic calculus. The actual possibilities range from excessive paranoia to extreme naïveté. In addition, for a country like Taiwan that depends on outside powers like the United States for security, it is also necessary to assess how much to depend on Washington. Fears of abandonment and entrapment are the price of security dependence, and again both paranoia and naïveté are possible.

Taiwan's Strategies for Coping with Beijing's Ambition

Even as the PRC's ambition concerning Taiwan has remained constant, its economic and military power has grown, darkening the shadow of insecurity under which the island's leaders and public exist. Material power is the most obvious way in which the balance of power has shifted in Beijing's favor, and material power can be both military and economic. Militarily, the PLA began a steady, systematic campaign in the late 1990s to build up and improve its military capabilities. Elements of the campaign included weapons platforms (air, surface, and subsurface), long-range precision-strike weaponry, an integrated system of surveillance, reconnaissance, intelligence, and communications, and the ability to fight as a truly joint force. Capabilities do not dictate intentions, but there is no question that if the PRC decided that it needed to attack Taiwan and block a U.S. intervention, it is more capable of doing so now than it was when the buildup began.

At the same time, the mainland economy has been important to Taiwan's prosperity since the early 1990s, as a market and as a platform for the production and assembly of goods (see chapter 4). For more than a decade, around 40 percent of Taiwan's total exports have gone to the PRC.[6] Many of the island's residents (though not all) are relatively well off because of the business opportunities that the mainland has provided. Is there a point at which Beijing tries to leverage that interdependence to extract political concessions? It is already using its growing financial resources to induce the countries with which Taiwan still has diplomatic relations to switch their support to the PRC.

Material power aside, there is a psychological dimension as well. The less confident Taiwan people are about their ability to continue their opposition to unification, the easier it will be for Beijing to bring that about. During the 2020 election campaign, people made references to "mango strips" (*manguogan*). That term was a homophone for *wangguogan*, which refers to an anxiety or fear of looming national destruction. Some citizens believed that national despair would only grow if the KMT returned to power.[7] Others thought that would happen under continued Democratic Progressive Party (DPP) rule.

How, then, can Taiwan's leaders balance economic and security imperatives and still maintain public support and confidence? Even if there is no precise deadline for unification, unlimited PRC patience cannot be assumed. Some in Taiwan may believe that Xi Jinping meant what he said in his January 2019 speech: "The long-standing political differences between the two sides of the Strait . . . should not be passed down generation after generation."[8] Chinese leaders may be overconfident about their ability to place more emphasis on the "hard" hand in its two-handed policy, relative to a reliance on persuasion. They may not take enough account of the dynamics of Taiwan's democratic system. But polling indicates that almost half of the public believe that unification is fairly likely, so Taiwan's leaders cannot be complacent about the future.[9] Taiwan leaders need to think carefully about their options, the costs and benefits of each, the difficulties of forging a consensus around the best—or least bad—option, and the dangers of inaction. Taiwan probably has to do more than simply reject what it opposes and think more about how to defend what it has. Not surprisingly, there is an internal debate over how to reduce insecurity. How to cope with the PRC has been, and still remains, the most salient issue in Taiwan politics.[10]

Thinking Analytically

In 1999 Randall Schweller, a professor at Ohio State University at the time, theoretically derived an inventory of the ways that a state can respond to the insecurity created by a rising power.[11] The variables that generated the options for coping were the fundamental intentions of the adversary—whether it was more revisionist or less so—and whether the adversary was risk-averse or risk-accepting:

- The sensible response by a target state to a power that is both revisionist and risk-accepting is preventive war. If there is a belief that conflict is inevitable, the defender should act while the power balance is more in its favor.

- If the adversary is revisionist and risk-averse, the sensible response for the defender is some combination of containment and balancing.

- Regarding an adversary that has only limited goals (that is, is not revisionist) but is risk-accepting, the proper coping response is either containment and balancing or engagement through strength.

- Finally, for an adversary that is non-revisionist and risk-averse, the defender can choose among engagement, binding the adversary to the existing order, or a mixture of the two.[12] Appeasement is one form of engagement.

Whether states respond to a powerful adversary's challenge as theory would dictate rests on two assumptions. The first is that the defender has an accurate assessment of the adversary's intentions and its approach to risk. Neville Chamberlain's evaluation of Adolf Hitler was wrong on both counts, which led to the failure of his appeasement policy.[13] After 9/11, the United States arguably exaggerated the threat that Iraq's Saddam Hussein posed to its interests and therefore undertook a preventive war at great cost.

The second assumption is whether the defending state has the capability and will to respond as circumstances dictate, even if it has a clear understanding of the threat posed. Poland discovered in the fall of 1939 that its military capabilities were lacking and that its attempt to be part of an anti-Nazi balancing group were unavailing. The factor that Schweller probably should have considered but did not is the adversary's approach to time—whether its door to achieving its goals vis-à-vis the defender remains open or is closing. This factor is related to an adversary's approach to risk but is analytically distinct.[14]

In addition, the subjectivity of judgments on security or lack thereof makes it difficult for decisionmakers to decide just how much security is sufficient. Their judgment may be subject to bias, either excessive fear or unrealistic hope. Moreover, even though leaders may believe their management of insecurity is "good enough," they may not be able to convince politicians and citizens to share their confidence.[15]

Competing Taiwan Views

What does all of this mean for Taiwan? Several illustrative points of view can be identified, three of which represent small minorities and two associated with major blocs. In terms of Taiwan's political color spectrum, two views are aligned with the Deep Blue camp, and one each with Light Blue, Light Green, and Deep Green camps.

Minority Views

The first minority perspective is that of the Deep Blues, and the first Deep Blue view to discuss comes from the New Party, which was established in 1993 by conservative members of the KMT who disapproved of then president Lee Teng-hui's policy direction. The New Party does not see Beijing's intentions as threatening to Taiwan's interests and is willing to accept unification. In August 2019, party chairman Yok Yu-min called for peaceful national unification that went a long way to accommodating Beijing. Yok envisioned a post-unification China that was an entity the PRC and Republic of China (ROC) shared, essentially "one country, two governments." Each side would respect the other's economic and political system. Taiwan would still have multiparty competition, but Taiwan independence and its political forces would not be allowed. Taiwan representatives would be included in the PRC delegation to the United Nations. The two sides would end the state of hostilities that technically still exists; Taiwan's armed forces would be reduced, and acquisition of American weapons would cease.[16]

Yok's proposal may have been intended as a response to Xi Jinping's call for a Taiwan-specific approach to 1C2S. Even he was unwilling to give up the Republic of China. But it would be fair to call this plan a policy of appeasement.[17] Many people on Taiwan would probably call it capitulation. For that reason, the New Party enjoys only a low level of political support.

Another Deep Blue proposal came from National Taiwan University professor Chang Ya-chung, who has thought for many years about how the two sides of the Strait might reduce the mistrust and tensions between them. He went so far as to prepare a draft agreement in the early 2010s. In terms of Taiwan's legal status, his draft called for what might be called "one whole China, two constitutional orders." This is one way to thread the needle between Beijing's insistence, on the one hand, that there is one China and Taiwan is part of its sovereign territory, and Taiwan's claim, on the other, that it is a sovereign entity. Based on this compromise, the two sides would cooperate as much as possible in expanding cooperation (including Taiwan's participation in international organizations) and by reducing mutual military tensions. His idea on the latter issue is that each side would pledge not to use or threaten force against the other, something Beijing has never been willing to do concerning Taiwan.[18] Chang's starting assumption was that Beijing is conciliatory enough to entertain a compromise that accepts conceptual parity on the legal identity of the two sides ("two constitutional orders"). As with Yok's proposal, Chang's has gotten little traction in Taiwan public opinion.

Yet even if Taiwan's larger political parties and the public have an aversion to some form of accommodation, this is not an approach that can be totally dismissed out of hand. One can imagine a hypothetical situation in which outright rejection of unification is no longer feasible: the PRC's military power vastly outmatches Taiwan's, the capability and will of the United States to come to Taiwan's defense is in serious doubt, Taiwan's prosperity is still highly dependent on the PRC, and Beijing's leaders become increasingly impatient and risk-accepting. At that point, would the Taiwan people run a significant risk of military conflict? Or would they with hard-headed realism seek through negotiations to resolve the fundamental dispute with Beijing on the best possible terms in order to preserve peace? That scenario may be highly unlikely, but that is not a reason to ignore its implications.

The second minority perspective is that of the Deep Greens, the original proponents of a Republic of Taiwan. Independence remains their goal, and from the perspective of both Beijing and Washington, they are the revisionists. For Beijing, a Republic of Taiwan would fundamentally contradict its position that the island is a part of state called China. For Washington, a push for an independent Taiwan would be contrary to its long-standing interest in regional peace and security. In the Deep Greens' view, however, it is the PRC that is revisionist and the KMT that remains an enemy. For them, the best way to secure their preferred Taiwan is simply to declare it, preferably through a referendum. As for the risks involved, as American political scientist Nathan Batto states, "even today independence fundamentalists are often stunningly dismissive of the threat from China and aggressively confident in the USA."[19] In short, they propose a kind of political preemption, driven by a revisionist goal and a dangerous willingness to take risks.

Majority Views

That leaves the two dominant approaches to security, which are well represented by Ma Ying-jeou and Tsai Ing-wen and their administrations. Both understood that the PRC's ultimate objective for Taiwan has been unification, and both opposed the 1C2S formula on which Beijing insists. Both knew that to some degree, the PRC's stated objective for Taiwan was revisionist. Both understood the strength of anti-unification sentiment among the public. Each understood that military power was needed to increase the costs for Beijing to conduct a military strike. Both have spent about the same amount of budgetary resources to create that power. Both understood that the capabilities of the PLA have grown beyond Taiwan's ability to keep up and that PRC leaders may choose to use military means to achieve its political goals. Yet each has deployed a different mix of responses to cope with the danger that PRC intentions posed.

Ma placed more emphasis on engaging Beijing and creating a web of economic, social, and institutional linkages in the hope that Beijing would regard the cost of destroying the web of interdependence as excessively high. For Ma, reassurance was an important part of engagement, and to that end he was willing to explicitly accept the 1992 Consensus, which Beijing set as the minimum for engagement. This was based on an ambiguous formulation about "one China" that was developed in the early 1990s to facilitate initial cross-Strait interactions. Ma also swore off independence as a policy option during his term of office. In stating his views on these points, Ma was accommodating to Beijing's tactic of requiring a party that it does not control to declare its stance (*biaotai*).[20] He believed that Taiwan could shape Beijing's behavior for good or ill by how it stated its reassurances, and he attributed the moderation that Beijing showed during his time in office to that pledge on his behalf. (To put it differently, he believed that Taiwan could better encourage Beijing to accommodate to the status quo by avoiding the impression that the island's leaders have revisionist intentions, something he believed the DPP had done.) For domestic political reasons, however, he also foreswore unification, even though he did not rule it out as a possibility someday and even thought that it could occur, given the right terms. In the near term, not ruling out unification was an element of reassurance. As he said after he left office, "Taiwan should never let Beijing and the mainland people feel that eventual reunification with Taiwan is absolutely impossible."[21] We might call his approach "engagement with reassurance."

However, Ma's case for reassurance glosses over a couple of key points.

First, he had declared that Beijing accepted his formulation of the 1992 Consensus as "one China, different interpretations" and specified that the Republic of China was his interpretation of one China. But Beijing has never agreed to that "different interpretations" formulation and holds to the view that the ROC does not exist. By January 2020, Ma appeared to acknowledge that harder line when he said publicly that Beijing had "skewed" the meaning of the consensus by saying only "one China" and dropping "different interpretations."[22] Second, the implication of Ma's way of reassuring the PRC is that the 1992 Consensus may be used for all aspects of cross-Strait relations, including political issues. Yet for Beijing, the 1992 Consensus was specifically designed as the framework for addressing economic, social, and cultural relations only, before more specifically defining Taiwan's legal status through political talks.

In effect, Ma created something of a box for himself and his party. Through the first half of his second term, the 1992 Consensus proved to be an acceptable basis for his administration to tackle economic and cultural issues, which were easier to resolve than political ones. Leaders of the PRC were most likely willing to tolerate his rhetorical sleights of hand about "different interpretations" not because they agreed with him but because they trusted his intentions. But even during Ma's first term, Beijing began to push for political talks, for which the 1992 Consensus probably would not have been a sufficient basis. The proposition was not tested because Ma, understanding that public opinion on Taiwan was not ready for such talks, deflected the request.

Tsai Ing-wen, the 1992 Consensus, and the Status Quo

To win the presidency in the January 2016 elections, DPP leader Tsai Ing-wen had to reassure Taiwan voters, the United States, and the PRC that she did not intend to be the ideology-driven troublemaker that Chen Shui-bian had become after a couple of years. But her reassurance did not copy that of Ma: she did not overtly accept the 1992 Consensus. Instead, she constantly repeated the vague mantra that she would not change the status quo. She sometimes offered hints as to what that meant. At a speech at the Center for Strategic and International Studies in Washington, D.C., in June 2015, she said, "Therefore, if elected President, I will push for the peaceful and stable development of cross-strait relations in accordance with the will of the Taiwanese people and the existing ROC constitutional order."[23]

But Beijing wanted more. It did not trust that Tsai or the DPP would not challenge its interests concerning Taiwan, so it demanded that she offer reassurances that the PRC would formulate and do so in an explicit way. Specifically, the PRC authorities set two preconditions on which Tsai would have to declare herself (*biaotai*) if she wished to continue the sort of economic and political interactions with the Chinese mainland that had occurred during Ma Ying-jeou's presidency. The first precondition was the same as that which the PRC laid down for Ma: adherence to the 1992 Consensus. The second precondition was Tsai's acceptance of what Beijing called the "core connotation" of the 1992 Consensus and its one-China principle, that Taiwan was part of the sovereign territory of China. Tsai had at least two reasons to spurn Beijing's demands. First of all, the two points on which Beijing insisted were controversial within her party, particularly with the Deep Green faction. Most objectionable for them was the PRC position that Taiwan was part of Chinese sovereign territory. To have explicitly accepted it, as Beijing required, would have alienated elements in the DPP that she needed to win power over and then govern. Second, the DPP has long been wary of accepting the PRC's principles (such as its one-China principle) at the beginning of an interaction because doing so would constrain it in later negotiations.[24] At the same time, she understood that if there were any chance that Beijing would coexist with her administration, she would have to provide some degree of reassurance (without, of course, undermining herself politically).

Tsai used her inaugural speech to address the elements of the PRC's preconditions without meeting its requirements in the explicit way that it desired her to do. Regarding the 1992 Consensus, she cited the various "joint acknowledgements and understandings" reached by the ROC's Straits Exchange Foundation and the PRC's Association for Relations across the Taiwan Straits in November 1992, which occurred in "a spirit of mutual understanding and a political attitude of seeking common ground while setting aside differences." She acknowledged that since 1992, "over twenty years of interactions and negotiations across the Strait have enabled and accumulated outcomes which both sides must collectively cherish and sustain."[25]

Regarding the "core connotation" of the 1992 Consensus, she said that she was "elected president in accordance with the Constitution of the Republic of China," which is understood to be a one-China document, and that it was therefore her "responsibility to safeguard the sovereignty and territory of the Republic of China." Moreover, she pledged that "the new government will conduct cross-Strait affairs in accordance with the Republic of China Constitution, the Act Governing Relations Between the People of Taiwan Area and the Mainland Area, and other relevant legislation." The references to the two "areas" can be taken to imply that they are part of the same country.[26]

Tsai's public statements were not all that she did to allay Beijing's concerns. Well before the election, she had a channel that she believed reached into the PRC system. The messages she received through that channel were more moderate than Beijing's public statements.[27] At the time of her inauguration, Taiwan officials believed that her speech was enough to get relations off to a good start and that a trust-building process would ensue. In some circumstances, moreover, PRC officials understand that this sort of mutual accommodation and trust building is a good way to solve problems. On North Korea, for example, Fu Ying, a veteran of the Chinese Foreign Ministry, advised Pyongyang and Washington (but especially Washington) that "the parties are well counseled to avoid trapping themselves by making demands that are impossible to meet at the current state. Some room should be left to make both parties comfortable enough to allow the process to proceed. . . . As the Chinese saying goes, 'Three feet of ice does not form in a single day.'" Solving the North Korea dispute, she advised, will require "goodwill, patience and perseverance."[28]

When it came to Tsai Ing-wen, however, PRC leaders made demands that were impossible for her to meet, given the views of some people in her party. Perhaps their moderate, private messages to her were not sincere. Perhaps they were so locked into the idea that de jure independence was her fundamental and immutable objective. Perhaps they believed that because they had the power advantage, accommodation was not necessary. Also, I speculate that Beijing decided that it did not want to coexist with Tsai and that painting her as an adversary would help define the boundaries of what was acceptable behavior on Taiwan's part. Whatever the combination of reasons, PRC leaders set the *biaotai* bar high enough that they could be confident that she could not comply. As a result, even as Tsai sought to reassure Chinese leaders, she and her administration adopted a more hedging approach to Beijing and relied more on the U.S. relationship to balance against Beijing.

Not surprisingly, Ma Ying-jeou criticized Tsai for dismissing the value of the 1992 Consensus. He claimed that his acceptance of the formula in 2008 transformed cross-Strait relations from the peril of the Lee Teng-hui and Chen Shui-bian years to tension-free stability. "A flashpoint of conflict [was transformed] into an avenue of peace," he said. Tsai's refusal to meet PRC preconditions, he argued, suddenly converted "a peaceful and prosperous cross-strait relationship . . . to a cold peace, and later, cold confrontation."[29] In August 2020, as tensions in the Strait temporarily increased, Ma warned that war was becoming more likely, because Tsai had refused to accept the 1992 Consensus and had aligned too closely with the United States and its anti-China policy. Tsai quickly rejected Ma's allegation.[30]

Yet Tsai's approach to security policy was not fundamentally different from Ma's. Even though she understood the political risks of economic dependence on the mainland economy, she was also well aware that continued access to the PRC economy remained a driver of Taiwan's economic growth. Her administration did not constrain cross-Strait economic relations but instead sought to expand Taiwan's economic space with initiatives such as the New Southbound Policy (see chapter 4). She had tried to reassure Beijing about her intentions, but it chose not to take "yes" for an answer. So she created a bifurcation in her PRC policy between economics and politics.

As her first term progressed, moreover, Tsai's view of PRC intentions evolved. Her major speeches chart this trajectory. Tsai used her inaugural address on May 20, 2016, to address the preconditions that Beijing had laid down for a continuation of the Ma-era cross-Strait relations. She also said that leaders on both sides of the Strait "must set aside the baggage of history, and engage in positive dialogue, for the benefit of the people on both sides."[31] In her 2017 speech on the ROC's national day (celebrated annually on October 10), she asserted that she had exerted "maximum goodwill" and worked to "safeguard the peaceful and stable development of cross-Strait relations." But she also emphasized the need to strengthen military capabilities and to protect Taiwan's "freedom, democracy, and way of life" and protect "the Taiwanese people's right to decide their own future."[32]

In her 2018 national day speech, she stated new concerns about the PRC's regional ambitions, its challenge to cross-Strait stability, and its "unilateral diplomatic offensive and military coercion" against Taiwan. At the same time, to reassure Beijing and the Taiwan public, she pledged that her administration would "neither act rashly to escalate confrontation, nor will we give in." She said she would not be "provoked into confrontation . . . nor deviate from the will of the people and sacrifice Taiwan's sovereignty."[33] In her 2019 national day speech, given three months before the 2020 election, she ramped up the rhetoric yet again: "China is still threatening to impose its 'one country, two systems model for Taiwan.' . . . As President, standing up to protect national sovereignty is not a provocation—it is my fundamental responsibility."[34]

In short, the longer Tsai's term ran, the more she used rhetoric that described the PRC as a revisionist power against which Taiwan had to stand guard. And the way to stand guard, she felt, was to align more closely with the United States. Her attempts to reassure the PRC had given way to more balancing against it, but she exercised sufficient restraint that Beijing could reasonably conclude that she was deterred from challenging its fundamental interests.[35]

The U.S. Factor and Taiwan's Security

Whatever their differences on how Taiwan should strengthen security in light of the PRC's goals, Ma Ying-jeou and Tsai Ing-wen, along with their parties, have long understood that the backing of the United States is a key factor. As Foreign Minister Joseph Wu put it in a July 2018 interview with CNN, "If the Chinese see the vulnerability of [a] Taiwan [that is] not getting U.S. support, then they would be thinking about starting scenarios where they would be able to take Taiwan over."[36]

Indeed, Taiwan has depended on the United States for security since the beginning of the Korean War in June 1950, but the nature of that dependence has changed over time. From 1954 to 1980, the U.S.-ROC Mutual Defense Treaty formalized a commitment that Washington would come to the island's defense if it were attacked. In the 1970s and early 1980s, Taipei grew increasingly anxious about the credibility of the U.S. commitment as the Nixon and Carter administrations moved gradually to end diplomatic relations with the ROC and then formally establish them with the PRC, which it did on New Year's Day 1979. Gradually thereafter, Taipei regained confidence: Congress passed the Taiwan Relations Act later that year. Beginning with the Reagan administration, Washington worked to strengthen Taiwan's security through policy statements and actions (for example, arms sales).

Taiwan's democratization transformed the U.S. relationship, giving the island's leaders and politicians a degree of agency that they never had before. Political forces on Taiwan now had the freedom to advocate for Taiwan independence or at least oppose too-rapid movement in cross-Strait relations. Lee Teng-hui capitalized on the growing sense of Taiwan identity to secure reelection in 1996, and Chen Shui-bian was the first president from the DPP, with its history of advocating independence. In different ways, Beijing worried that Lee and Chen were separatists, and the Clinton and George W. Bush administrations sought to restrain them to protect U.S. interests in peace and stability.

Since 2008, in contrast, the Ma and Tsai administrations have each given Washington little or no reason to think it might provoke a conflict. Each has acted with restraint regarding the politics of cross-Strait relations and Taiwanese nationalism. The approach of each reflects the public's status quo sentiments when it comes to the long term. In return for this moderation, both the Obama and Trump administrations intensified security ties between the U.S. and Taiwan militaries with the aim to raise the cost that Beijing would bear if it made any attempt to achieve its unification goal by force.

The Taiwan Public's Views of the PRC

How do people in Taiwan evaluate Taiwan's security vis-à-vis the PRC and how they should cope with its insecurity? The results of a variety of Taiwan surveys indicate how citizens in Taiwan's democratic system feel about different aspects of this issue. Taken together, they suggest a mix of realism, fear, hope, and pragmatism.[37]

The Pace of Cross-Strait Relations

The first issue is how the public feels about the pace of cross-Strait exchanges: Is it too slow, too fast, or just right?[38] Since the 1990s, the Election Study Center of National Chengchi University has conducted periodic polls on behalf of the Mainland Affairs Council that pose that question. Figure 8-1 shows the results from April 2009 to March 2020. A number of points stand out.

The share who believed that the pace of cross-Strait developments was just right oscillated between 36 and 48 percent during the Ma period, with the only extended low period occurring at the time of the Sunflower movement of early 2014. It then dropped to as low as 31.3 percent in January 2017 (one year after Tsai's election) but then climbed to the low forties in the two surveys in 2019. In March 2020, the figure was 45.1 percent.

The share who believed the pace was too fast was around 33 percent in 2009 and then rose to about 36 percent before and after the Sunflower movement. However, it then dropped steadily, to as low as 6.7 percent one year after Tsai was elected. By March 2020, the share was at 12.9 percent.

Conversely, the share who thought cross-Strait relations were developing too slowly remained below 20.0 percent until the time of Tsai's election, rose to as high as 45.0 percent in June 2017, and then dropped to 26.6 percent in March 2020.

Since Tsai's election in 2016, an average of 73.6 percent of those polled believed that cross-Strait relations were developing just right or too slowly. This combination varied from poll to poll, but generally people thought the pace was too slow in her first two years and just right in the last two. These are suggestive of how much people supported economic engagement with the mainland.

The topic of cross-Strait exchanges is very general, and the question posed did not probe what aspects respondents had in mind in their opinion on pacing. The safe guess is that they were thinking mainly about economic rela-

FIGURE 8-1. **Pace of Cross-Strait Exchanges, 2009–2020**

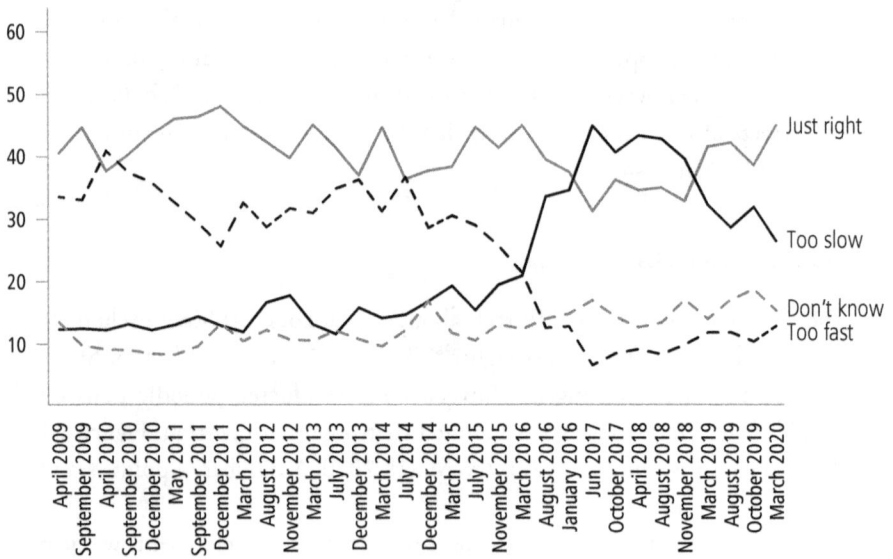

Source: "Public's View on Current Cross-Strait Relations," Mainland Affairs Council, Republic of China (Taiwan) (www.mac.gov.tw/en/Content_List.aspx?n=433E0B702064 D807).

a. The Mainland Affairs Council conducts surveys about five times a year. Those that cover public attitudes on Chinese hostility are conducted about three times a year.

tions because that was most likely to affect their personal situation. Although there were times when some people were dissatisfied with the pace, thinking it either too fast or too slow, the mainstream view was acceptance of status quo of the moment.

The PRC's Hostility toward Taiwan

Since the 1990s, the Election Study Center has also conducted polls for the Mainland Affairs Council on the degree to which the public believes that Beijing was unfriendly or friendly (*youshan*) toward both the Taiwan people and the Taiwan government.[39] The results of these surveys from 2009 on are shown in figure 8-2. Several key points on PRC unfriendliness toward Taiwan stand out.

The public consistently believes that the PRC is friendlier to the "people of the ROC" than it is to the government. The gap between unfriendly toward the government and toward the people remained modest during the Ma Ying-jeou period, generally less than 10 percent. It widened after Tsai Ing-wen became president—generally around 20 percent and as high as 24.1 percent in the summer of 2018. By August 2016, more than 60 percent believed Beijing was unfriendly to the Taiwan government, and the figure jumped to 76.6 percent in March 2020. The share of the public that believed Beijing was unfriendly to the Taiwan people ranged from 40 to 50 percent through the entire decade, except for August 2019, when it reached 51.4 percent, and then March 2020, when it rose to 61.5 percent.[40]

Thus a significant share of the Taiwan public believes that the Beijing regime is unfriendly toward their own government. Why respondents perceived a higher level of PRC hostility across the board in early 2020 is not clear. One reason, no doubt, was Beijing's reaction to Tsai Ing-wen's reelec-

FIGURE 8-2. **Beijing's Hostility toward Taiwan, 2009–2020[a]**

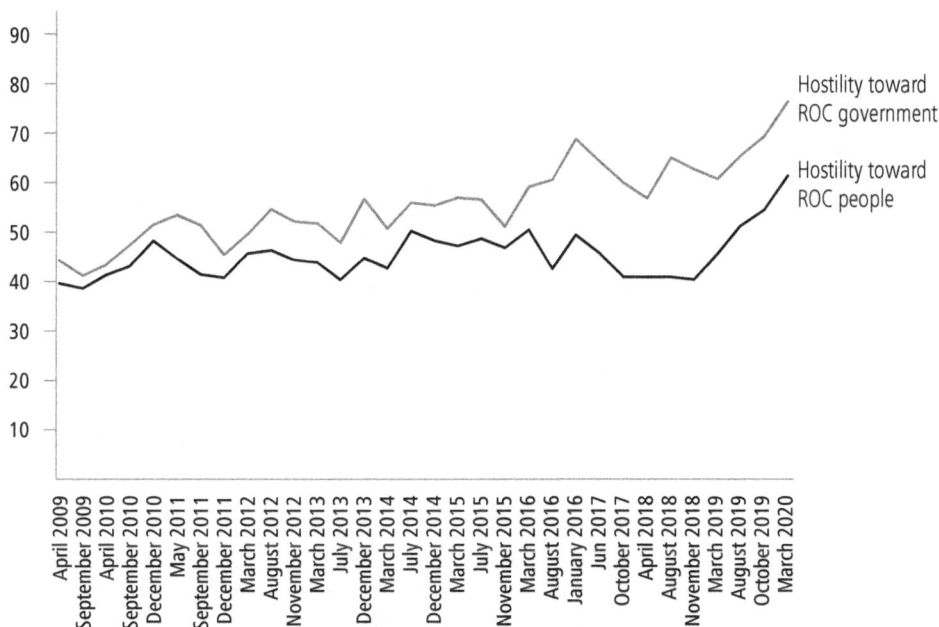

Source: "Public's View on Current Cross-Strait Relations," Mainland Affairs Council, Republic of China (Taiwan) (www.mac.gov.tw/en/Content_List.aspx?n=433E0B702064 D807).

a. The Mainland Affairs Council conducts surveys about five times a year. Those that cover public attitudes on Chinese hostility are conducted about three times a year.

tion. Another may have stemmed from events in Hong Kong in 2019 and the difficulties that the Taipei government had in getting business executives and others who lived on the mainland back home after the outbreak of COVID-19 in 2020.

Coping with PRC Ambition

As general as these two polls are, they highlight Taiwan's dilemma. Interactions with the mainland are satisfactory, but the Beijing government has been seen as unfriendly, particularly toward the Tsai government. What to do? One answer lies in people's current preferences about the longer-term future. Since the 1990s, the Election Survey Center has conducted a poll that asks respondents to choose among a series of options that essentially ask which outcome they prefer—unification, independence, or the status quo—and in what time frame. Figure 8-3 charts the trends from 1994 to 2019.[41] The following shows the options and shares of those surveyed in December 2017, eighteen months after Tsai Ing-wen took office:

- unification as soon as possible: 2.2 percent
- independence as soon as possible: 5.0 percent
- maintain the status quo, then move toward unification: 10.3 percent
- maintain the status quo, then move toward independence: 17.2 percent
- maintain the status quo, then decide later: 33.2 percent
- maintain the status quo indefinitely: 25.1 percent

This poll has a significant drawback in that the terms are not defined. The "status quo" category is particularly vague. Also unclear is whether those who favor unification now or later interpret that to mean unification under 1C2S, though it seems plausible that they do, since no other formula is discussed in Taiwan or the PRC. This poll, at least, indicates that people disfavor unification by almost an eight-to-one margin. The approximately 10 percent support rate for unification now or later has been consistent over time. The only time it reached 15 percent in the last decade was in 2018.[42]

But the message from this distribution of opinion, which has remained stable since 2009, is that a broad consensus exists in favor of the status quo and in opposition to unification. Security, it appears, can best be achieved by charting a path between capitulation to Beijing, on the one hand, and not provoking war, on the other. Indeed, a risk-averse stance makes perfect sense.

FIGURE 8-3. **Taiwan Attitudes Concerning Unification, Independence, and the Status Quo, 1994–2020**

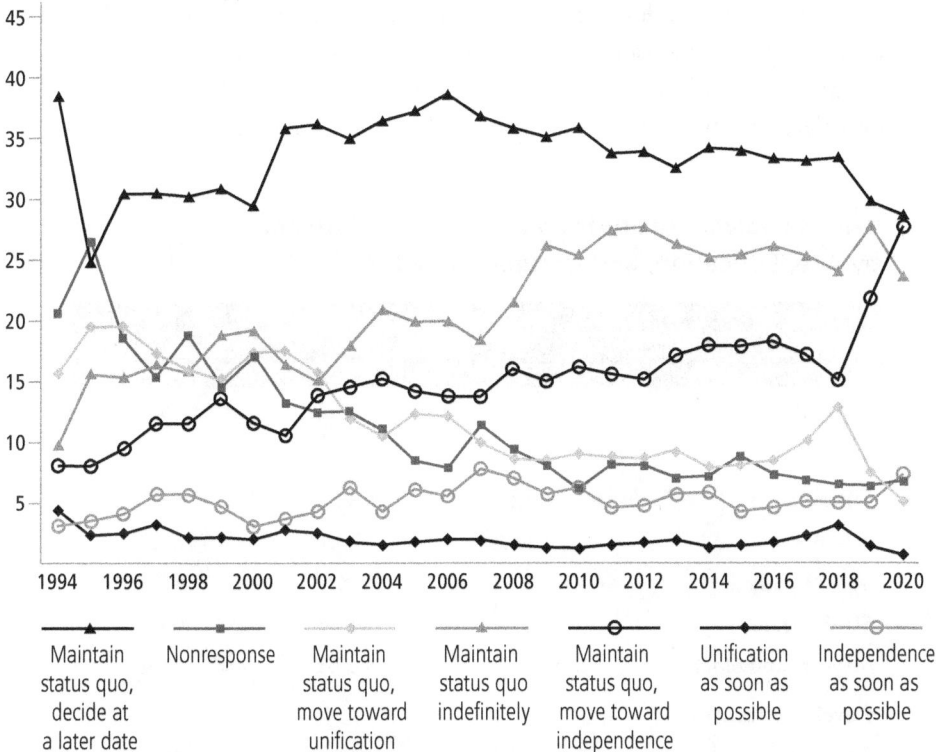

Maintain status quo, decide at a later date | Nonresponse | Maintain status quo, move toward unification | Maintain status quo indefinitely | Maintain status quo, move toward independence | Unification as soon as possible | Independence as soon as possible

Source: "Changes in the Unification-Independence Stances of Taiwanese as Tracked in Surveys by Election Study Center, NCCU (1994–2020)," Election Study Center, National Chengchi University (www.researchgate.net/figure/Changes-in-the-Unification-Independence-Stances-of-Taiwanese-as-Tracked-in-Surveys-by_fig3_327048040).

Why should Taiwan people trade what they have now, even with its problems and unresolved dilemmas, for an uncertain and perhaps dangerous future?

There has been something of a silver lining for Beijing, and that is the relatively low share of those surveyed who favored de jure independence either right away or in the future: only 22.2 percent in the December 2017 poll. More worrisome to the PRC were the results of the June 2020 iteration of this survey. The share of those who favored independence now or later increased to 36.1 percent; and 28.7 percent favored maintaining the status quo and then moving toward independence. The share who favored some version of the status quo declined to 51.3 percent, and those who favored unification now or later fell below 10 percent. These shifts may be a temporary response to the harsh policies that Beijing imposed on Hong Kong beginning in the summer of 2019, but the trend certainly bears watching.

Table 8-1 breaks down the views on different cross-Strait outcomes but controlling for generation, education, and occupation type. Support for the status quo remains generally strong no matter the controlled variable. The only clear exception concerns young people's views on independence: 35.4 per-

TABLE 8-1. **Taiwan Attitudes on Cross-Strait Outcomes, by Age, Education, and Occupation, 2017**

	Percent		
	Unification[a]	Independence[a]	Status quo[b]
Sample	13.9	19.4	59.8
Age			
20–29 years	8.6	35.4	53.2
30–39 year	12.8	23.1	62.2
40–49 years	17.0	14.5	66.0
50–59 years	17.8	10.2	64.8
60 years and older	13.3	17.5	53.4
Level of education			
Primary and below	8.9	15.6	46.3
Junior high	13.8	10.3	72.3
High school	13.1	17.7	64.2
Technical college	18.0	16.3	63.9
University and above	14.7	26.9	55.8
Occupation type			
White collar	11.6	24.6	60.3
Blue collar	8.2	22.1	61.8
Student	5.1	42.4	48.9
Retired	16.5	16.5	58.2

Source: "Telephone and Mobile Phone Survey of the Presidential Satisfaction, Twenty-Second Wave," Taiwan's Election and Democratization Survey, December 2017 (http://teds.nccu.edu.tw/main.php).

a. Now or later.
b. Indefinitely or forever.

cent of respondents age twenty to twenty-nine and 42.4 percent of students favored independence now or later. In addition, 26.9 percent of those with a university education and above wanted independence. This is consistent with the observation, common after the Sunflower movement of 2014, that young people naturally were advocates of independence (*tianrandu*). Whether they maintain that view as they age is an open question.

Amplifying a generally risk-averse approach are the results of polls sponsored by the Taiwan National Security Survey since 2002 that have measured in greater detail the public's sense of insecurity and how to manage it. The answers to several questions shed interesting light on how Taiwan people view the island's strategic situation.[43]

Economic growth is seen as a function of cross-Strait political relations. In the 2017 poll, 69.1 percent of those surveyed said that Taiwan's economic situation would get worse if cross-Strait political relations got worse, while 20.1 percent predicted no impact, and 1.5 percent expected improvement.

At the same time, overreliance on the mainland economy can put Taiwan in a vulnerable position. In the 2017 poll, slightly more than 50 percent believed that if Taiwan becomes too dependent economically on the mainland economy, Beijing will leverage that dependence to extract political concessions. Thirty-five percent disagreed. Despite that potential vulnerability, 53.3 percent thought that Taiwan should strengthen economic ties with the mainland, and only 21.6 percent thought such ties should be reduced.

The PRC political system and economic level affected respondents' attitude toward unification, but by only a modest degree. Of those surveyed, 58.3 percent disapproved of unification if the political, social, and economic gap between the two sides of the Strait was still very large, while 24.5 percent approved despite the large differences. The number who would approve if convergence between the two systems occurred increased only to 33.1 percent, while 52.7 percent still opposed unification.[44]

People polled in 2016 were realistic about the cross-Strait balance of power and how to address the military threat of the People's Liberation Army. Of those polled, 66.8 percent preferred a more moderate policy, presumably one relying on negotiations, and only 22.4 percent advocated increasing the military's strength. Fewer than 4 percent favored a combination of the two.

Most surprising is the response to a question in the 2017 poll that asked respondents about the probability of unification. The survey used a zero-to-ten scale, and 28.1 percent picked the middle point of five, that is, the odds of unification were even; 32.2 percent thought the probability was less than 50 percent; and 29.3 percent believed it was more than 50 percent. The average score on the scale was 4.73, a bit less likely than even odds.[45] To put it differently, only a third of respondents were confident that unification could be avoided over the long term.

When it comes to dialogue and negotiations between Taipei and Beijing, the most hotly debated question on Taiwan has been whether the island's leader should accept the 1992 Consensus as a basis for interacting with the PRC. Presidents Ma Ying-jeou and Tsai Ing-wen took different positions on this question. Ma explicitly accepted the Consensus when he became president in 2008, but Tsai did not in 2016. Public views seemed to favor Ma's approach. In 2012, halfway through Ma's presidency, a poll by Taiwan's Election and Democratization Survey (TEDS) asked respondents about using the formula. Those who had a view on the matter favored accepting it by a two-to-one margin over those who wanted to reject it. Four years later, when Tsai became president, there was still relatively little change in what people thought: 59.8 percent of those surveyed who had a view still supported use of the 1992 Consensus.[46]

Beneath the surface of the overall result, generational differences were at play. While no generational group was a major outlier in the 2012 poll, the 2016 poll demonstrated a divergence among particular age groups. For those who had a clear view, respondents older than thirty-nine were still in favor of using the 1992 Consensus, by about a five-to-three margin. Only a bare majority of the thirty- to thirty-nine-year-old group (53.4 percent) still approved it. But 54.1 percent of the twenty- to twenty-nine-year-old cohort said the 1992 Consensus should be rejected.[47] The likely reasons for these shifts were growing concerns about economic dependence on the PRC.

Despite the still fairly strong support for using the 1992 Consensus, these results may exaggerate people's hope that a constructive dialogue with Beijing is possible. These polls did not define the 1992 Consensus but left respondents to do so for themselves. On Taiwan, the conventional definition of the formula is the one that Ma Ying-jeou has used: "one China with each side adopting its own interpretation." It is likely that many respondents adopted the same meaning. But that is not a definition that the PRC has ever accepted, so public support for the formula may contribute less to Taiwan's security than people think.

Another idea for enhancing cross-Strait security that has been around for a long time is that the two sides reach a peace accord of some sort. One version of that idea is that the PRC would pledge not to use force and Taiwan would agree not to pursue independence. Opinion polls on Taiwan find support for this type of peace accord: 78.1 percent approved the idea, while 16.7 percent disapproved.[48] Whether such a formula would be mutually acceptable is unknowable, but it is based on the premise that what Beijing does is a function of what Taipei does and vice versa. The problem with this arrangement is that the PLA would continue to increase its capabilities overall, many of which are relevant to a Taiwan contingency, whether or not Taiwan pledged a change in its intentions. Whether the Taiwan public would actually support a peace accord once it saw the details is also relevant.[49]

Conclusion

Taiwan's leaders are divided on how to cope with the security challenge that the PRC poses. On one side is the Blue camp, with its emphasis on accommodation, reassurance, and engagement. On the other is the Green camp's more distanced stance of refusing to accept Beijing's preconditions, keeping economics and politics separate, exercising restraint when it comes to the PRC bottom line of independence, and relying on the United States to balance Beijing's power over Taiwan.

Each camp's approach has a downside. Ma Ying-jeou had hoped that in return for accommodating and reassuring Beijing, mainland China would not block his administration from having greater participation in international organizations and from negotiating free trade agreements. But the PRC was grudging in how far it allowed Ma to go in both arenas. If he wished to go further, the PRC insisted, he would have to begin political talks to better define Taiwan's legal status from Beijing's point of view. Tsai Ing-wen may have expected that any cost to Taiwan would be tolerable if she declined to *biaotai* in the way the PRC wanted. Beijing might follow the same playbook it had during the Chen Shui-bian administration: suspending the institutional communications mechanisms between the two sides, getting one or two of the countries with which Taipei had diplomatic relations to switch support to Beijing, and providing political support to the DPP's domestic rivals. The PRC's response to her election was much more robust (see chapter 12).

The different ways that the Ma and Tsai administrations have sought to preserve Taiwan's security relate to a question about the source of the PRC's Taiwan policy. Put simply, Is Beijing driven by fear or greed?[50] If fear is the motivation, then the sensible response from Taiwan is to offer reassurances to assuage PRC anxieties. If, on the other hand, Beijing is motivated by greed, then deterrence is Taiwan's best option, with the United States making a major contribution. If greed is Beijing's motivation, then reassurances will only whet its appetite. For Taipei to use deterrence to respond to PRC fear will only deepen those fears.[51]

The evolution of PRC policy indicates a migration from fear to greed. From around 1994 to 2008, it appears its leaders were motivated more by fear, while the policies of Lee Teng-hui after 1994 and Chen Shui-bian after 2002 contained some degree of greed. The Ma administration emphasized reassurance as Beijing's confidence in its growing power led it to be less fearful and more greedy. Yet the Ma administration did not solely rely on reassurance. Ma rejected Beijing's demand for political talks, certainly an example of PRC greediness. Conversely, Tsai did not solely rely on deterrence. She did make an effort to reassure Beijing before and after her election. The issue is the relative balance between the two approaches. With Tsai Ing-wen's election, Beijing initially behaved as if it were afraid—for example, by insisting that Tsai declare herself in ways that it probably knew she could not meet. But its actions thereafter were more consistent with greed than fear. The increase in independence sentiment in Taiwan during 2020, perhaps temporary, might suggest that Beijing's fear will be triggered again. But if PRC policies themselves—such as its harsh repression of political freedoms in Hong Kong—turn out to be the cause of that shift in Taiwan sentiment, then Beijing will have only itself to blame.

9

Taiwan's Military Defense

The goal of the People's Republic of China (PRC) regarding Taiwan is clear: ending the island's separate existence and incorporating it into the People's Republic of China system under the "one country, two systems" (1C2S) model. The PRC would prefer to achieve this objective without war, but it has refused to abandon the use of force, believing that the threat of force is necessary to dissuade Taiwan leaders from moving to de jure independence. This raises the question, Is there a point where Chinese leaders judge that the modernization of the People's Liberation Army (PLA) not only enables them to deter what they fear (Taiwan independence) but also gives them the capacity to compel what they want (unification)? Of course, capabilities do not dictate intentions; but lacking capabilities constrains intentions, as has been the case in the past. How Taiwan copes with PRC ambitions—deflecting or provoking them—will be a factor. So will the commitment of the United States to Taiwan's security. Yet it is a reality that PRC leaders are closing in on being able to use military means to compel Taiwan to accept unification. Of course, Taiwan strongly opposes Beijing's objective, at least on the terms proffered. The question is whether Taiwan can deter what it fears.

PRC Military Capabilities

The systematic modernization of the PLA is now more than two decades old. Twenty years on, the U.S. Defense Intelligence Agency's 2019 report on PRC military power painted a clear picture of the ways the expanding set of tools that could enable the PLA to conduct warfare well beyond PRC shores. Its basic finding: "PLA ground, air, naval and missile forces have become increasingly able to project power during peacetime and in the event of regional conflicts." This buildup began in the late 1990s, when Beijing concluded, whether rightly or wrongly, that Lee Teng-hui was moving toward independence and that the best way to stop him was to modernize the PLA. Indeed, the agency's report asserts that "Beijing's longstanding interest to eventually compel Taiwan's reunification with the mainland and deter any attempt by Taiwan to declare independence has served as the primary driver for China's military modernization."[1]

Military modernization has yielded surface ships with greater fire power that can sail farther and longer, high-tech submarines that patrol in the East China Sea, more advanced equipment for the air force, and longer-range, more accurate missiles. Equipment that can project power even further— longer-range bombers, transport aircraft, aircraft carriers—are in the works. By increasing the tempo of its exercises in the air and waters around Taiwan, the PLA is turning equipment into capabilities.

Also significant in an era when networked communications are increasingly important in warfighting, the PLA's growing cyberwar capabilities enhance its ability to collect and process intelligence, gain information dominance at the beginning of a conflict, disrupt Taiwan's defenses, and amplify the effectiveness of more conventional capabilities.[2] Taiwan's vulnerability is exacerbated by the success of Chinese intelligence agencies in stealing the island's defense secrets. Scholar Peter Mattis writes, "Despite Beijing's relentless and sometimes fruitful efforts to penetrate the most sensitive of Taiwan's national security institutions and society, Taiwan's leaders have not been able to push forward a stronger legal foundation for counterintelligence." The problem is not just legal but also political. Mattis says that "the problem is worsened because the Kuomintang and the Democratic Progressive Party struggle to find common ground despite their shared interest in not allowing Beijing to decide Taiwan's future."[3]

Just as important as the modernization of PLA equipment, or "hardware," is the transformation of its institutions, or "software." These include a reduction in the primacy of the ground forces relative to the navy, air force, and missile forces; the creation of theater commands that assemble forces so that they are best organized to meet possible security challenges; an unprecedented effort to develop tenable joint war-fighting that integrates the operations of various services; and a modernization of command and control.[4] All of these would be important in fighting a war over Taiwan. In addition, in 2020 the PLA undertook a more aggressive program of exercises that are relevant to conducting military operations against Taiwan.[5]

If and when these reforms are successfully implemented, they will deepen Taiwan's vulnerability. Until now, one of Taiwan's hidden advantages was that the PLA did not know how to fight on a joint basis to conduct difficult operations such as a naval quarantine or an amphibious landing. That may be changing, and Taiwan cannot assume the PLA will fail. The assessment of Taiwan's Ministry of National Defense (MND), in its 2017 Quadrennial Defense Review, is realistic about the ways the PLA is getting stronger: "Mainland China continues to invest heavily in military modernization, vigorously undertaking military force transformation and reforming into theater commands, and is gradually acquiring force projection capability west of the Second Island Chain, adding uncertainties to the security environment in the region."[6]

Beijing's Red Lines for the Use of Force

Leaders of the PRC declare that their fundamental policy regarding Taiwan is "peaceful reunification." At the same time, they have never renounced the use of force. Beijing regards the Taiwan matter as an internal affair, for which force is an acceptable response to solving the dispute. Technically, the state of hostilities that existed between the forces of Mao Zedong on the mainland and Chiang Kai-shek on Taiwan in the 1940s still exists. Most serious from the PRC perspective are the existence on Taiwan of "independence forces." If these forces were successful in advancing their independence objective, Beijing would regard the move as a casus belli.

Twice in the past twenty years, the PRC government has authoritatively set forth the circumstances under which it would abandon "peaceful reunification" and undertake a military campaign against Taiwan to subdue it. The first was the State Council Information Office's Taiwan White Paper of February 2000, issued one month before the election that brought Chen Shui-bian to power, and the second was the 2005 Anti-Secession Law.[7] The key provisions of the white paper and the Anti-Secession Law are presented in table 9-1.

TABLE 9-1. **The PRC's Redlines for the Use of Force**

	2000 White Paper	2005 Anti-Secession Law
Condition 1	If "a grave turn of events occurs leading to the separation of Taiwan from China in any name," or	If "the 'Taiwan independence' secessionist forces should act under any name or by any means to cause the fact of Taiwan's secession from China," or
Condition 2	"Taiwan is invaded and occupied by foreign countries,"[a] or	"Major incidents entailing [or leading to] Taiwan's secession from China should occur," or
Condition 3	"The Taiwan authorities refuse, *sine die*, the peaceful settlement of cross-Straits reunification through negotiations,"	"Possibilities for a peaceful reunification should be completely exhausted,"
Threat of action to follow	Then "the Chinese Government will only be forced to adopt all drastic measures possible, including the use of force, to safeguard China's sovereignty and territorial integrity and fulfill the great cause of reunification."	Then "the state shall employ non-peaceful means and other necessary measures to protect China's sovereignty and territorial integrity."

Sources: "The One-China Principle and the Taiwan Issue," Taiwan White Paper, Taiwan Affairs Office and the Information Office of the State Council, Embassy of the People's Republic of China in the United States, February 21, 2000; and "Anti-Secession Law (Full text)," Embassy of the People's Republic of China in the United States, March 15, 2005.

a. This formulation follows the PRC's description of the U.S. security relationship with Taiwan up through 1978.

The Anti-Secession Law's way of stating the conditions that would trigger the use of nonpeaceful means is exceedingly vague. The conditions are more general than those enunciated in the 2000 White Paper, and even those were not a picture of clarity. Quotations from the 2005 law, which is more authoritative than the White Paper, demonstrate the haziness of its conditions:

- *Condition 1, "the fact of Taiwan's secession from China":* If, as this phrasing implies, secession can take forms other than a declaration of independence, how precisely would Beijing define the actions that Taiwan should not take?

- *Condition 2, "major incidents entailing Taiwan's secession from China should occur":* Could Beijing judge that joint exercises conducted by U.S. and Taiwan armed forces meet this condition? Can Washington and Taipei assume that such exercises would not lead to that judgment?

- *Condition 3, "the possibilities for a peaceful reunification should be completely exhausted":* Would Beijing judge that this condition was met if the Taipei government—even a Beijing-leaning government—were unwilling to conclude or even enter into unification negotiations because Taiwan's leaders judged PRC terms to be unacceptable and the public opposed such talks?

Stating these red lines ambiguously makes sense from a PRC point of view. If red lines are to be drawn, doing so with a certain amount of fuzziness can enhance deterrence. One that is too precise will be read by a risk-accepting adversary as a license to go right up to the line and not cross it. That was Chen Shui-bian's style during his presidency (2000–2008), and it posed dilemmas for Beijing. Should Beijing have acted preemptively because Chen was testing the limits of PRC policy? Should it have accommodatingly pulled the line further back, because the risks of war were just too great? Should it have stated clearly what it could not tolerate and been prepared to risk all on enforcing that clear line? So far, Beijing has relied on the law's vagueness to serve as a kind of strategic ambiguity.

Aside from the definitional vagueness, there are three problems with the way the Anti-Secession Law seeks to limit Taipei's actions. First of all, it leaves it up to the PRC government—and only the PRC—to decide when a use-of-force condition has been met. How Beijing might define the fact of secession from China or the complete exhaustion of possibilities for peaceful reunification is very different from how Taipei or Washington might define them.

Second, the tendency of PRC analytic and policy agencies and of its top leaders to read the worst into developments that might conceivably challenge the regime's fundamental interests makes it more likely that they would exaggerate the boundary-crossing character of an edgy Taiwan or American initiative. For example, Beijing asserts that when a Green administration in Taiwan revises textbooks in ways that play down Taiwan's link with the mainland, that helps lay the foundation for independence. Chinese scholars have argued that referendums and judicial interpretations in the direction of independence might expand that foundation.[8] Moreover, Chinese leaders interpret a closer U.S.-Taiwan security relationship as evidence of strengthening the Taiwan independence forces. Since Beijing will be the one to interpret the actions of a Green administration, and since it refuses to talk to a Green administration that does not meet its preconditions, a PRC miscalculation about Taipei's intentions cannot be ruled out.

Third, at the end of the day, if senior Chinese leaders decide that Taiwan has gone too far, whatever the circumstances, neither the vague language of the Anti-Secession Law nor the reality on Taiwan will matter. But the law's red lines at least reveal what most concerned decisionmakers when the law was enacted in 2005.

War Scenarios

How might the PLA's developing capabilities be used to compel Taiwan to surrender or negotiate on Beijing's terms if Chinese leaders decided that war was its only option? The annual report by the U.S. Office of the Secretary of Defense (OSD) posits four different military options that the PRC leadership might order the PLA to undertake, either separately or in combination.[9]

The first is an air and maritime blockade. Based on PLA writings, it would begin with larger-scale missile strikes and then move to blockades of air and maritime traffic, in addition to cutting off Taiwan's access to key imports. If necessary, the PLA's navy and air force, complemented by a variety of electronic and information warfare operations, would continue as long as necessary to subdue Taiwan. The second option would be a limited campaign in which PLA units would conduct "a variety of disruptive, punitive, or lethal military actions . . . probably in conjunction with overt and clandestine economic and political" information operations to "shape perceptions or undercut the effectiveness or legitimacy of the Taiwan authorities." These could include cyberattacks on critical infrastructure, to degrade public confidence in the government. The third option is an air and missile campaign that would attack air defense systems "to degrade Taiwan's defenses, neutralize Taiwan's leadership, or break the Taiwan people's resolve."

The fourth and most difficult operation would be an amphibious invasion of Taiwan. The most frequently discussed scenario for this option "envisions a complex operation relying on coordinated interlocking campaigns for logistics air, and naval support, and electronic warfare." Once shore defenses were breached and beachhead established, troops and materiel would land at designated sites at the northern and southern ends of the island and then proceed to attack and take key targets.

In each of these scenarios, the PLA would most likely conduct information operations, including use of cyber weapons, to disrupt Taiwan communications and disable critical infrastructure. According to the OSD report, PLA writings "identify [information operations]—comprising cyber, electronic, and psychological warfare—as integral to achieving information superiority and as an effective means for countering a stronger foe." The PLA, the report warns, could use cyber weapons to attack logistics, communications, and commercial activities and to enhance the effectiveness of other capabilities in an armed conflict.

Even as the PLA turns its modern equipment into capability, and assuming that Taiwan does nothing that is an explicit move to independence, what are the prospects that Chinese leaders would undertake one or more of the above options? One part of the answer would be an assessment of whether the PLA today can undertake an amphibious invasion. As damaging as the non-invasion options are both in material or psychological terms, they may not be sufficient to get the Taiwan government to sue for peace. Only a successful invasion can guarantee victory. On this, the OSD report is skeptical: "Large-scale amphibious invasion is one of the most complicated and difficult military operations. . . . An attempt to invade Taiwan would likely strain China's armed forces and invite foreign intervention. These stresses, combined with China's combat force attrition and the complexity of urban warfare and counterinsurgency, make an amphibious invasion of Taiwan a significant political and military risk."[10]

Yet while the report outlines why it would be difficult for the PLA to mount an amphibious invasion, it does not state any qualifications concerning the other three scenarios, which implies that the OSD believes that the PRC is already capable of carrying them out successfully. Taiwan's Ministry of National Defense speaks to those vulnerabilities and reaches a pessimistic conclusion. It judges that the PLA can impose a blockade on Taiwan itself, seize the small islands off the coast of Fujian province that Taiwan controls, hit the entire main island with short- and medium-range ballistic and cruise missiles and do so with increasing accuracy, and use its cyberattack capability to disrupt the Taiwan military's surveillance, reconnaissance, and command and control systems.[11]

But the larger security context remains important, and the OSD report judges the PLA's options in light of the PRC's political objectives. It says, "China appears prepared to defer the use of military force *as long as it believes that unification with Taiwan over the long-term remains possible and the costs of conflict outweigh the benefits.*" That is, until PRC leaders judge that the door to unification is definitely closing, then they do not need to undertake a war of necessity. Moreover, they can take some confidence that "the credible threat of force is essential to maintain the conditions for political progress and prevent Taiwan from making moves toward independence."[12] The views of the Taiwan public seem to provide confirmation of this judgment.

One key factor in a PRC assessment about the risks and benefits of going to war is that of U.S. intervention. I have long believed that despite the ambiguity of U.S. declaratory policy on defending Taiwan, PRC leaders prudently assume that Washington would act to save Taiwan; hence their commitment of significant resources to make intervention as difficult as possible.[13] The Defense Intelligence Agency's report inventories the PLA's progress. As of 2019,

> China has closed many of the gaps in key warfare areas, such as air defense and long-range strike, that would support countering third-party forces in regional campaigns. China has built or acquired a wide array of advanced platforms, including submarines, major surface combatants, missile patrol craft, maritime strike aircraft, and land-based systems that employ new, sophisticated anti-ship cruise missiles and SAMs. China also has developed the world's first road-mobile, anti-ship ballistic missile, a system specifically designed to attack enemy aircraft carriers.[14]

The cyber and counterspace capabilities of the PLA would also be relevant in countering U.S. intervention.[15]

In 2015 the RAND Corporation developed a scorecard of U.S. and PLA capabilities relevant to the Taiwan conflict. It predicted the shifts in the superiority of U.S. military capabilities vis-à-vis the PLA that would occur between 2003 and 2017, ranking them according to the degree of the U.S. advantage. The United States had a major advantage in 2003 in U.S. attacks on PRC airbases, U.S. antisurface warfare, and cyber warfare with the PRC and only an advantage in 2017. The United States had a major advantage in 2003 but was at a disadvantage in 2017 with respect to PLA attacks on U.S. airbases in East Asia. In air superiority and PLA counterspace, the United States had an advantage in 2003, but there was approximate parity in 2017. The United States had an advantage in 2003 but was at a disadvantage in 2017 in PLA anti-surface warfare. Parity has prevailed over the whole period in the U.S. ability to penetrate PRC airspace. And the United States was at a disadvantage in 2003 and was at parity in 2017 in U.S. counterspace.

This evolution affects how well U.S. capabilities and perceived intentions will deter the PLA, the risks that Beijing is willing to run, and the nature of the conflict should deterrence fail. Any U.S. effort to help Taiwan defend itself will only get costlier and more time-consuming as PLA capabilities improve. Even if a U.S. intervention succeeded militarily, the political and economic consequences for the PRC, the United States, and Taiwan would still be significant.[16] This reality has led some in Taiwan and the United States to warn that the PLA may have the ability to launch a surprise attack against the island and achieve victory before U.S. armed forces could mobilize for an intervention (assuming that civilian authorities ordered such a response).[17]

Taiwan's Defense Tasks

What, therefore, does Taiwan need to do to strengthen deterrence so that PRC leaders do not take that risk of mounting a major military campaign? U.S. policymakers in several administrations have pointed to at least two issue areas that Taiwan needs to address to achieve such outcomes: defense spending and defense strategy.

Taiwan's Defense Spending

Taiwan's democratization permitted debate on a new range of policy issues and crystallized a broad social consensus that was suspicious of the PRC and opposed to unification on Beijing's terms. But this political transformation also handicapped defense capabilities. The public's demand for social benefits such as health care was satisfied by taking money from the military. Opposition parties were able to use their power in the legislature to block costly initiatives proposed by the government, and the average politician has neither much knowledge about military matters nor any political incentive to support increased spending (Taiwan's defense industry lacks the political clout that its American counterpart enjoys). Some members of the Democratic Progressive

Party recall the military's negative role during the authoritarian period and question its commitment to defend the country. Young people are generally antimilitary.[18] Taiwan's defense ministry is well aware of the negative political environment in which it operates: "Many of our fellow citizens have gradually lost awareness that the two sides of the Strait remain military adversaries, and that the risk of war still exists. Some have ignored the widening gap of military capabilities and increasing menaces from Mainland China, undermining their support for defense affairs."[19]

The usual metric for evaluating how much Taiwan spends on its military is defense spending as a share of GDP. That is the basis on which President Trump judged the commitment of the U.S. NATO allies to be wanting. Several Taiwan administrations have struggled to raise defense spending to a level that exceeds 2 percent of GDP. But expenditures should be based on the extent of the threat and not an artificial percentage share of the total economy, which, among other things, can create perverse effects. If the economy declines but defense spending stays the same, the latter will increase as a percentage of GDP without any change in capability. Jessica Tuchman Mathews has observed when discussing the U.S. defense budget that using GDP as the denominator is misleading: "The valid measure of affordability is defense spending as a share of the federal discretionary budget."[20]

Defense spending as a share of government spending is a better metric because it reflects the choices that officials and politicians make concerning resource allocation. Given a finite amount of resources from revenues and borrowing, a New Taiwan dollar spent on education or social welfare is a dollar unavailable for defense, and the reverse is also true. Table 9-2 shows how much of Taiwan's total government budget goes for protecting the island, from 2009, the first year the Ma administration formulated the budget, through 2019. What it shows is that defense varied between a low 10.85 percent in 2018 and a high 11.52 percent in 2015. The average was 11.14 percent, and the Ma administration did a better job of staying above that amount than the Tsai administration did in the three budgets that it formulated and the Legislative Yuan approved (10.96 percent in 2017, 10.85 percent in 2018, and 11.04 percent in 2019).

Even more meaningful than percentage indicators in assessing the Taiwan government performance is the absolute amount expended. The average amount for this period was NT$301,429 billion. Before 2015, that figure was exceeded only once, in 2012. Thereafter, the total varied between NT$304 trillion and NT$315 trillion. During the 2009–2019 period, Taiwan's average annual inflation rate was 0.91 percent. So in the years when actual defense

TABLE 9-2. **Taiwan's Defense Spending as a Share of Government Spending, 2009–2018**

Year	Total government expenditures (NT$)	Defense expenditures (NT$)	Defense as share of government expenditures (percent)
2009	2,670,898	297,746	11.15
2010	2,566,804	286,929	11.18
2011	2,612,947	288,889	11.06
2012	2,677,984	303,903	11.35
2013	2,665,241	292,646	10.98
2014	2,645,712	291,418	11.01
2015	2,645,189	304,636	11.52
2016	2,745,305	314,847	11.47
2017	2,778,361	304,632	10.96
2018	2,844,538	308,571	10.85
2019	2,911,645	321,506	11.04
Average	2,705,875	301,429	11.14

Source: Taiwan Statistical Data Book 2019 (Taipei: National Development Council, R.O.C. [Taiwan], 2019), table 9-3a, "Net Government Expenditures of All Levels by Administrative Affair."

spending declined, the real value declined even more, and increases in spending were not as significant in real terms as the annual figures might suggest. In effect, defense spending has been essentially stagnant over a period when PLA capabilities continue to grow. The Tsai administration was able to get an increase for defense in the 2019 budget, when the final expenditure amount was NT$326 trillion. It proposed $341 trillion for 2020 and received $325 trillion, a decline from 2019. For 2021, it requested $352.3 billion for 2021.[21] As a proportion of the central government budget (not the total budget), these figures constituted 17 percent of the total, where previously the share was 16 percent or less.

In addition to the regular budget, Taiwan's MND sought a special budget to cover major purchases of weapons systems from the United States. Thus in November 2019, the legislature passed a NT$247 billion budget to pay for sixty-six F-16 C/D Block 70 fighter planes over a seven-year period.[22] The key point, however, is that even with periodic special budgets, the modest increase in the amount of defense spending is occurring at a time when the modernization of PRC capabilities is making Taiwan significantly more vulnerable.

Then there is the matter of what defense funds are spent for. In fact, there is an imbalance in the distribution of resources within the Taiwan defense budget away from equipment and readiness. This occurred because Taiwan's political leaders decided in 2009 to move from a conscripted force to an all-volunteer force. There was little support for increasing the budget to facilitate the costly transition, so the only way out was to reduce the size of the active duty force, from the 188,000 billets authorized in 2019 to 175,000 at some time in the future. Whether this 7 percent reduction in the force was militarily sound in light of the growth of PLA power is an unaddressed question. To make matters worse, the resources that the MND had available for personnel were insufficient to attract volunteers. The bottom line, according to the Pentagon, is that "the unanticipated magnitude of transition costs has led Taiwan to divert funds from foreign and indigenous acquisition programs as well as near-term training and readiness."[23]

But does increased personnel spending on a volunteer force actually create military capabilities? In 2013 the period of mandatory training was reduced to four months, hardly enough to create combat-ready soldiers. There have been complaints that the training that occurs entails busy work, not the inculcation of military skills. The *Taipei Times* complained editorially, "How was [four months of training] supposed to create a motivated, effective reserve force? It was a waste of time and money, and only served to exacerbate the sense of pointlessness in the endeavor when its purpose—protecting Taiwan's freedoms and way of life—should have been explicit."[24]

The budgetary resources allocated for defense is the result of a set of political choices designed to balance competing priorities. Those priorities include meeting the needs of an aging population and funding the educational needs of young people, both of which are understandable concerns.[25] But defense is another priority. At the same time, the government has accommodated the public's general reluctance to provide through taxation the revenues that the government needs to address adequately all the priorities that compete for resources. The principal reason why the Taiwan military's share of the budgetary pie is relatively low is that the pie is too small. Despite the growing danger from the PRC, the public is unwilling to provide more in taxes to respond to that danger.

Taiwan's Defense Strategy

The second issue area deals with whether the Taiwan armed forces have adopted an optimal defense strategy, one that takes into account the new threat environment created by the PLA's increasing ability to project military power and the limited budgetary resources currently available. Taiwan's long-standing defense strategy envisioned an air and sea battle against the PLA, with the Taiwan Strait as the battlefield.[26] This entailed "symmetrical war-fighting of surface action groups, fighter planes, or tanks slugging it out" in a war of attrition.[27] Historically, that made sense because Taiwan's equipment was technologically more advanced than that of the PLA and also because an island possesses natural defensive barriers. But PLA modernization has closed or eliminated that qualitative gap and is creating a new gap in its own favor, one that increases Taiwan's vulnerability. A strategy of attrition no longer works to Taiwan's advantage.

Hypothetically, Taiwan might restore the balance in capabilities by relying on advanced American equipment, as it lacks the indigenous ability to produce advanced platforms itself. But even if Washington were willing to brook the wrath of the PRC by effectively arming its cross-Strait adversary, U.S. platforms are expensive. Acquiring them in the numbers required to fit an attrition strategy is beyond the reach of Taiwan's constrained budget. Moreover, U.S. platforms are good for projecting power on offense; what Taiwan needs are capabilities that mount an effective defense against a large, aggressive adversary. Taiwan's air fleet is also increasingly vulnerable to bombardment of airfields by PLA missiles and bombers and to the PLA's increasingly sophisticated air defenses covering the Taiwan Strait.

The MND has taken some steps to compensate for the growing disparities between its armed forces and the PLA (for example, building war reserves, improving joint operations, strengthening the officer and noncommissioned officer corps, and improving the reserve forces). But according to the OSD report, "these improvements only partially address Taiwan's declining defensive advantages."[28]

Moreover, Taiwan's defense planning must take into account an undeniable reality: even if U.S. leaders decided that it should use the armed forces to respond to an unprovoked PRC attack on Taiwan, the U.S. armed forces could not intervene right away. On this, geography—the immense size of the Pacific Ocean—is the PRC's friend and America's enemy. The working estimate is a number of months at a minimum, which is why Washington has worked for several years to encourage Taiwan's MND to acquire the capabilities it needs to hold on for that long.

This need for strategic endurance was the origin of the Overall Defense Concept, a strategy that sought to exploit the PLA's vulnerability in a campaign to take Taiwan, rather than trying to oppose the PRC where it is strong. Instead of trying to contend with the PLA in the entire Taiwan Strait, this strategy would draw an outer defense perimeter in the waters off Taiwan's western coast, about 100 kilometers out into the Strait. In this outer littoral, Taiwan would place sea mines and large surface ships equipped with anti-ship cruise missiles (which Taiwan does produce) that could destroy at least some of an approaching invasion force. The second phase of the defense would occur in the beach flats, which stretch out forty miles from dry land. Again, an array of mines, fast-attack boats, and shore-launched cruise missiles would degrade the invasion force. For such a campaign, the weaponry Taiwan needs is short-ranged and defensive, and much of it can be produced indigenously. Mines and missiles would also be useful in countering a blockade. In this regard, Taiwan's 2019 decision to purchase 108 M1A2 Abrams tanks (at a cost of approximately NT$66 billion) does not seem like a cost-effective way to strengthen shore defense, which is their most likely use in the defense against an amphibious invasion.

The Overall Defense Concept thus has a dual purpose: first, to increase the difficulty of a PLA invasion or blockade to such an extent that Beijing concludes that the risks are too high, and second, to give the U.S. military time to intervene in force through tactics such as the suppression of the PLA counter-intervention capabilities to complete the defense of the island (assuming a U.S. decision to intervene at all).

The U.S. government's support for this strategy was conveyed at a defense industry conference in October 2019 by David Helvey, principal deputy assistant secretary of defense for Indo-Pacific security affairs. Referring to the approval of the sale of Abrams tanks and F-16 fighters, he acknowledged the need for Taiwan to "recapitalize select elements of its legacy force structure." The fighters, he noted, would enhance deterrence in peacetime. But Helvey also spoke of the need to build out the Overall Defense Concept and ensure that Taiwan is "fielding a combat-credible force proficient in asymmetric warfare, force protection and littoral battle."[29] He emphasized the need to spend sufficient resources on the right things. He called for "a distributed, maneuverable, and decentralized force—large numbers of small things—that can operate in a degraded electromagnetic environment and under a barrage of missile and air attacks. . . . These include mobile coastal defense cruise missiles, short-range air defense, naval mines, small fast-attack craft, mobile artillery, and advanced surveillance assets."[30]

Speaking at the same conference was General Chang Guan-chung, Taiwan's vice minister for armaments. He echoed Helvey's emphasis on the Overall Defense Concept and the need to take advantage of the island's natural buffer zone. "We adopt innovative and asymmetric concepts," he said, "to focus our investment on systems that are mobile, hard to find, agile, cheap, numerous, survivable, and operationally effective."[31] Chang divided Taiwan's force buildup into conventional, asymmetric, and force protection categories. Despite Chang's endorsement of the Overall Defense Concept, the Pentagon is concerned that Taiwan's army, navy, and air force are too interested in acquiring advanced conventional capabilities such as tanks, F-35s, and indigenously produced submarines and that the cost of those systems will crowd out money for personnel, readiness, and training associated with building asymmetric capabilities—even though the cost of the U.S.-supplied platforms will be spread over several years.

At the 2020 iteration of the same defense industry conference, Helvey reiterated these priorities and added a couple of elements. First, concerning weaponry, he placed specific emphasis on "highly-mobile coastal defense cruise missiles" and revealed that the United States had "encouraged Taiwan to acquire as many as possible—both foreign and indigenously produced." Second, he stressed the importance of strengthening the reserve forces, which have suffered from neglect. Helvey then noted that reserve training would serve not just a military purpose but a political one as well; it would "show how the creativity, resourcefulness, the ingenuity and the patriotism of the Taiwan people can be catalyzed to signal that Taiwan and the very idea of Taiwan is something that's worth fighting for."[32]

At its core, the argument over defense strategy reflects several institutional weaknesses. The first is an imbalance in civil-military relations. Both before and long after 1949, when national security was the most salient policy issue, the armed forces were a dominant actor in the Kuomintang regime. Even after 1979, when the threat from the PRC declined somewhat, and despite the decline in its budget, the military continued to have substantial autonomy to define defense strategy or, more precisely, to treat strategy as a function of its procurement preferences rather than derive it from the threat. Since Chiang Ching-kuo's passing, moreover, Taiwan's presidents have not had expertise on national security and so had to defer to the military on matters of strategy.

Second, the policy formulation process is not integrated to the extent it usually has been in the United States. Because the military sought to preserve its monopoly over national security, it was always difficult to blend its view of defense and military strategies within the broader framework of national security. Philip Caruso, a fellow at the Carnegie Council for Ethics in International Affairs and a former U.S. Air Force officer, concludes that "while the need for such an asymmetric defense is obvious, the present political prospects of reforming the MND and enlisting public support are weak. The MND has adopted a stubbornly resistant institutional position. Criticism of the MND's approach has not resulted in major change, in part because these alterations require public discussion that would refute the MND's claims that its strategy and structure are already optimal."[33] Consequently, the United States has sometimes played an outsize role in Taiwan's deliberations over national security.

Polling on Defense Issues

Clearly, Taiwan's political and military leaders have a way to go in funding and implementing a defense strategy that is apposite to the threat the PLA poses. Getting strategy and resources right is both difficult and essential. Suboptimal performance will only increase Taiwan's vulnerability. One factor in securing sufficient funding will be the degree of public support for this priority. The best source of information on what the Taiwan public think regarding issues of war and peace is the Taiwan National Security Survey (TNSS), which is conducted by Emmerson Niou of Duke University, in collaboration with the Election Study Center of the National Chengchi University.[34]

On a fairly basic level, there are contradictions in the public's views. One is the gap between perceived will and capability. On the one hand, a majority of respondents believed that in the event of a mainland attack, regardless of the circumstances, the Taiwan people would "resist." Of those surveyed in 2016, 62.7 percent agreed with that statement. The percentage dropped to 52 percent in 2017 (the first full year that Tsai Ing-wen was president) but then rebounded to 61.6 percent by 2019. On the other hand—and quite startling— the public has serious doubts about the ability or capacity (*nengli*) of Taiwan's armed forces to defend the island. That was the view of 81.5 percent in 2016, 77.5 percent in 2017, and 69.6 percent in 2019. Part of the contradiction here is that it is not clear how civilians can resist a well-trained, well-supplied, modern army when, in their own estimation, Taiwan's military is weak.

Then there is the difference between what people want as a long-term outcome and what they expect. A large majority of respondents are strongly opposed to Beijing's ultimate political objective of unification. Only 2.2 percent of those polled in December 2017 wanted that outcome right away, and an additional 10.3 percent wanted it at an indefinite point in the future. However, respondents in the 2017 TNSS had serious doubts about avoiding the outcome they opposed. They indicated that the odds that unification would occur sometime in the future were about even.

Moving to more detailed defense issues, opinions display a realistic sense of caution. A significant share of those surveyed understood that independence is the third rail of cross-Strait relations. Generally, 49.4 percent of respondents believed in 2017 that the "independence-unification issue" could lead to war, and 50.5 percent agreed in 2019. Two particular findings demonstrate the sentiments surrounding independence and the threat of war: Presented a scenario in which Taiwan declared independence and Beijing did not attack, as high as 80 percent of those surveyed in 2011 and an average of 63.4 percent in the 2016, 2017, and 2019 surveys would opt for independence. But in a scenario in which declaring independence would spark a war, the share of those polled in 2016 who opposed independence grew to 57.1 percent, with only 30.9 percent supporting it. The ratio in subsequent years was also around two to one: 59.1 to 26.3 percent in 2017, and 60.3 to 29.8 in 2019. Moreover, almost half of respondents—41.3 percent in 2017 and 49.9 percent in 2019— agreed with the statement that independence would lead to war.

Clearly, restraint is the Taiwan mainstream's watchword on this key strategic question. The public would ideally prefer an independent Taiwan, but people know that they do not live in an ideal world. True, around 30 percent would still want independence even if it meant war, probably because they believe that Beijing's threats are only bluffs. But at least half of those who answered believe that Beijing is not bluffing and that independence is a clear red line for China and a trigger for war.

It is worth noting that the TNSS survey questions do not fully capture the ambiguity in Beijing's stated redlines. The third condition—that force would be justified if "possibilities for a peaceful reunification [had been] completely exhausted"—implies that Beijing might employ nonpeaceful means not because Taiwan leaders declare independence, but because they are unwilling to resolve the basic cross-Strait dispute through negotiations. Would a Taiwan refusal to even begin political talks, as Ma Ying-jeou did, justify the use of force as far as Beijing was concerned? Given these ambiguities, the Taiwan people should perhaps be even more cautious than they already are.

The Taiwan public has also come to understand that whether Washington will intervene in a cross-Strait conflict is a function of how war would begin—specifically, whether Taiwan provoked the fight in the first place. In both 2011 and 2019 surveys, three-fifths of the TNSS respondents believed that Washington would intervene if Taiwan maintained the status quo (defined as no declaration of independence) and China attacked anyway. But if a Taiwan declaration of independence triggered a PRC attack, the share expressing confidence in U.S. action declines, to 47.7 percent in 2016, 40.5 percent in 2018, and 48.5 percent in 2019. Even in the scenario in which Taiwan maintained the status quo, a full 40 percent either doubted U.S. intentions (24 percent) or did not respond (14.5 percent). However, 71.9 percent of those who gave an answer believe that the United States would intervene, while 28.1 percent do not.

Given respondents' lack of confidence in Taiwan's armed forces, the ambiguities in Beijing's red lines for the use of force, the modest Taiwan doubts about U.S. intervention, and the growing difficulties in carrying out an intervention, one might expect there would be strong support for strengthening the armed forces as a way to enhance deterrence against war. But according to the TNSS polls, only a minority—22.4 percent—favor an increase in military strength, while 66.8 percent prefer the adoption of "a more moderate policy," and 3.7 percent want both. When the MND highlighted the public's lack of "defense awareness" in its 2017 *Quadrennial Defense Review*, it knew whereof it spoke. Yet public doubts about the defense of the island, divisions concerning defense strategy, and the limits on the military budget only strengthen the hands of the adversary.

10

Taiwan's Political Defense: National Identity

Faced with a fraught security environment, Taiwan opinion is divided on how to respond. What is the proper mix of accommodation, reassurance, distancing, and balancing? Confronting a growing imbalance in the military power of the People's Republic of China (PRC), and even assuming a firm defense commitment by the United States, how do the Taiwan armed forces adequately deter an attack from the People's Liberation Army and then continue the fight until U.S. armed forces can intervene? Can Taiwan's leaders convince the public of the need to pay more in taxes to strengthen the armed forces? Can they allay public doubts about the military's capacity to mount a defense if deterrence fails? None of these questions are easy to answer under the circumstances, but they must be addressed seriously to enhance Taiwan's security. In developing a defense strategy to deter the PRC from using military means to achieve its political goal of unification, the recent trend in Taiwan's military establishment has been not to try to challenge the People's Liberation Army where it is strong and getting stronger but to confront it asymmetrically, to take advantage of its weaknesses.

Beginning in the 1990s, as Taiwan was making its transition to a democratic system, Taiwan's civilian leaders and the public at large have discussed and debated whether there is an asymmetric, *political* approach with which to challenge Beijing's unification objective. Taking that tack makes a certain amount of sense. The cross-Strait dispute is fundamentally political in character. Although it has a military dimension that cannot be ignored, Taiwan has tried to build political defenses, as well. The focus has been on Taiwan's identity as a nation and state, raising a number of questions. Are the island's people Chinese or Taiwanese? Are they some combination of both? Is there a Taiwan nation? What is the island's international legal status? What is its legal and political relationship with the state China? What should it be? Is Taiwan a state? Is it a Chinese state called the Republic of China (ROC), on a par with the PRC? Or is it just Taiwan?

From Beijing's perspective, there is only one set of answers to these questions: there is one Chinese state in the world, and most, but not all, countries recognize the PRC government is the sole legal representative of that China in the international community. In Beijing's view, the ROC government ceased to exist in 1949, and the territory that the Taiwan "authorities" control—Taiwan and its associated islands—is part of the sovereign territory of China. Residents of these islands are members of a Chinese nation. The cross-Strait dispute is the result of a long-running political confrontation and not a dispute over sovereignty and nationhood. Finally, the only basis for reconciling cross-Strait differences is the one country, two systems (1C2S) formula.

People on Taiwan reject some of these PRC points out of hand. Some people reject all of them. Many other issues are contested. That should be no surprise, given the island's political history of division between the Kuomintang (KMT) and the Democratic Progressive Party (DPP) and the long-term cross-Strait rivalry. That very disagreement limits the utility of devising political defenses in the first place. Internal divisions regarding identity and legal status have constrained the island's ability to act externally. Often, one faction's principled position is another's reckless provocation.

In addition to commanding broad public support, these political defenses must be clear and credible in substance. But history and cross-Strait mistrust are not the only reasons that Taiwan people and political parties cannot agree on these fundamental questions. Conceptual complexity also makes it harder to come to a shared understanding of what Taiwan is. Taiwan people, most of whom are not political scientists or lawyers by training, can be forgiven for conflating concepts that even analysts do not always keep distinct. Complicating matters even further is that while good data for Taiwan exist on some of these issues—especially national identity—there is less information on others. Yet Taiwan can no longer afford to make do with substantive ambiguity in coping with the PRC's demands for unification on the basis of 1C2S, as it has tried to do so far.

What is clear is that if new formulations on the issues of nation and state are to be effective defenses against Beijing, the failure to form a consensus on them may deepen insecurity rather than reduce it. It is therefore useful to explore in depth how questions of nation and state identity have been discussed and to inventory public views on those matters as much as possible.

Basic Concepts

This chapter addresses the issue of national identity; chapter 11 examines that of the state. We begin with a discussion of conceptual and historical background, recount the ways in which the authoritarian period shaped later attitudes, and examine the evolution of Taiwan identity during the democratic period. The concepts are identity, the nation, the state, sovereignty, and the melding of state and nation.

Identity

Identity is one way that individuals or groups of people specify who they are and how others define them. Identity refers to different aspects of social existence and the social roles that people fill. Consequently, one individual has multiple identities. I, Richard Bush, am a male Caucasian; a senior citizen; a husband, father, and grandfather; a member of the upper-middle class; a Ph.D.-holding China specialist; a citizen of the United States of America; a veteran; a registered Democrat; a taxpayer; an atheist; and so on. Some identities are ascriptive, things that I cannot change, such as my age cohort. Other identities are the result of my choices and efforts, for instance, that I am a China specialist with a Ph.D.

A key point here is that each individual's various identities are mutually compatible in some ways and conflict in other ways. Some people are able to manage their various identities and maintain some degree of balance among them. Others are not.

Also, individuals will rank their identities according to a perception of their relative importance. How one spends one's time each day and over time will be a function of that ranking. Moreover, people will change their rankings according to changes in circumstances and act accordingly. For example, the late sociologist G. William Skinner explored how the Chinese community in Thailand, which before the twentieth century was a collection of organizations based on different Chinese dialects and places of origin in

China, evolved to emphasize a common Chinese identity with organizations to match. The community created this greater ideational and institutional unity to defend against adverse Thai government policies.[1] Another example would be competition within and between political parties. I may have disagreements with my fellow Democrats about which policies and candidates our party should promote, but we are likely to close ranks vis-à-vis Republicans, at least on issues that divide people by party.

A signal development in the making of the modern world was the priority placed on national identity relative to other types. First in Europe and North America, then in Latin America, Asia, the Middle East, and Africa, people were encouraged to see themselves first and foremost as tied to a specific national territory and political unit—a nation.

The Nation

Regarding the nation, scholars have adopted essentially two viewpoints: essentialism (also termed primordialism) and instrumentalism. Essentialism has a longer history and argues that national identities form from a natural process where "certain 'givens' of social existence into which one is born determine one's group loyalties."[2] These ascriptive "givens" may include language, religion, culture, race, and history. Thus, leaders in Beijing stress the common ethnicity of people in the PRC and people in Taiwan as the basis for national unification.

The instrumental approach is different. Based on the ideas of Benedict Anderson, this approach views the nation is an "imagined political community, based on a set of national narratives and symbols."[3] That is, the nation is a product of social construction (to use social science jargon) and, more concretely, political struggle. Any group claiming to be a nation must contend with its rivals for ideational primacy. Canada, with its British and French colonial legacy, was once described as "two nations warring within the bosom of a single state."[4] The winner of these struggles imposes its own definition of the nation on everyone else, in a process that has "the effect of removing differences within the political community and replacing them with a common hegemonic order of signs, symbols, and values."[5]

For example, the United Kingdom resulted from English suppression of the separate identities of Wales and Scotland and the transformation of their peoples into Britons (Ireland was a totally different story).[6] In a separate example, Chinese national identity emerged and was shaped from a series of political struggles: against Western penetration in the nineteenth century, against the Qing (Manchu) dynasty in the late nineteenth and early twentieth centuries, against Japanese invaders and occupiers in the 1930s and 1940s, against the United States in the Korean War, and in the struggle between the KMT and the Chinese Communist Party (CCP) from the 1920s to the present.[7]

The State

The concept of the state has several manifestations. It can refer to a country's central political institutions, which govern within a defined territory. It can also refer to a country's status as a full, legitimate member of the international community. Thus the United Nations Charter says that membership is open to "peace-loving states which accept the obligations contained in the present Charter and, in the judgment of the Organization, are able and willing to carry out these obligations."[8]

In characterizing the state as a governing institution, Frances Fukuyama draws on German sociologist Max Weber to define the state as "a human community that [successfully] claims the monopoly of the legitimate use of force within a given territory." Fukuyama continues to say that "the essence of stateness is, in other words, *enforcement*: the ultimate ability to send someone with a uniform and a gun to force people to comply with the state's laws."[9] By extension, it is the ability of the tax collector to collect the revenue that the law requires, or of the official of a regulatory agency to get the entities it regulates to do what the rules require.

Once established, states, particularly modern states, build institutions to perform a variety of tasks. Examples include external and internal security; government finance; providing public goods such as the rule of law, establishment and enforcement of property rights, education of the young, recruitment of public officials, and regulation of economic and social life; limiting the ability of social groups to undermine the state through corruption; and so on. Each state will choose which tasks to perform and which to ignore. It may do some well and others badly. Moreover, Charles Tilley's insight concerning the history of Western Europe—that "war made the state and the state made war"—suggests that there may be a sequence in the performance of state tasks: for example, achieving internal and external security first and then moving on to economic development, rule of law, accountability, and so on.[10] Finally, Fukuyama usefully distinguishes between the scope of the state and its strength.[11] Scope refers to the tasks that the state undertakes. Strength pinpoints its capacity to implement and enforce the tasks that it chooses to fulfill.[12]

Sovereignty

Associated with the concept of the state is that of sovereignty, which parallels the different dimensions of the state. Stephen Krasner posits three elements of sovereignty. One is domestic sovereignty, which refers to "the authority structures within a given state and to their actual capacity." That is, it covers the same issues as the state qua domestic institutions. The second element is international legal sovereignty, which refers to "juridically independent territorial entities [that] merit recognition and with it such rights and privileges as membership in international organizations, . . . the ability to sign contracts or treaties with other states and entities, and so on." That sense of sovereignty refers to states as full-fledged members of the international system. The third element is what Krasner calls "Westphalian-cum-Vattelian sovereignty," meaning that within its own territory, "each state has the right to determine its own authority structures, which implies that states should avoid intervening in each other's internal affairs."[13] A similar definition equates sovereignty with independence, in the specific sense of "the fundamental authority of the state to exercise its authority without being subservient to any outside authority."[14]

State and Nation

The nation and the state combine together, but in different ways and in different circumstances, to form a two-fold concept. The common term for this combination is the nation-state. The order of the two words suggests that the nation precedes the state, which is then congruent with the nation. In some cases, the nation indeed begets the state. From this perspective, modern history is a story of how nations—in the sense of imagined communities—created, seized, or received a state that was aligned with them. Thus the Jewish nation, particularly its Zionist wing, decided in the nineteenth century that it needed a state. Not all Jews agreed, but beginning in the twentieth century, Zionists mounted a campaign for a Jewish homeland and then for the State of Israel itself.

Yet countries do not necessarily or precisely fit in this nation-to-state template. In nineteenth-century Europe, the Italian and German nations had already been imagined through language and culture, but it took the initiative of the state of Piedmont to create a unified Italy and the relentless effort of Otto von Bismarck's Prussia to bring about a united Germany. After World War I, Woodrow Wilson sought to use the Treaty of Versailles of 1919 to create states for national communities in Central and Eastern Europe that had previously been parts of old empires.

Moreover, as Brian McVeigh, a Japan specialist, notes, the idea that "a particular culture (nation) and bounded state (polity) should be congruent" is actually a myth, albeit a powerful one.[15] Indeed, much of modern history has actually seen the imperfect alignment of state and nation. Versailles allocated some Germans to Czechoslovakia and so gave Adolf Hitler a pretext to push to the brink of war in 1938. Many of the countries that emerged from post–World War II decolonization were congeries of different ethnic groups, which at times led to civil war and instances of large-scale violence, such as during the partition of India. Zionists secured a state for the Jewish people, but the Muslim Palestinians who resided in the territory of that state soon aspired to create their own nation-state at the expense of Israel.

There are also cases where state precedes nation, such as the United States. Harvard-based American historian Jill Lepore has argued that what was created in Philadelphia in 1787 was a state, and a federal state at that. The American nation did not yet exist, in part because people lacked a common ancestry, coming as they did from various ethnic backgrounds and because at least until the Civil War they regarded the subnational state in which they lived—for example, Virginia, Georgia—as their "country." Lepore writes, "The United States ... was a state before it became a nation," which was a process that took several decades.[16] State institutions later played a role in reinforcing American nationalism. One pillar of the state that inculcated a sense of belonging to the United States was the school system. Political parties also incorporated successive waves of immigrants of different ethnic backgrounds to participate in the democratic system to instill a common identity.

Singapore is another example. After its expulsion from Malaysia in 1965, it remained a strong unitary state, but the population it governed was composed of Chinese, Malays, Indians, and others. The state used the education system, housing policy, national service, and the ruling People's Action Party to build a sense of nationhood on a civic, rather than ethnic, basis.[17] Finally, China itself is an example. One might argue that although Chinese nationalism began to flourish among the politically conscious in the first half of the twentieth century and animated both the KMT and the CCP, it was only after the establishment of the PRC that the CCP was able to "nationalize" Chinese nationalism beyond the elite.

Application to Taiwan

These concepts are all related, but they should be kept distinct when being applied analytically. That is particularly true for Taiwan, where ambiguity and analytical conflation affect how Taiwan people think about Taiwan and how it relates to the PRC.

Unfortunately, the Chinese language almost guarantees that discussions of nation and state will be muddled. In a current Chinese-English dictionary, the Chinese word *guo* (國) is translated into English as "country, state, nation." The same is true for the word *guojia* (國家) and for *bang* (邦) and *bangguo* (邦國).[18] In the common-sense understanding of those Chinese words, they all refer to the same thing. For social scientists, however, only country and state are the same; nation is something different. Moreover, in Chinese, the word *minzu* (民族) is used to convey "people," "nation," "nationality," and "ethnic community." The term *minzu guojia* (民族國家) is rendered "nation state."[19] Then there is the tendency on both sides of the Strait to render complex concepts as expressions composed of four or eight Chinese characters, for example, "one China, different interpretations" (一個中國各自表述 or 一中各表). Adding even more to the language complications is the fairly common tendency among people in Taiwan to equate the word for China (中國) with the People's Republic of China.

Taiwan, Nation and State

Before the beginning of Japanese colonial rule on Taiwan in 1895, there were four principal social groups. The first was made up of groups of non-Han (as opposed to ethnic Chinese), indigenous tribes whose ancestors were present on the island thousands of years before, and each of which had their own identity and territory. The other three groups were Han people who began arriving in Taiwan in the seventeenth century. What distinguished them were the three places in southern China from which they came: Quanzhou and Zhangzhou prefectures, in Fujian province, and the Hakka areas of eastern Guangdong province.[20] For many years, there was social conflict among these four groups, divided against one another in different combinations. Finally, from the end of Japanese rule in 1945 through the defeat of the KMT regime on the mainland in 1949, around 2 million ethnic Chinese descended on Taiwan. They hailed from all over China and were associated with the ROC state, dominated by the KMT. They joined the approximately 6 million people who were already living in Taiwan in 1945. The long-time residents were labeled "native Taiwanese" (*benshengren*, people of this province), and the recent immigrants were termed mainlanders (*waishengren*, people of an outside province). For several decades after 1949, the mainlander-Taiwanese distinction became the most important for delineating in-groups and out-groups in defining the nation.[21]

The Evolution of the ROC State

Once the Nationalist regime escaped to Taiwan in 1949, it undertook a series of tasks in clear sequence.[22] The first was to ensure external defense, achieved as a result of the Korean War and the growing defense relationship with the United States, which forced the PRC to abandon any thought of invading Taiwan. The second priority was to restore even basic capacity of the KMT state, whose severe decay was on display in the predatory and violent way that Nationalist forces took over the island, alienating the Taiwanese population. Chiang Kai-shek authorized his son, Chiang Ching-kuo, to remedy many of the organizational problems in state institutions, including corruption and communist penetration.[23] The KMT regime also made efforts early on at social transformation through land reform and local elections and continuing the universal primary education begun by the Japanese. Yet as far as Chiang Kai-shek was concerned, these reforms were a means to achieve the illusory goal of "mainland recovery." Economic policy emphasized import substitution to help build the military, and much of the government budget still went to the armed forces. Strengthening national defense included the suppression of internal political dissent, on the grounds that the KMT was still at war.

The 1960s saw a significant shift in priorities that increased the scope and capacity of the ROC state. The ROC regime shifted its economic strategy from import substitution to export-led growth, based on the rationale that the KMT could best compete with the CCP by improving life on Taiwan. It created an economic technocracy to staff and direct the developmental state, and the Examination Yuan fostered a more talented and professional civil service.[24] Mainland recovery remained the stated goal, but gradually the national-security establishment shifted its mission from preparing for an attack on the mainland to defending Taiwan from a mainland attack. Politically, Chiang Ching-kuo undertook the co-optation of successful and loyal Taiwanese into the ROC system, thereby broadening the base of its still authoritarian rule.[25] Elections were now used not only to penetrate local society but also to monitor regime performance and to facilitate co-optation.

Elections also encouraged habits of political competition, the emergence of a proto-opposition party, and the demands for further democracy.[26] Still, the institutions for political participation and for checking the arbitrary exercise of state power were limited, at best.

On one issue, the KMT regime did not change. That was its rigid view that there was only one government of the state recognized internationally as China, and that government was the ROC. The government in Beijing asserted from 1949 on that the PRC was the sole government of China. When it came to diplomatic relations with other countries, those governments had to choose either the PRC or the ROC. Dual recognition with embassies in both Beijing and Taipei was not an option. But there was no justification in international law for such a zero-sum approach. Indeed, in the late 1950s and early 1960s, U.S. diplomats created a legal rationale for having both the PRC and the ROC represent China in the United Nations. They tried to convince Taipei that such an approach was in its interests, but to no avail.[27]

The ROC State and the Taiwanese Populace

For purposes of this chapter the most significant initiative of the ROC state during the authoritarian period was its effort to turn Taiwanese into good Chinese nationalists. When the KMT regime took control of Taiwan in the fall of 1945, only weeks after the end of World War II, there seemed to be no reason to doubt the loyalty of Taiwan people to the Chinese nation. Steven Phillips, of Towson State University, writes, "Publicly, most Taiwanese enthusiastically supported reunification under the Nationalist government. A mania for learning Mandarin Chinese . . . , the officially sanctioned dialect of the Nationalists, swept the island. Acceptance of Sun Zhongshan's [Sun Yatsen's] political ideology became an important symbol of loyalty to China and confidence in the future under Chiang Jieshi's [Chiang Kai-shek's] Nationalist government."[28] There was also hope among Taiwan people that the ROC state would grant this "model province" greater autonomy than that enjoyed by provinces on the mainland.

Yet the reality of KMT rule quickly destroyed any expectation that Taiwan's assimilation would be easy. Some of the abuses that the KMT inflicted on the Taiwan population and the desire for justice—and even vengeance— that they ultimately engendered have been noted (see chapter 6). Moreover, KMT leaders worried not only about political opposition from disgruntled Taiwanese but also doubted whether their new citizens were truly Chinese. Japan had ruled Taiwan from 1895 to 1945, fostering social and economic development and integrating Taiwanese into the Japanese empire to some extent. Crucially for the KMT, however, that same Japanese empire had carried out military aggression against China and had imposed a brutal occupation on most of the eastern part of the country. Chinese collaborators assisted the Japanese overlords. Meanwhile, on Taiwan, many young men were drafted into the Imperial Japanese Army. Not surprisingly, therefore, not a few officials in the KMT questioned the loyalty of the Taiwanese that they ruled from 1945 on.

Consequently, one goal of the ROC state was to instill in the minds of the Taiwanese public a strong identity with China after a half-century of separation. (A secondary purpose of this effort, as Christopher Hughes, of Warwick University, points out, was to mute the provincial differences that existed among the people who had come from the mainland in the 1940s, but the Taiwanese-mainlander distinction remained the most salient one politically.)[29] The KMT campaign to reshape Taiwanese consciousness occurred first through propaganda and the education system. Mandarin Chinese, or *Guoyu*, became the language of instruction in schools, even though Mandarin and the native dialects of most Taiwanese were mutually unintelligible. The history that students learned in schools was Chinese history, not Taiwan history; geography was mainland China's geography, not Taiwan's; and so on. Sun Yat-sen's Three Principles of the People was the only political program that could be discussed, and even then, within ideological boundaries. In addition, mandatory military service for young Taiwanese men was an opportunity for mainlander commissioned and noncommissioned officers to drive home the need for conscripts to be loyal to the ROC and the KMT regime.

Yet there was no effort to create one, integrated society. For example, Taipei, the "provisional" capital city, was divided into mainlander and Taiwanese residential areas, with significant educational and occupational segregation.[30] Ordinary citizens had to remember that the security services, charged with arresting people suspected of communist or Taiwan-independence sentiments, monitored their public behavior on a constant basis.[31] Fostering national identity was definitely a top-down, regime-led enterprise, with a state-to-nation dynamic at play.

Vestiges of the KMT regime's aggressive enforcement of a Chinese nationalist template on the Taiwanese population lingers to this day, and people live in something of a political time warp. The national anthem of the ROC is actually the KMT's party anthem (its first line is, "The Three Principles of the People are our party's objective"). The national emblem is the KMT's emblem. Sun Yat-sen is pictured on the New Taiwan $100 bill, and Chiang Kai-shek is on the $200 bill. For many years after 1949, years was rendered not according to the Western calendar but counting from the founding of the ROC. In this method, year one was 1912, the year that the ROC was founded. Thus 1975 was *Minguo 64 nian* (sixty-fourth year of the ROC).

National holidays that are not derived from traditional Chinese culture, such as the Mid-Autumn Festival, are linked to the KMT and its time in China. January 1 is the day the ROC was founded in 1912. Arbor Day is celebrated on March 12, the date that Sun Yat-sen, the founder of the KMT, died in 1925. Armed Forces Day is September 3 and celebrates Japan's surrender to the Pacific allies at the end of World War II. The ROC national day is October 10, which celebrates the start of the rebellion against the Qing (Manchu) dynasty in 1911, in which followers of Sun Yat-sen participated. Retrocession Day, October 25, was established by the KMT regime to celebrate the return of Taiwan to China after Japanese rule, according to its version of history. November 12 is Sun Yat-sen's birthday. Constitution Day celebrates the adoption of the ROC Constitution (and happens to be Christmas Day). The only holiday that really speaks to the Taiwanese experience is Peace Memorial Day, on February 28, established in 1995, which marks the beginning of the incident in 1947 that led to massive resistance against KMT abuses of power, resulting in widespread and indiscriminate killing of Taiwanese.

Even street names are reminders of the KMT and mainland China. As early as November 1945, the ROC state terminated the use of Japanese or traditional Chinese street names and ordered the adoption of names that were closely related to the KMT and to mainland China. Thus every town in Taiwan has a *Zhongshanlu*, a reference to Sun Yat-sen, and a *Zhongzhenglu*, a reference to Chiang Kai-shek. There are streets named after Sun's Three Principles of the People (for example, People's Livelihood Road, *Minshenglu*). Moreover, by the early 1950s, many Taipei streets were named after places across the Taiwan Strait, with the names in each quadrant of the city replicating places in the appropriate quadrant of the Chinese map.[32] The state's political message was clear: we are part of China.

But the campaign to socialize the Taiwanese populace into a conservative Chinese identity largely failed. The late Alan Wachman summed up the effect of the ROC state's early policies. They "directly and indirectly reinforced distinctions between Mainlanders and Taiwanese in a way that undermined the party's goal of social integration. These institutionalized manners of distinction have contributed to the emergence and sustenance of Taiwanese identity. . . . Surely, by viewing the Taiwanese as a group that needed to be assimilated forcibly, the KMT inadvertently nourished the Taiwanese sense of distinctiveness that was the seed of the Taiwan independence movement." It also would later foster widespread opposition to unification.[33]

How widespread or how deeply felt the underground construction of this Taiwan national identity was within the island's population is not known. Certainly, some chose to regard themselves as Taiwanese after their experiences at the hands of a repressive regime that sought to impose a Chinese identity. Others concluded that accommodating overtly to the regime's definition of the correct national identity was a reasonable price to pay to protect one's family and to promote the state's economic well-being, at least as long as doing so increased one's personal security. What is known is that democratization freed people to reveal thoughts they had previously kept hidden out for fear.

The early surveys that the Election Study Center (ESC) of National Chengchi University conducted about national identity provide some evidence of the limited impact of the KMT policies. In 1992 elections for the Legislative Yuan were first conducted on a popular basis on Taiwan, as well as the first identity poll by ESC. In that year, only 25.5 percent of those surveyed said they were Chinese. Many of these people were probably the mainlanders who come to Taiwan in the late 1940s, about 15 percent of the population. Of the remainder, 46.4 percent said they were both Chinese and Taiwanese, while only 17.6 percent dared to say they were Taiwanese. Five years later, the share who said they were Chinese had dropped to 5.3 percent, and the share who said they were Taiwanese had risen to 34 percent. The "both" category had dropped to 41.4 percent. Clearly, the KMT campaign of Sinification had failed, and a resilient Taiwanese identity emerged in spite of the prior state-to-nation effort.

As the sense of being at least both Taiwanese and Chinese naturally grew, some political leaders played up Taiwanese consciousness in election campaigns and policy formation. Thus Lee Teng-hui spoke in 1994 about "the sorrow of being born a Taiwanese," and Chen Shui-bian called himself "a son of Taiwan."[34] There were also efforts to mute the differences between the two sides for the sake of national unity. The most intriguing was a theme that was developed first by Peng Ming-min, a senior DPP leader who favored independence, and later by Lee Teng-hui. This drew on the ideas of Ernest Renan in his *What Is a Nation?* The nation is defined not by ethnicity or language but by a people's strong belief that they are "a community of shared destiny" (*mingyun gongtongti*). Lee drew on the concept of a "living community" (*shengming gongtongti; gemeinschaft,* in Lee's translation).[35] Lee even anointed Ma Ying-jeou as a "new Taiwanese" in 1998. The actions of the PRC also had an impact on the emerging balance of identities. Its threats to Taiwan security (such as the People's Liberation Army military exercises) or perceived offenses to the sense of dignity of its citizens (such as inducing the countries with which the ROC had diplomatic relations to switch to the PRC) strengthened the belief that Taiwan was different from the PRC, whether the threat perceived or the offense taken was justified or not.[36] After 2008, as mainland tourists began to flood Taiwan, people on the island quickly observed that the visitors were loud and sometimes boorish. The two sides of the Strait were two different societies.[37]

Identity Today

The ESC's survey on identity asks this question: "In our society, some people say they are Taiwanese (*Taiwanren*; 台灣人), some say they are Chinese (*Zhongguoren*; 中國人), and yet others say they are both (*doushi*; 都是). Do you think you are Taiwanese, Chinese, or both?" Figure 10-1 maps the responses. The main trend is the gradual climb of identification as Taiwanese only, the fall of Chinese identity to a low level, and a middling variation claiming both. By 2009 a stable balance of identities had emerged. The Chinese share was stuck at under 5 percent. Taiwanese identification was dominant and ranged between 50 and 60 percent. The "both Taiwanese and Chinese" category varied from 30 and 40 percent. Combined, these latter two responses constituted a consistent share of about 90 percent. (In this process of identity evolution, the old distinction between mainlanders and Taiwanese lost its political salience.)[38]

Also worth noting are differences according to age group, education, and occupation. Table 10-1 presents findings on these categories, drawn from the 2017 survey of the Taiwan Election and Democratization Study. Respondents under forty years of age were most associated with the "Taiwanese only" category, followed by those sixty and over. Respondents in their fifties also identified predominantly as Taiwanese, but at a lower rate. The share of those in their forties who identified as both Chinese and Taiwanese exceeded the share who said they were Taiwanese only. Identification as Chinese only was low across the board but especially with those under thirty.[39]

Regarding education, those who went no further than primary school were the most strongly identified as Taiwanese only (69.1 percent), and those who had graduated from a technical college were the least (46.7 percent). Generally, the more educated people were, the more likely they were to pick a dual identity. Again, fewer than 5 percent said they were Chinese only.

FIGURE 10-1. **Taiwanese/Chinese Identity, Taiwan, 1992–2020**

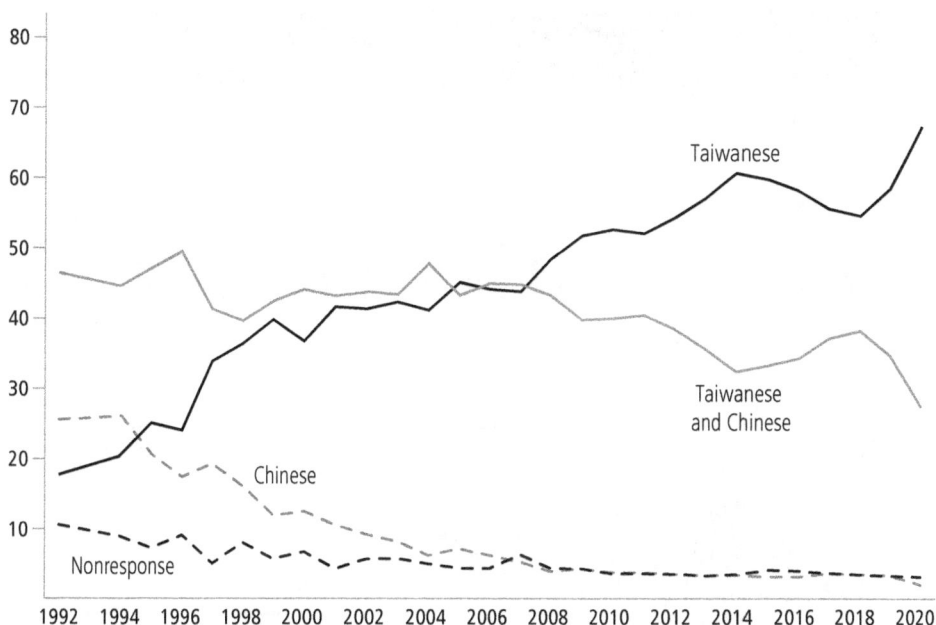

Source: Election Study Center, National Chengchi University (https://esc.nccu.edu.tw/course/news.php?Sn=166).

Regarding occupation, students were the clear outliers. Among the college students surveyed, 72.9 percent regarded themselves as Taiwanese only, compared with 49.9 percent of white-collar workers, 56.8 percent of blue-collar workers, and 53.5 percent of retired people. Only 27.1 percent of students defined themselves as both Taiwanese and Chinese, but in each of the other groups, 37 to 42 percent picked a dual identity. No student respondents said they were Chinese only, while 6.3 percent of retirees said they were, and the share for both white- and blue-collar workers was less than 5 percent.

Shelley Rigger of Davidson College provides greater precision to generational analysis. She differentiates the political generations of the native Taiwanese based on their respective experiences after they came to political consciousness and the views they formed as a result. The first and second generations came of political age during the Japanese and authoritarian periods, respectively. The third and fourth did so from the mid-1980s, when both economic engagement with the PRC and the democratic transition began.

TABLE 10-1. **Differences on Identity: Age Group, Education, and Occupation**

Category	Taiwanese only	Chinese and Taiwanese	Chinese only
Age group			
20–29 years	70.0	27.1	1.0
30–39 years	65.9	30.1	1.2
40–49 years	44.2	48.8	2.9
50–59 years	48.1	40.6	5.0
60 years and older	56.3	32.4	5.2
Education			
Primary and below	69.1	18.5	3.9
Junior high school	58.2	34.2	1.9
High school or vocational	55.9	36.9	3.2
Technical college	46.7	45.4	4.8
University and above	56.6	46.9	3.2
Occupation			
White collar	49.9	42.0	4.1
Blue collar	56.8	38.0	2.1
Student	72.9	27.1	0.0
Retired	53.5	37.0	6.3

Source: "Taiwan Telephone and Mobile Phone Interview Survey of Presidential Satisfaction—The Twenty-Second Wave," Taiwan's Election and Democratization Study, National Chengchi University, survey conducted December 2017 (http://teds.nccu.edu.tw/main.php).

The fifth generation was born after 1982 and came of age in the early years of this century, after the first transition of power from the KMT and the DPP. Rigger draws a sharp contrast between the second and fifth generations:

> Taiwanese who came of age in authoritarian Taiwan were forced to choose between identifying with Taiwan or with China. "Gen Fivers" have never been asked to make that choice. For them, identifying with Taiwanese is natural. But so too is engaging with China. For their second-generation grandparents, "China"—the China within Taiwan

[that is, the KMT regime before democratization] even more than the China on the other side of the Strait—was a cauldron of confusion and regret, hope and humiliation, anger and fear. To the "Gen Fivers," China is just a nearby country that offers both opportunities and risks, ones they are free to explore from the secure platform of Taiwan, their home.[40]

The first political generation shares the anti-KMT and anti-PRC views of the second. The third and fourth generations share the pragmatism concerning mainland China that "Gen Fivers" exhibit.

For several reasons, however, there is a limit to how much can be read into these figures. First of all, the basic terms used in the survey were not defined, and respondents were left to interpret the question for themselves. Particularly ambiguous is the category "both Taiwanese and Chinese." It could mean Chinese ethnically and Taiwanese in every other respect. It could mean Chinese ethnically, socially, and culturally but Taiwanese when it comes to politics. It could mean Taiwanese by virtue of residence and Chinese for everything else. Note also that the terms for Taiwanese and Chinese (literally, "Taiwan person" and "Chinese person") put Taiwan and the PRC on a par but leave that par undefined. Does it refer to geographic entities or political ones?[41] Moreover, putting *Taiwanese* first in the question's list of choices may bias the result. So too may be the fact that many in Taiwan associate the word *Chinese* with the People's Republic of China and everything associated with that regime. Yet "China" and "Chinese" can be conceived culturally without reference to one state or the other. These definitional problems obscure what exactly is being measured in the ESC poll.

Compounding the ambiguity, the "Taiwanese only" and "both Taiwanese and Chinese" figures vary somewhat according to circumstances. Thus "Taiwanese only" peaked at 68.6 percent in 2014, when public criticism of the Ma administration's policy of economic engagement with Beijing reached its height, but then dropped after President Tsai took office and Beijing took a number of actions to punish and pressure her administration. At that point, the "both" share rose somewhat and the "Taiwanese only" share declined commensurately. What is significant, however, is that the combination of percentage shares for "Taiwanese only" and "both" has remained stable in the low 90s since 2009.

To gain a more nuanced sense of how respondents viewed these categories, Harvard political scientist Alastair Iain Johnston and Dartmouth professor George Yin employed a different methodology. Using the survey platform of the *Meilidao Dianzibao* (usually translated as *Formosa Magazine*), they asked respondents to allocate ten points across the three options. Assigning all ten points to Taiwanese identity meant exclusively Taiwanese, while assigning all ten points to Chinese identity signified the opposite.

About 53 percent of respondents allocated points to both Taiwanese and Chinese identities. This was around twenty points higher than the same category in the ESC surveys in recent years. Of these 53 percent, around 50 percent identified themselves as evenly Taiwanese and Chinese (allocating five points each to both identities). Only about 47 percent of those surveyed identified themselves as exclusively Taiwanese (that is, they did not allocate any points to being Chinese), which is around ten points lower than recent results in the ESC polls. For those who identified with both nationalities, the average number of points allocated to their Taiwanese identity was around six, and the average number of points allocated to their Chinese identity was around four. Only 2.3 percent allocated ten points to the Chinese category.

In short, the sense of being both Chinese and Taiwanese may be stronger than what the results of the ESC polls would suggest, particularly relative to the "Taiwanese only" category. Yet again, the *Formosa Magazine* poll leaves it up to respondents to define the terms, which creates uncertainty about what their responses mean. Moreover, this approach has been applied only once, so it is not possible to get a sense of evolution over time.[42]

Three surveys in the 2010s explored views on the cultural and ethnic dimensions of Chineseness and Taiwaneseness. The first was led by Zheng Sufen of the ESC at National Chengchi University, where surveys were conducted in 2013, 2014, 2017, and 2018. It posed an either-or question: Is Taiwan culture (*Taiwan wenhua,* 台灣文化) the same as Chinese culture (*Zhonghua wenhua,* 中華文化) or not? The responses are summarized in table 10-2.[43]

TABLE 10-2. **Is Taiwan Culture the Same as Chinese Culture? (Percent)**

	2013	2014	2017	2018
Identical/the same	45.1	41.5	53.1	53.0
Not the same	45.4	36.9	39.5	40.7
No response	9.6	11.9	7.4	6.2

Source: Zheng Sufen, "Jiexi 'Taiwanren/Zhongguoren' renting de chixu yubianyi" [Analyzing continuity and change in "Taiwanese/Chinese" identity], paper presented at the "Symposium on Taiwan's Democratization and Free Elections" at the Election Study Center of National Chengchi University, Taipei, Taiwan, May 25, 2019.

Around half of those surveyed believed that the two cultures were the same. Moreover, there is a modest inverse correlation between views on the identity of the two cultures and the policies of the party in power. That is, the sense of sameness of both cultures was lower in the last years of the Ma administration, which had engaged the PRC, and higher during the Tsai administration, which Beijing opposed.

The second survey that investigated cultural and ethnic dimensions of identity in Taiwan was conducted in 2013 by the Taiwan Election and Democratization Study. Instead of posing a forced choice, it asked a question that offered a range of possible answers concerning Chinese and Taiwanese culture. Among respondents, 5.3 percent said the two cultures were completely the same, 47.6 percent said they were mostly the same, 3.4 percent said they were "half and half," 26 percent answered that they were only a little the same, and 11.7 percent denied any similarity at all.[44]

The third survey was conceived by Yang Zhong of Jiaotong University in Shanghai and conducted by the Taiwan Indicators Survey in 2014. It had a somewhat different focus, that is, membership in the "Chinese nation" from the perspective of "blood and culture." The term it used for "the Chinese nation" was *Zhonghua minzu* (中華民族), where *Zhonghua* refers to China in a cultural sense and *minzu* can be translated as "nation" but also as "people" and "ethnic community." In the poll, 53.8 percent of Taiwanese surveyed claimed membership in *Zhonghua minzu*, 3.2 percent just said they were Chinese, 25.2 percent said they were both, and 11.0 said they were neither. Combining the first three categories, Yang concludes that "the majority of Taiwanese people do not reject their Chinese ethno-cultural identity."[45]

In contrast, committed Taiwan nationalists who stress essentialist or primordial factors point to evidence that contemporary native Taiwanese incorporate in their DNA the genes of the indigenous people who lived on the plains of the western side of the island and intermarried with settlers from China beginning around the seventeenth century. For them, Taiwanese are ethnically different from Chinese and therefore embody a separate nation (even though some of the descendants of those indigenous tribes oppose that political use of their genetic heritage).[46]

In the Zheng and Taiwan Election and Democratization Study polls, therefore, a bare or clear majority believed that Chinese and Taiwanese cultures were the same or quite similar. The Yang Zhong survey showed that 80 percent of respondents associated themselves with Chinese ethnicity and culture. All three polls are consistent with the Johnston-Yin findings on the greater strength of a dual identity. The strength of an exclusive identification with Taiwan depends very much on how the question is asked and how respondents interpret terms such as *Taiwanese, Chinese,* and *both.*

The precise contours of political identity on Taiwan are at least confused, if not contested. That a great majority of the Taiwan public identifies at least partially with Taiwan can serve as a shield to fend off Beijing's unification goal and foster a sense of resentment about some PRC policies regarding the island. But the significant share that has a personal sense of being Chinese creates a barrier against independence. It is clear what Taiwan people are against, but it is far from certain what they are for. Dual identity seems to be the default stance, but it is inherently ambiguous. Is it possible to reduce that ambiguity? Is there another basis for defining what it means to be Taiwanese besides the usual polling questions? What is more certain is that the creation of a more common, shared sense of who the island's people are will help their leaders better address the challenge that the PRC poses.

National Narratives and Symbols

Taiwan has competing narratives on its society's past, present, and future. If Taiwan is to be, as Anderson envisions, a strong, effective imagined political community, do its people share a dominant, widely shared narrative? The answer to that question, at least for an outsider, seems to be "not really." There are debates about how much Taiwan and its people are part of Chinese history and culture. Taiwanese nationalists claim that there is a distinctive ethnicity, while their opponents assert that the Taiwan people and their culture are, at best, a regional variant of Chinese ethnicity, specifically southern Fujian and eastern Guangdong provinces. Is the island's folk culture to be interpreted as Chinese culture with Taiwanese characteristics or Taiwanese culture with Chinese characteristics?[47] Is the folk religion one sees in Taiwan more Taiwanese or more Chinese?[48]

Similar differences appeared in school curriculum after democratization. During Lee Teng-hui's time in office and during DPP administrations since, textbooks were revised to place greater emphasis on Taiwan and reduce the focus on mainland China. During the Ma administration there was a move back to a more China flavor.[49] Each political camp objects to the textbook changes of the other. For example, the high-school history curriculum developed by the Tsai administration provoked KMT ire by including the view that Taiwan had legally not been returned to China after World War II and that its status was thus "undetermined," which was contrary to the traditional view of the KMT.[50]

As this example suggests, on the question of Taiwan's history, the answers often reflect somewhat the political views of the historian. Toward one end of the spectrum is Su Beng, a Marxist and Taiwanese nationalist who lived for much of his adult life in Japan. There he devoted himself to studying and recounting Taiwan's history from the seventeenth century on from a more Taiwanese point of view.[51] In his telling, the Taiwanese people were predominantly of "mixed Han lineage," joined by a small number of mixed Malayo-Polynesian aborigines. For him, what constructed Taiwanese nationality was the experience of living under the colonial rule of a succession of outside overlords: the Dutch, Ming loyalists led by Zheng Chenggong, the Qing dynasty, imperial Japan, and Chiang's KMT. These periods of domination were characterized by rule by foreign regimes and class exploitation by external economic forces. Taiwanese, writes Su, engaged in 400 years of struggle against colonialism and, as a result, "developed the unique economic, social, and psychological character of Taiwanese society."[52]

Similarly, there is a tendency in the DPP and the broader Green camp to regard Taiwan's history as one of victimhood. This theme of the "sorrow of being Taiwanese" also frequently appears often in the pages of the *Taipei Times*, the newspaper that often reflects the views of the most pro-Taiwanese people on the island. Extracts from two of the paper's editorials exemplify their understanding of the past:

> [Chiang Kai-shek] then occupied Taiwan and included it in Chinese territory. In doing so, he completely ignored the will of Taiwanese and deprived them of their right to choose to establish their own nation after the war, as countries in the region established their independence one after another. . . . Chiang ruled Taiwan as a despot and based on a "Greater China" attitude. . . . The result is that Taiwan to this day continues to lack the normal status of a regular nation, while it remains under the shadow of Chinese threat. Chiang was not the protector of Taiwan; he was guilty of bringing disaster to all Taiwanese.[53]

> After the end of World War II, the Sino-centric policies that were imposed on Taiwan [by the KMT] resulted in the removal of Taiwanese elements from Taiwan's social development. Whether it was culture, the arts or fashion, anything Taiwanese was looked down upon, while everything Chinese was praised. Sino-centrism was incorporated into

the educational system beginning from elementary school and was pervasive in subjects such as history, geography and language. It was as if a Chinese chip was implanted in every student's brain. The nation's people, history, geography and other aspects of Taiwanese identity were disdained and marginalized.[54]

The implication of assertions that the Taiwan people were victims of domination by outsiders is that they had been denied their own nation.

On the Blue side of the spectrum, the traditional view has been that people in Taiwan are part of the larger Chinese nation. When former vice president Lien Chan spoke at Peking University in May 2005, he referred to "23 million Taiwan compatriots and 1.3 billion mainland compatriots" (that is, members of the same nation). For him, what divided the two sides of the Taiwan Strait was "civil war thinking" and the legacy it created, and he urged the two sides to work for the "people's welfare . . . and the interests of the future of *the nation*, based on mutual goodwill and trust."[55] Chang Ya-chung, a professor at National Taiwan University, has a similar view of what is and is not the source of cross-Strait division. He writes, "Both sides see the reality of separate political rule, but also agree that they are both a part of and represent the Chinese people." This is to say that their separation is only one of governance, and that, from a nationalistic perspective, they are part of the same "family."[56] Many Taiwanese, including those who acknowledge a common ethnicity with people in the PRC in mainland China, would not accept the idea that they are part of the same nation or "family."

Taiwan politicians do not have the luxury of adopting one or the other of these mutually exclusive narratives. To do so would alienate those who believe in the opposite one. Instead, some have sought to formulate and propagate a more inclusive understanding of where the people of Taiwan have been and where they are going. That requires winning over skeptics.

One attempt came from Chen Shui-bian to balance or diffuse the Taiwanese nationalism that was normally his forte. In his second inaugural address in May 2004, he played out the theme of Taiwan as an immigrant society:

> It was several hundred years ago that the generations before us traversed the "Black-water Channel" [Taiwan Strait] or crossed the great ocean to find a safe haven in Taiwan. No matter what year they arrived, regardless of their ancestral origins and their mother tongues, and despite their different hopes and dreams, all are our forefathers. All settled down here and together faced a common destiny. Whether they be

indigenous peoples or "new settlers" [Han people], expatriates, foreign spouses or immigrant workers who labor under Taiwan's blazing sun—all have made a unique contribution to this land and each has become an indispensable member of our family known as "New Taiwan." Because of their disparate histories and distinctive cultures, different ethnic groups understandably hold divergent views and values. Recognizing such inherent differences, we should embrace one another with more tolerance and understanding.[57]

Chen's theme of Taiwan as a nation of immigrants gained no traction, in part because creating mutual tolerance is a long-term process and in part because his subsequent deeds did nothing to encourage "understanding" on the part of the mainlanders to whom he was presumably appealing. When Ma Ying-jeou became president in 2008, he faced a different challenge: reassuring people outside of the KMT that he himself was not an outsider, despite the fact that his family came from mainland China and he was born in Hong Kong. At least rhetorically, he made a good case in his first inaugural address, giving Taiwan credit for his own personal success and for the revival of a defeated ROC:

> Taiwan is not my birthplace, but it is where I was raised and the resting place of my family. I am forever grateful to [Taiwan] society for accepting and nurturing this post-war immigrant. I will protect Taiwan with all my heart and resolutely move forward. . . . The Republic of China was reborn on Taiwan. . . . This democratic republic, the very first in Asia, spent a short 38 years on the Chinese mainland, but has spent nearly 60 years in Taiwan. During these last six decades, the destinies of the Republic of China and Taiwan have been closely intertwined. Together, the two have experienced times good and bad. On the jagged path toward democracy, the ROC has made great strides. Dr. Sun Yat-sen's dream for a constitutional democracy was not realized on the Chinese mainland, but today it has taken root, blossomed and borne fruit in Taiwan.[58]

Ma was also careful not to state explicitly, as Lien Chan had, that the people on the two sides of the Strait were all part of the Chinese nation. Instead, he spoke of their "common Chinese ethnic heritage" and noted that they shared "common blood lines, history and culture."[59]

Johnny Chiang Chi-chen, who was a generation younger than Ma, became chairman of the KMT in March 2020 and offered a personal narrative similar to Ma's. However, he fully exploited the ambiguity surrounding Taiwan, asserting that he was both Taiwanese and Chinese. "I was born and raised in Taiwan. [Therefore] I am Taiwanese.... From the perspective of blood origin, culture and history, I am also Chinese.... On the basis of the Constitution of the ROC, I am an ROC national."[60]

When Tsai Ing-wen became president in 2016, she did not dwell on issues of ethnicity or historical background. In her inaugural addresses in both 2016 and 2020 she spoke of "the Taiwanese people" or "the people of Taiwan," but did not politicize the terms. She pledged that her administration would be guided by the ROC Constitution and legislation that suggested that Taiwan was a part of China (see chapter 8). But Tsai adopted a new approach to the question of identity and unity, and that was to emphasize Taiwan's democratic system and what some have termed "civic nationalism."[61] This approach to identity came through clearest in a talk she gave to the Copenhagen Democracy Summit in June 2020. In the 2020 elections, she said, "the Taiwanese people chose democracy as our common denominator. Democracy is in our DNA. It is what makes us Taiwanese.... National identity does not necessarily flow from ethnic, religious, or social background. It can be founded on the belief and attachment to the democratic system itself.... Taiwan is one of the important examples of this phenomenon."[62]

Ma Ying-jeou also highlighted the importance of Taiwan's democratic system. In his second inaugural address, he said,

> We are a family and Taiwan is home to us all. We strongly believe that no matter what political differences there may be between the ruling and opposition parties, we are still one family. Despite the many difficulties over the past several years between the ruling and opposition parties, I believe we share a common commitment to democracy. On this foundation, we can surely seek consensus and work together to solve problems.

Treating democracy as Taiwan's primary basis of political identity is certainly plausible. The system is a source of pride within the ethnic Chinese world and is the reason for other democracies to support Taiwan. That the public strongly opposes unification on Beijing's terms and that constitutional procedures must be followed to bring about significant political and legal change creates real limits on the island's leaders in their conduct of cross-Strait relations. That the people of Taiwan elect leaders and the people of the PRC do not further legitimize Taiwan's negotiating position. There is no ambiguity about Taiwan's democratic system, whereas the focus on Taiwanese, Chinese, and dual identity is beset by problems of definition and measurement.

Yet for Taiwan to base its identity on its political system also has its limitations. Tsai Ing-wen and Ma Ying-jeou take very different positions on substantive policy issues. That is understandable, because democracy is a system that actually encourages conflict, even as it hopes to facilitate political outcomes that enjoy political legitimacy, because the leaders who formulate those outcomes are selected by the people. Yet there is no guarantee that a popularly elected government will be an effective government, and that the legitimizing norms and procedures of elections, legislatures, and judiciaries will not themselves become the objects of political combat. Even if leaders agree on the importance of democracy in principle, as Ma Ying-jeou and Tsai Ing-wen do, that does not mean that they will agree on the fundamentals of policy, which they do not, however beneficial that would be.[63]

Disagreements over identity, historical narratives, and political symbols all attest to the continuing conflict over what Taiwan is and the degree to which it should be the touchstone of political identity. Since the early 1990s, the content of Taiwan's "imagined community" has been up for grabs, and it is not yet settled. These disagreements constitute obstacles to the construction of a single, dominant national narrative. To mute this conflict, there appear to be two options. One is to continue the struggle within Taiwan between the two political camps until one is the clear victor. Each side would stress what divides them concerning issues of nationhood and attempt to establish dominance over the other. Many in the DPP would continue to assert a narrative of victimhood, focus on what the KMT and the PRC have in common, and even accuse the KMT of doing the PRC's dirty work. The KMT would warn about the DPP's purported goal of separatism and the damage that would be done by denying the Chinese content of Taiwan society. The other option would be for the two camps to stress what they have in common, such as a shared success in building a prosperous society and a democratic system, plus a common understanding of the challenge that the PRC poses. The former would be politics as usual. The latter would require a commitment to convergence.

11

Taiwan's Political Defense: The State

As Taiwan's domestic institutions evolved from an authoritarian regime to full democracy, and as views about national identity were debated, there was a parallel struggle, both within the island's political system and between Taipei and the People's Republic of China (PRC) regime, over Taiwan's legal status. This was a complicated process, which I recount in excruciating detail through 2004 in my book *Untying the Knot*.[1] It was complex partly because the issues involved were not simple and partly because the definition of "Taiwan" was quickly becoming politicized. The key point of difference between Beijing and Taipei was whether Taiwan was a sovereign entity (or state) for purposes of clarifying its international role and in any negotiations on political issues with the mainland. How Beijing interpreted Taipei's claim that it was a sovereign entity was also a factor. Within Taiwan, the issue was whether the Democratic Progressive Party (DPP) would advocate de jure independence to create a state for its imagined Taiwan community or take a more flexible position that aligned it closer to the Kuomintang (KMT).

The PRC's own unification proposal increased the salience of this issue. From the beginning, the Taipei government rejected how Beijing had grouped Taiwan with Hong Kong and Macau as the targets of the one country, two systems (1C2S) proposal. From Taiwan's perspective, Hong Kong and Macau had been colonies and not sovereign entities, whereas the Republic of China

210

(the official name of the Taiwan government) had existed since 1912 and had been a World War II ally against Japan and a founding member of the United Nations. But under 1C2S, Taiwan would merely be a special administrative region of the PRC. It would possess autonomy and not be ruled as Beijing ruled regular provinces. But autonomy was not the same as sovereignty. As far as Beijing leaders were concerned, the PRC was a unitary state, in which the central government was the sole sovereign. The powers that any subordinate units possessed, whether provinces, autonomous regions, or special administrative regions, were delegated from the center.

Taiwan officials from both the KMT and DPP administrations consistently stress Taiwan's sovereignty, although in not precisely the same way. An oft-stated formulation of Republic of China (ROC) officials is that, according to the conventional translation, "The ROC/Taiwan is an independent sovereign state" (*Zhonghua Minguo/Taiwan shi yige zhuquan duli de guojia*). In September 2008, President Ma Ying-jeou told a reporter from Mexico that Taiwan's dispute with Beijing was over sovereignty, but that the time was not right to try and solve it.[2] Beijing objects to this Taiwan view, as, for example, President Xi Jinping did in January 2019, when he blamed "long-standing political differences between the two sides of the Strait," a result of the late-1940s civil war, for the lack of progress on cross-Strait relations.[3] By implication, differences over sovereignty were not to blame. It is striking that Ma Ying-jeou himself, who sought to improve cross-Strait relations wherever he could, would directly challenge the PRC view that the dispute was over political differences. That places in sharp relief the importance of sovereignty to Taiwan, regardless of party.

Some elaboration on the phrase "independent sovereign state" is required. At least when used by KMT spokespersons, this formulation does not assert that the ROC or Taiwan is an independent country with no political or legal connection to China. A more precise translation would be "the ROC is a country whose sovereignty is independently derived." The idea here is that the ROC is not subordinate to any higher authority and certainly not to the PRC, a meaning that is similar to what Stephen Krasner calls "Westphalian-cum-Vattelian sovereignty" (see chapter 10).[4] Moreover, this is not a recent formulation. Its earliest use (at least that I have found) occurred in a statement by Chiang Kai-shek at the time the ROC was forced to leave the UN (and Chiang was certainly no advocate of independence).[5] In fact, the statement is made most regularly to challenge the restrictions on Taiwan's participation in the international community, a subject on which Taiwan people have a right to complain.

But the formulation serves an internal political purpose as well as an external one. In the mid-1990s, when the DPP had emerged as Taiwan's principal opposition party, it was associated with the goal of de jure independence. The KMT under Lee Teng-hui saw a need to dilute public support for the DPP and its objective. So they engaged in a verbal sleight of hand by using this formulation, arguing that because the ROC was already an independent sovereign state, it did not need to declare independence. Later, the moderate wing of the DPP was able to use a version of the formulation to deflect demands from the Deep Green wing that it do more to promote real independence. Beijing appears to have understood the political games that were being played, because it has never made a big issue of the formulation.

The Taiwan public certainly endorses the assertion that the ROC or Taiwan is a sovereign state. The Taiwan National Security Survey asked respondents whether they agreed with the view statement, "Taiwan is an independent sovereign state whose current name is the Republic of China and so does not need to declare independence." In three different surveys, summarized in table 11-1, more than 60 percent of those polled agreed with the proposition to some extent.[6] How well they understand the proposition, though, is not certain.

Yet Taiwan has been at a distinct disadvantage in claiming that it was a sovereign entity for purposes of its international role. The PRC has long campaigned to restrict its formal participation in the international system, either as a member of international organizations or through establishing diplomatic relations with other countries. The ROC had been a founding member of the United Nations and in the 1950s had diplomatic relations with a majority of the existing countries in the world. But its dominance vis-à-vis the PRC changed in the 1960s, as African colonies became independent and tended

TABLE 11-1. **Is Taiwan an Independent Sovereign State and So Does Not Need to Declare Independence?**

	2016	2017	2018
Especially disagree	11.6	9.0	8.6
Disagree	15.7	13.4	12.8
Agree	37.3	38.5	38.9
Especially agree	28.5	28.5	30.9

Source: "Taiwan National Security Survey," Program in Asian Security Studies, Duke University (https://sites.duke.edu/pass/taiwan-national-security-survey/).

to recognize Beijing as the government of China. A key turning point came in October 1971, when the PRC replaced the ROC as the government representing China in the United Nations, by which time most countries had established diplomatic relations with Beijing. Another came in 1979, when the United States, which had maintained relations with the ROC after 1949 and helped defend its position in the United Nations, terminated relations with Taipei and established them with Beijing, recognizing the latter as the sole legal government of China. With limited exceptions, Taiwan was forced to leave those international governmental organizations of which it had been a member. As of the fall of 2020, Taipei has diplomatic relations with only fourteen countries and the Vatican.

The question of whether Taiwan was a sovereign entity for either international or cross-Strait purposes became more salient in the early 1990s when, after more than four decades without any interaction, the Taipei and Beijing governments began to lay the foundation of their economic relationship. In preparation, Taipei crafted its opening position in the form of the National Unification Guidelines, issued in February 1991, and in a resolution that the National Unification Council passed in August 1992. The guidelines endorsed the principle that the Chinese mainland and Taiwan were parts of China and that unification was the responsibility of all Chinese. Unification should also promote the people's welfare, Chinese culture, democracy, human rights, and the rule of law. In addition, the ROC should have an international role. The resolution asserted that "China" meant the Republic of China and that the ROC's sovereign territory still encompassed all of China while its jurisdiction—the area over which it exercised control and governance—covered only Taiwan and its associated islands. China, the guidelines said, was a divided country with two political entities (the implication being that the two entities were legally equal). In effect, the Lee Teng-hui administration was putting forward a position of one country, two sovereign governments, to contrast with Beijing's one country, two systems formula.

Beijing rejected the Taiwan position out of hand. It opposed the idea that there were two Chinas and reaffirmed one country, two systems. Still, the two governments created semiofficial organizations that were clearly the agents of the two governments: Taiwan's Straits Exchange Foundation and the PRC's Association for Relations across the Taiwan Strait. In late 1992, they were able to form an understanding that was sufficient to begin talks between them to address practical issues. Known as the 1992 Consensus, the agreement was a set of parallel, general statements that spoke positively about "one China" and unification but in no way reflected agreement on how Taiwan would fit within that unified China. The 1992 Consensus made it possible for the heads of the Straits Exchange Foundation (Koo Chen-fu) and the Association for Relations across the Taiwan Strait (Wang Daohan) to meet in Singapore in April 1993. They reached some modest agreements and created some optimism that further progress was possible. The key point for purposes of this chapter, however, is that in crafting the 1992 Consensus, the two sides reached no agreement resolving the question of Taiwan's legal political status.

Meanwhile, the DPP was trying to stake out its own position on Taiwan's status and policy toward the PRC. In the run-up to the National Assembly elections in December 1991, the party adopted a resolution that, in effect, called for a Taiwan nation-state:[7]

> In accordance with Taiwan's actual sovereignty, an independent country should be established and a new constitution promulgated in order to create a legal and political system appropriate to the realities of Taiwan society, and to return to international society in accordance with principles of international law.... Based on the principle of popular sovereignty, the establishment of a sovereign, independent and self-governing Republic of Taiwan should be carried out by all residents of Taiwan through a national referendum.[8]

That is, the territory of Taiwan was not a part of China, and its government was not a government of China.

Instead, the DPP proposed creation of a new, sovereign state—the Republic of Taiwan—with all the rights of full members of the international community. The DPP wanted to reverse the process undertaken by the authoritarian KMT after 1949, through which the ROC state tried to impose a Chinese national identity on the Taiwanese that it now ruled. The DPP in 1991 called for the creation of a new state that was based on what it believed was a preexisting but repressed Taiwanese nation. (Requiring that this state be created through a referendum was a mechanism to liberate that repressed nation.) In part because of this proposal, which was well outside the mainstream of Taiwan opinion, the DPP suffered a serious defeat in the National Assembly elections of late 1991. For at least a decade thereafter, it therefore muted the Taiwan independence element of its political brand.

Still, Lee Teng-hui had to contend with several pressures. First, the DPP criticized his policy toward the PRC and advocated a more aggressive approach to getting back into international organizations, including the UN. Second, Lee himself increasingly objected to Beijing's Taiwan policy—because it did not treat the ROC as a sovereign entity and did not include, as Taiwan had asked, a PRC renunciation of the use of force. He objected especially to Beijing's opposition to an international role for Taiwan.[9] Third, in 1993 Lee still needed the moderate wing of the DPP to support him and the moderate wing of the KMT to complete the transition to democracy, which was accomplished in 1994 with a constitutional amendment that authorized direct presidential elections. Finally, he began preparations to run in that first popular election, to be held in March 1996.

Responding to these pressures, Lee aligned himself with the sufferings of the Taiwanese under the KMT authoritarian regime, which was one of the elements of the emerging Taiwanese narrative. He spoke of the "sorrow of being Taiwanese" and tried to challenge Beijing's embargo on Taiwan's international role (outflanking the DPP in the process). Reentering the UN then became a policy objective of the KMT government, as it had been a DPP priority. Lee also engaged in "golf diplomacy," traveling to various countries of Southeast Asia to play with their leaders. As the elections approached, his top priority was to visit the United States and give a speech at his alma mater, Cornell University. He pulled this off by getting friendly members of Congress to exert pressure on the Clinton administration. That tactic was effective, and the visit occurred in June 1995. Lee in effect was telling Beijing, "If you won't acknowledge Taiwan's sovereignty and therefore its right to a place in the international system, I will grab a place despite your objections."

The PRC read the worst into Lee's travel diplomacy, accusing him of promoting Taiwan independence, and it triggered a downturn in cross-Strait and U.S.-Taiwan relations. Around the time of the elections, the People's Liberation Army conducted displays of force that included firing dummy missiles near Taiwan, in the hope of scaring the Taiwan public. Washington was unhappy that Lee had undercut its one-China policy and undermined cross-Strait peace and stability. For their part, Taiwan voters confirmed Lee for another term by a wide margin. Lee was then conciliatory in his inaugural address, stating, among other things, that "we do not need to declare independence." The crisis subsided, and it appeared that cross-Strait dialogue was back on track. Koo Chen-fu and Wang Daohan met in the PRC in October 1998, and there was an agreement that Wang would visit Taiwan in the fall of 1999.

Territory as an Element of Taiwan's Sovereignty Claim

Lee Teng-hui assumed that political issues would be discussed in depth during Wang Daohan's visit, which triggered the need for Taipei to better define its legal status. Beijing had clear views on that subject, which were unacceptable to Taiwan, so Lee could not afford to have fuzzy views. He had said on a couple of public occasions that Taiwan lacked a definite international status. In June 1998, he opined that the "two sides should talk about international law. In doing that, we would also be talking about sovereignty," or statehood.[10] He created a team of experts to research the issues and make recommendations, one member of which was Tsai Ing-wen. The report submitted to Lee included a draft statement stating key policy principles that he should present to Wang and a set of recommendations for follow-up actions, including proposals for constitutional amendments. Lee approved the package, which was to be reviewed by senior officials.

Then on July 9, 1999, Lee jumped the gun and used part of the draft statement to answer questions from a visiting reporter of the German TV network Deutsche Velle.[11] For our purposes, what is important about the statement was its content concerning the ROC's legal status and territory. Its key parts are as follows:

> Since the PRC's establishment, the Chinese communists have never ruled Taiwan, Penghu, Jinmen, and Mazu, which have been under the jurisdiction of the Republic of China. In 1991, our country amended Article 10 of the Constitution . . . to reduce its effective area [*diyu xiaoli*] to Taiwan; to recognize legality of the rule [*tongzhiquan*] of the People's Republic of China on the Mainland; and to put elections of the president and to the National Assembly and Legislative Yuan on a direct, popular basis. As a result, these so-constructed [Taiwan] national institutions represent only the people of Taiwan. The legitimacy of the rule of the country comes from the mandate of the people and has absolutely no connection with the people of the Mainland. Since the 1991 constitutional amendments, cross-Strait relations have been the relations between two states [*guojia*], or at least a special state-to-state relationship, and not a type of internal relations under One China, [such as] between a legal government and a renegade group, or between a central and local government. . . . The Republic of China has been an independent sovereign state since 1912.[12]

The statement is occasionally muddled in its terminology, but two points stand out. The first is that Lee was at pains to distinguish the jurisdiction of the ROC government over Taiwan and that of the PRC government over the mainland (recall that sovereignty and jurisdiction are distinct concepts). But this was not a new assertion, nor was his later assertion that the ROC is an independent sovereign state. What was new was the link he drew between the territory where elections take place (only on Taiwan and its associated islands) and the enhanced legitimacy of the ROC government. It was through that linkage, he extrapolated, that the amendments concerning elections transformed cross-Strait relations into special state-to-state relations.

What is the basis for that last leap of logic? My guess is that it stemmed from the four requirements for statehood in the Montevideo Convention of 1933: a permanent population, a defined territory, a government, and a capacity to enter into relations with other states. Of those four, the one on which Taiwan's claim of statehood was the weakest was the definition of territorial scope of the ROC. The traditional view of the KMT regime was that both the mainland and Taiwan were ROC's sovereign territory. But the ROC had governed Taiwan only since 1949. Lee's stress on the PRC's and ROC's totally separate jurisdictions and the assertion that the ROC government derived its legitimacy from elections held only on Taiwan suggests that he was, in effect, redefining the sovereign territory of the ROC.[13] To put it differently, if sovereignty derives from the people by their voting in elections, then where the people vote defines the territory of the state. (Note that Lee's emphasis on elections implies a popular-sovereignty basis for state formation.)[14]

That Lee was, in fact, trying to redefine the sovereign territory of the ROC became clear later. In the first decade of this century, information came out about the changes in nomenclature, laws, and the constitution that Lee's team of experts had proposed to supplement the principles in Lee's statement. These included the revision and ultimate abolition of the National Unification Guidelines, seen as a one-China document, and a halt in the use of various formulations that assume or imply a one-China framework (such as "one China, different interpretations" and "one China is the ROC"). The most significant of the suggested changes concerned Article 4 of the ROC Constitution of 1946, regarding the ROC's territorial scope. That article does not actually specify geographically what the national territory is, but the thrust of later articles was that it included mainland China. The draft amendment read, "The territory of the Republic of China consists of areas effectively governed by this Constitution," that is, "Taiwan, Penghu, Jinmen, and Mazu."[15] If passed, this measure would have removed the mainland from ROC territory.

These changes never happened because Lee's surprise statement created a strong negative reaction from Beijing and Washington and led to a downturn in Taiwan's relations with both. In particular, the proposed amendments were never sent forward to the National Assembly. More broadly, it is hard to see how the supporting argument for the special state-to-state formulation could gain traction in the international community. The PRC government has consistently asserted that sovereignty over (or ownership of) the territory of Taiwan was effectively transferred to the state China through the Cairo and Potsdam Declarations, which was also the traditional, pre-1999 view of the KMT. Beijing's long-term goal has been to end the ROC government and its political claims and incorporate Taiwan in the PRC system. If Taiwan were to act on the state-to-state formulation and seek membership in international governmental organizations from which Taiwan is presently excluded, the PRC would use its firmly entrenched position in those organizations to defend its firm position that neither the ROC nor Taiwan is a state and block Taipei's efforts. The legal position of the United States is that Taiwan's legal status is to be resolved through negotiations between Beijing and Taipei (in effect, it is undetermined). The Clinton administration's negative response to Lee's statement stemmed from his failure to consult with Washington in advance and a fear that it might lead to a cross-Strait conflict.

Lee Teng-hui was not the first person to latch onto the issue of territory as a way to assert sovereignty for Taiwan. Many in the DPP and the broader Green camp focus on what they see as the muddled legal treatment of Taiwan after World War II. They point to the fact that immediately after the beginning of the Korean War, the Truman administration abandoned its previous position that Taiwan was a part of China and announced that "the determination of the future status of Formosa must await the restoration of security in the Pacific, a peace settlement with Japan, or consideration by the United Nations."[16] They also note that at American instruction, the peace treaties Japan concluded after World War II said that Japan gave up sovereignty over Taiwan but did not say to whom sovereignty would be transferred.[17] Based on these starting points, some Taiwan nationalists assert that the position of the PRC government and the traditional claim of the KMT—that Taiwan is a part of China's sovereign territory—has no basis and that the people of the island should be allowed to create their own state. Some suggest that since the United States was the occupying power over Japan, it has a stronger claim as Taiwan's sovereign than any other state. These approaches to Taiwan statehood are as unrealistic as they are creative, because they encounter two fundamental obstacles.[18] First, there is no international court that would take such cases without Beijing's consent (an impossibility). Second, it is highly unlikely that Washington would support such a novel claim, given its long-standing legal position.

There was one more chapter in the saga of Lee Teng-hui's struggle with the issue of territory. On April 24, 2000, about one month after Chen Shui-bian's election as president and twenty-six days before his inauguration, the National Assembly passed new amendments to the constitution and, among other things, created a detailed process for changing the national territory. The 1946 Constitution said merely that such a change would have to occur pursuant to a resolution by the National Assembly. The 2000 amendment provided greater specificity and added the Legislative Yuan to the process. First, the Legislative Yuan had to pass the proposal by a three-fourths majority of members present, with a quorum of three-fourths of all the members required. Second, passage of the territorial change needed a three-fourths majority of the National Assembly, with two-thirds of the members present. Politically, given the growing parity between the two political parties, no such measure could have passed without the support of both KMT and DPP members in the Legislative Yuan and the National Assembly.[19] The net effect of this amendment was that any territorial change would be highly unlikely.

Post-Lee Presidents on Taiwan's Legal Status

While the Lee Teng-hui administration was formulating its statement on cross-Strait relations, the DPP was preparing for the 2000 presidential elections. For it to have any chance of winning, two things had to happen. The first was that the KMT had to split over who should be Lee's successor.[20] The party kindly obliged: Lee wanted Vice President Lien Chan to be the nominee, but Soong Chu-yu, a rival to be Lee's successor, insisted on running. In the end, Lien and Soong split the KMT vote, and the DPP candidate Chen Shui-bian won the presidency with just under 40 percent of the votes. If the KMT had been united, the DPP would not have come to power.

The other requirement for a DPP win was that the DPP moderate its own position on cross-Strait relations. It released on May 8, 1999, a "Resolution on Taiwan's Future," which had been the subject of an intense intra-party debate.[21] The resolution did help the DPP reduce the electoral vulnerability that its past advocacy of de jure independence had created. What was not noticed at the time, at least by the U.S. government, was a less-than-reassuring statement in the DPP platform for the 2000 elections. In Chinese it read, "In accordance with the reality of Taiwan's sovereignty, the scope of Taiwan's sovereignty over the land and the people should be redefined."[22] In short, the DPP was explicitly declaring as its objective what Lee planned to do following his July 1999 statement (the English version of the DPP declaration, as disseminated, used the lesser term "jurisdiction").

Once Chen Shui-bian was elected, he sought further to reassure the Taiwan public, Beijing, and the United States. In his inaugural address, he stated five steps he would not take while in office as long as Beijing did not intend to use force: He would not declare independence, change the national title (ROC), push to include Lee's two-state formula in the constitution, promote a referendum on independence or unification that would change the status quo, or abolish the National Unification Guidelines or Council. (But Chen did not foreswear an attempt to make a change in the national territory.) Chen hoped, to no avail, that these assurances would elicit cooperation from the KMT and the PRC. He thus concluded that the best way for him to win reelection in 2004 was to play to the party's independence-inclined base. He knew that the United States expected consultation on sensitive matters, so he chose to leave Washington in the dark, believing that even if he received a U.S. pushback after his provocative move, he would come out in a better position in the long run.

Over several years, therefore, Chen made statements and took actions that took the DPP back to its early years regarding what Taiwan should be:

- In August 2002, he declared that there was one country (*guo*) on each side of the Strait.
- In May 2003, he called for referendums on domestic policy issues and Taiwan's participation in the World Health Organization (the latter issue entailed sovereignty).
- In September 2003, he called for a new constitution that would, among other things, make Taiwan a normal country.
- In October 2003, he said that the one-China principle and Taiwan's sovereignty were mutually contradictory.
- In January 2006 he effectively terminated the National Unification Council.
- In the fall of 2007, he promoted a referendum to be held at the time of the March 2008 presidential elections, calling for Taiwan to enter the UN under the name Taiwan, in effect asserting that Taiwan was a new state internationally.

After starting out as a relative moderate within the DPP, therefore, Chen, by his statements and actions, had reassociated his party with the idea of a Taiwanese nation-state that was politically disconnected from the state China in all ways.

In the end, the referendum failed, and Ma Ying-jeou, the KMT candidate for president, defeated his DPP rival, Hsieh Chang-ting, with 58.4 percent of the vote. To the extent that this outcome reflected voters' judgment of Chen's policy toward the PRC, and it did to some extent, they had clearly repudiated him. At the time of Ma's election, the share of people who told pollsters that they were Taiwanese only was 48.4 percent, while those who identified as both Chinese and Taiwanese represented 45.1 percent (the share saying "Chinese only" was 4 percent).

Despite the intense rivalry between the KMT and the DPP while Chen was president, the two parties did cooperate in June 2005 to amend the constitution regarding the process for doing so and for altering the national territory. They terminated altogether any role for the National Assembly, which, as of the 2000 amendments, still retained the power to ratify such changes as approved by the Legislative Yuan (the National Assembly thereafter ceased to function). Moreover, the 2005 amendments made the process more democratic. Specifically, passage of a constitutional amendment now required a three-fourths majority in the Legislative Yuan, with three-fourths of the membership voting, and then a majority of eligible voters voting yes in a referendum. That same mechanism was applied to any changes in the national territory.[23] These new procedures ensured that a very broad public consensus would be needed for constitutional and territorial changes. This, in turn, probably guarantees that the national territory of the ROC will not be changed, frustrating Lee Teng-hui's hope to do so in 1999, unless the KMT changes its fundamental position on the legal relationship between Taiwan and mainland China.

Ma Ying-jeou's Presidency

On the legal status of Taiwan, Ma Ying-jeou returned to the orthodoxy that had prevailed before Lee Teng-hui enunciated the two-state theory. Taiwan and the mainland were "two areas" of one China, not two states.[24] Neither side denied, he said, that the government on the other side had jurisdiction under its control, and neither acknowledged the sovereignty of the other. His guard rails for cross-Strait relations were "no independence, no unification, and no war." He accepted the 1992 Consensus, with its one-China connotations, to be the basis of normal, cooperative cross-Strait relations, at least in the economic and social sphere. But he was very clear on how he interpreted the Consensus. As he said in his second inaugural address in May 2012,

> When we speak of "one China," naturally it is the Republic of China. According to our Constitution, the sovereign territory of the Republic of China includes Taiwan and the mainland. At present, the ROC government has authority to govern only in Taiwan, Penghu, Kinmen and Matsu. In other words, over the past two decades, the two sides of the Taiwan Strait have been defined as 'one Republic of China, two areas.' This status has remained unchanged throughout the administrations of the past three presidents.[25]

Ma also affirmed the fundamental soundness of Taiwan's democratic system. He hoped to expand Taiwan's international space by consulting Beijing, not circumventing it.

Ma would later reveal his rationale for emphasizing "different interpretations" of "one China." In July 2020, he said that the 1992 Consensus was "the most circumlocutory way *of achieving the goal of bringing China* [that is, the PRC] *to concede the ROC's existence.*"[26] The likely reason that Beijing never accepted Ma's framing of the 1992 Consensus and his interpretation of one China is that it recognized his hidden agenda. The best short formula to reflect Ma's thinking is perhaps "one Chinese nation, two sovereign governments."

Apparently, Ma's reaffirmation that the two sides of the Strait were areas of one China is not a belief that the Taiwan public shared. The surveys conducted by Zheng Sufen of the Election Study Center at National Chengchi University, cited in the previous chapter, asked whether respondents thought that China (that is, the PRC) and Taiwan were the same *guojia* (國家, country, nation, or state) or different ones.[27] The responses in four separate waves of the survey can be found in table 11-2.

Although the question is not posed in terms of territory specifically, its implication is that if the PRC and Taiwan are the same *guojia*, then, Taiwan and the mainland both belong to the same state. If they are different countries, then Taiwan is not a part of China.

Ma took an interesting stance on the question of nationhood. He definitely praised Taiwan's economic and political achievements. It was on Taiwan, he said, that the ROC was reborn. But he also said that in the years before his election, "the people . . . rediscovered Taiwan's core values of benevolence, righteousness, diligence, honesty, and industriousness."[28] These happened to

TABLE 11-2. **Are China and Taiwan the Same Country or Different Ones?**

	2013	2014	2017	2018
Same country	20.3	18.9	23.6	22.7
Different country	68.1	70.3	66.5	67.5
No response	11.6	10.8	9.9	9.9

Source: Zheng Sufen, "Jiexi 'Taiwanren/Zhongguoren' renting de chixu yubianyi" [Analyzing continuity and change in 'Taiwanese/Chinese' Identity], paper presented at the "Symposium on Taiwan's Democratization and Free Elections" at the Election Study Center of National Chengchi University, May 25, 2019.

be traditional Confucian values. He called Beijing and Taipei to make contributions to the international society based on "our common Chinese heritage." Unquestionably, Ma regards himself as a patriotic Chinese. Yet instead of taking significant, path-breaking steps on issues related to state and nation, Ma chose to consolidate and improve the status quo. Rhetorically, he sought to say enough to reassure both Beijing and the Taiwan public. But when Beijing tried on several occasions to get him to begin political talks to go beyond the 1992 Consensus as the basis of cross-Strait relations, Ma refused on political and substantive grounds. He understood, it seems, that the Taiwan public was reluctant to have him enter political talks and that the difficulties that Taiwan leaders had faced in defining the island's legal status since the early 1990s persisted. At the time Ma left office, 54.3 percent of those polled said they were Taiwanese only, 3.6 percent said they were Chinese only, and 38.5 percent said they were both.

Tsai Ing-wen's Presidency

As noted earlier, Tsai Ing-wen's tried to reassure Beijing about her intentions both before and after the 2016 elections, and Beijing insisted that she declare herself explicitly on certain issues of principle. One of those issues specifically relevant to defining the status of Taiwan is the PRC's position that the geographic entity of Taiwan was part of China's sovereign territory. If cross-Strait relations were to continue as they had under Ma, Beijing insisted, Tsai had to state publicly that Taiwan was a part of China. If she had done that, however, it probably would have split the DPP. Tsai addressed that in her inaugural address by pledging to conduct cross-Strait relations on the basis of the ROC

Constitution and the law governing relations between Taiwan and the mainland, both of which Beijing could have accepted as meeting its requirement but chose not to.

Once in office, Tsai's basic approach to cross-Straits relations was characterized by caution and moderation. She did permit some projects to be undertaken to accommodate the fundamentalist wing of her party, such as those involving transitional justice. Mainland observers argued that these proved that Tsai's true intention was de jure independence, but the charges were not convincing. Some in the DPP pushed for changes on language and culture, reflecting a more primordial approach to nationhood, but they did not get much traction.[29] On the basics of policy, including issues of state and nation, she did not make an overt challenge to Beijing's position. The proof of her moderation was that William Lai Ching-te, who acknowledged that he was a "worker for Taiwan independence," challenged her for the DPP nomination for president for the 2020 elections, doing so just after stepping down as her premier. He lost that contest.

Conclusion

The subject of this and the previous chapter is how Taiwan leaders and the public identify themselves and how they define the nature of the Taiwan nation and state as a way to strengthen the island's security and to shield against PRC ambition. Given Beijing's clear, consistent, and self-serving definition of what Taiwan is and what it is not, Taiwan needs an understanding of itself that is equally clear and consistent.

Polling suggests that Taiwan people share a broad consensus on issues regarding nation and state, as they do on Taiwan's security environment and what to do about its vulnerability. To sum up the findings of the last four chapters, a majority of the public display the following tendencies:

- a strong sense of identification with Taiwan, but one that is combined with a Chinese identity in ways that are not precisely clear;

- opposition to both unification and independence and a preference for an undefined status quo (by wide margins);

- an understanding that Taiwan's prosperity depends on its trade with and investment in the PRC, which cannot be divorced from political relations, and that this economic interdependence creates an opening for Beijing to exert pressure on political issues;

- a belief that cross-Strait relations could develop faster than they have this far;

- an awareness that the degree of PRC friendliness or hostility depends on which party is in power, the DPP or the KMT;

- recognition that a declaration of independence would lead to war, a conflict in which the United States would probably not intervene on Taiwan's side;

- a belief that if Taiwan preserves the status quo but is subject to attack from the People's Liberation Army, the United States would probably come to its defense;

- serious doubts about the ability of the Taiwan armed forces to defend Taiwan;

- a preference for a moderate approach on the part of Taiwan's leaders in dealing with Beijing, exercising restraint concerning its red lines and relying more on diplomacy than on its military; and

- a belief that Taiwan is a sovereign state and a different country from the PRC.

However, because of methodological questions regarding the polling on which these judgments are based, there is actually more disagreement on identity than what is apparent at first glance. Specifically, what does it mean for someone to say that they are both Taiwanese and Chinese, or have a dual identity? Which part of that dual identity governs politics and Taiwan's relations with the PRC? When people identify just with Taiwan, it probably reflects their reaction to the PRC's unification goal and its offensive PRC actions. Yet any formulation of an affirmative policy toward Beijing probably requires a clearer definition of dual identity.

On the issue of the state, there is even greater lack of clarity. Polls indicate that a significant majority, including people in the DPP, agree with the idea that the ROC or Taiwan is an independent sovereign state called the Republic of China, even if they do not necessarily understand the international law behind the statement. The KMT and many in the DPP have a rather fundamental disagreement over whether Taiwan is a part of China's sovereign territory. A majority of the public aligns with the DPP in disagreeing with the idea that the two sides of the Strait are part of the same country (*guo*), but that may reflect a commonsense view about the nature of the two political systems rather than a legal viewpoint. It is certainly a good thing that Taiwan's two most recent presidents have followed a policy course that does not go against domestic public opinion or provoke a harsh reaction from Beijing or Washington. But as reassuring as a commitment to a vague status quo may be, it does not indicate more specifically how Taiwan should cope with the demands about the island's legal character that lurk in PRC policy and how to mobilize broad public support behind such an approach.

Lee Teng-hui's "two-state theory" aside, all that Taiwan leaders have done to reconcile contending views about the state is through verbal formulas that combine the words "Republic of China" and "Taiwan" in different ways. Lee himself spoke of the Republic of China on Taiwan. The DPP's 1999 resolution on Taiwan's future stated that, "Taiwan is a sovereign and independent country . . . named the Republic of China."[30] In his 2008 inaugural address, Ma Ying-jeou stated that, "The Republic of China was reborn on Taiwan."[31] The Tsai administration first used "Republic of China, Taiwan," and then shifted to "Republic of China (Taiwan)." The Deep Green *Taipei Times* objected editorially to the order of these terms and said that it was time to use "Taiwan (Republic of China)." It wrote, "Reversing the order of 'Taiwan' and 'ROC' would be a minor change, but it would have a profound effect on helping the nation gain international visibility, and is worth the government's every effort."[32]

Put differently, the Taiwan public's broadly held but rather vague and sometimes conflicting views about nation and state have been effective in defending against what it opposes: the PRC's unification 1C2S proposal. But they are not so useful in clarifying what it is that Taiwan should realistically seek. Taiwan people, based on the strength of their Taiwanese identity, would be happy to turn their de facto independence into de jure independence, but that is a nonstarter, since the PRC rejects this outcome as strongly as Taipei rejects 1C2S. Beijing tried to get Ma Ying-jeou—who was quite likely the most accommodating Taiwan leader it will ever have—to engage in political talks to clarify Taiwan's legal identity in ways that would be conducive to unification. Ma correctly spurned these overtures, but that they occurred at all should be a warning sign that this part of the PRC agenda will not go away. Taiwan's leaders have to go beyond using rhetorical devices to define the nation and the state and clarify the in-depth substance of those terms in order to fortify its negotiating position for the time that it is needed. They will also need to educate the public on these complex issues. If novel thinking on nation and state is to be effective as a defense against PRC political ambitions, greater consensus on its content will be necessary.

12

The PRC's Asymmetric Offense

In the early 1980s, I heard an anecdote about how people in the PRC viewed their government's Taiwan policy at that time. This was the period after the Carter administration had cut off diplomatic relations with Taipei and terminated the mutual defense treaty, and the Reagan administration had consented to a communique with Beijing that appeared to set limits on U.S. arms sales to the island's military. It was also when Beijing began promoting the one country, two systems (1C2S) formula for unification. There was understandable hope in Beijing that Taiwan would soon concede defeat. And yet it did not happen. Taiwan president Chiang Ching-kuo had rejected 1C2S out of hand, and the Reagan administration was taking steps to strengthen Taiwan's security, despite the absence of diplomatic relations.

In this context, a large gathering of officials gathered in Beijing to hear a speech by the Deng Xiaoping, the paramount leader of the People's Republic of China (PRC). The speech, as I recall, was about domestic issues, not Taiwan. After Deng concluded his remarks, and following a few approving statements from the audience, a voice rang out from the back, "*Taiwan zenma yang?*"—literally, "What's going on with Taiwan?" (台灣怎嗎樣). Yet the underlying meaning was, "Why haven't we made any progress toward unification?"

It is a question that could still be asked today, almost four decades later, and probably is being asked. Patient persuasion has not worked to bring about unification. Indeed, achievement of that goal is probably more distant than it was in the early 1980s or 1990s. Taiwan's democratization meant that the island's leaders no longer had the power to make the final decision; the people did. Vibrant discussions about Taiwan identity and the definition of the Taiwan state—the island's asymmetric defenses—had effectively countered the rationale for Beijing's unification appeals: that people on both sides of the Taiwan Strait were Chinese and that the incentives built into 1C2S should be enough to justify Taiwan's becoming a special administrative region of the PRC. The optimism with which PRC leaders had viewed the election of Ma Ying-jeou had turned to pessimism after the success of the Sunflower movement and the clear-cut victory of Tsai Ing-wen and the Democratic Progressive Party (DPP) in 2016. Repeatedly, they had to justify their Taiwan policy to domestic audiences. Indeed, Xi Jinping's long speech on January 2, 2019, was yet another answer to the very short question, "*Taiwan zenma yang?*"

Beijing's Taiwan Options

Taiwan's multifaceted efforts to enhance its security—militarily, politically, and so on—and the DPP's continuing ability to win elections creates a serious quandary for Beijing. Put simply, does Beijing have to choose between accommodating Taiwan, which is strongly opposed to unification, and a costly war?

Accommodation is unlikely. Having staked out unification as a principal goal of the regime, PRC leaders are unlikely to accept Taiwan as it is and abandon the objective. Hypothetically, Beijing might keep the one country, two systems slogan but radically change its content to make it more appealing to the Taiwan public. Yet there is no sign of movement in that direction. Such a shift would deflate the expectations the regime has raised domestically about the unification of Taiwan and most likely lead to demands from Hong Kong and Macau for the same treatment. On the other hand, going to war to compel unification is replete with uncertainties. How well will the People's Liberation Army (PLA) fight, having undertaken no major military campaign since its 1979 war with Vietnam? How well will the Taiwan armed forces mount an initial defense? Will the United States intervene, and to what effect? Will a war to take Taiwan strike fear in the hearts of other countries in East Asia and complicate the domestic rule of the Chinese Communist Party (CCP)? The uncertainties are not trivial.

In the months after Tsai Ing-wen's reelection in January 2020, it seemed that the chances of war were increasing. There was hawkish rhetoric about the need to robustly respond to the activities of "Taiwan independence forces," without providing any objective and credible evidence that such activities were actually occurring and that de jure independence was Tsai Ing-wen's aim. Planes of the PLA Air Force increased the frequency with which they crossed the center line of the Taiwan Strait, contrary to established practice in more relaxed times.[1] In September 2020, the PLA air force intruded into Taiwan's Air Defense Identification Zone twice in two days, with more planes than ever before. At a minimum, these flights allowed the PLA air force to test how the Taiwan Air Force might respond in a real conflict.[2]

Although some American commentators echoed the warnings of war, analysts with solid track records argued that the probability of full-scale war was low. Taiwan-based scholar J. Michael Cole argues that "the threat of military action, while serious, remains a somewhat distant one."[3] American defense scholar Ian Easton concurs, stating that contrary to PRC propaganda that an attack is imminent, "the reality is that China will probably not attack Taiwan in such a radical and high-risk fashion."[4] University of Maryland professor Scott L. Kastner suggests that "recent trends in the Taiwan Strait are reducing the likelihood of the cross-Strait conflict that, arguably, most worried analysts prior to 2008—a revisionist Taiwan crossing PRC redline, thus triggering a military response."[5] Finally, Bonnie Glaser and Matthew Funaiole, of the Center for Strategic and International Studies, argue that the justification for war put forward by hawks in Beijing—an imminent Tsai move to independence—is an imaginary horrible. In their view, "Beijing has already effectively deterred Taipei from declaring de jure independence."[6]

But despite the PRC's inability to shape Taiwan leadership and mass opinion sufficient to advance its unification goal, and despite its failure to weaken U.S. support for the island's defense, Beijing does have an alternative to accommodation and war. It has its own asymmetric option, one that it has implemented since the beginning of Tsai Ing-wen's first term. It is what I call "coercion without violence." That is, Beijing uses its power to take actions that punish, pressure, or marginalize the Tsai administration for its failure to meet Beijing's preconditions; to try to coopt sectors of Taiwan society to the PRC's benefit; and to interfere in Taiwan's democratic system. Such an asymmetric approach runs fewer risks than war and, over time, may lead to the outcome it wants at acceptable costs. It also targets not Taiwan's armed forces and its territory but rather the self-confidence of Taiwan's civilian populace. June Teufel Dreyer, a political scientist at the University of Miami, aptly terms this an "Anaconda strategy," whereby Taiwan is squeezed by PRC pressure until it is forced to surrender.[7]

Taiwan officials have clearly understood Beijing's strategy. On the military front, in November 2019, Taiwan's minister of national defense, Yen De-fa, told the Legislative Yuan that during the previous few years the PLA had sent about 2,000 reconnaissance aircraft and warplanes over the Taiwan Strait each year and sailed its aircraft carrier through the Strait.[8] This was not the use of force but rather the display of force. The intention was not to attack Taiwan physically but to deplete public confidence by reminding the people that the PLA had the ability to mount an attack if the PRC leadership gave the order to do so. For example, on September 14, 2020, the PRC launched a rocket on a course over Taiwan. This was not a part of a military exercise; its purpose was to launch satellites. There may well have been a technical reason for directing the rocket over Taiwan, but PRC leaders responsible for Taiwan policy likely would not have minded if the action unnerved the island's public psychologically."[9] Displays of force and other forms of intimidation and manipulation test the people's ability to endure in the face of hostile but nonviolent action and could foster the sentiment that resistance is futile. This is the stratagem of the fifth century BCE strategist Sun Zi, to "subjugate the enemy without fighting."[10] This does not mean that Taiwan's armed forces do not have to prepare for war to better deter attack. They do, and they share the *para bellum* paradigm in Western strategic thought: "If you want peace, prepare for war."[11] There is a nontrivial possibility that the combination of the aggressive patrolling near Taiwan by the PLA Air Force and the scrambling of Republic of China Air Force jets to protect the island's airspace could lead to an accidental clash that would then escalate. In July 2020, Joseph Wu, Taiwan's foreign minister, warned that the risk of a military clash was "rising precariously."[12] Yet Taiwan's leaders and many in the public understand that they are already in a different kind of war that Beijing probably hopes will achieve its political objectives without firing a shot.

True, some of the war-fighting scenarios previously cited do have a significant psychological purpose. A naval quarantine is one. An aerial bombardment of key points of Taiwan is another. Seizing the Taiwan-controlled small islands off the coast of Fujian and Mazu is yet another. But each of them also has a kinetic element that risks bringing about a military intervention by the United States, which remains a serious point of vulnerability for the PRC. Coercion without violence reduces that risk. The trick for Beijing, therefore, is to create enough coercion against Taiwan to deepen the island's *wangguogan* (the feeling that the country is lost) but eschew the violence that could trigger a U.S. decision to enter the fight.[13]

The PRC's rulers have long understood the value of influence operations in warfare and political struggles. Reportedly, PRC scholars have sought to deepen the conceptional basis of influence operations under the term "cognitive domain operations." Scholar Nicholas Beauchamp-Mustafaga summarized the concept as follows: "The goal of cognitive domain operations is 'mind superiority' (*zhinaoquan,* 制脑权), using psychological warfare to shape or even control the enemy's cognitive thinking and decision-making. . . . Cognitive domain operations represent the next frontier of warfare domains."[14]

Confirming Beijing's preference of coercion without violence, Vincent Chen, deputy director-general of Taiwan's National Security Bureau, presented an authoritative inventory of PRC actions to distort political opinion on Taiwan in an October 2019 speech to a conference sponsored by the Jamestown Foundation in Washington, D.C.: "CCP's Taiwan policy . . . dictates PLA's military coercion, external isolation of Taiwan, infiltration and subversion, united front interaction, cyber activities, and disinformation dissemination. From the cognitive perspective, all these activities are incorporated in a propaganda framework intended to shape Taiwanese mindset."[15] Chen reports that Beijing had set up a cross-department task force to influence Taiwan's elections in 2018 and 2020 by "financing pro-China parties, supporting mainland spouse groups, aboriginal talk show hosts and website writers." The PLA's Strategic Support Force was to coordinate propaganda and cyber activities, and the Taiwan Affairs Offices in PRC provinces and cities, along with the CCP's United Front Work Department, were to conduct "cognitive warfare" to shape Taiwan public opinion. Pro-China traditional media, along with social media, would be exploited to bias the terms of political debate. The regime "worked with China's own information technology companies to categorize constituents, design issues, evaluate manipulation, and modify strategies accordingly. . . . These activities constituted a new modus operandi of CCP's cognitive warfare against Taiwan which challenges Taiwan's response capacities." The objective: "annexing Taiwan without bloodshed."[16]

A Multipronged Attack on Taiwan's Confidence

Tsai Ing-wen's victory in the 2016 presidential election and the DPP's simultaneous emergence as the majority party in the Legislative Yuan almost guaranteed that Beijing would turn to coercion without violence against the new government and the island's people. Otherwise, they would perceive the mainland's passivity as accommodation or even appeasement. So, to sap Taiwan's self-confidence, Beijing has used multiple tools: economic, diplomatic, civil society, cyberwarfare, social media, and military displays of force. The Tsai administration was able to compensate or defend against some of these moves but not others. The most remarkable—and least noted—aspect of this campaign is that Beijing chose to inflict far more punishments in the first year of the Tsai administration than it did during Chen Shui-bian's two terms. Yet objectively Chen acted more provocatively in challenging Beijing's interests.

Suspension of Institutional Contacts

Not long after Ma Ying-jeou took office in May 2008, Taiwan's Straits Exchange Foundation and China's Association for Relations across the Taiwan Straits, the semiofficial organizations charged with cross-Strait interaction on an institutional basis, began regular contacts. On behalf of their two respective governments, the two groups reached twenty-three agreements on a variety of subjects, mainly economic.[17] In February 2014, the directors of Taiwan's Mainland Affairs Council and China's national-level Taiwan Affairs Office—the official agencies of the two governments responsible for policy toward the other—met for the first time. In November 2015, Ma met with Xi Jinping in Singapore. The last time that the leaders of the two sides had met was in the 1940s. The stated basis of these semiofficial and official interactions was Ma Ying-jeou's willingness to state that he would adhere to the 1992 Consensus. Even before the 2016 election, Beijing stated that these institutional contacts would only continue if Tsai Ing-wen promised to adhere to that precondition and another one regarding Taiwan's legal relationship with China. After Tsai Ing-wen chose to address these issues in her own elliptical way rather than adopt Beijing's language, the scene was set for the suspension of interaction between the Straits Exchange Foundation and the Association for Relations across the Taiwan Straits, to say nothing of the Mainland Affairs Council and the Taiwan Affairs Office. The PRC declared the suspension in June 2016.

Diplomatic Raids

At the end of the Ma Ying-jeou administration, twenty-two countries still recognized the Republic of China as the government of China and maintained diplomatic relations with it. Just about all of these were in Africa, Latin America and the Caribbean, and the South Pacific. Ma had reached an understanding with PRC leaders that neither Beijing nor Taipei would poach the diplomatic partners of the other, which allowed Taiwan to maintain those that it had. Two months after Tsai was elected president—and even before she had been sworn in—Beijing had announced that it was restoring relations with The Gambia. The Gambia had broken relations with Taipei in 2013, but

China had done nothing in response while the Kuomintang (KMT) was still in power. In Beijing's eyes, the DPP's election victory negated its reason for restraint. Thereafter, it picked off seven more of Taiwan's diplomatic partners: Sao Tome and Principe in December 2016, Panama in June 2017, the Dominican Republic and Burkina Faso in May 2018, El Salvador in August 2018, and the Solomon Islands and Kiribati in September 2019.

A variety of factors determined at least the timing of these flips in diplomatic relations. The decision on The Gambia occurred at the time of a conference of African leaders in Beijing. El Salvador switched as a leftist government was about to transfer power to a rightist one and not long after Tsai Ing-wen made a trip to the region. However, the main factor was money. The PRC now has a lot of cash it can use to induce needy and sometimes corrupt governments to switch diplomatic relations. Conversely, Taiwan has less funds and is less inclined to engage in bidding wars than it was in the twentieth century. This means that if Beijing wishes to take away Taiwan's remaining diplomatic partners, it will be able to do so sooner or later. The only possible exception is the Vatican, for which money is probably not a factor. More important is Pope Francis's desire to end the division between Beijing and the Vatican. That, in turn, hinges on whether the PRC is willing to give Rome an acceptable role in the appointment of all Catholic bishops in mainland China.

Imposing Economic Costs and Offering Benefits

Beijing sought to exploit the economic dependence of specific sectors of Taiwan society on the mainland to apply pressures and incentives. One was the tourist sector, which was opened early in Ma Ying-jeou's administration. Subsequently, there was a jump in the number of Chinese tourists coming to Taiwan, both in groups and as individuals. According to Taiwan government tourism statistics, between 2009 and 2015 (the six full calendar years of the Ma administration), the number of Chinese tourists to Taiwan jumped from 953,009 in 2009 to 4,143,836 in 2015, for an average of 2,996,094. The average for the last four of these six years, after the numbers had built up, was 3,370,112. But for the two full years of Tsai Ing-wen's presidency for which data are available (2017 and 2018), the average was 2,678,849.[18] That is, the annual average dropped by 20.5 percent from the last four full years of Ma to the first two full years of Tsai. It so happened that the numbers increased again in the first nine months of 2019 to 2,375,252, which, on an annualized basis, would be more that 3,500,000, well above the Tsai average.[19] That may explain why in August 2019, the PRC government announced a temporary suspension of permits for independent travel to Taiwan, to hurt Taiwan's tourism sector. The other reason, though, would have been to limit the number of PRC citizens who might go to Taiwan to witness the upcoming elections.[20]

After Tsai took office and the number of Chinese tourists declined, her administration took steps to soften the economic impact on the tourism sector, which includes hotels, restaurants, and luxury stores. It did so by making it easier for travelers from other countries to visit—for example, by expanding Taiwan's visa-waiver program. That effort proved to be successful. The total number of tourists in 2015, the last year of the Ma administration, was 10.4 million. By 2018, that number had risen to 11.1 million, an increase of 6 percent.

It was also in the economic sphere that the PRC made its greatest effort to offer positive incentives for Taiwan people. These were the so-called 31 Measures that were rolled out in late February 2018. Drafted by more than thirty agencies of the PRC, their stated purpose was to create a more level playing field for Taiwan individuals and businesses for their activities in mainland China. In effect, they gave Taiwan people national treatment relative to mainland actors, and they were ostensibly intended to provide better opportunities for Taiwanese businesses and individuals. On the business side, the measures were aimed at sectors such as manufacturing, infrastructure, finance, the professions, and entertainment and the arts. Concerning education, the new policies made it easier for Taiwan students to matriculate in mainland institutions. At a minimum, the new policies aggravated the brain drain that worried Taiwan officials and economists in 2018.[21] Roughly half a million Taiwan residents moved to China to work.[22] The incentives might strengthen opposition to the DPP in future elections. Beijing announced an additional twenty-six measures in October 2019, three months before the Taiwan presidential elections.[23]

Taipei responded to the first round of the 31 Measures with an announcement of measures of its own. On March 17, 2018, the minister of economic affairs announced eight policies intended to promote four goals. The policies included increasing incentives for scholars, improving defenses against corporate threat, and enhancing industrial innovation. The goals were to encourage quality schooling and employment, retain talent, maintain Taiwan's advantage and global supply chains, promote capital market expansion, and strengthen cultural industries, especially film.[24] This program made good sense, particularly because a brain drain of Taiwanese talent was already underway (the question is why the program had not been undertaken before). Another response by Taipei was to make the case to the Taiwan public that not many Taiwan people were taking advantage of Beijing's incentives and that Beijing had another motive for offering them. They argued with some merit that changes in the business environment in mainland China had led to disenchantment among foreign investors, which forced Beijing to reach out to Taiwan. Most likely, the economic and political reasons for the measures reinforced each other. Finally, the trade disputes between the PRC and the United States since Donald Trump had become president added to the incentives of Taiwan companies to either move back to Taiwan or relocate their supply chains elsewhere.[25]

Detaining Taiwan Residents Visiting China

In September 2019, the Straits Exchange Foundation announced that since Tsai Ing-wen had become president in May 2016, it had received 149 reports of Taiwan citizens who were missing in the PRC. The situation of 67 of those people was unknown at the time of the announcement. One, Li Mingju, a local government adviser, was last seen in Hong Kong in August 2019. He had expressed support for the protest movement there on his Facebook page. Cai Jinshu, chairman of the South Taiwan Cross-Strait Relations Association, was last seen in Xiamen in July 2018. Shi Zhengping, a retired National Taiwan Normal University professor and economist at a business conglomerate, went missing one month later. Confirming the detentions, a Taiwan Affairs Office official suggested that their "crime" was "endangering national security." That offense is defined broadly by the PRC regime to include what would be regarded in democratic systems as peaceful exercise of political rights.[26]

The most notorious case, however, was that of Lee Ming-che. Lee was a human rights activist affiliated with Wenshan Community College, who previously had been a DPP staff person. According to his wife, he went to the PRC in March 2017 "to 'preach' and 'share' Taiwan's experience of democratization with his Chinese friends" and was last seen in Macau. In late November, he was held incommunicado and then put on trial for "state subversion." After making what was most likely a coerced confession, he was convicted and sentenced to five years in prison. Lee's supporters in Taiwan mounted pressure on the Tsai administration to make a tough response against Beijing, which put the government in a quandary because it did not wish to aggravate Lee's plight.[27]

The specter of more detentions darkened because of developments in Hong Kong. In the second half of 2019, the city was plagued by regular demonstrations that sometimes turned violent. The trigger for the protests was the Hong Kong government's proposal to pass an extradition law that Hong Kong people feared would be used to violate their political rights. But the campaign broadened to include abuses by the police and the fundamentals of Hong Kong's own one country, two systems arrangement. Beijing became convinced that the Hong Kong government could not itself restore order and decided to impose a national security law.[28]

Of importance to Taiwan, one of the crimes the new law established was "colluding with foreign or external forces." This prohibited Hong Kong residents from requesting support from outsiders in such activities as "(1) rigging or undermining an election, (2) imposing sanctions or 'engaging in other hostile activities [against Hong Kong or the PRC],' or (3) 'provoking by unlawful means' hatred among Hong Kong residents towards the governments of China or Hong Kong." As George Washington University legal scholar Donald Clarke emphasized, "Clearly this kind of language, as with many other key terms in the law, is open to very broad interpretation."[29] The *Global Times*, an official PRC newspaper, warned Taiwan people that the "National Security Law of Hong Kong provides clear punishment provisions for the actions of 'Taiwan independence' chaos in Hong Kong that jeopardizes national security, making this law formally a legal sword that cuts off the DPP authorities' chaos in Hong Kong."[30] Taiwan's Mainland Affairs Council warned that, based on the law, Beijing was asserting the authority to seek the deportation to China of Taiwan individuals from countries with which it had extradition agreements, based on those individuals activities in and about Hong Kong.[31] (It is worth noting that although some people from Taiwan may have sought to assist the protest movement, there is no evidence that the Taiwan government was involved. This provision reflects a predilection of the PRC regime to blame outsiders like the United States for the failures of its own policy.)

Disinformation: Traditional Media

One PRC target for "shaping hearts and minds" has been the traditional media, and its biggest success story has been the outlets of the Want Want China Times Media Group. Want Want, owned by Tsai Eng-meng, began as a Taiwanese food company that catered to the mainland market. From 2006 to 2008 (the final years of the Chen Shui-bian administration), the firm bought two television stations—CTV and CTi-TV—and the venerable *China Times* newspaper. The *China Times* had supported moderate political reform in the 1980s and the Blue camp after the transition to democracy. But since its purchase by Want Want, writes Kathrin Hille of the *Financial Times,* "the

China Times has morphed from a mainstream publication into what critics call a mouthpiece for the Chinese Communist Party."[32] Want Want China Holding's financial records show that the company received US$586.7 million in subsidies from 2004 through 2018.[33] Although Want Want denies that the payment was a quid pro quo for pro-PRC coverage, the editorial managers at the *China Times* and CTi-TV reportedly receive tasking from Beijing's Taiwan Affairs Office concerning what to cover.[34] As reported in the U.S. State Department's report on human rights in Taiwan in 2019, PRC authorities exerted pressure on companies to withdraw advertising from Taiwan media outlets whose coverage diverged too much from their policies.[35]

In May 2019, Tsai Eng-meng led a delegation of anti–Tsai Ing-wen Taiwan media executives to Beijing. It was received by Wang Yang, the member of the CCP Politburo Standing Committee responsible for Taiwan policy after Xi Jinping. They laughed as Wang made fun of Tsai Ing-wen and then listened as he reminded them of their role as an instrument of PRC policy: "As we want to realize peaceful unification, one country, two systems, we need to rely on the joint efforts of our friends in the media. History will remember you."[36] They also listened as Wang explained why Taiwan should not rely on the United States: America had not been able to stop the communist victory in 1949 or to win victory in Korea. "They didn't defeat us when we were very poor, so what will happen when they face China today? Will they have the courage to fight us?"[37] Wang's remark is probably the clearest admission of the PRC's intention to interfere in Taiwan politics for its own revisionist ends and its lack of genuine respect for Taiwan public opinion. Not surprisingly, the PRC media report was removed from the internet almost as soon as it was posted.

Disinformation through Social Media

The 2016 U.S. presidential election demonstrated how effectively an external adversary can distort and disrupt a democratic political system through social media platforms. Taiwan is probably more vulnerable than America in this regard. It provides an open field for a bad actor, with an internet penetration rate of 92.78 percent and a mobile-phone subscription rate of 123.66 percent in 2018.[38] The fact that the bad actor (in this case, Beijing) and the victim (Taiwan) share a common standard spoken language, known as Mandarin in the West, as well as two versions of the same writing system, makes PRC manipulation of Taiwan's online discourse easier than, say, Russia interference against America.

Indeed, according to University of Gothenburg's 2019 annual report on the world's democracies, Taiwan's democratic system is one of the most exposed to foreign government dissemination of false information worldwide.[39] This judgment has been confirmed by other independent observers. A study by Lauren Dickey, a Washington-based China specialist, provides a good description of the various channels by which PRC actors probably try to manipulate Taiwan public opinion. She acknowledges that successful disinformation campaigns usually exploit "preexisting divides" by providing content for which an audience already exists.

> In the case of Taiwan, disinformation campaigns carried out by China seek to further divide support for any pro-Taiwan platforms and, instead, create a narrative that supports Beijing's political objective of unification. These efforts take the DPP as a primary target because the DPP's platform is viewed by Beijing as "stubbornly [sticking] to 'Taiwan independence'". . . [while] the KMT . . . is a benefactor of disinformation and social media campaigns believed to originate from China.[40]

Similarly, Paul Huang, a free-lance journalist based in Taipei, did a forensic analysis of the role of social media manipulation in the 2018 Kaohsiung mayoral race, in which Han Kuo-yu won by riding a populist wave. A number of factors contributed to his victory, but Huang argues that "Han's rise from obscurity to superstardom had a little help: a campaign of social media manipulation orchestrated by a mysterious professional cybergroup in China."[41]

The most authoritative statement to come from outside the Taiwan government was made by James Moriarty, chairman of the American Institute in Taiwan, the organization through which the U.S. government conducts substantive relations with Taiwan in the absence of diplomatic relations. In an interview with the TVBS television network two weeks before the Kaohsiung election, Moriarty said, "There obviously are attempts by external powers here in Taiwan to try and alter the debate and to spread false information, and those are dangerous." The TVBS network, which is associated with the Blue camp, posted the interview on its website but then pulled it a few days later. The Taipei office of the American Institute in Taiwan then posted it on its Facebook page.[42]

Not surprisingly, the anti-DPP forces fought back against the government's charges that the PRC was engaged in a massive disinformation campaign, along with the government's efforts to counter it. An extract from one *China Times* editorial published a month after the 2018 elections provides a flavor of the rhetoric: "The government controls massive resources accumulated through taxes paid by the entire public, and many government agencies use public funds to maintain press and PR spokespersons. . . . There is no way to provide correct information winning the people's trust, but [if looked at differently,] in a reverse manner, [as] restricting citizens' freedom of speech and freedom of the press, it is veritably confirming the government's incompetence."[43] Striking a balance between freedom of speech and limiting politically motivated disinformation is certainly not easy. The attribution question—identifying the source of disinformation—is a problem that will always exist. Even if PRC actors abstained from participation in Taiwan's social media debates, domestically generated disinformation would exist. It has been a constant in the rough and tumble of democratic politics (though given who is shaping its content, the *China Times* is probably not the most credible judge here).

Both inside and outside the Taiwan government, there were efforts to limit the impact of disinformation. Within the government, combating fake news became a priority for various agencies, particularly those responsible of national security. Fact-checking became an important line of defense. For example, the Executive Yuan's homepage has a subpage that collects erroneous reporting about government agencies and then works with affected agencies to quickly post corrections. Both the Executive and Legislative Yuans have revised existing laws to create broader authorities to combat disinformation. As a result, the government has fined some television stations for not checking their content and for spreading information that harms the public interest. Social media platforms in the private sector have developed mechanisms to screen out fake news, and two civil society organizations created the Taiwan FactCheck service to provide real-time corrections of inaccurate content.[44] According to one evaluation, "Taiwan harnessed citizen-built and operated platforms, powered by voluntary reporting to check and rebut false claims. The citizenry also collaboratively designed and quickly deployed a media-literacy curriculum ahead of the election."[45]

At the end of the day, there is the question of the impact of disinformation. It is not the only source of information for voters, and it may only reinforce the views that most people already hold. The main impact may be on undecided voters in a close election. Moreover, not all the disinformation that afflicts Taiwan comes from outside, and political campaigns can be exercises in misleading voters. Yet there is a fundamental difference between domestic disinformation and its negative impact on electoral outcomes, on the one hand, and meddling by an outside power that seeks to determine who holds power in Taiwan and what they do with it, on the other.

The United Front

Whenever a Leninist party encounters a political force which it cannot control by direct, institutional means but would like to do so indirectly, it seeks to create a "united front" with sympathetic elements within that political force in order to undermine it from within. Thus before it won power in 1949, the CCP created the United Front Work Department that sought to win allies in urban areas controlled by the KMT, such as students, intellectuals, and business owners, and isolate those who would oppose the new PRC regime.[46]

Even before that regime was founded, the CCP linked up with elements in Hong Kong society that were opposed to British colonial rule. Taiwan after 1949 was a more difficult challenge because of the authoritarian controls of the KMT regime, but democratization created new possibilities. Business executives who had set up operations on the mainland made up one target group. Conservative politicians who were unhappy with Lee Teng-hui's Taiwanization of the KMT and who created splinter parties that were more open to unification made up another. Beijing's hope was that these groups would work in parallel with it, first to oppose independence and then to promote unification. Where it was possible to bring new allies into the united front, that was done. The enemy against which the united front was formed was demonized and, it was hoped, isolated. If unification were to happen under one country, two systems, the Taiwan individuals who had been a part of the united front would be candidates to govern Taiwan on behalf of the sovereign authority in Beijing.[47]

Beijing did not need to stress the united front in Taiwan during the presidency of Ma Ying-jeou because his policies toward the PRC contributed to what Beijing called "peaceful development," the intermediate phase that would precede and prepare the way for unification. But it became a more central part of PRC policy toward Taiwan after Ma left office, as it was when Chen Shui-bian was president.

The first element of the united-front strategy is to demonize the adversary. So Beijing unleashed a steady stream of criticism against Tsai Ing-wen herself. This passage from the 2019 version of the PRC's biennial national defense report was just one of many attacks:

> The Taiwan authorities, led by the Democratic Progressive Party (DPP), stubbornly stick to "Taiwan independence" and refuse to recognize the 1992 Consensus, which embodies the one-China principle. They have gone further down the path of separatism by stepping up

efforts to sever the connection with the mainland in favor of gradual independence, pushing for *de jure* independence, intensifying hostility and confrontation, and borrowing the strength of foreign influence. The "Taiwan independence" separatist forces and their actions remain the gravest immediate threat to peace and stability in the Taiwan Strait and the biggest barrier hindering the peaceful reunification of the country.[48]

This screed badly misrepresents reality, including the fact of Tsai's consistent caution and Beijing's refusal to recognize how unpopular 1C2S is among the Taiwan public, including those voters who elected her.

Having demonized Tsai, the thrust of Beijing's united front was to gain allies within Taiwan to check her alleged moves toward independence and to work to drive her party from power. So it was not surprising that allegations regarding such activities surfaced from the time she took office. The National Security Bureau's Vincent Chen asserted that Beijing was creating links with local jurisdictions not controlled by the DPP, directing benefits their way. It had

24 business media and semi-official representatives in Taiwan, cultivating a wide connection, and some of them have engaged in activities beyond their stated mission. There are at least 22 pro-unification organizations and political parties and we have identified a number of those with connections to organized crime [that] further extend their networking to local temples, Taiwan businessmen in the mainland, or Taiwanese youth.[49]

The most interesting of these parties is the China Unification Promotion Party, headed by a former gangster, Chang An-le, a.k.a. "White Wolf." In the 1980s, Chang was a member of the Bamboo Union, one of Taiwan's three main criminal Triads, which had connections to the Taiwan security services. In October 1984, Chang participated in a plot to kill Henry Liu, a Chinese-American author living in Daly City, California, who was working on a book that was going to portray KMT leaders in an unfavorable light. After the killing, U.S. intelligence got evidence that this was not a random murder but had been directed by an agency of the Taiwan government. That finding prompted action by the Reagan administration and criticism in the U.S. Congress.[50] The murder also broke a stalemate in the KMT regime between the security services that wished to maintain tight internal control and political reformers. President Chiang Ching-kuo sided with the reformers, reduced the power of the security services, and set Taiwan on the course toward democracy.[51]

Fast forward to 2005, when Chang founded the China Unification Promotion Party. Its goal is clear from its name—promote unification—and it accepts the one country, two systems formula. What is more, it has engaged in political actions that disrupt Taiwan society. In 2017, for example, party members attacked students of National Taiwan University who had demonstrated against a PRC-sponsored event on campus. Six members were convicted of assault and extortion.[52] Officials of the Tsai administration, including the Vincent Chen, have credibly alleged that PRC funding supports the activities of these parties. Taiwan business leaders on the mainland are said to be the channel by which this money flows.[53]

It was the KMT that Beijing regarded as the political party most likely to win power and to steer Taiwan's cross-Strait policy in a direction in line with its objectives and so an optimal partner for the united front. In the early 1990s, the Lee Teng-hui administration had been willing to cooperate with Beijing in removing obstacles to better economic ties. Those parts of the business community that were moving operations to the mainland supported the KMT. And it was the KMT administration of Ma Ying-jeou that made the most progress toward improving cross-Strait relations. Yet as already discussed, Beijing's plan was disrupted by Taiwan's domestic politics, and it had some doubts about whether Ma and the KMT would be willing to move from economic issues to political ones and ultimately to unification. The Taiwanese wing of the party was imposing constraints, and the party's disastrous showing in both the 2016 and 2020 elections raised questions about its staying power.

There were occasions when the PRC undermined its own united-front strategy. One occurred in September 2020 concerning the annual cross-Strait forum on the mainland that KMT leaders attended. On this occasion, the leader of the delegation was to be Wang Jin-pyng, the leader of the southern, Taiwanese faction of the KMT and someone who Beijing needed to cultivate. But in discussing the visit, an anchorperson of the official China Central Television referred to it as the KMT's coming to "sue for peace." This set off a firestorm in Taiwan, and the KMT had no choice but to cancel its participation in the forum as a party. Individual members were not barred from attending in their personal capacity.[54]

As noted, political parties are not the only Taiwan organizations that are targets of the united-front campaign. Temples and associations of workers in farming and fishing industries are important and influential actors in Taiwan politics, making them useful sympathetic elements for the PRC. The former are able to deepen their connections with sister temples in the PRC that worship the same gods, and the latter get offers to sell to the mainland market at favorable prices, .[55] Schools also receive invitations and funding to make field trips across the Strait. The key facilitator is money, which Beijing's network of Taiwan Affairs Office branches have to spend.

Beijing also employs culture for political purposes. In October 2019, a dance troupe affiliated with the PRC government performed in Kaohsiung, where KMT presidential candidate Han Kuo-yu was mayor at the time, and three other KMT controlled counties. The troupe, organized by a group connected to the CCP's United Front Work Department, was permitted to register with the Taiwan government as an art education exchange. The Taiwan sponsor was a foundation under the China Youth Corps, which, in turn, is affiliated with the KMT. The title of the performance was "The Love of a Chinese Family, A Celebration of Taiwan." The first part of the title easily evoked one of the central themes of Xi Jinping's Taiwan policy, that the two sides of the Strait were all part of one Chinese family. Implied in that characterization is a view that a separate Taiwanese identity was illegitimate, because it is contrary to a Chinese identity, and also perhaps that Taiwan people should accept the authority of the "family patriarch," Xi Jinping. That the performances came less than three months before the Taiwan presidential election was most likely not a coincidence.[56]

To deter and punish various forms of PRC interference in Taiwan's political system, both through traditional media and united front alliances, Taiwan's legislature on the last day of 2019 passed an anti-infiltration bill. The goal of the legislation was "to prevent meddling by external hostile forces, ensure national security and social stability, and uphold the sovereignty of the Republic of China, and its democratic and constitutional institutions." It focused specifically on efforts by an external source to direct or fund political activity within Taiwan.[57] Tsai Ing-wen called the act a "democratic defense mechanism," but leaders of the business community called it vague and a danger to routine cross-Strait economic relations because prosecutors might misinterpret the financial transactions of companies in China. "Amid fears that they will be easily criminalized by the law due to a lack of a concrete definition, Taiwanese companies could stop conducting exchanges across the Taiwan Strait," said Lai Cheng-yi, chairman of the General Chamber of Commerce of the Republic of China.[58] The KMT also criticized the legislation. Two weeks later, after she had been reelected, Tsai sought to calm the growing concern by pledging that the act would not target normal cross-Strait exchanges but constrain "making political donations; engaging in electioneering; sabotaging legal assembly; [and] lobbying and interfering with elections" when directed or funded by the PRC.[59]

Cyber Warfare

Probably the most effective nonviolent weapon at Beijing's disposal is cyber activity, in terms of both PRC capabilities and Taiwan's relatively weak defenses. Taiwan has the dubious distinction of being one of the top targets globally of cyberattacks. In 2017 there were double- and triple-digit percentage increases in malware infections of Taiwan IT devices and a 600 percent increase in internet-of-things attacks. While China is not the only source of these attacks, it is certainly a significant one. In 2017 the PRC's "internet army" was responsible for 21 percent of the internet-of-things attacks and for 288 successful attacks on Taiwan government agencies. Researchers from the Taiwanese cybersecurity firm CyCraft discovered a PRC-based hacking campaign that attacked at least seven Taiwanese chip firms during the 2018–2020 period. The goal was to steal as much intellectual property as possible, including source code, software development kits, and chip designs.[60]

At a September 2019 event in Taipei, Brent Christensen, director of the Taipei office of the American Institute in Taiwan, announced that mainland cyberattacks on Taiwan were seven times greater in 2018 than in 2017 and that attacks in 2019 were projected to be another twenty times greater in 2020.[61] Christensen reportedly said that people use the openness of the internet to sow division, create polarization, and spread outright falsehoods to make people begin to lose faith in democratic institutions. The PRC also performed cyberattacks to threaten Taiwan's economy, particularly on the semiconductor, smart machinery, and electronic component industries.[62]

Yet the greatest danger is probably to Taiwan's critical infrastructure, both governmental and private. In June 2019, hackers compromised the personal information of almost a quarter of a million civil servants. In 2016 an Eastern European gang penetrated First Bank's network and caused its ATMs around Taiwan to emit cash. The bank lost US$2.3 million. In October 2017, cyber thieves stole around US$60 million from overseas branches of Far Eastern Bank. Warnings have been raised about Taiwan telecommunications companies' incorporating components manufactured in PRC companies such as Huawei. Compounding the vulnerability of infrastructure, their control systems often still use antiquated software.[63]

The Taiwan government has taken several steps to mitigate the cyber threat. It adopted a national strategy for cybersecurity and integrated the relevant firms into its broader industrial development plan. It has created a cadre of talented white-hat hackers. President Tsai rhetorically equated information security with national security. Her administration sought to standardize and simplify cybersecurity protocols for government agencies. It drafted and then passed a cybersecurity management act specifically to protect critical infrastructure in December 2018. The administration created a command in the armed forces to consolidate existing components that previously were separate and a civilian Communications and Cyber Security Center to protect critical infrastructure. The Executive Yuan drafted a control regime to reduce the use of PRC information and communications products in both central and local government agencies and issued guidelines to that effect in April 2019. It created a security clearance system for all government agencies, based on the sensitivity of the information they handled. Finally, it stepped up cooperation with the United States on cybersecurity.[64]

But the danger to Taiwan's core infrastructure and to public confidence persists. Tzeng Yi-suo, a scholar at the Institute for National Defense and Security Research, a Taiwan defense think tank, has suggested two ways that the PRC could undertake a cyberattack on Taiwan. The first is by cutting the undersea cables and their four landing stations, thus ending Taiwan's communications with the outside world that uses those cables. Second, it could force Taiwan to shut down domestic internet services in response to a large-scale disruption caused by Chinese cyberattacks and disruption of service.[65]

Beijing need not continue these attacks for long. It merely needs to demonstrate the ability to shut off electricity or disable ATM machines or interrupt electronic payments by the government to have a psychological effect on the populace.

Conclusion

One value of a coercion-without-violence strategy for those who employ it is that it does not have to work right away. The objective is to wear down the psychological confidence of the target society. If it yields a quick success, fine. But it is the long game that is important—as long as the target lacks the capacity and will to take actions that close the door on the attacker's achieving ultimate victory.

In the Taiwan case, the medium- and long-term goal of the PRC's asymmetric offense is to socialize the Taiwan public to the inevitability of unification and the need to accept it. The danger that the government in Taipei might move toward de jure independence is low, whatever PRC propagandists have to say. So in the short term, Beijing's goal was twofold: to punish the Tsai administration and, by implication, the voters who empowered them in

2016, and to drive the DPP from office. Whether success in that endeavor would have yielded a Blue leader who had a policy program similar to that of Ma Ying-jeou was an open question. Yet a KMT victory in 2020 would have boosted Beijing's confidence in the future and allowed a shift from coercion back to persuasion. From the PRC perspective, a weak Blue leader would have been more malleable than Tsai Ing-wen.

But it was not to be. Tsai won the presidency by a bigger margin in 2020 than she had in 2016. The DPP preserved its Legislative Yuan majority. Yet that was not a total disaster for Beijing. As noted, coercion without violence can sometimes work in the short term, but it is a strategy more suited to the long term. Asymmetric offense is the most plausible PRC option for as long as Tsai is in office. It is low risk and potentially high gain because it targets what is a real point of vulnerability: the long-term confidence of the public. Beijing can play for time, at least through Tsai's second term to see if and to what degree public sentiment on Taiwan will shift in its direction, as it did after eight years of Chen Shui-bian.

It is the medium-term scenario that is most likely to worry PRC leaders. Tsai Ing-wen picked William Lai Ching-te, a former mayor of Tainan and her premier from 2017 to 2019, to serve as vice president during her second term. Lai is generally regarded as more committed than Tsai to de jure independence, and he will quite likely try to position himself for a presidential run in 2024. If he were to win, Beijing could well conclude, rightly or wrongly, that the Taiwan public will not revert in a Blue direction and that the door to unification is closing.

Taiwan's leaders and the public cannot operate under any illusions about PRC intentions and what it takes to induce its restraint. Beijing chose to inflict far more punishments in the first year of the Tsai administration than during Chen Shui-bian's two terms. Objectively, however, it was Chen who acted more provocatively in challenging PRC interests. This contrast reflects, I believe, the shift in the motivation of Beijing's Taiwan policy from fear to greed.

That, in turn, raises the question of how Taiwan is to strengthen its security in the face of PRC greed and in the domestic political and policy context. The Green camp believes that Beijing is motivated by greed, but at least some in the Blue camp think that fear is still its driving motivation, and that it is up to Taiwan to reduce that fear. Hence their criticisms of Tsai's PRC policy. Beijing's military buildup and its campaign of coercion without violence against the Tsai administration constitute a double warning for Taipei. On the one hand, it has to enhance deterrence against a military attack by strengthening its military defenses, and do so in a way that is appropriate to the threat environment. On the other hand, it must also continue to develop counter-measures against Beijing's asymmetric offense and sustain public confidence in the government's security policies. Taiwan's politics complicate any effort to carry out those two tasks. Which offers the better chance of success? A regular rotation of power with attendant swings in security policy, in which either the DPP or the KMT ultimately emerges as the dominant power? Or is greater consensus and enduring security more likely to result from a conver-gence of the two major parties, in terms of politics and policy, whichever party wins the presidency?

13

Taiwan's Democratic System

Uniquely, Taiwan has included its democratic system in its security toolkit. The mandate that voters deliver every four years and the findings of regular opinion polls are held up as reasons that Beijing should exercise restraint toward Taiwan and be more accommodating (it also gives the United States a reason to support Taiwan). Thus Tsai's reelection victory in 2020 could be read as a popular response to the pressure and intimidation that the People's Republic of China (PRC) executed during her first term and confirmation of a preference for her policies of separating economics and politics, eschewing the need to match every PRC provocation with one of its own, and relying on the United States to balance somewhat against Beijing (as opposed to the more accommodating stance of the Kuomintang, or KMT). As Hoover Institution scholar Kharis Templeman concluded, "In the end . . . Taiwan's democratic institutions held up. The Taiwanese state showed its underlying strengths: regulatory bodies with broad powers, independent and energetic prosecutors' offices, and above all an excellent system of election management."[1]

Hence democracy is a tool that Taipei uses in conducting cross-Strait relations. Beijing, on the other hand, is likely to read it as the manipulation of public opinion, framing the contest as a referendum on Beijing's one country, two systems formula. An editorial in the PRC's *Global Times* asserted at the time of Lee Teng-hui's death in September 2020, that the democratization he engineered "has greatly increased the resistance to China's rise . . . Lee Teng-hui pushed Taiwan to a dead end, using deformed democracy to help 'Taiwan independence' drink poison to quench its thirst."[2]

Taiwan's Challenges and Its Democratic System

So far, this book has produced several basic findings. First, Taiwan faces a medium- or long-term existential challenge. The PRC wishes to transform the status quo of Taiwan's existence by making it a special administrative region similar to Hong and Macau. The Republic of China (ROC) would legally cease to exist and, based even on the original Hong Kong model of one country, two systems, the island's democratic politics would be constrained.

Second, public opinion surveys find that Taiwan people are relatively united on a number of issues, both on social and cultural values and on political matters such as national identity, state identity, and preferences for the future. Even discounting for the imprecision of pollsters' terms, respondents tend to see themselves as an undefined mix of Taiwanese and Chinese; they prefer democracy, warts and all; and they prefer the status quo to moving into the unknown of unification or independence.

Third, however, on a number of public policy issues there is division. Competing views exist among government agencies, politicians, civil society, and the public on matters such as budget priorities, energy, the economy, and transitional justice. On issues directly related to the PRC, beyond the basic issues of political identity and independence versus unification versus status quo, the disagreements are more profound. That is understandable. Because the policy issues are complex and Beijing's challenge is existential, determining how to address them is not easy.

Fourth, from 1979 on, PRC leaders hoped to persuade their Taiwan counterparts that its approach—one country, two systems (1C2S)—was the best option for the island's future. Yet those appeals have fallen on deaf ears. Only a small minority support unification either now or later. To make matters worse for the PRC, from around 1995 to 2008 it appeared that Taiwan leaders were taking Taiwan in the direction of de jure independence. Based on those fears, in the late 1990s the People's Liberation Army began developing military capabilities to deter such an outcome.

Fifth, since 2008 the objective danger of a move to independence has receded—and it was probably not that high anyway. Presidents Ma Ying-jeou and Tsai Ing-wen sought to allay Beijing's fears through accommodation, though they disagreed on how to do so. Ma's accommodation was more flexible, and Tsai's was more skeptical. Beijing accepted Ma's approach but interpreted—or misinterpreted—Tsai's election as new momentum toward separatism. It chose not to believe Tsai's stated commitment to preserve the status quo.

Sixth, objectively speaking, Beijing's reliance on persuasion has not worked so far. The Taiwan public is no closer to accepting 1C2S than it was in the early 1990s. At the same time, PRC leaders have not resorted to using military force to get their way. That is a risky option, in part because Beijing cannot rule out the possibility of U.S. intervention. Nor can it be confident that it would achieve its goal.

Seventh, during Tsai's first term the PRC resorted to intimidation, pressure, isolation, cooptation, and interference in Taiwan's affairs. This coercion without violence is a "just-right" way to cope with Taiwan's refusal to move toward unification and its purported fears that Tsai's goal is independence. It is less risky than going to war, and it is more likely to achieve its goal than simply accepting the Taiwan public's opposition to unification. Coercion without violence attacks a weaker target, the Taiwan populace's psychology (military force would target the island itself and the armed forces defending it). If people lose confidence in the ability to withstand the challenge coming from across the Taiwan Strait, Beijing wins. If Taiwan's leaders and citizens are divided on what to do, Beijing also wins.

Tsai's reelection in January 2020 probably means that PRC leaders will continue coercion without violence. But even if KMT candidate Han Kuo-yu had won the 2020 election and then accepted the 1992 Consensus in the way that Ma Ying-jeou did, cross-Strait relations probably would not have returned to the early Ma pattern for very long. Even during his first term, Beijing began pressuring Ma Ying-jeou's to begin political talks. Beijing's logic appears to be that because it is strong and getting stronger in terms of material power and Taiwan is weak and supposedly getting weaker, Taiwan will submit sooner or later in the face of PRC power. Beijing has not yet gotten its way with Taiwan, but it believes that its ability to do so has grown.

Taiwan faces a challenge in reconciling contending priorities not just because policy issues are substantively complex but also because the resulting dilemmas must be addressed within the island's democratic political system, if they are tackled at all. During the authoritarian period, a relatively small group of officials made key decisions: military officers and diplomats on national security issues and technocrats on economic issues. But democracy is all about expanding the circle of policy contenders and stakeholders, which complicates the task of resolving differences.

To even pose these questions contradicts democratic Taiwan's positive reputation. It was a poster child for the global "third wave" of democratization that occurred in the 1980s and 1990s. Social and economic modernization, a growing political opposition, and a decision in 1985 by Chiang Ching-kuo, the leader of the KMT, combined to produce a transition to liberal, popular rule that was negotiated between regime and opposition and was gradual and peaceful.[3] More than two decades after the completion of the democratic transition in 1996, Taiwan's democracy still gets high marks from outside observers. Government officials in the United States regularly praise its political progress. According to the State Department's annual report of human rights practices, civil and political rights and the rule of law are well protected, a finding that Freedom House's annual rankings for civil and political rights confirms. Elections are free and fair and highly competitive.[4] There have been three presidential transfers of power, usually a sign of democratic consolidation. The party system is institutionalized and stable, with two large, distinctive parties whose leaders and loyal followers accept that elections are the legitimate way to select Taiwan's leaders.[5]

In one assessment of the quality of democratic governance around the world (defined as the level of state capacity and degree of democracy), Taiwan scores high on both measures. In that ranking, it is firmly in the company of European democracies, Japan, and South Korea.[6]

Moreover, Taiwan has so far avoided the worst phenomena associated with the global "democratic recession" that began earlier in the 2010s: coups; weakening of electoral integrity, the rule of law, and democratic freedoms; overall bad governance owing to corruption and abuse of power; and a resurgence of authoritarian regimes.[7] In addition, based on surveys by Transparency International, Taiwan is perceived to have been doing better on reducing corruption, always the scourge of a democratic system. In 2007, the last full year of Chen Shui-bian's administration, Taiwan had a score of 57 on Transparency's index and a global ranking of thirty-fourth. Twelve years later, its score was 65 and its ranking was twenty-eighth.[8]

Despite the high marks that Taiwan's democratic system has received, it must be assessed in light of the challenges it faces and what is at stake. If Canada's political system does not work well, the impact on its national security will most likely be limited, since its external threats are modest at most. In Israel, however, domestic dysfunction has weakened the country's ability to survive in a fairly hostile neighborhood.[9] Former U.S. National Security Advisor Susan Rice wrote in September 2020,

I have long viewed domestic division as our greatest national security vulnerability. Political polarization is a "force multiplier" that worsens other threats and cripples our ability to combat them. Stoked by leaders who profit from divisive politics, our polarization prevents us from effectively confronting vital challenges . . . Our own fissures also create easy openings for Russia to inflame Americans' fears of one another and to erode our faith in democracy by using social media to spread disinformation and sow distrust.[10]

When the stakes are high, the challenge to the political system grows accordingly. As the PRC's ambitions create a high-stakes challenge for Taiwan, the outcome may permanently define the island's future. This in turn poses questions about the quality of Taiwan's democratic system, through which the challenge will be met. Does it mitigate difficult policy dilemmas or exacerbate them? Does it facilitate consensus on how to approach the challenges of the future, or does it intensify the disagreements and create gridlock?

A Brief Introduction to Taiwan's Democratic System

Taiwan's democratic system was the product of four different legacies: the political ideas of Dr. Sun Yat-sen, the ROC Constitution of 1946, the character of the Leninist authoritarian regime and of the democratic transition that followed it, and the Confucian idea of calling things by their proper name. Consequently, the political leaders who engineered the democratic transition in the late 1980s and early 1990s did not start with a blank slate.

Sun Yat-sen

Sun Yat-sen was the founder of the Kuomintang and its leader until his death in 1925. He is known as the father of the Republic of China. As he thought about government in this new China, Sun borrowed a lot from the U.S. system. He advocated an Executive Yuan (EY), a Legislative Yuan (LY), and a Judicial Yuan, replicating the three branches established in the 1789 U.S. constitution (*yuan* means council). But he added an Examination Yuan to recruit the civil service and a Control Yuan to serve an ombudsman function. These latter two institutions were copied from Imperial China's examination system and censorate. Sun also proposed the mechanisms of direct democracy—suffrage, recall, initiative, and referendum—having been impressed by their operation in Western Europe and the United States. Once the Kuomintang movement, led by Chiang Kai-shek, Sun's successor, seized control of the ROC government in 1928, it established Sun's "five-power system" and added the office of president to serve as the chief of state.

The 1946 Constitution

But the post-1928 KMT regime was not able to enshrine these institutions in a constitution until 1946, beset as it was by challenges from domestic militarists and by war with Japan.[11] It made attempts in the intervening period, but none came to fruition. Devising the right set of powers for the top civilian leader proved difficult, particularly since Chiang, the top military leader, had a stake in the outcome, and he usually dominated the system, whichever formal positions he held. The constitution that emerged in 1946 included Sun's five powers, or branches, authorized an elected national assembly to pick the president and to enact constitutional amendments, and specified various civil and political rights, including suffrage, recall, initiative, and referendum.[12] The civil and political rights enshrined in the constitution were suspended in May 1948, during the mainland civil war, and not restored on Taiwan until 1991. After the KMT retreated to Taiwan, elections for most seats in the National Assembly and the LY were suspended on the grounds that the ROC was the government of all of China but did not control the Chinese mainland, where most of the election districts were. Popular elections on Taiwan for the LY were first held in 1992 and for president in 1996. Legislation to implement initiative and recall was not enacted until 2003.

Today, the president nominates the leaders of all yuans except the LY, which picks its own leaders. The LY must also approve the president's choices for the Executive, Judicial, Control, and Examination Yuans. Grand justices are nominated by the president and approved by the LY. For the unicameral LY itself, seventy-three seats are chosen by popular elections in geographic districts. Thirty-four are drawn from lists of candidates compiled by each political party, based on the share of the vote that each political party receives in a separate tally from the district contests. Six seats are reserved for members of aboriginal communities.

That the KMT's leaders had only suspended the constitutional provisions concerning elections and civil and political rights in the late 1940s and did not terminate the charter altogether had great significance some forty years later. Once the KMT leadership decided to make the transition to democracy, the basic template already existed. For some provisions, such as those concerning civil and political rights, the act of lifting the 1948 suspension started a process of defining those rights in detail. For other matters, passage of amendments was necessary to take account of the passage of time. For example, the amendments concerning elections that were enacted in the 1990s and 2000s were written to be implemented only on Taiwan and its associated islands (which were called the "free areas"). If it had been necessary in the early 1990s to draft an entirely new constitution through a constituent assembly, it would quite likely have stimulated a broad discussion on the nature of state and nation. The Democratic Progressive Party (DPP) undoubtedly would have welcomed that debate, but the transition probably would have been more complicated than was actually the case (which was complicated enough).

KMT Authoritarianism and the Democratic Transition

A critical feature of Taiwan's transition from authoritarianism to democracy was that the authoritarian party—the KMT—was a participant in and beneficiary from that evolution. For example, the KMT retained the presidency for another thirteen years after the end of martial law and regained the presidency in 2008 for another eight years. Only in 2016 did the KMT lose control of the LY. This type of transition is very different from other authoritarian systems, where the ruling power is overthrown, the former authoritarian party disappears, and a new system is created from scratch. That the KMT survived in power for so long was the result of several significant factors: a positive record on economic development, a well-established organization with roots into society, and substantial resources.[13] But its authoritarian past had a couple of enduring consequences.

First of all, some Taiwan people still feel bitterness as a result of being victims of the KMT regime during the authoritarian period. It is because the KMT still exists that transitional justice became a salient issue in the 2016 election and thereafter.

Second, that the KMT was a Leninist party organizationally, even though it was anticommunist ideologically, has affected post-democratization politics. During the authoritarian period, the tentacles of the KMT organization penetrated the executive, the military, and all other political and social institutions in Leninist fashion. For example, military officers had a presence on college campuses. The system also created incentives for civil servants, military personnel, teachers, and so on to become KMT members, in part to demonstrate loyalty and in part to enhance their career prospects. Consequently, the institutional apparatus of the executive branch, including the military and the intelligence services, did not have a history of political neutrality. When the DPP won the presidency in 2000, the individuals that President Chen Shui-bian appointed to lead bureaucratic institutions doubted that career officials would follow their policy direction. Conversely, the people who staffed state institutions may have questioned the qualifications and loyalty of their new political masters to the ROC. In every democratic system, of course, there is a tension between the technocracy, whose officials are selected on the basis of merit and whose work is directed at solving problems in a technical manner, and the heads of agencies, who are picked on the basis of politics. But in Taiwan, history exacerbated this mutual mistrust. The DPP members recalled KMT repression, and people in the KMT believed (correctly or incorrectly) that the goal of the DPP was independence.

Rectifying Names

Finally, Deep Green Taiwanese nationalists stress the need to use the term "Taiwan" as much as possible in official documents and in the title of organizations (for example, the Chinese Petroleum Company). They want to dissociate what they regard as their homeland from China in general and the ROC in particular. To be sure, this was a response to the KMT regime's practice during the authoritarian period of using the term "China," to fortify the claim that the ROC was the government of all of China. With the transition from authoritarianism to democracy, it was people in the DPP for whom names became a political issue.

For example, the administration of Chen Shui-bian, a leader of the DPP, sought to change the titles of Taiwan's state-owned enterprises, which included the word "China," a legacy from early KMT rule. In 2020 some DPP legislators tried to revive this practice by proposing that the English name of the Academia Sinica, a prestigious research organization founded in Nanjing in 1928, be changed to Academia Taiwan or "Taiwanica."[14] (The Chinese name of the organization does not include a word for "China.") Later that year, there was a move in the LY by some in the DPP to highlight the name "Taiwan" on passports and on China Airlines, Taiwan's flag carrier (there had been a similar action on passports in the Chen Shui-bian administration). The LY passed resolutions encouraging the EY to take those actions but did not require them. Even so, the administration announced in September 2020 that it would go ahead and carry out the passport change."[15]

The reasons for this advocacy are several: resentment that the Taiwan government's official name is the Republic of China, which suggests that the island is a part of China; memories of the suffering under the ROC regime during the authoritarian regime; and fear that Beijing will try to carry out its unification objective and that leaders of the KMT might help them do so, to the detriment of the population's interests. At a minimum, use of the term "Taiwan" by Taiwanese nationalists is a clear assertion of identification with Taiwan itself and of differentiation from China. In this spirit, pro-independence members of the DPP in 2003 created the Taiwan United Nations Alliance to lobby for UN membership. Its fundamental objective was creation of a "Taiwan Republic" (*Taiwanguo*), which will allow "name and reality to converge" (*mingshi heyi*).[16] There is an irony here: the idea that words should reflect reality is a fundamental principle of Confucius, a quintessentially Chinese philosopher.[17]

System Dynamics

Taiwan's system may be visualized mentally in different ways. A constitutional perspective emphasizes the relationship among institutions, particularly between the executive and legislature. A political one focuses on the clash of camps and parties within those institutions and especially at election time. A functional perspective yields a set of concentric circles. The circle at the center is the political leadership, composed of the president and the senior officials that she or he appoints to lead and direct executive agencies. The leadership claims its authority mainly from having won elections. The second circle is made up of those executive agencies, including military and security institutions. Each has its mission and policies, its set of technocratic tasks to implement, and its cadre of professional experts to carry them out according to established routines. The third circle is an arena of accountability, providing a check on the political leadership and the technocracy. The legislature is the key institution here, but the courts, the Control Yuan, and the mass media can impose accountability as well. Elections render the ultimate verdict.

Among the concentric circles different dynamics are possible. For example, during Chen Shui-bian's presidency, the KMT-controlled LY and the KMT-inclined technocracy kept the political leadership on the defensive. When Ma Ying-jeou was president, he tried to unite the bureaucracy and the KMT-controlled legislature behind his policy of mainland engagement. In the Tsai era, the political leadership and the DPP-dominated legislature has squeezed the technocracy.

How the political system processes any specific issue can vary according to the nature of the issue, the actors that contend over it, and the broader political environment. The issues discussed in earlier chapters, five in particular, illustrate the point that each issue has its own politics: the budget, economic policy, energy policy, transitional justice, and relations with the PRC.

On the budget, the office of the president can reset priorities to some extent to reflect leadership priorities, but it is the EY's Directorate-General for Budget, Accounting, and Statistics and the Ministry of Finance that have a dominant position. Expected revenues, the requirements of entitlement programs, and the past division of the budget pie define how each year's budget is crafted. Since the LY can only reduce specific allocations, its elected members are constrained somewhat from reshaping the budget to reflect popular and party preferences. Proposals to change policy on matters like pensions can spark public protests.

When it comes to setting policy on the economy, competing priorities and near-immutable constraints make choices difficult. There are trade-offs between growth and equity, between the needs of big business and of small enterprises, and between the needs of the aging and those of youth. The political leadership's willingness to accommodate Beijing politically can affect Taiwan's growth and its ability to conclude bilateral trade agreements and participate in multilateral arrangements such as the Regional Comprehensive Economic Partnership. The president and the ministry of economic affairs dominate basic policy, while legislators seek resources to benefit their districts. At election time, voters can remove an administration that they believe has failed to meet their expectations regarding the economy, their top priority.

Energy policy was originally formulated by the national political leadership and carried out by agencies of the EY. Beginning in the 1980s, this technocratic approach came under fire from the DPP and civil society, particularly over the safety of nuclear energy. The information technology sector supported nuclear power because it was more likely to meet its need for a constant supply of electricity. Policy changed as political power shifted from KMT to DPP and back again, and current policy calls for total elimination of nuclear power, even though the outlook for renewables' filling the gap is uncertain. Meanwhile, no political leaders were willing to brook public anger by raising electricity prices.

The initiative for the transitional justice project came from within the DPP during the 2016 presidential campaign. Tsai Ing-wen treated it as an important issue and, once the DPP gained power, she appears to have accommodated the strong desire of its caucus in the LY to give it priority. Because the DPP had a parliamentary majority, it was able to designate who would implement the project and what norms it would follow. The EY had almost no role because it had not had responsibility for such issues in the past. The KMT's only "ally" in this struggle was the judiciary, which blocked the party assets commission and the transitional justice promotion committee from carrying out some of its proposed actions.

On policy toward the PRC, it was political parties and their leaders that debated how much to accommodate Beijing. The business community favored a policy that facilitated cross-Strait trade and investment. Other groups worried about a slippery slope from economic dependence to political subordination. The public supported a restrained policy that did not provoke hostile action from Beijing. The military was divided over defense strategy and what advanced equipment was needed to create a sufficient deterrent. Paying for that deterrent was caught up in broader budget politics—low revenues and the division of the spending pie.

Early 2020 provided another test of the Taiwan political system—COVID-19—and it performed exceptionally well. As of mid-2020, Taiwan had registered only 473 cases and seven deaths.[18] It successfully employed border controls, testing, contact tracing, and quarantines to keep the number of cases low. Several features of the political system's response contributed to this success. The leadership of the Tsai administration was united, serious, and transparent. Members of the public, who habitually use masks when they get a cold, did not need much official persuasion to do the same when it came to the coronavirus. Members of the LY did not politicize the issue, perhaps because they understood the stakes. (That is, on this issue Taiwan had both good leaders and followers.) But the most important factor was the improvement of Taiwan's public health agencies in responding to contagious diseases. They had not performed well after the outbreak of the SARS outbreak in early 2003, but thereafter it identified deficiencies, corrected its standard operating procedures, and raised readiness to a high level. In short, the political leadership, the technocracy, politicians, and the public worked together to create an exemplary result.

Citizens' Attitudes toward Taiwan's Democracy

The Taiwan public has mixed and complex views about their political system. The best source of information on attitudes is the Asian Barometer Survey, which has queried Taiwan attitudes on four different occasions: summer 2001 (one year after the DPP won the presidency for the first time), winter 2006, winter 2010 (two years after the KMT took back the presidency), and summer 2014.[19] The results concerning democracy in general, plus the Asian Barometer poll of South Koreans in 2015, for comparison's sake, are in table 13-1.

TABLE 13-1. **Attitude toward Democracy, Taiwan, and South Korea, 2001–2015, Various Years (Percent)**

	Survey				
	Taiwan Summer 2001	Taiwan Winter 2006	Taiwan Winter 2010	Taiwan Summer/Fall 2014	South Korea Fall 2015
Attitude toward democracy in general					
Democracy may have problems; still best form of government			90	88	89
We should get rid of parliament and elections and have a stronger leader decide things	22	18	17	16	20
Only one political party should be allowed to stand for election and hold office	18	12	10	8	15
Army should come in to govern the country	8	7	5	4	9
We should get rid of elections and parliaments and have experts make decisions on behalf of the people	17		14	12	21
Attitude toward Taiwan's democratic system					
Satisfaction with the way democracy works	53	59	70	64	63
Democracy is capable of solving problems in society	58	62	65	61	76
Democracy is suitable for our country	59	68	74	78	84
How much of a democracy is our country? (full or with minor problems)		53	63	60	68
Democracy is more important than economic development	11	16	16	19	23
Protecting political freedom is more important than reducing economic inequality			17	21	16
Democracy is always preferable	45	50	52	47	63

Source: Yun-han Chu, and others, "Re-assessing the Popular Foundation of Asian Democracies: Findings from Four Waves of the Asian Barometer Survey," Working Paper Series 120 (Asian Barometer, 2016).

The polls conducted in 2010 and 2014 showed that, as a general matter, Taiwan citizens strongly support the idea that democracy is still the best form of government, whatever its problems (90 and 88 percent, respectively). They oppose a number of alternatives to democracy: rule by a strongman, by the military, by a single party, and by technocrats. Of these alternatives, the clearest points of reference are the authoritarian systems in Taiwan through the late 1980s and in the PRC today.

The most recent wave of the survey in Taiwan found that 64 percent of those polled were satisfied with how democracy works in Taiwan, and more than three-fourths of respondents thought that it was suitable for Taiwan. There were some discordant notes, however:

- Only 60 percent said that their political system was a full democracy or one with minor problems.

- Only 47 percent said that democracy was always preferable.

- A mere 19 percent said that democracy was more important than economic development.

- Only 21 percent thought that political freedom was more important than reducing economic equality.

On some questions, Taiwan respondents in late 2014 were less positive about their democratic system than people in other countries around the same time. For example, only 61 percent of people in Taiwan agreed that democracy is capable of solving problems in society, whereas 77 percent of Japanese, 76 percent of South Koreans, 87 percent of Indonesians, 82 percent of Malaysians, and 65 percent of Filipinos thought so.

The 2012 World Values Survey asked respondents about the essential elements of democracy. It used a zero-to-ten scale, ten being absolutely essential. The elements that received the strongest support, all with an average score above eight, were that people chose their leaders through free elections, that civil rights existed to protect against government oppression, and that men and women were recognized as equal. There was more moderate support (averages between 6.44 and 7.43) for government policies that equalized wealth and income and aided the unemployed.[20]

An analysis of the 2007 Asian Barometer Survey data by Chu Yun-han and Huang Min-hua, two democracy scholars in Taiwan, sought to measure respondents' general support for democracy, on the one hand, and their adherence to liberal democratic values, on the other. Respondents therefore fell into four groups: "consistent democrats" (gave high support for democracy and liberal values), "nondemocrats" (gave low support on both variables), "superficial democrats" (paid lip-service to democracy but held many anti-liberal attitudes), and "critical democrats" (believed in liberal democratic principles but also "harbor[ed] some reservation about democracy's desirability, suitability, efficacy, or priority in a specific historical context"). The results demonstrated that half of Taiwan's citizens surveyed were critical democrats and one-quarter were consistent democrats. That is, three-quarters of respondents believed in liberal, democratic values, but two-thirds of that group had a degree of skepticism about democracy's value in practice. (One-sixth of people surveyed were nondemocrats, and 8 percent were superficial democrats.)[21]

The World Values Survey asked people about their confidence in domestic institutions. In 2012 it found that institutions associated with democracy did not rate well. Respondents had a "great deal" or "quite a lot" of confidence in other institutions:

- banks, 76.1 percent
- environmental organizations, 73.6 percent
- the central government, 44.8 percent
- the civil service, 59.4 percent
- religious organizations, 66.7 percent
- the police, 62.1 percent
- the armed forces, 52.9 percent
- the courts, 47.5 percent
- the press, 28.4 percent
- the Legislative Yuan, 27.6 percent
- political parties, 22.4 percent[22]

The low level of support for the press, the LY, and political parties is not surprising, since those institutions generally do not have good reputations. Yet it is still intriguing that people have more confidence in environmental organizations than they do the police and the armed forces, more in religious organizations than the courts, and more in the civil service than in the legislature or political parties. Also intriguing is that, at least in 2012, respondents twenty-nine years of age and younger had either equal or greater confidence in political institutions than did older cohorts. Yet it should be a matter of concern that institutions that play key roles in grappling with Taiwan's problems (the LY and political parties) inspire so little confidence.

One reason for the low respect in which Taiwan's legislators are held is their reputation for corruption, which seems to be well earned. It was noted earlier that Taiwan's ranking in Transparency International's Corruption Perceptions Index (CPI) had improved since 2007. In 2019, it ranked Taiwan twenty-eighth in the world. Within East Asia, excluding Australia and New Zealand, it was fourth after Singapore, Hong Kong, and Japan. Its score was 65 out of 100. The score was 85 for Singapore, 76 for Hong Kong, and 73 for Japan.[23] The gap with Singapore and Hong Kong suggests there is room for improvement.

Of course, the CPI examined more than the public views of parliamentarians, but there is much anecdotal evidence that it is a serious problem. In September 2020, for example, prosecutors charged three LY members and one former member with violations of the anti-corruption act for their involvement in business disputes. Two were members of the KMT and one each were from the DPP and minority New Power Party.[24] The larger significance of such behavior is that when government personnel use their official positions to increase their private wealth, they may be distracted from addressing issues that affect Taiwan's future. They also weaken confidence in the integrity of the system. Taiwan is not the only democratic system to be weakened by corruption. The United States is certainly not a shining example of political probity. Yet under its unique circumstances, can Taiwan afford for its politicians to ignore the big picture and spend their time in rent-seeking?

When it comes to types of political participation, the World Values Survey shows a variation in which ones Taiwan people value. For sure, they place a high value on voting in elections: 59.6 respondents said that they always voted in local elections, and 70.6 percent said they did so in national elections. Only 10.3 and 5.2 percent, respectively, said they never participated in local and national elections. Moreover, 81.8 percent believed elections offered voters a genuine choice either very often or fairly often. A greater number, 85.9 percent, believed that elections were very or rather important in making it possible for their families to make a good living (thus linking politics to economic aspirations). However, 71 percent of those respondents reported either modest or no interest in politics. Around a quarter of them signed petitions and attended peaceful demonstrations.[25]

That only 61 percent of people in Taiwan agreed that democracy is capable of solving problems in society and only 47 percent thought that it was always the preferable system is revealing.[26] Chang Yu-tzung and Chu Yun-han, two political scientists associated with the Asian Barometer Survey, warn that, "The most alarming trend is the rapid depletion of public trust in some key democratic institutions, such as the president, the central government, the leg-islature . . . and political parties. . . . The recurring pattern of dramatic swings of the pendulum . . . after each rotation of power has done a lot of damage to the foundational legitimacy of the democratic regime."[27] The analysis in pre-vious chapters of the dysfunctional politics surrounding policy issues suggests that there is a basis to the survey results. Looking in more depth, moreover, there are several features of Taiwan's contemporary democracy that can dilute public confidence. Some stem from the way the system was designed. Others are part of citizens' attempt to circumvent the institutions and procedures of the representative system.

Institutions as Sources of Suboptimal Performance

Since the transition to democracy, it has been institutions that shape politics. Elections set the relative power of political parties, and, more than anything else, the interaction of the executive and the legislature determined policies. Some facets of Taiwan politics stem from the design of those institutions. They are polarization, majoritarianism, the formation of third parties, and the power of veto players.

Polarization

In the book *Democracies Divided: The Global Challenge of Political Polariza-tion*, Thomas Carothers and Andrew O'Donohue present a systematic and comparative analysis of the trend toward zero-sum politics in many democra-cies. Obviously, some polarization is inevitable in democratic systems as par-ties seek to differentiate themselves from their rivals. Competition is not a bad thing, particularly if it enhances performance of the political system. But in *Democracies Divided,* the authors focus on what they call "severe polariza-tion," where cleavages are no longer cross-cutting but have become cumula-tive. The members of each party have a high-level of agreement on all major issues. The difference between parties goes beyond "principled issue-based dif-ferences to a [split over] social identity."[28]

Does Taiwan qualify as a severely polarized democracy? The impression one gets from watching Taiwan politics is that it is very much a contact sport, and sometimes literally so. Politicians on one side often think the worst of their opponents' motives, even as they think the best of their own. On many policy issues, party affiliation determines one's substantive position. Debates over identity and political loyalty are a central part of political discourse. Compromise between the Blue and Green camps is difficult. The mass media, thriving as it does on conflict, exacerbates the polarization in political circles. The result is often a zero-sum contest ("you-live-I-die"; in Chinese, *nihuo wosi*). The PRC factor does add a significant layer of complexity, but it is not the sole source of division.

Majoritarianism

Related to polarization is the majoritarianism that has marked the Taiwan political system since 2008. The bias in the system of electing the president on a first-past-the-post system favors the selection of a candidate who can win a clear majority. The 2005 reforms of the system for legislative elections, which replaced multi-member districts with single-member ones, had a similar impact. Since 2008, one party has controlled both the presidency and the legislature at the same time. The KMT held sway from 2008 to 2016, even as it was plagued by internal conflicts. The DPP defeated the KMT in both the presidential and LY contests in 2016 and will hold sway until 2024.

Majoritarian systems have some built-in advantages. They tend to produce fewer parties, or at least fewer large parties, because election outcomes are on a winner-take-all basis. Fewer parties mean fewer policy programs from which voters must choose. There may be value in thus reducing the number of policy programs in competition when a country faces an existential challenge as Taiwan does. Too many proposals can produce confusion and gridlock. A small number of parties in the legislature means less time is needed for forming ruling coalitions. In addition, when legislators are selected from simple territorial districts, they are more likely to be responsive and accountable to their constituents than legislators who are picked in multi-member districts. In the latter case, when a group of parliamentarians represents a single large district, the incentives for each legislator to be attentive to the needs of constituents is lower than if she or he were the only representative.

Yet majoritarian systems have their downsides. Legislative elections skew the results in favor of the winning party. Thus in 2016, the DPP got 44.6 percent of the single-member LY vote but won 68.5 percent of those seats. A majoritarian system for Taiwan's legislature fosters a zero-sum character in politics, one that is magnified by the winner-take-all nature of the presidential election, which is held on the same day.[29] Taiwan's electoral system for the LY does seek to mitigate the distortions of majoritarianism by marrying it with proportional representation for thirty-four seats, based on a separate vote for political party. But there is still a distortion. In 2016, for example, the DPP won 44.1 percent of the party vote and got 52.9 percent of those seats.[30]

When it comes to accountability, the worst feature of executive-legislative majoritarianism is that the ruling power of the moment has the opportunity—and temptation—to enact as much of its agenda as possible during its time in office, in hopes that most or all of it will survive the next transfer of power. In Taiwan, that period of opportunity lasts at least four years and perhaps eight years, because the president may serve for two terms.

A majoritarian configuration of power, particularly one in which the executive and the majority caucus in the LY are working with close coordination, can create deep frustration within the minority party. It has little or no impact on administration policy, and it lacks the votes to change or block bills put forward by the majority if the majority is determined to ram the legislation through. Street protests and support from some segments of the media can compensate somewhat for this imbalance of power, but they do not negate the opposition party's frustration.

The incentives to mount disruptive challenges grows. For example, in June 2020, the LY was scheduled to consider President Tsai's nominations of individuals to be the president and members of the Control Yuan, the ombudsman institution. Tsai's candidate for president was Chen Chu, who had been an opponent of the KMT regime from the 1970s and spent time in jail as a consequence. More recently, she had served two terms as mayor of Kaohsiung and then as Tsai's chief of staff. The KMT caucus chose her confirmation as an issue to mount a strong challenge to the DPP, arguing that Chen's administration in Kaohsiung had been so marred by official misbehavior that the Control Yuan was the last institution that she should lead. To express their opposition, some KMT members of the LY occupied its chamber on the afternoon of Sunday, June 28. They secured the doors to the chamber with chains and piled up chairs as a second set of obstacles. Late morning on June 29, DPP members cut the chains and moved into the chamber. Scuffles ensued, and it was not until an hour later that they gained control of the speaker's podium.[31] After a few more struggles, the DPP majority prevailed and the nominees were confirmed. [32]

Of course, the DPP is not blameless when it comes to such methods. It used the same tactic many times back when it seemed to hold permanent minority status. With the Sunflower movement of 2014, civil society got into the act of LY occupation, with no small degree of assistance from the DPP caucus. Despite the frustration that produces these eruptions, and whatever the media publicity that the instigators attract to their cause, respect for the norms of a regular legislative process suffers. In turn, respect for the idea of representative government that a legislature symbolizes declines as well.

Limits on Polarization and Majoritarianism

Qualifying the hypothesis that Taiwan is severely polarized and the victim of majoritarianism, it is clear that the Blue and Green camps are not as unified as they seem on first glance. As already noted, each camp is divided into subcamps defined by degree of ideology and pragmatism. The spectrum runs from the unification-inclined Deep Blues, through the more pragmatic Light Blues and Light Greens to the pro-independence Deep Greens. Within each camp, there have been struggles for power on some issues.

But these struggles occur in different ways in each major party. Within the KMT, the Light Blue, more Taiwanese wing of the party can try to block a Deep Blue leadership from adopting policies that are too accommodating to the PRC. On the Green side of the spectrum, a Light Green leader is more likely to be electable as president, in part because she or he usually appeals to middle voters to win election. As a result, that person will come under Deep Green pressure to move faster toward independence and to pursue other objectives that lie more outside the public mainstream. But the ultimate check is the ruling party's fear that voters will punish it for going outside the mainstream of public preferences. The results of the 2008 and 2016 elections reflected voters' belief that first Chen Shui-bian and then Ma Ying-jeou had gone too far in one direction or another. That check exists, but the party in charge still has at least four years and perhaps eight to chalk up a positive performance. It may also do a lot of damage before voters can replace incumbents.

One example of intraparty power struggle occurred in Ma Ying-jeou's second term, when he sought to purge legislative Speaker Wang Jin-pyng. The ostensible reason was alleged mishandling of classified information, but the real reason was Ma's deep frustration that the Light Blue Wang was using his position to frustrate his legislative program. Wang fought back, and Ma had to back down.

Then in 2015, the KMT had a hard time picking its candidate for president. The more likely potential candidates with mainstream views held back, perhaps believing that Tsai Ing-wen was certain to win. Seeing no takers, Hung Hsiu-chu, a Deep Blue unknown, stepped forward and won the nomination without a contest. But her views on the PRC were quite forward leaning, even for the KMT. The more that party members heard about her views, the more concerned they became. The Light Blue wing of the party, who tended to be Taiwanese from the south and regarded Wang Jin-pyng as their leader, mobilized opposition to Hung. In October 2015, three months before the election, the KMT replaced her with Chu Li-luan, the mayor of New Taipei City. The intra-KMT contention over the nomination was one of the reasons that Tsai beat Chu in a landslide.

Another example of party infighting took place after the DPP suffered a clear defeat in the 2018 local elections. The Deep Green wing of the party blamed Tsai Ing-wen, claiming that the policies she had pursued were too moderate, especially on issues connected with their independence agenda, and that she should have done more to challenge Beijing's Taiwan policy. That the United States under Donald Trump appeared to be showing unprecedentedly strong support for Taiwan strengthened that belief. Some Deep Greens went so far as to try to pressure Tsai not to run for reelection. To that end, they encouraged William Lai Ching-te, who had been serving as Tsai's premier, to challenge her for the presidential nomination. Tsai's supporters were "outraged at the viciousness of the smear campaign" waged by Lai's older Deep Green backers, "especially since this was a contest between 'comrades' of the same party." In the end, Tsai won the nomination and picked Lai to take the vice presidential slot on the ticket.[33]

Division in the DPP concerning the PRC gets played out on other issues. Party leaders must avoid creating the impression that they do not care about the economy if they are to gain and keep power. Because the mainland has such an outsized impact on Taiwan's prosperity, and because the economy is the top priority for voters, the DPP must find ways to separate business promotion from ideology. Magistrates and mayors of the DPP have understood that their performance depends, in part, on maintaining favorable economic ties between their jurisdictions and the mainland economy. Similarly, civil society groups, which had formed coalitions with the DPP in the 1990s, abandoned the party at the beginning of the new century because they concluded that the Chen Shui-bian administration had sacrificed the interests of the people to accommodate large corporations.

In short, the KMT cannot win at the national level unless it is able to forge unity within the party between mainlanders and Taiwanese, between the North and the South, and between the party center and the local branches. The DPP cannot win at the national level unless it mutes the differences between Light Greens and Deep Greens and thereby appeals to a broader swath of the electorate.

These divisions can also limit the political impact of the party controlling both the presidency and the legislature. The Ma administration was unable to push through some of its agenda, in part, because it could not treat the KMT caucus in the LY as a unified bloc committed to supporting it down the line. Speaker Wang Jin-pyng exemplified this legislative independence, but he was only the most obvious example.[34] The DPP came into office in 2016 with the intention of enacting a bill to strengthen LY oversight over cross-Strait economic agreements, the proposal that Speaker Wang had negotiated to end the Sunflower movement two years earlier. Yet legislation did not advance, in part because of splits within the Green Camp.[35]

This episode illustrates some of the ways in which the character and norms of the LY can limit the dominance of the majority party. National Chengchi University political scientists Huang Shih-hao and Sheng Shing-yuan document how "parties of all different sizes, as well as individual legislators, can exert influence over legislation" with multiple points of access. As a result, much is proposed and relatively little is accomplished. "Influence over legislation is relatively evenly distributed across parties, and the legislative advantage of the executive branch and the majority party is small."[36]

Not only are the two political camps not as unified as they might seem, there is also evidence that the public is not as polarized as politicians are. The finding of the more rigorous surveys on perceptions of national identity is that people see themselves not as either Chinese or Taiwanese but rather as some combination of the two. The World Values Survey found that by and large respondents tended to take a centrist position on issues such as income inequality, private versus government ownership of business, and whether the government or the people themselves should be responsible for people's welfare.[37]

In addition, the findings of the Taiwan National Security Survey concerning party loyalties suggest that a significant part of the public is not strongly tied to just one side, the DPP or KMT, or the Green camp or Blue camp (see table 13-2a). This part of the survey asked whether they "especially supported," "generally supported," or "inclined toward" the main political parties. Looking only at respondents who associated themselves with one of those parties, the distribution seems bimodal, with 73 to 83 percent either strongly supportive or generally supportive of their camp. Yet around 50 percent of respondents overall said they were "neutral," or did not answer, or said that they associated with another party (most of which are tiny). If that group is factored in, the resulting distribution is more unimodal, with a fairly large group of neutral or independent voters in the middle. This distribution is merely illustrative, since it is impossible to know how many of this "neutral" group were true independents. National Chengchi University political scientist Yu Ching-hsin has addressed this issue with more precision, and he estimates, based on elections up through 2012, that true independents make up at least 25 percent of the electorate.

Recent elections appear to confirm the picture of an electorate that is divided among Blue loyalists, Green loyalists, and true independents. This estimated distribution of sentiments, combined with changing political circumstances, affects the results of presidential elections. Thus in 2008, after eight years of DPP rule under Chen Shui-bian, Ma Ying-jeou won the presidency in 2008 with 58 percent of the vote. By the election in 2016, the next one in which there was no incumbent in the race, the KMT's popularity had shrunk badly, and it did not mount a strong challenge to Tsai Ing-wen. She therefore won with 56 percent. Then, in the 2018 local elections, excluding independents and small parties, KMT candidates won 55 percent of the vote and DPP

TABLE 13-2A. **Party Loyalty, Blue and Green Supporters and Neutral Voters (2017)**

	Support level	Total %
Blue		
	Consistent[a]	16.7
	Weak	6.2
	Total	22.9
Green		
	Consistent[a]	19.6
	Weak	3.7
	Total	23.3
Neutral[b]		50.5

TABLE 13-2B. **Party Loyalty, Blue and Green Supporters Only (2017)**

Support level	Blue %	Green %	Total %
Consistent[a]	33.7	39.6	73.3
Weak	12.5	7.5	20.0

Source: Taiwan National Security Survey, Program in Asian Security Studies, Duke University (https://sites.duke.edu/pass/taiwan-national-security-survey/).

a. "Especially" or "generally" supported the camp.
b. Neutral or supported another party.

candidates got 45 percent.[38] But fourteen months later, Tsai was re-elected with a larger percentage than she scored in 2016. This pattern suggests that although some voters vote their party regardless of circumstances, a significant share cast their ballots based on the performance of the incumbent party. As Yu Ching-hsin writes, "Political independents frequently play a pivotal role in deciding the final outcome of a close election. They also function as a vital balance in an otherwise polarized society. This is especially important for a nascent democracy like Taiwan, where the party system has not yet stabilized."[39]

Third Parties

Splinter parties regularly emerge to fill niches that the major parties have left open. As a result, they weaken the cohesion and solidarity of the camp to which they are most closely aligned on policy issues and create a degree of fragmentation of the political system writ large. The existence of third parties also demonstrate that the Blue and Green camps are not as solid as they might seem, and that polarization is actually weaker than it seems on first glance.

Splinters occur for different reasons. One is an ideological split within one of the large parties. For example, the Deep Blue conservatives left the KMT in 1993 to form the New Party because they did not like Lee Teng-hui's increasing emphasis on Taiwanese identity. Political experience can be another stimulus. The young people who formed the New Power Party after the 2014 Sunflower movement wished to capitalize on the success of that movement. Its leaders also believed that neither of the main parties cared about the interests of the working class, so the New Power Party tried to fill that niche. In other cases, new parties appear as vehicles for politicians who have been marginalized from the dominant two-party system to remain relevant. Thus Lee Teng-hui formed the Deep-Green Taiwan Solidarity Union after he stepped down as president in 2000. The same year, James Soong formed the Deep-Blue People First Party.

As a result, the KMT and DPP cannot rely on the absolute loyalty of their various leaders and factions, because they have the option of going off on their own. The 2020 election produced another splinter party, the Taiwan People's Party. This was both an organizational vehicle for the independent mayor of Taipei, Ko Wen-che, and a reflection of rising populist sentiments.

Support for third parties is strongest soon after their formation, as they present what appears to be a positive alternative to the DPP and KMT. Yet none of the third parties that have emerged since the mid-1990s got very

large, because they face built-in limits to growth. They often lack the organization needed to elect a president or legislators from geographic districts.
What allows them to exercise influence at all is the party-list feature of legislative elections, whereby voters cast a ballot for their preferred party as well
as for the representative of their geographic district. If a small party can get
more than 5 percent of the total party-list vote, it is given seats based on the
share of that vote. For example, until 2020 the People First Party got sufficient
support from Deep Blue voters to win a few LY seats, and party leader James
Soong often tried to enhance that support by running for president. The legislators that small parties control then bargain with the two larger parties for
their votes.

The party-list vote in the 2020 legislative elections updated the relative
strength of the large and small parties. The DPP received only 34 percent of
the party vote, which was 23 percent less than Tsai Ing-wen's vote total. The
KMT received 33 percent, and all other parties got the remaining third. Neither the People First Party nor the Taiwan Solidarity Union received more
than 5 percent of the party vote and so neither won seats. The New Power
Party fell from five seats to three, but Ko Wen-che's Taiwan People's Party
(TPP) got 11 percent of the party vote and five seats. The most plausible explanation for these results is that a significant share of voters (probably young
people) wanted Tsai to continue as president, or wanted to prevent Han Kuo-
yu from becoming president, but were not happy with the DPP's performance.
Casting their party vote for the TPP was a way to convey that message.

Small parties have the greatest leverage when neither of the major parties
has an absolute majority of seats in the LY. In that circumstance, the majority
party must negotiate with them to secure majorities on an issue by issue basis.
As an editorial in the *Taipei Times* notes, small parties together can form a
third force that, it asserts, can have a positive impact on the LY's culture. "The
nation's politics suffers from ineffectual partisan blockades, and embarrassing
legislative and council floor tussles, exacerbated by the stagnant tribalism of a
purely polarized approach to every single issue. Having minor parties whose
vote could mean the difference between the success or failure of a government
proposal would arguably encourage more rational debate."[40]

Vetocracy

Between elections, opponents of the ruling majority's program can exploit
various openings in the system to block it. A notorious example of this phenomenon was the manipulation of the process in the LY to delay, dilute, or

block legislative initiatives. This was most common during the Ma Ying-jeou period, when the KMT had a significant LY majority and should have been able to pass any bill that it wanted. But before a bill could go to a final vote, it was subject to discussions in the "consultation committee" (*xieshang huiyi*). Political parties that had at least three LY seats had equal representation on the committee, in which case it did not matter how large the majority party's LY margin was. The irony of this setup was that it was led by then Speaker Wang Jin-pyng, a KMT vice chairman and the leader of the Taiwanese wing of the KMT. He used his role to enhance his power relative to that of President Ma and the executive branch and benefited the DPP in the process.[41] When the DPP assumed control of the LY in 2016, it reduced the potential for that sort of antimajoritarian tactic by making the meetings of the committee available to the public.

There are other ways in which majority initiatives can be frustrated. Legislators from opposition parties—or even from a faction of the majority party—can submit EY officials to public criticism during periodic interpellations or committee meetings. Legislative Yuan members can threaten to cut the budget for specific programs. Through demonstrations and other types of public actions, civil society groups can put the administration on the defensive. Large-scale protests can have the same effect, and the mass media can amplify the causes of protesters.

This illustrates the power of veto actors. The more or less consistent division of the budget pie year after year suggests that coalitions of agencies, legislators, and interest groups are able to preserve their relative share of the budget and block others from expanding their share. The capacity of any administration to make policy changes is constrained by the strong aversion of corporations and the public to increases in taxes and electricity prices. The KMT was able to use the courts to block some of the moves in the transitional justice campaign.

Obstacles to government action can be erected preemptively. The most significant example was an amendment to the Act Governing Relations between the People of the Taiwan Area and the Mainland Area that the LY passed in May 2019. The amendment established the process for considering any draft agreement with the PRC that had a "major constitutional or political effect." It was enacted at a time that the ruling DPP was worried it would lose power after the 2020 presidential and legislative elections and the incoming KMT government would negotiate a peace accord with Beijing.[42] The steps required to approve any agreement were as follows:

- There would first be a determination of whether the proposal had "major constitutional or political effect" (those terms were not defined, nor was a process established for making the determination).

- Then, there would be a submission by the EY to the LY of a "signing plan" and "political impact assessment report" at least ninety days before negotiations were to begin.

- Next, there would be an approval of the plan by three-quarters of the LY at a meeting attended by three-quarters of the membership.

- Once talks with Beijing begin, the lead agency would make "timely reports" to the LY. If the EY decided that the negotiations were not feasible, it could terminate them. If the LY reached the same conclusion, it could cancel the talks by a majority vote.

- If a draft agreement was reached, it hopefully was to be published within fifteen days of the presidential signature.

- For the agreement to go into effect, it would have to be passed by a three-quarters majority in the LY with three-quarters of the membership LY attending and then approved in a referendum by half of eligible voters.[43]

Practically speaking, the net result of this series of procedural steps is that no agreement can ever go into effect without the support of all major political parties, in which case legislative and public approval would be more likely. (This act was not the legislation that Wang Jin-pyng promised to the leaders of the Sunflower movement to get them to end their occupation of the LY. That piece of legislation governed economic agreements and is still in limbo.)

Veto players also have an outsize degree of power in the United States, a trend that the Stanford University scholar Francis Fukuyama has criticized, on the grounds that "vetocracy" is one of the key ways that a developed political system can undergo decay. He writes, "A well-functioning and legitimate regime needs to achieve balance between government power and institutions that constrain the state. Things can become unbalanced in either direction, with insufficient checks on state power on the one hand, or excessive veto power by different social groups on the other that prevent any sort of collective action."[44] Fukuyama would most likely attribute the imbalance in Taiwan's political system to the second of these imbalances.

Circumvention of Institutions

The premise of the democratic system established in the early 1990s was that politics would flow through institutions, particularly parties and the LY, and that voters would judge performance in elections. Yet there was no reason to believe that those institutions would command respect forever, particularly if performance was unsatisfactory. In that case, new modes of politics would emerge and place a burden on existing institutions to adapt if they are to remain effective and relevant.[45] For example, changes in information technology have altered the kinds of political participation that people prefer. Huang Min-hua, a political scientist at National Taiwan University, finds a trade-off in Taiwan between voting and forms of civic activism like demonstrations. He writes:

> The changes of social communication . . . [have a] salient impact on political participation: people tend not to be satisfied with the conventional channels to engage in politics and incline to adopt a direct means to voice out their political views and influence politics. . . . The rise of the internet expedites the flow of information and breaks spatiotemporal restriction of communication, which together make collective action easier to organize and therefore, allow people to engage in political affairs through a more direct and instant measure by activist participation, comparing to the traditional way of electoral participation. This trend is particularly prominent within younger generations.[46]

Three modes of circumvention have become more common since 2008: a protest culture (the aggressive exercise of political rights), promoting the use of the right of referendum to decide policy issues, and voters' attraction to populist, non-establishment politicians.

The Emergence of a Protest Culture

During the latter part of Taiwan's authoritarian period, social protest movements arose that complemented the periodic efforts of the political opposition—the *dangwai*—to open the political system. One of the most prominent movements occurred in the town of Lukang in Changhua County in 1986. Residents protested the construction of a Dupont titanium oxide plant in a local industrial zone because they feared that the resulting pollution would hurt fishing, damage temples, and suppress the tourism industry. The protests, which lasted into early 1987, led DuPont to abandon its plan to build the plant in Lukang.[47] Thereafter, civil society groups proliferated on a variety issues. One faction of the DPP, which coincidentally was established in 1986, advocated cooperation with civil society groups as the most effective way to gain political power.

Yet from the completion of the transition to democracy until the late 2000s, politics usually flowed through political parties—essentially the DPP and the KMT—and not outside them. Representative democracy, via elections of the president and legislators, was the norm, not direct democracy through mechanisms such as initiative, referendum, and recall. Debates over policy occurred within the LY and between it and the agencies of the executive branch (the technocracy). The civil society sector existed and provided some checks on the legislative-executive duopoly, but it was still relatively weak. Even when the DPP government won power in the 2000 election and civil society groups had high hopes for more political impact, they were soon disappointed because the Chen Shui-bian administration ignored their agenda and tilted increasingly to accommodating business interests (he used referendums for political, not policy, reasons).[48] To the extent that protests occurred, they were focused on policy issues rather than targeted on authority itself.

The conduct of politics through parties began to change after Ma Ying-jeou took office in 2008. The number of protests in Taiwan had reached almost 800 in 2006 before dropping to more than 400 in 2008 and 2009. They then picked up again, climbing to between 500 and 600 in 2012 and 2013. In those last two years, more than thirty events attracted in excess of 1,000 participants. From 2010 on, there were about 100 "confrontational protest events" that involved clashes with the police.[49]

New activist groups sprang up around an array of issues such as food safety, environmental protection, and historic preservation. Young people fired by idealism and mobilized by social media provided the leadership of these groups, not political professionals.[50] "Flash" events became the principal mode of political action, replacing manifestos and the press conferences of more conventional civil society groups. They were different from the staider demonstrations that were a regular, almost routinized part of Taiwan's politics. Among other things, they benefited from Taiwan's hyperactive mass media, which amplified the message of the new-style politics, and the increasing use of social media to mobilize supporters. For example, in 2013 an obscure group named Citizen 1985 called for a candlelight vigil on the evening of Saturday, August 4, in front of the Office of the President to mourn the death of Corporal Hung Chung-chiu, who had died under suspicious circumstances. Even the organizers were surprised when more than 200,000 people showed up, and the minister of national defense soon resigned, taking responsibility for the death.[51]

Over time, there emerged a loose set of leaders, organizations, and networks devoted to political action outside the normal system. Each movement yielded lessons that were applied to the next one, with amalgamated learning that ultimately culminated in the Sunflower movement.[52] Yet even if we stipulate that representative democracy was not effective in addressing policy issues, direct democracy did not work particularly well, either. Mass protests were more effective in blocking what they opposed than in promoting what they desired (if they had a program at all). The complex interaction of political parties, the legislature, executive branch officials, the mass media, and twenty-first-century social movements have now made more difficult the achievement of outcomes that enjoyed broad political support.

The Sunflower Movement

The rebirth of civil society groups was, in part, a response to the Ma Ying-jeou administration's conservative ideological bent and its policy of normalizing economic relations with the PRC, pursuing economic interdependence through liberalization of trade and investment.[53] More than twenty cross-Strait agreements had been signed by June 2013, when a cross-Strait agreement on trade in services was concluded. For a couple of reasons, it soon provoked opposition.

First of all, various economic sectors became concerned that the agreement would leave them at a competitive disadvantage against mainland competitors. For example, printers objected to allowing mainland investment in Taiwan's printing industry as long as PRC censorship restricted the mainland market for their materials. The administration compounded these fears by its failure to explain in advance what was in the agreement.

More broadly, the DPP and civil society groups argued that Ma's economic engagement of Beijing was benefiting wealthy individuals and large corporations only, at the expense of the rest of the population. Opponents feared the hollowing out of the Taiwan economy and claimed that growing economic dependence on the PRC would put Taiwan in a weak position when it came to negotiating political issues (even though the Ma administration had rejected Beijing's attempt to start political talks). A later poll, taken at the end of 2015, would find that 62 percent of those surveyed thought that Taiwan had become too economically dependent on the mainland.[54] Established nongovernmental organizations banded together in a Democratic Front against the agreement. A key group established by student activists was the Black Island National Youth Front.

Procedurally, the Ma administration made the mistake of trying to avoid a detailed review of the agreement. It claimed that this was an executive order that only had to be submitted to the LY "for the record," as opposed to more extensive review. Some KMT members of the LY objected on institutional grounds to being bypassed in this way. Speaker Wang Jin-pyng, who was embroiled at the time in a bitter political dispute with Ma, weighed in and brokered an understanding between the DPP and KMT caucuses of the LY that the agreement would be reviewed on an article by article basis.[55]

Beginning in July 2013, twenty public hearings were convened to solicit opinions on various parts of the pact (a KMT legislator chaired twelve of them, and a DPP legislator, eight). Disagreements between the KMT and DPP came to a head in mid-March 2014, when the period for hearings ended and it was time to move to the second reading of the agreement. Ironically, a poll conducted by the DPP's Poll Center found the public actually favored the KMT cross-Strait policies over those of the DPP. For example, when asked, "Which party's cross-Strait economic policy is closer to yours?" 44.7 percent of respondents picked the KMT, and 25.5 percent picked the DPP.[56]

Yet this assessment of the public mood had no impact on the contention between the KMT and DPP legislators charged with reviewing the service-trade agreement. The KMT caucus suddenly asserted on March 10 that, pursuant to a provision of the law governing the operation of the LY, the time had long since expired for reviewing the agreement. The DPP caucus countered, probably correctly, that the provision cited did not apply in this case. Some in the KMT agreed.[57] The DPP called for the review to be conducted according to the principles of reciprocal market opening, fair competition, public livelihood, and national security, all of which were arguably biased against approval of the agreement.[58]

Also on March 10, an intense argument began as to which party would be in the chair for the plenary review on a provision-by-provision basis.[59] According to the LY's rules, the chair of committees rotates between the leading majority party (in this case, the KMT) and the leading minority party (then the DPP). At the point that hearings ended, a DPP legislator was in the chair of the committee of jurisdiction (Internal Administration). The KMT caucus thought that it was inappropriate for the opposition party to set the agenda for a plenary consideration of the agreement, so it delayed the proceedings until one of its legislators, Chang Ching-chung, could assume the chair.

That annoyed the DPP, which created its own procedural obstacles on the grounds that the Ma administration had kept its negotiations with China in a "black box."[60] On the evening of March 11, the DPP occupied the meeting room so that KMT legislator Chang Ching-chung could not take the chair.[61]

On March 12, according to the *Taipei Times,* the meeting, at which a DPP legislator presided, was marked by chaos, conflict, and a standoff between the pan-Green and the pan-Blue camps, during which Chang grabbed the sign-up sheet so that DPP members could not register to speak.[62] On the same day, the DPP called for a renegotiation of the agreement.[63]

The session on March 17 was also chaotic, with DPP members tackling Chang Ching-chung when he tried to convene the meeting. The arguments went on for three hours, at which point an angry Chang grabbed another microphone, invoked the questionable provision of the law governing legislative operations, and announced that the second reading was complete and that the agreement would be forwarded to the plenary session of the LY for final consideration.[64] Three DPP legislators decided to undertake a hunger strike the next day.

A central problem here was a lack of clarity over how to apply the rules of the legislative process to this situation. Compounding matters was the well-established norm of sharing the convening powers between the KMT and the DPP, which deprived the majority party of control over the agenda. That would not create a problem on issues that were not too controversial, but it was a problem when the stakes were high. (When the KMT became the LY minority in 2016, it used the same obstructionist tactics.)[65]

The Black Island National Youth Front had remained in the background, so Chang's attempt to speed up consideration of the bill took it by surprise. But the group quickly swung into action. Late in the day on March 18, the forces it mobilized occupied the LY chamber, which they held until April 10. Their principal justification for the action was that the Ma administration had handled the service-trade agreement in a black box, without transparency, and the Black Island National Youth Front was bringing sunshine to the process. Their movement was thus dubbed the Sunflower movement. Speaker Wang Jin-pyng had the authority to request that police end the occupation of his chamber, but he chose not to use it, probably because of his personal and political dispute with Ma Ying-jeou referenced earlier.

Having been preempted by the students, the DPP shifted position. The party decided to oppose the service-trade agreement rather than tolerate arguing against the bill in a plenary session. To ensure that Sunflower occupiers would have continuing access to the chamber, DPP legislators worked in shifts to guard the doors. Party staff also ensured that the activists would have the supplies they needed.

On the evening of March 23, a Sunday and a public holiday, the Black Island National Youth Front escalated by carrying out a sit-in in the courtyard in front of the EY. Thereafter, some of the demonstrators broke into the EY building. The police intervened to retake the building, and the episode turned violent. The occupation of the LY only ended on April 10, when Speaker Wang Jin-pyng, without consulting President Ma and the EY, worked out a deal whereby no action would occur on the service-trade agreement until the LY first passed an agreement concerning cross-Strait economic agreements. As noted, that bill was stuck in the LY as of late 2020.

Also lingering six years later were court cases regarding the actions of protesters and government officials and, by implication, who should be held accountable for what actions. In April 2020, the Taiwan High Court sentenced seven Sunflower Movement activists who had led the attempted break-in of the Executive Yuan to two to four months in prison. This was after they had been tried and acquitted in a lower court. In September, in a civil case before the Taipei District Court, Ma Ying-jeou, Chiang Yi-huah, who was serving as Ma's premier at the time, and two senior police officials were found not guilty of using excessive force in the same incident.[66]

The Sunflower movement has inspired a lot of analysis and commentary.[67] It was the most significant mass movement in almost a decade and the culmination of a series of civil society actions waged against politics as usual. Moreover, it was highly successful in blocking what it opposed. Retrospective accounts by commentators sympathetic to the movement justify it as an appropriate response to the Ma administration's lack of transparency, the growing danger of PRC penetration of the society, the failure of the DPP and other opposition parties to check KMT policies, and the episodes of police violence, which purportedly evoked Taiwan's authoritarian past.

But beyond blaming the DPP for its inability or unwillingness to promote the goals of civil society groups and check the Ma administration's policies, none of the commentaries evaluate this episode of direct democracy for Taiwan's established system of indirect democracy and for the rule of law. Whether the opponents of the service-trade agreement liked it or not, Taiwan's voters had twice entrusted Ma Ying-jeou with the office of the president and the KMT with a majority in the LY. True, the administration may have done a poor job of explaining why the agreement would benefit Taiwan's economy and why it would not put Taiwan at risk. But the norm of a representative system is that if the minority cannot change the majority's policies through the checks accorded in the constitution, gaining power by winning elections is the proper and ultimate response, as difficult as that response may be in the short term. For a relatively small share of the citizenry to preempt the work of the citizenry's representatives, however defectively that work is conducted, is to deprive them of their ultimate authority.[68] Engaging in such actions only sets a precedent for political forces on the other side of the public debate to act in the same way. Moreover, for a relatively small group of citizens, no matter how convinced they are of the rightness of their cause, to occupy public buildings, particular the building where representative government is exercised, is, strictly speaking, a violation of the law.

These precedents aside, there is no denying that social organizations like the Sunflower movement do reflect "a sense of disillusionment with mainstream party politics" and with the weakness of the LY's procedures and norms. Civil society organizations can strengthen democracy by challenging the legislatures and major political parties to do their job.[69] But using questionable means to accomplish purportedly worthy ends can weaken democracy, whereas working to legitimize valid means can strengthen it.

Even granted the public dissatisfaction with politicians (to the point that polls found that only 27.6 percent of respondents had a "great deal" or "quite a lot" of confidence in the legislature), it was still a representative body. More than 65 percent of the LY's members represented geographic constituencies, and most of the rest reflected popular alignment with a political party. Who, one might ask, did the people who occupied the LY chamber represent? They most likely—and no doubt sincerely—believed that they were acting on behalf of the people as a whole against the Ma administration and the KMT caucus in the LY. But on what basis did they make that claim? President Ma and all the members of the LY could cite the democratic legitimacy they had earned by being elected. The Sunflower activists could make no such claim and merely arrogated to themselves the right to take an extreme political action. After the movement stood down, some of its veterans moved from protest to electoral politics. Young people mobilized themselves to participate in the 2014 local elections, throwing their support to the DPP. Later, Sunflower leaders formed the New Power Party, which won five LY seats in 2016 but then dropped back to three in 2020. In 2019 Lin Fei-fan, one of the movement's leaders, was honest enough to acknowledge that Sunflower had failed in making connections with the public on whose behalf they were acting. "We failed to communicate at the grassroots level, so that's why a lot of people remain conservative and unwilling to accept reformation."[70]

The Right of Referendum

As Sun Yat-sen thought about the design of the ROC political system, he advocated a central government with five branches (*yuan* in Chinese): executive, legislature, judiciary, examination, and control. However, he also called for the inclusion of four mechanisms of direct democracy: suffrage, recall, initiative, and referendum. Sun had gained some understanding of how these mechanisms operated in Switzerland and some U.S. states and believed that through them the people could check and balance the administration, which would be staffed by experts and prioritize efficiency, and the legislature. It was no surprise, therefore, that when the 1947 constitution of the ROC came to be written, Article 17 read, "The people shall have the right of election, recall, initiative and referendum" and Article 136 prescribed that "the exercise of the rights of initiative and referendum shall be prescribed by law."[71] Yet because the KMT ruled on an authoritarian basis for the next four decades, the regime never got around to enacting those laws.

When Taiwan made the transition to democracy in the early 1990s, the emphasis was on establishing the institutions of representative, or indirect, democracy and the rules for elections. Nothing was done right away to pass legislation to enable the other three mechanisms of direct democracy. Of these, the right of referendum was most salient, but establishing it might not have occurred had it not been for the single-minded efforts of independence advocate Tsai Tung-jung. He romanized his name as Trong Chai, which is what I use here. He also had the nickname "Tsai gongtou" (Referendum Tsai). It happens that Chai drew me momentarily into his campaign for a referendum law.

Trong Chai was born in 1935 in what is now Chiayi County. Chiayi was one of the places where the ROC military's repression after the February 28 (1947) incident was most severe. Chai was in fifth grade at the time, and his teacher, who had opposed the ROC military, disappeared. For him, as for many Taiwanese, bitterness about the KMT crackdown was personal and life-transforming. He went to the United States for graduate school in 1960, and after a few years he was drawn into anti-KMT political activities. A key point came in 1982, when he and other exiled Taiwanese formed the Formosan Association for Public Affairs as an instrument for changing Taiwan's political system. The organization would support pro-democracy members of the U.S. Congress, and they would try to exert pressure on the KMT regime directly and through the executive branch of the U.S. government. One of those members was Stephen J. Solarz, a Democrat from Brooklyn who, in

January 1981, became chairman of the House Subcommittee on Asian and Pacific Affairs. Solarz was unwilling to promote Chai's ultimate goal of de jure independence, but he was more than willing to work for Taiwan's democratization and greater protection of human rights. I was a member of Solarz's subcommittee staff from 1983 to 1993, and in that capacity was Chai's point of contact.

In April 1988, Chai suggested that Solarz initiate a congressional resolution calling for a plebiscite on whether Taiwan should be a part of the PRC. The focus on a plebiscite reflected Chai's long-standing desire to facilitate an act of self-determination for the people of Taiwan. But there was also his more proximate concern about the growth of cross-Strait social and economic contacts. I happened to believe that promoting a plebiscite would do more harm than good for Taiwan, but in the spring of 1990 Solarz went ahead and introduced a resolution with the operative clause: "It is the sense of Congress that in determining the future of Taiwan, the will and wishes of the people on the island should be taken into account through effective democratic mechanisms, such as a plebiscite."[72] Beyond introducing the resolution, no further action was taken, and no real damage was done.

But the idea did not die. In June 1990, the KMT regime allowed Chai, who had long been on its blacklist of overseas dissidents, to return temporarily to Taiwan for humanitarian reasons. Once Chai got to Taiwan, he stayed and became active in politics as a member of the DPP. His hand is obvious in this sentence in the DPP's 1991 party charter: "Based on the principle of popular sovereignty, the establishment of a sovereign, independent, and self-governing Republic of Taiwan should be carried out by all residents of Taiwan through a national referendum.[73]

The rationale for instituting the right of referendum stemmed from a belief among DPP members that the existing system was stacked against them. Back in the 1990s, the KMT dominated the executive, legislature, and judiciary. It did so by a variety of advantages, such as party-owned assets to fund electoral campaigns and a network of political brokers at the local level. With electoral dominance, the KMT controlled government policy. Taiwanese nationalists like Chai believed that the public was more anti-KMT than election results would suggest, so holding referendums could check KMT power and policies and do so in a way that had democratic legitimacy.[74] Most important for him and other Deep Green members of the party, a referendum was a way to block any move by a KMT government toward unification with the PRC. But more was going on than simply creating a way to mitigate KMT dominance.

First of all, it is worth noting that the current, common term for referendum is *gongmin toupiao* (or *gongtou,* for short), which simply means "citizens cast a vote." But the term for referendum used in the ROC constitution is *fujue,* which has the connotation of reconsideration by a direct popular vote of a measure proposed or approved by the legislature. In addition, Article 12 of the constitution, regarding amending of the constitution, says that after the LY has approved an amendment, it will be subject to review or referendum (*fujue*) by a vote (*toupiao*) by eligible voters of the "free area" of the ROC (that is, Taiwan and its associated islands).[75] But the strongest advocates of the right of referendum believed that the device should be used for purposes other than the review of legislation or an LY-passed draft constitutional amendment, such as defining Taiwan's legal relationship with the state China.[76]

It is also worth noting that in current usage in Taiwan, *gongmin toupiao* can refer to both a referendum and a plebiscite, but in English there is at least a nuance of difference between the two. A referendum reviews legislation. A plebiscite can have that same meaning, particularly as it relates to a major policy issue, but it also can refer to a much more consequential political act, that is, an act of self-determination by the members of one political unit about its future. It was this latter purpose that the strongest advocates of the right of referendum, including Tong Chai, wanted to enable.

As the 2004 presidential election approached, Chen Shui-bian revived the referendum issue. He did so primarily to mobilize the Deep Green base of the DPP, which had been unhappy with his relatively moderate policy approach during the first two years of his first term. Chen made proposals that Beijing interpreted as steps toward independence, with a referendum as the way to negate the check imposed by the KMT-controlled LY. In May 2003, he called for referendums on the issues of nuclear power, the size of the legislature, and whether Taiwan should participate in the World Health Organization. The last issue was sensitive for Beijing because, depending on how the question was worded, it could touch on Taiwan's legal identity. In September 2003, Chen called for a new constitution, in order to, as he put it, make Taiwan a normal country (in effect, an independent country), and to approve the new charter through a referendum.

In the fall of 2003, the DPP proposed a referendum bill in the LY (Trong Chai, then an LY member, was one of the proponents). The draft authorized referendums on changes of the national frontiers, the national flag, and the official name of the country. It also allowed permissive provisions on how many people had to vote for the referendum to be considered valid. The KMT and the People First Party, a KMT splinter, had the votes to kill the bill, but they worried that voters would punish them in the presidential election in March

2004. So a compromise was reached that tightened the turnout provisions and excluded subjects such as the official name of country.[77] Chen took advantage of a provision in the bill authorizing a "defensive referendum," and he proposed including questions having to do with national security. Yet given the way he formulated the questions, there was little doubt about what the public felt, so his motivation for calling the referendum was obviously political. In the event, not enough people voted in the referendum, so it was invalid.[78] Chen tried another referendum for the 2008 election to help the DPP presidential candidate. The question this time was more controversial, proposing that Taiwan enter the United Nations and that "Taiwan" be used instead of "Republic of China." That could be interpreted as changing the name of the country and unnecessarily provoking Beijing. Again, the referendum failed for lack of sufficient turnout.

When the DPP returned to power in 2016, there was renewed pressure from within the party to change the law, making it easier to use referendums to change government policy, and the LY passed amendments in December 2017. As a result, petitions to hold a referendum would need signatures of only 0.01 percent of the total number of eligible voters in the previous presidential election, rather than 0.1 percent, as before. The number of signatures needed to pass approval at the second stage was reduced from 5.0 to 1.5 percent of eligible voters (about 280,000 signatures). For a referendum to pass, 25 percent of eligible voters had to cast ballots, not 50 percent as before, and a majority of them had to cast "yes" votes. (Referendums on sensitive sovereignty and constitutional issues, such as cross-Strait issues and territorial changes, were not allowed.) The amendments also lowered the voting age for referendums from twenty to eighteen.[79]

The KMT and its allies then used the referendum—the Deep Green's political weapon of choice—against it. Using the law's looser provisions for approving the placement of questions on the ballot, there were ten referendums on the ballot. Three targeted the DPP's energy policies, particularly on nuclear power. Five concerned same-sex marriage, three of which were sponsored by well-funded and well-organized conservative votes, the other two put forward at the last minute by defenders of marriage equality. One referendum concerned food safety, specifically banning imports of food from the prefectures of Japan affected by the nuclear disaster of March 2011, based not on scientific evidence that the food was contaminated but on the mere fact that it was from one of the affected prefectures. Finally, Deep Green politicians promoted a measure that would require the Taiwan Olympic team to use the name "Taiwan" rather than "Chinese Taipei," which was the name sanctioned by the International Olympic Committee and accepted by the PRC and which had been in use since 1984.

The results of all but the last of the referendums were a big blow to the policy program of the Tsai administration, held as they were at a time when opinion about its performance was generally negative. All three energy measures passed, with the most important one calling for cancelation of the 2025 date for ending the use of nuclear power, which was the administration's priority. The three conservative measures opposing same-sex marriage passed, while the two sponsored by proponents failed.[80] The referendum banning affected Japanese imports passed, which brought to a halt any improvements in Taiwan-Japan relations, also an administration priority. The measure changing the name for the Olympic team failed, which was a no-brainer since the International Olympic Committee had made clear that the team could compete under "Chinese Taipei" or not at all, but it left the Deep Green sponsors angry at Tsai and the DPP leadership for the neutral stance it had taken on the measure.

The DPP complained that it had been hoisted on its own petard. Chou Chiang-yeh, the DPP's spokesman, said these actions "ran counter to the spirit of referendums, causing a tool originally designed to facilitate public dialogues to degenerate into one used to divide society."[81] So in the summer of 2019, the DPP-controlled LY made some changes that it hoped would make it more difficult to use referendums as political weapons. National referendums would be held every two years at the end of August, instead of simultaneously with national elections. The Central Election Commission would have sixty days, instead of thirty, to verify the identities of people who endorsed referendum petitions. Finally, the substance of referendums would be made public ninety days before voting day, instead of twenty-eight, to allow more time for public discussion.[82]

Every political procedure designed to reflect the popular will is subject to some distortion. Legislative elections based in single-member districts give a structural advantage to the party that wins a majority. Referendums benefit active minorities over passive and inattentive majorities. In commenting on the November 2018 referendums concerning energy policy, Taiwan-based American political scientist Nathan Batto registered three objections. First, they do not force voters to consider trade-offs. Second, they ask voters to pick short-term solutions to issues that must be addressed with a long-term calculus. Third, they assume that voters have a lot more information than they can reasonably be expected to have. His conclusion: "Referendums are a terrible way to make public choices."[83] In a longer essay entitled, "Do Referendums

Reflect Public Opinion?," his judgment was that "ultimately, . . . most people don't know enough or don't care enough about specific policy questions to make a good decision. It sounds high-minded and democratic to bypass the elected politicians and put a question directly to the people, but, in practice, 'direct democracy' is a disaster."[84]

Populism

For democracy scholars in the West, a principal cause of the current, general democratic dysfunction is populism. One of those scholars, Marc F. Plattner at the National Endowment for Democracy, defines populism as a tendency for leaders to press what they assert to be the will of the majority without much regard to "liberalism's emphasis on procedural niceties and protection of individual rights."[85] For Jan-Werner Mueller, who teaches politics at Princeton University, populism constitutes an attack on elites but also against the pluralism that makes democracy possible, and so would like to see the exclusion of their enemies from political life. He writes, "Populists are not against the principle of political representation: they just insist that only they themselves are legitimate representatives" of the people."[86] Dutch political scientist Cas Mudde defines populism as "an ideology that considers society to be ultimately separated into two homogeneous and antagonistic groups, 'the pure people' versus 'the corrupt elite,' and which argues that politics should be an expression of the *volonté générale* (general will) of the people."[87]

Hsin-huang Michael Hsiao, a prominent Taiwan sociologist, takes a similar view.[88] For him, populism includes charismatic leadership to mobilize the masses, and a "style of rhetoric reflecting [the] principle that 'the people'—especially the 'common people'—and not the elites should rule all aspects of politics." Populist "followers," says Hsiao, "are prone to be attracted or mobilized by 'easy or empty slogans.'"[89] Taiwan political scientist Nathan Batto agrees with this perspective: "Populism is a way of framing political competition as a *moral* question. Populists champion the *real* people, who they see as morally pure and homogenous. . . . The populist insists that he alone defines who constitutes the real people."[90]

Since democratization, Taiwan's politics have often had a streak of populism. In their electoral campaigns, both Lee Teng-hui and Chen Shui-bian played up Taiwanese identity (thus claiming to define who "the people" were). Politicians who worked to facilitate holding referendums assumed that the best and most accurate statement of the popular will was when "the people" were allowed to directly express their preference on policies, not just who should be president or their local legislator. The leaders of the Sunflower movement became the self-appointed spokespersons for the public interest on the service trade agreement.

It was in the wake of the Sunflower movement that a Taiwan-style populism began to surge. The first manifestation was Ko Wen-che, a surgeon at National Taiwan University Hospital, who ran for mayor of Taipei as an independent. Ko had an off-the-cuff, tell-it-like-it-is political style, very different from the more programmed practice of most politicians. But he was not an agitator, either. In his races for Taipei mayor, first in 2014 and then again in 2018, he employed television and social media to appeal to young people and middle-class professionals with simplistic slogans.[91] In particular, he did not portray himself as specifically a champion of the people against elites. But his appeal was large enough that he became one of three Taiwan politicians to make populist challenges to the dominance of party organizations and to President Tsai herself.

The second was Han Kuo-yu, a sometimes KMT politician whom the party put forward as its candidate in the 2018 Kaohsiung mayor's race, not expecting him to win in a DPP stronghold. But he did win with his own slogans, and by proposing simple solutions to difficult problems and playing on the frustration of "common people" (*shumin,* 庶民). His aggressive corps of netizen supporters helped him dominate social media, and local political allies helped with mobilization. He had no sooner taken office when he began making moves to run against Tsai. The third populist was Terry Gou Tai-ming, the founder of Foxconn, which does contract manufacturing in China for Apple and other information technology companies. A billionaire, he was an unlikely populist, but he could credibly claim to the young and the underemployed that he had the talents and connections to turn the Taiwan economy around (he had met with both Xi Jinping and Donald Trump). Ko, Gou, and Han spent the first nine months of 2019 maneuvering for position. Han and Gou competed for the KMT nomination, along with a few more traditional politicians, and Han eventually won. Ko and Gou talked about an alliance to run as independents, but in the end neither ran.[92]

Political analysts have presented competing views of the characteristics of people who constituted the Han wave and responded to his populist appeal. Lin Fei-fan, a leader of the Sunflower movement, offered an anti-government perspective: "Frustration towards the government pushed [many people] to join the populist movement."[93] In another view, Han's "common people" were teachers, military people, and civil servants who are often KMT supporters. In another, it is the elderly, the middle-aged, and young people with only a secondary school education. In yet another, it is older, generally working-class people (laborers, farmers, and workers in the fishing industry) and people from military-family backgrounds. These groups, it seems, combine nostalgia for a simpler past and patriotism associated with the Republic of China with the desire for a better political and economic life.[94]

What was remarkable about the populist challenge to Tsai Ing-wen's presidency and the larger political establishment was how quickly it petered out. Han received the KMT nomination for president on July 28, and by early September Tsai had opened up a double-digit lead that widened further as the election grew near. In a comprehensive, late-October poll by the My Formosa organization, Tsai was leading in all age and education categories.[95] That is, the groups associated with Han no longer supported him as strongly.

As far as many people in Taiwan were concerned, the main reason for Han's collapse was the PRC. Xi Jinping's major policy speech on January 2, with its emphasis on unification under the one country, two systems formula, put the KMT and the individuals contending to be its presidential nominee on the defensive. Xi's clear focus on unification as his desired end made it harder for KMT leaders to argue that once their party returned to power, cross-Strait relations would return to the situation that prevailed during Ma's first term, and there would be no demands from Beijing that Taipei make concessions on the political front. In June, protests began in Hong Kong against a draft bill to authorize the rendition to jurisdictions with which Hong Kong did not have an extradition agreement of individuals accused in those jurisdictions and detained in Hong Kong. Tsai used these negative results of the one country, two systems model to again put the KMT on the defensive. Finally, she successfully made the case that her policies as president were doing more for the common people than Han's performance as mayor of Kaohsiung.[96]

In the January 2020 presidential election, Han lost to Tsai by 1.65 million votes. He then was the target of a recall campaign and was removed from office in June. It is conceivable that populism may only be in hibernation, however. Ko Wen-che could mount another populist challenge in the 2024 presidential campaign. The Taiwan People's Party, which he formed in 2020, could help propel that challenge by giving Ko an organizational base that he has so far lacked. For now, at least, reducing politics and governance to a simplistic split between the elite and the "common people" seems to have run its course.

Conclusion

Polarization is stronger between the two camps of Taiwan politicians than it is in the public at large. But it is not severe. Each political camp has its internal divisions. Since 2008, the political system has had a majoritarian character, with all the attendant advantages and disadvantages, but it still has access points that allow opponents of the incumbent administration some opportunities to block its initiatives. But veto actors and protest leaders face the same dilemma: they may be able to stop what they do not like, but they are unable to act successfully on what they prefer. Promoters of the rights of initiative and referendum may have thought that these mechanisms were the essence of democracy, but they did not anticipate that their opponents could use those same instruments against them and the administration they supported. Populism seemed to get a good start in Taiwan, but it could not gain traction for the presidential race once the Hong Kong protests began.

As a result, Taiwan's existing political system, based on representative government, retained its dominance. True, its democratic deficiencies were not as serious as in some other democracies or pseudo-democracies. But the dissatisfaction of some elements of the public had shown no signs of abating. The polarization between political camps—but not necessarily within the public at large—persisted. Attempts to circumvent the institutions of representative democracy were symptoms of those institutions' underlying dysfunction. A failure to make the system more capable will only invite new challenges.

It is particularly telling that a mere 19 percent of respondents in the 2014 Asian Barometer Survey said that democracy was more important than economic development and that only 21 percent thought that political freedom was more important than reducing economic equality (table 13-1).[97] These findings no doubt reflect the importance that Taiwan people place on development and on reducing inequality. But they also speak to the tension between two different kinds of legitimacy a political system can possess (legitimacy is usually defined as the rulers' right to rule and the citizens' obligation to obey).[98] One concerns process and the other performance. Process legitimacy refers to how political leaders are selected (both executive and legislative) and then how much elected leaders follow the rules and norms governing their offices. Performance legitimacy concerns what political leaders accomplish and whether they are responsive to society's needs.[99] The survey findings suggest that for Taiwan's citizens, outcomes are more important than—or at least as important as—the process by which leaders are selected and that policies are enacted.

This should not be a huge surprise. Citizens in democracies everywhere want their elected leaders to deliver on their promises and to address the problems that society is facing. They are probably not ready to sacrifice democracy for a meritocracy like Singapore, which focuses much more on policy outcomes and less on ensuring a democratic process.[100] Yet the prolonged disagreements in Taiwan over issues such as energy security, economic growth and equality, the size and allocation of budgetary resources, the salience of the past for the future, and, most of all, how to secure the society vis-à-vis the PRC indicate that the democratic system could perform better than it has done.

Of course, Taiwan's political system is not alone in experiencing polarization, veto actors, protests, and populism. The society shares with most other advanced economies (including the United States) the consequences of success that have fostered suboptimal performance by institutions and popular efforts to circumvent those institutions. But as much as Taiwan is similar to South Korea, Japan, the United States, Canada, and the countries of Western Europe, it faces a special challenge: the PRC. Beijing's objectives are clear. Its patience is not unlimited. It has shown through its coercion-without-violence campaign against the Tsai administration the ways in which it is willing and able to challenge the status quo that Taiwan people want. That unique, existential challenge increases the stakes for the democratically elected leaders whose responsibility it is to address it. If the issues the political system faces were simply the problems of postmodernity, then a suboptimal system might be tolerable, and the society could muddle through. But because Beijing does pose a unique challenge, suboptimal performance by Taiwan, which makes Beijing's job easier, is therefore not "good enough."

14

United States Policy

The United States cannot help Taiwan mitigate the problems of its political system. In truth, we cannot seem to remedy the dysfunction in our own system, so it is unclear why anyone else would take the advice of the United States. But how Taiwan's political system has sought to enhance security in the face of the challenge posed by the People's Republic of China (PRC) since the 1950s has often affected U.S. interests. Washington has remained committed to protect Taiwan, first through the mutual defense treaty (1954–1980) and thereafter through policy statements and actions. Whether Taiwan's political system was authoritarian or democratic did not completely dictate American policies, but it did have an impact on how Washington managed their effect.

Taiwan's default answer to the question of how it can ensure its security has always been to rely on the United States, as Foreign Minister Joseph Wu appeared to confirm in a July 2018 interview with CNN: "If the Chinese see the vulnerability of Taiwan not getting U.S. support, then they would be thinking about starting scenarios where they would be able to take Taiwan over."[1] That said, and as previous chapters have noted, there are divisions within Taiwan over how much to accommodate the PRC and how much to deter it, how much to spend on defense, and what might be the most effective strategy for the use of defense resources. Those divisions have implications for U.S. interests. Furthermore, Americans are often divided about policy toward Taiwan.

Current U.S. and Taiwan officials regularly say that the bilateral relationship has never been better, and since 2008 there has been a lot of truth in such statements. Taiwan leaders matured in their management of the politics of security policy, and U.S. and Taiwan interests became more closely aligned. On closer inspection, however, some elements of the Trump administration's approach to Taiwan have called into question the "never been better" judgment and should lead Taiwan leaders to ponder how changes in American democracy have affected their interests, for good and ill.

Historical Background

In early 1950, the Truman administration was initially willing to accept the fall of Taiwan to Mao Zedong's forces. But North Korea's invasion of South Korea in June 1950 changed how Washington policymakers assessed Taiwan's strategic value to U.S. interests in East Asia. They began rebuilding the U.S. security relationship with the Kuomintang regime. In 1954 the Eisenhower administration formalized the commitment to come to the defense of Taiwan itself and the Penghu Islands through a mutual defense treaty. But the United States never had to honor that pledge because the PRC lacked the capabilities to seize Taiwan.[2] Taipei became very anxious about the credibility of the U.S. commitment to its security in the 1970s and early 1980s, as the Nixon and Carter administrations moved gradually to end diplomatic relations with the Republic of China and then formally establish them with the PRC on New Year's Day 1979. In the process, Washington terminated the mutual defense treaty with Taiwan and replaced it with only a declaratory statement of the U.S. abiding interest in the "peaceful resolution" of the cross-Strait dispute. Congress added security language to the 1979 Taiwan Relations Act, which created the framework for unofficial relations with Taipei that appeared to replace the treaty commitment but really did not.[3] The Carter administration and the Taiwan Relations Act pledged that arms sales would continue, but the Reagan administration appeared to set the United States on a path to terminating them.[4]

Over time, however, the American commitment to Taiwan's security and confidence was restored. Washington toughened its declaratory policy, and the value of arms sales increased rather than declined. Substantive exchanges between the U.S. military and the Taiwan armed forces, which essentially ended in 1979, resumed in the late 1990s. Beijing's effort to change U.S. intentions had not succeeded. And through the 1990s, U.S. military capabilities clearly outmatched those of the People's Liberation Army (PLA).

Taiwan's democratization and the new ideas it produced about the island's future changed the calculus in Beijing and Washington. Before the mid-1990s, both the United States and the PRC could work on the assumption that Kuomintang leaders in Taipei would continue to agree with Beijing that Taiwan was a part of the sovereign territory of the state of China and that some sort of unification was the ultimate goal. But political forces on Taiwan now had the freedom to advocate for Taiwan independence or at least oppose unification. This was despite—or because of—its expanding economic relationship with mainland China. Lee Teng-hui's initial openness to engaging Beijing on political issues waned as his time as president went on, and he had domestic electoral reasons for appealing to the burgeoning Taiwanese identity. Beijing, in turn, worried that Lee was moving down the road to independence. It became even more worried when Chen Shui-bian, the leader of the at least nominally pro-independence Democratic Progressive Party, became president in 2000.[5]

Since 2008, in contrast, both the Ma and Tsai administrations have given Washington little or no reason to think Taiwan might provoke a conflict. Each has acted with restraint regarding the politics of cross-Strait relations and Taiwanese nationalism, in recognition of the public's status quo and risk-averse sentiments, which the polling results cited in chapters 8 and 9 illustrate. Taiwan voters want their government to act in a restrained way vis-à-vis Beijing. In return for this moderation on Taiwan's part, both the Obama and Trump administrations intensified security relations between the U.S. and Taiwan militaries with the aim of raising the cost that the PRC would bear if it made any attempt to achieve its unification goal by force. President Tsai was so cautious that she had to overcome a challenge to her renomination from the Deep Green wing of the Democratic Progressive Party, which believed that she could have exploited American support to move in an independence direction.

The Trump Administration's Policies Concerning Taiwan

The plural "policies" is used deliberately here because the Trump administration's approach to Taiwan went in several different directions at once. Moreover, the reality was less a matter of what the administration said than of what it did or did not do.

Declaratory Policy

In their speeches, senior administration officials usually aligned the United States with Taiwan in its fraught relationship with Beijing. In October 2018, Vice President Mike Pence condemned "the Chinese Communist Party" for inducing three countries to shift diplomatic relations from Taipei to Beijing. In addition, he affirmed that, "while our administration will continue to respect our One China Policy, as reflected in the three joint communiqués and the Taiwan Relations Act, America will always believe that Taiwan's embrace of democracy shows a better path for all the Chinese people."[6]

In February 2019, Randall Schriver, then a senior Pentagon official, declared that the United States "continue[s] to support Taiwan through faithful implementation of the TRA [Taiwan Relations Act] to ensure they have the needed capabilities to deter aggression from China. . . . The TRA gives us the flexibility to provide Taiwan weapons of a self-defensive character for Taiwan's sufficient self-defense." As the threat from across the Taiwan Strait has grown, he said, "things we do with Taiwan have also naturally evolved."[7]

In March 2019, David Stilwell, whom the Trump administration had nominated to be its assistant secretary of state for East Asia and Pacific affairs, told the Senate Foreign Relations Committee that "China . . . should stop its pressure and coercion and resume dialogue with the democratically elected authorities on Taiwan."[8]

In October 2019, Vice President Pence asserted that "we've stood by Taiwan in defense of her hard-won freedoms. Under this administration, we've authorized additional military sales and recognized Taiwan's place as one of the world's great trading economies and beacons of Chinese culture and democracy."[9]

In congressional testimony in July 2020, Deputy Secretary of State Stephen Biegun pledged that "the U.S. commitment to implementing the Taiwan Relations Act is firm, as is our commitment to the U.S. One China policy, including our insistence that cross-Strait issues be resolved peacefully and without coercion or intimidation." He specifically mentioned Washington's desire that Taiwan be allowed to participate more fully in the international community and the need to assist in improving the island's defenses.[10]

The Free and Open Indo-Pacific Strategy

Perhaps the most significant statement of Trump administration policy was the "Indo-Pacific Strategy Report," issued by the Department of Defense in June 2019.[11] This document provided a more detailed elaboration of U.S. policy than the administration's "National Security Strategy" and "National Defense Strategy" documents, completed in late 2017 and early 2018, respectively, which mostly offered general statements of principles. In addition, it placed Taiwan in the context of broader strategy and policy toward the Indo-Pacific region.

The basis for the strategy was an assessment of the PRC's intentions, which were deemed to be highly threatening. That assessment began with the report's transmittal letter, by Acting Secretary of Defense Patrick Shanahan: "Inter-state strategic competition, defined by geopolitical rivalry between free and repressive world order visions, is the primary concern for U.S. national security. In particular, the People's Republic of China, under the leadership of the Chinese Communist Party, seeks to reorder the [East Asia] region to its advantage by leveraging military modernization, influence operations, and predatory economics to coerce other nations."[12] In addition, the title of the report's section on the PRC referred to the Chinese Communist Party as a "revisionist power," and that section made a clear statement of Beijing's objectives: "As China continues its economic and military ascendance, it seeks Indo-Pacific regional hegemony in the near-term and, ultimately global pre-eminence in the long-term."[13]

With respect to Taiwan, the report attributed these objectives to Beijing's military buildup: "The PLA continues to prepare for contingencies in the Taiwan Strait to deter, and if necessary, compel Taiwan to abandon moves toward independence. The PLA is also preparing for a contingency to unify Taiwan with the mainland by force, while simultaneously deterring, delaying, or denying any third-party intervention on Taiwan's behalf." In light of the increase in PLA capabilities, the report said, it was U.S. policy to "ensure that Taiwan remains secure, confident, free from coercion, and able to peacefully and productively engage the mainland on its own terms" by commensurately stepping up defense engagement with Taiwan and providing it with defense articles and services.[14]

The report did not state explicitly that Taiwan could contribute to U.S.-PRC security competition, but it did so indirectly. It designated Taiwan as a security partner (not an ally), along with Singapore, New Zealand, and Mongolia, and then states the contribution that allies and partners could make:

"Mutually beneficial alliances and partnerships are crucial to our strategy, providing a durable, asymmetric strategic advantage that *no competitor or rival* can match."[15] In this framing, therefore, Taiwan was a strategic asset of the United States.

To some extent, the Trump administration's Free and Open Indo-Pacific strategy and the documents associated with it were a rhetorical rationalization of the actions that it had undertaken. It was developed as an alternative to President Obama's "rebalance to Asia," with which it was similar in many ways. The biggest difference between the two administrations' strategies was how they concern themselves with the PRC. Obama sought to preserve and enhance some areas of cooperation between Washington and Beijing, regarding climate change, Iran, and North Korea. It sought to manage the competition in areas such as East Asia's maritime domain. For Obama, cooperation was good for its own sake, but it also provided balance to the relationship and kept it from tipping into mutual conflict. Many parts of the Trump administration, however, took a zero-sum approach to U.S.-PRC relations, which placed Taiwan in a more positive light.

Yet the clear implication of the Pentagon report that Taiwan was a strategic partner of the United States stood in sharp contrast to the view of President Trump himself. John Bolton, who served as national security adviser from April 2018 to September 2019, reported in his memoir, *The Room Where It Happened*, that Trump's assessment of Taiwan's strategic value to the United States was low at best. Bolton wrote, "One of Trump's favorite comparisons was to point to the tip of one of his Sharpies [felt-tip pen] and say, 'This is Taiwan,' then point to the historic Resolute desk in the Oval Office and say, 'This is China.' So much for American commitments and obligations to another democratic ally." Trump's attitude toward Taiwan, he remarked, was "particularly dyspeptic."[16]

Security

Declaratory policy aside, the Trump administration continued to support Taiwan's security in several ways. The first was by working with Taiwan's high command to ensure that it was making effective adjustments to its defense strategy in response to the changing threat environment. The second was by maintaining arms sales. By February 2020, the Trump administration had made available US$9.5 billion in weaponry; the principal items were F-16 fighters, main-battle tanks, and anti-tank missiles.[17] The third was by increasing operations by the U.S. Navy and Air Force in Taiwan's vicinity that were designed to signal American support for the island in the face of PLA exercises that increase the island's sense of vulnerability. Finally, and just as important, the administration continued the array of exchanges that occur between the U.S. and Taiwan militaries, all of which are designed to improve Taiwan's ability to fight. As with previous administrations, the Pentagon under Trump conducted enhanced security cooperation with Taiwan, quietly for the most part. It assumed that Beijing knew these activities were happening but avoided creating public, diplomatic disputes.

The big question mark concerns U.S. intentions in the event of a PRC attack. Washington's long-standing interest regarding Taiwan has been to preserve peace and security in the Taiwan area. The underlying purpose of U.S.-Taiwan security cooperation in its various guises is to better deter Beijing from trying militarily to resolve the cross-Strait dispute in its favor. But if Beijing were to conclude that Washington would not intervene to save Taiwan, deterrence would be weakened.

There are some in Taiwan, the PRC, and the United States who believe that the TRA requires that Washington come to Taiwan's defense in the event that the PLA attacks the island. As a matter of law, the TRA does no such thing. As a matter of policy, the act states the U.S. expectation that the Taiwan issue will be resolved peacefully, but the only thing that it requires the executive branch to do if conflict breaks out is to report to Congress.[18]

At the time the TRA was drafted, moreover, the authors of the legislation only anticipated that the PRC would unilaterally attack Taiwan; they did not contemplate the possibility that war might start because Taiwan leaders took actions that PRC leaders believed, rightly or wrongly, challenged its fundamental interests and so required a forceful response.

It was the PRC's definition of and reaction to Lee Teng-hui's that led the Clinton administration to revise that assumption. Secretary of State Warren Christopher elaborated U.S. declaratory policy on this issue. In a May 1996 speech, Christopher said, "We have emphasized to both sides the importance of avoiding provocative actions or unilateral measures that would alter the status quo or pose a threat to peaceful resolution of outstanding issues."[19] Chen Shui-bian's provocative pronouncements prior to the 2004 Taiwan presidential elections led the George W. Bush administration to further expand this view in April 2004, in congressional testimony by Assistant Secretary of State for Asian and Pacific Affairs James Kelly:

> Our foremost concern is maintaining peace and stability. . . . Because the possibility for the United States to become involved in a cross-

Strait conflict is very real, the President knows that American lives are potentially at risk. Our one-China policy reflects our abiding commitment to preserve peace in the Taiwan Strait so long as there are irreconcilable differences. . . . President [George W. Bush]'s message on December 9 of last year [2003] . . . reiterated the U.S. Government's opposition to any unilateral moves by either China or Taiwan to change the status quo. This message was directed to both sides. The President and the senior leadership of this administration consistently make clear to Chinese leaders that the United States will fulfill its obligations to help Taiwan defend itself, as mandated in the Taiwan Relations Act. At the same time we have very real concerns that our efforts at deterring Chinese coercion might fail if Beijing ever becomes convinced Taiwan is embarked on a course toward independence and permanent separation from China, and concludes that Taiwan must be stopped in these efforts.[20]

The unstated implication of both the Christopher and Kelly statements is that Washington would not necessarily intervene in a military conflict to help Taiwan if it judged that Taipei's actions stimulated that conflict, but that it would intervene if the PRC mounted a unilateral attack. This is a posture of dual deterrence. Of course, the object of U.S. deterrence warnings depends on which side of the Strait—Taiwan or the mainland—creates the greater danger to peace and stability. The moderation of Taiwan's leaders that began in 2008 diminished the need to warn them to avoid challenging Beijing's interests. Moreover, the Trump administration's relatively dire statements about PRC capabilities and intentions ("the PLA is also preparing for a contingency to unify Taiwan with the mainland by force") meant that the need for U.S. deterrence toward Beijing and Beijing alone increased.

A wild card here, again, was Trump himself. Since the late 1980s at least, Trump has had an aversion to U.S. alliances and the defense commitments that come with them, along with a resistance to the deployment of U.S. troops overseas and U.S. intervention in conflicts like Iraq and Afghanistan.[21] This long-standing attitude has implications for Taiwan. In *Fear: Trump in the White House*, his account of the first year of the Trump administration, Bob Woodward recounts a January 19, 2018, meeting at the White House where Trump and his national security team discussed—not for the first time—the rationale for the United States defending allies and partners. In this particular argument, Trump first asked, "What do we get by maintaining a massive military presence in the Korean Peninsula?" He then asked, out of the blue, "Even more than that, what do we get from protecting Taiwan, say?"[22] Three points about this statement are worth noting. The first is that President Trump actually appeared to believe that past administrations had some sort of commitment to come to Taiwan's defense, though the situation was more complicated than that. The second was the very transactional use of the word "get" in evaluating a U.S. pledge to protect Taiwan. Third, there is the implication that even if Beijing chose to undertake a cross-Strait war, Trump might be skeptical about intervention on Taiwan's behalf.

Diplomacy

The Trump administration's State Department was more forward leaning in its relations with Taiwan. The level of civilian officials who traveled to Taiwan increased. Cooperation on issues such as cybersecurity expanded. Washington, responding to Beijing's inducement of countries to switch diplomatic relations with the Republic of China to the PRC, sought to discourage those that remain from "flipping" to Beijing. Long overdue, a new building for the Taipei office of the American Institute in Taiwan, the nongovernmental organization through which the United States conducts substantive relations with Taipei, opened in 2019, a visible—and expensive—symbol of the American commitment. The State Department could reasonably argue that it had stayed within the basic limits of the U.S. one-China policy—that is, the recognition of the PRC government as the sole legal government of China and its pledge to conduct relations with Taiwan on an unofficial basis—even as it expanded the definition of what "unofficial" means. Moreover, it had taken these steps fairly quietly.

Again, President Trump sometimes went his own way. As president-elect, he seemed to tilt toward Taiwan by taking a phone call from President Tsai Ing-wen on December 2, 2016 (a call he later regretted). Nine days later, however, he talked as if he wanted to use Taiwan merely as leverage against Beijing on trade and North Korea. Thereafter, it seemed that Trump had been willing to defer to PRC President Xi Jinping on matters concerning Taiwan. In a September 6, 2018, column in the *Washington Post*, Josh Rogin reported this statement from a "senior administration official": "This administration, from a personnel perspective, has the most hawkish Taiwan team ever. . . . But if Xi calls [Donald Trump] and complains, the president's instinct is to defer to that because there is always some pending issue in which we want something from the Chinese."[23] More ominous for Taiwan was the possibility that Trump would seek a concession from Xi Jinping on something important to him that would open Trump up to a demand from Xi for a compensatory concession. Trump's June 2019 plea to Xi for Beijing to buy more American agricultural goods to help Trump in the 2020 election, as reported in John Bolton's memoir, was a case in point.[24]

Economic Policy

The positive trend in the diplomatic and security dimensions of U.S. policy is not manifest in economic policy, which should be puzzling. With a population of only 23 million people, Taiwan is the world's fifteenth-largest exporter and nineteenth-largest importer.[25] In 2019 it was the tenth-largest important trading partner of the United States globally, with $54.3 billion in exports (rank thirteenth) and $31.2 billion in imports (rank fourteenth).[26] Taiwan's economic strategy since the 1960s has been to meet the demand of large retailers in more advanced economies, especially the United States. Its entrepreneurs implemented this strategy first by producing products in Taiwan and being quick to adapt to changes in external demand. Starting in the 1980s, the island's companies maintained their global competitiveness by moving some operations—mainly production and assembly—to other places, especially mainland China. As a result, the figures for Taiwan exports to the United States are an understatement, because a significant share of PRC exports to the United States are produced in wholly owned Taiwanese factories there. Taiwan is the seventh-largest sender of students to America, with 23,369 in the 2018–2019 academic year.[27] Many of the best and brightest in Taiwan's information technology industry trained in the United States and worked in Silicon Valley.

Yet there is a serious disconnect between the Taiwan policies that the economic agencies of several U.S. administrations have pursued and the strategic value that other parts of the U.S. government have placed on the island, especially during the Trump administration. Taiwan has long sought for significant improvements in economic relations with the United States. Until the Trump administration withdrew from the Trans-Pacific Partnership in early 2017, Taipei had hoped that Washington would facilitate its inclusion in the pact in negotiations on accepting a second group of members. More recently, Taiwan has sought a free trade agreement with America, but the prospects of early negotiations were decidedly slim.[28] Given that the Trump administration starts, in the words of Derek Scissors, of the American Enterprise Institute, from a stance of "trade-balance protectionism," Taiwan's US$53 billion surplus with the United States would be a serious impediment to initiating any talks.[29] Then again, that the Trump administration was willing in 2020 to begin talks with Kenya on a free trade agreement, reportedly to "counter China's influence in Africa," raised questions about why the same logic did not lead it to start free trade agreement negotiations with Taiwan.[30]

Moreover, since the Ma administration, the office of the U.S. Trade Representative (USTR) had held that Taiwan reneged on commitments regarding market access for beef and pork, specifically meat exports that contain the additive ractopamine. The Taiwan administration has the authority to lift restrictions on pork imports, as it did for most beef imports, but deferred a decision because pork farmers are an important political constituency in Taiwan, as they are in the United States. Moreover, civil society groups that advocate strict measures to ensure food safety also opposed to pork imports, even if the levels of ractopamine are below the level that international organizations have scientifically determined to be safe for consumption. As of early 2020, the prospects for significant U.S.-Taiwan economic agreements seemed gloomy, particularly if USTR insisted that the pork and beef issue be resolved first. Conversely, the American Chamber of Commerce in Taipei concluded that this approach "has not achieved positive results" and advocated beginning talks on a free trade agreement "with the clear understanding that these [agricultural] issues would need to be resolved as part of the negotiations.[31] (Also shaping the U.S. position on negotiations with Taiwan was a fear that they might complicate USTR's talks with Beijing.)

On August 28, 2020, President Tsai took the politically bold step of allowing imports of foreign pork whose amount of ractopamine was below the level judged by international experts to be safe for human consumption.[32] By meeting USTR's precondition for any forward-looking economic talks, including on an FTA, she had hit the negotiation ball into the U.S. court.

As an aside, this action stimulated actions by the KMT that displayed some of the dysfunctional features of the Taiwan political system discussed in the previous chapter. Its LY caucus used procedural tactics to block Premier Su Tseng-chang from making the traditional policy speech at the beginning of the new legislative session. To ensure greater media coverage, they brought a large plastic pig to the LY chamber during the episode.[33] The party resorted to direct democracy, applying to hold a referendum on Tsai's decision, despite the fact that she had the legal authority to act as she did.[34] Most disturbing, and a reflection of the polarization of Taiwan politics, the KMT called on local governments led by its members to enact ordinances to prohibit the sale of pork with ractopamine in their jurisdictions.[35]

The Trump administration presented Taiwan with other economic challenges, one of which stemmed from Donald Trump's promise during his campaign that he would radically raise tariffs on PRC imports as his way to reduce the American trade deficit with the PRC. He did not understand that bilateral trade balances are not the best or only measure of the balance of costs and benefits in an economic relationship. Nor did he understand that many U.S. "imports from China" are counted as Chinese goods because the PRC is where the final assembly takes place, which is the criterion U.S. Customs uses to decide where a particular good comes from, though much of the value of the product was added elsewhere. For example, a mountain bicycle that is labeled "Made in China" could be the product of a Taiwan company that produces the more sophisticated parts in Taiwan and assembles the bike in its wholly owned subsidiary on the mainland.

The Trump administration also threatened to raise tariffs on many electronic goods, such as iPads and iPhones, whose assembly occurs in mainland China with components from the United States, Taiwan, and other places, in a supply chain that is managed by Foxconn, a Taiwan firm. To have increased U.S. tariffs on the imports of such information technology products would have hurt American and Taiwan companies much more than Chinese companies. The administration's threat to impose those tariff increases was only withdrawn as part of the January 2020 "phase-one" trade agreement with the PRC.[36]

The large—and still growing—bilateral trade deficit aside, Trump administration officials had other goals in mind concerning economic relations with the PRC. One was to press it to reverse changes it had made in the business environment of foreign companies operating in mainland China. Beijing's move toward mercantilist industrial policies hurt all advanced economies, including Taiwan's, so returning to a more level playing field was a worthy objective. Many experts believed, however, that the Trump administration's reliance on increased tariffs on PRC goods, or even threatening to increase tariffs, was not the right way to achieve the objective. More effective, they thought, was to mobilize a united front of all affected companies against PRC policies.

Another goal of the Trump administration was to create pressures to move the global supply chains out of mainland China and, in a frequently used term, "decouple" the U.S. and PRC economies. On that objective they had some success, in part because the cost of doing business for foreign companies had been rising already and because the prospect of higher U.S. tariffs quickly became an added incentive. If companies in Taiwan or Korea moved their supply chains out of mainland China, all the better from the Trump administration's point of view. For Taiwan companies, just the uncertainty fostered by Trump's increase in some tariffs and the threat to increase them more created incentives to move operations out of mainland China. This may have created problems for the companies involved, but it worked to the advantage of Taiwan as a whole. Those firms sought to reduce their dependence on the PRC as a production platform by relocating their supply chains to other economies in East Asia, including Taiwan. As of August 2019, "reshoring" companies had invested almost US$500 billion in Taiwan's local economy, which would create an estimated 39,000 jobs.

The Tsai administration took steps to remedy shortages in land, water, and electricity and to ensure that the money coming in did not go into the real estate sector.[37] This was a short-term boon for the Taiwan economy. At the same time, the downside was that, because these were hardware companies that were relocating to Taiwan, their relocation may have reduced incentives for a longer-term integration of hardware and software (see chapter 4). Also, Taiwan does not have enough workers to meet the demand of all the reshoring companies.

The Trump administration's most far-reaching policy intention dealt with technology. The administration's economic and security officials believed that the United States was in an existential struggle with the PRC for economic and military dominance and that if the United States was going to win, it had to both acquire for itself the defining technologies of the twenty-first century and deny to the PRC those technologies that would aid it in closing its gap with America, and then forge ahead. The key U.S. weapon in this fight to the death was a technology control regime under which specified PRC "entities" would be denied American technologies and required Americans and perhaps others to obtain licenses to sell items on a long list of critical technologies to PRC customers. However, the implications of such policies are two-sided. Mainland Chinese companies such as telecommunications giant Huawei still depend on U.S., Taiwan, and other manufacturers for a wide array of parts and components, which means that those companies depend on the PRC market for part of their revenue stream. For example, the exports to mainland China of Taiwan Semiconductor Manufacturing Corporation (TSMC), the world's chip foundry, account for about 17 percent of the company's revenue. For the United States to cut the cord between U.S. and other tech companies and their mainland Chinese customers could well be the latter's kiss of death. But it would also hurt the suppliers' bottom line.[38]

The export control regime that the Trump administration developed was more complicated than just blocking the transfer of pieces of hardware from American producers to designated PRC customers. Because the United States no longer has a monopoly over the creation of the most advanced technologies, the question was how much extraterritorial reach Washington would extend to transactions between target PRC firms such as Huawei and its overseas suppliers. Under U.S. government pressure, for example, the Taiwan firm United Microelectronics Corporation terminated its cooperation with Fujian Jinhua Integrated Circuit Company in 2018 after Washington banned sales to Fujian Jinhua.[39]

Another approach focused on semiconductors produced by companies like TSMC and sold to PRC entities, and specifically the share of U.S-origin technology that was embedded in those chips. In mid-2019, U.S. policy required that a Taiwan company like TSMC would have to secure a license (a cumbersome process) in order to sell components to Huawei, whose American content was greater than 25 percent. There was some talk of reducing that limit to 10 percent, but that idea was set aside. More consequential was imposition of restrictions based on where semiconductors sold to PRC companies were produced and on the origin of the equipment that produced them. Originally, the Trump administration had required a U.S. company that produced chips in the United States to get a license from the Department of Commerce before it could sell those components to a company like Huawei. But that created a loophole. Companies outside the United States, including foreign subsidiaries of U.S. companies, did not require a license for the chips they produced in those plants with U.S.-origin equipment (as long as they preserved the limit of 25 percent American content of the final product). But in May 2020, the Trump administration closed that loophole and began to require a license for chips produced outside the United States with American equipment, whenever the equipment was purchased. This was a significant extraterritorial overreach on the Trump administration's part. Meanwhile, TSMC sought to hedge its bets with the Trump administration by deciding to build a chip plant in Arizona.[40] But TSMC Chairman Mark Liu warned of the dangers of increasing tariffs and restrictions on the free flow of information, both elements of the Trump administration policy. He said, "One thing is that competition will be stronger. Secondly, the cost of production or development will be higher because one cannot leverage the whole world like in the past.[41]

How the U.S. change in administrations will affect technology policy toward the PRC is in limbo. But it has already exposed Taiwan companies to friendly fire, whereby the Trump administration's tighter policies force them to choose between doing business with mainland Chinese counterparts and with American ones.[42] The uncertainty about the future of the policy alone affects those companies' calculus. Even though there is a need to tighten the regime governing the transfer of some technologies to the PRC by all advanced economies, it should be done in a way that strengthens relations with the friends and partners of the United States instead of damaging them.[43]

Congress

Members of Congress have sent many signals of support to Taiwan. Several resolutions and bills were enacted during Donald Trump's presidency. Most of what Congress has done was mainly a function of the anti-China mood on Capitol Hill. Beijing, for its part, believed that Congress actively contributed to the pro-Taiwan side of the Trump administration policy. Yet when it came to these congressional actions, it is important to read the fine print to assess the significance. Much of the legislation that Congress enacted was hortatory and lacked any binding effect on the executive branch. People in Taiwan are correct to take heart from the sympathy that members of Congress feel toward them, but they sometimes exaggerate the impact that these measures have on the conduct of U.S. policy.

For example, the John S. McCain National Defense Authorization Act had two sections concerning Taiwan.[44] The first, section 1257, was binding on the Trump administration, but all it required was a report that assessed Taiwan's military capabilities, offered "recommendations to improve the efficiency, effectiveness, readiness, and resilience of Taiwan's self-defense capability" in a number of areas, and developed a plan for carrying out those recommendations. One specific subject to be included in the plan was expansion of "senior military-to-military engagement and joint training by the United States Armed Forces with the military of Taiwan," ideas that defense experts who favored an upgrading of U.S.-Taiwan defense ties had discussed for some time. No doubt the PRC would respond vociferously if such senior-level engagement and joint training had occurred, at least rhetorically. But the legislation did not require that either of these activities occur; it only asked the Pentagon to report on them. Moreover, the executive branch already had the authority to undertake these initiatives. It had chosen not to do so as a matter of policy.

The second, section 1258, was a statement of the "sense of Congress on Taiwan." It set forth a number of steps that the executive branch should take, all of which were already current policy or made sense for the future. The most controversial was a clause that said that the Department of Defense "should consider supporting the visit of a United States hospital ship to Taiwan as part of the annual Pacific Partnership mission to improve disaster response planning and preparedness." This was sensitive because a visit by a U.S. military ship, even a hospital one, arguably would breach the normalization pledge on unofficial relations. But again, sense-of-Congress statements do not constitute orders to the executive branch.

Another example is the so-called Taiwan Travel Act, which Congress passed in early 2018. Its stated purpose was to "encourage visits between the United States and Taiwan at all levels." It made a statement of policy that U.S. officials at all levels should be allowed to travel to Taiwan and that high-level Taiwan officials should be permitted to travel to the United States. If the executive branch had adopted such a policy, it would have set aside the ways in which successive administrations had implemented the policy of unofficial ties for purpose of two-way travel by senior government personnel. Indeed, it is hard to see how the term "unofficial" would have had any enduring meaning. One cannot, of course, predict precisely how the PRC, which had insisted on lack of officiality in Taipei-Washington interactions, would respond if they believed the United States had reneged on that commitment. Substance aside, because the legislation only consisted of statements of policy and of the sense of Congress, it had no binding effect.[45] The president already had the authority to do what the act suggested.

A final example is the Taiwan Symbols of Sovereignty Act (S. 3310), introduced by Senator Ted Cruz (R-TX) in mid-February 2020.[46] In this case, the bill, by using the word "shall," took the form of an order to the executive branch. Specifically, "The Secretary of State and the Secretary of Defense shall permit members of the armed forces and government representatives from the Republic of China (Taiwan) or the Taipei Economic and Cultural Representative Office (TECRO) to display, for the official purposes set forth in subsection (b), symbols of Republic of China sovereignty, including (1) the flag of the Republic of China (Taiwan); and (2) the corresponding emblems or insignia of military units." This would go against the policy that the United States would conduct relations with Taiwan on an unofficial basis.

One reason that most of these measures have been expressed in a nonbinding form is that they would arguably encroach on the president's constitutional powers as commander in chief and head diplomat. President Trump's written statement concerning the National Defense Authorization Act for 2019, issued at the time of signing, included a section germane to section 1257:

> Several provisions of the bill, including sections 1207, 1241, 1257, and 1289, purport to dictate the position of the United States in external military and foreign affairs. My Administration will treat these provi-

sions consistent with the President's *exclusive* constitutional authorities as Commander in Chief and as the sole representative of the Nation in foreign affairs, including the authorities to determine the terms upon which recognition is given to foreign sovereigns, to receive foreign representatives, and to conduct the Nation's diplomacy.[47]

If the Cruz bill ever reached President Trump's desk, it would challenge the White House's definition of his constitutional authority. The executive branch would most likely ignore the measure and leave it up to Senator Cruz to challenge its nonaction in the courts. (The bill received no action.)

The upshot is that members of Congress can take credit for helping Taiwan by getting such measures passed, even as they probably know that they are unlikely to change U.S. policy. People in Taiwan are likely to believe that U.S. support for Taiwan is stronger than it is (the Taiwan government probably understands their true legal impact). The PRC government gets more alarmed than it probably should, fearing that whatever the import or lack of import of each individual measure, together they signal a negative trend in U.S. policy. In this aspect of U.S.-Taiwan relations, at least, theater has displaced serious policy formulation.

Policy Chaos

The divergence in U.S. policy toward Taiwan has been partly the result of an ongoing bureaucratic fight between trade agencies, on the one hand and diplomatic and security agencies, on the other. At play here is a quirk in the organization of the U.S. government. The Office of USTR is within the Office of the President, so how it sets its policies and carries them out is less subject to pressure from agencies such as the Departments of State and Defense. Moreover, USTR is very responsive to members of Congress who bring it specific concerns about market access in other economies. The USTR would conduct trade policy toward Taiwan within a broader strategic contest only if the president directed it to do so.

During the Trump administration, however, the institutional problems ran deeper. Briefly, the regular process of policymaking since the late 1940s has had these characteristics:

- It was inclusive. It allowed and required the different agencies who had a stake in any given issue to talk to one another and try to find policy consensus.

- The process was bottom-up. Issues requiring decisions were discussed at higher and higher levels, until recommendations reached the desk of the president.

- Because the process was bottom-up, it benefited from the expertise of officials at working levels. As a result, senior officials had a better sense of the consequences and trade-offs involved in any decision.

- It was institutionalized, enshrined in a set of rules that each new administration enunciated as it came into office.

This process broke down under the Trump administration. Decisions were not coordinated. Contending agencies could act independently. Mistakes were made. Both Taiwan and the PRC likely misperceived the true balance point in U.S. policy. A sound policy-formulation process does not guarantee good policies, but it is probably imperative if the conflict between our Taiwan security policy and our Taiwan trade policy is to be resolved. Without it, the schizophrenic way that Washington has treated Taipei is guaranteed to continue. The phenomenon of a U.S. president who placed high value on his personal relationship with PRC President Xi Jinping, who diminished Taiwan's strategic importance, who occasionally saw Taiwan as a source of leverage in negotiating with Xi, and who often made choices untethered from any institutionalized process was particularly dangerous.

Taiwan Perspectives

Broadly speaking, the Taiwan public has a positive view of the United States. In 2016 the Taiwan National Security Survey asked respondents how many points they would assign to the United States, with 0 signifying "especially dislike" and 10 denoting "especially like." The mean score was 5.53, meaning those who liked the United States were in a majority. A third of respondents picked the neutral score of 5, and 41.6 percent ranged from 6 to 10. On the question of whether the United States would come to Taiwan's defense when it did not declare independence, respondents in the 2019 Taiwan National Security Survey were quite confident that it would. Excluding those people who declined to respond or said they did not know, 10.5 percent of the remainder said America would "definitely not" intervene, 17.5 percent said it "would not" intervene, 34.2 percent said it "would" intervene, and 37.7 percent said that it "definitely would" intervene. The balance of sentiment, therefore, was 2.56 to 1.[48]

The Trump administration's conflicting signals about Taiwan and China policy stimulated a variety of views there concerning what should be done in response, and informed opinion was more divided. On one side were voices who saw a risk in relying too much on the United States for its security at a time that U.S.-PRC tensions were rising. Su Chi, who was Ma Ying-jeou's first Secretary General of the National Security Council, was one of those voices. Writing in October 2019, he criticized President Tsai for taking the U.S. side in what the Trump administration called "strategic competition" with Beijing. If Taiwan takes sides, he wrote, it will deny itself the "maneuvering room" that a more neutral stance would have allowed. Moreover, too clear an alignment with an overcommitted United States puts Beijing in a position where it has to respond, with consequences for the larger competition. If the PRC chooses confrontation vis-à-vis Washington and Taipei, as Su thinks is likely, then the United States will be put to the test. If Washington also chooses confrontation, then there will be war, and Taiwan "will surely suffer dire consequences." If Washington accommodates Beijing, then what Su sees as the Democratic Progressive Party's push for independence "will simply end up consummating reunification" (because, Su probably believes, the PRC would impose such pressure on Taipei that it would eventually capitulate). Whatever the outcome, Taiwan would have accelerated the U.S.-PRC competition and put itself in a "more precarious position" in the process.[49]

Parris Chang, who taught for many years at Penn State University and later served as an official in the Chen Shui-bian administration, read the strategic dynamics differently. A member of the Deep Green camp, he believed that Taiwan should have exploited U.S.-PRC competition and the Trump administration's perceived strong support for the island. Writing in the *Taipei Times* in August 2018, he recommended that Taipei should push Washington to conduct a thoroughgoing review of Taiwan policy, believing that Taiwan could only benefit from the outcome. He advocated passage by the U.S. Congress of a resolution that authorized the president to use military force to help defend Taiwan. He saw no legal or political reason why the United States could not or should not establish normal relations with Taiwan. As to why Taiwan has not pressed Washington for these steps already, he pointed the finger at President Tsai without explicitly identifying her. "Why is this? According to one US expert who has close connections in the Trump White House, Taiwan has so far been too reticent and polite to tell the US exactly what it wants or what role it is willing to play in the Indo-Pacific strategy. Could it be that some people are afraid of offending Beijing?"[50]

It appears that the Taiwan public is evenly split between these two views.

The 2019 Taiwan National Security Survey asked this question: "Some people say that Taiwan should strengthen its cooperation with the United States and Japan in confronting the Mainland. Do you agree or disagree?" In response, 46.6 percent agreed, while 45.4 percent disagreed.[51]

Neither Su Chi nor Parris Chang took note of how Xi Jinping could shape the calculus of Donald Trump. In a very real sense, Xi's most effective weapon in stopping U.S. initiatives regarding Taiwan that he did not like was the telephone. If, hypothetically, Tsai Ing-wen had abandoned her approach of maintaining a degree of balance between Beijing and Washington, or if the Trump administration had pushed her government toward a more anti-PRC position, Xi only needed to voice his objections personally to President Trump. How Trump would have responded would have depended on the context, of course, but the possibility that he might have sacrificed U.S. interests regarding Taiwan to please Xi cannot be ruled out.

What Washington Should Do

To say in 2020 that U.S.-Taiwan relations have never been better begs the question, "Better than what?" Officials in both capitals would acknowledge that there were rough seas that had to be navigated in the past. They cannot rule out the possibility of deterioration in the future, and this chapter has suggested examples of how that might happen. Moreover, just because there was a convergence of U.S. and Taiwan interests during recent Taiwan and American administrations, which was the reason for the positive state of affairs after 2008, is no reason that relations cannot be improved even more.

Policy Formulation and Implementation

Starting with process, the United States badly needs to correct the damage that the Trump administration did to the way that foreign policy and national security policy is made and implemented. This is true across the board, and not only regarding Taiwan. But Taiwan is a special case. To be sure, it benefited in some ways from trends in U.S.-PRC relations, especially on the security side. But it could also become the victim of that interaction (for example, technology transfer policy and Trump's off-and-on bromance with Xi Jinping). A return to the institutionalized, inclusive, bottom-up, and expert-based process of past administrations—Republican and Democratic alike—is absolutely necessary. This will not guarantee perfection in American policy, but it will reduce the probability of mistakes that damage Taiwan's interests in an irreversible way.

Inevitably, policy toward Taiwan will be a function of U.S. administrations' policies toward Beijing. That does not mean that the content and conduct of U.S. relations with the PRC will be at Taiwan's expense. It could be but does not have to be. Given the complexities of Beijing-Washington, Taipei-Washington, and Taipei-Beijing relations, the Biden administration will best assess and reconcile the substantive trade-offs through a process that is comprehensive in its scope. A good process does not itself guarantee good policy substance—and the proper protection of Taiwan's interests—but a ragged and disorganized process will surely not.

Economic Relations

The area where a better balance of priorities is necessary concerns trade, investment, and technology. Looking strategically, Taiwan's future is better assured if it has a strong, globally connected economy. That is important for its own sake but also because it fortifies public confidence. Beijing is working to control as much of the island's access to the global economy as it can, by blocking Taiwan's efforts to negotiate free trade agreements with third countries and to gain membership in multilateral economic groupings. The unstated message: the road to the international economy runs through Beijing. This campaign of marginalization has an economic impact, forcing Taiwan companies that might prefer to stay in Taiwan to move behind the tariff walls of other economies. But marginalization also has a political and psychological effect. Beijing, by demonstrating that it is in control, weakens the authority of the Taipei government and fosters hopelessness among the people.

Stealthily, therefore, Beijing is changing the economic status quo. Senior U.S. officials have said that Washington opposes a unilateral change in the status quo by the other side. If that warning extends to economics, as I think it should, then the United States should craft its economic policy toward Taiwan in ways that counter this trend and mitigate the island's marginalization. That would seem to be obvious if the United States were engaged in a hard containment of the PRC in the name of strategic competition. Because the PRC is Taiwan's adversary, it becomes a partner in containment. But even if U.S. policy is not as zero-sum as containment implies, accepting the possibility and even necessity of cooperation with Beijing in some fields, it is still in the interest of the United States to aid Taipei in strengthening its economy and to give it new avenues to the international economy.

The most effective way to do this would be through a free trade agreement or its functional equivalent, that is, a series of negotiated agreements that would be equivalent to the chapters of a free trade agreement. Even announcing the beginning of negotiations would give a morale boost to Taiwan's political leaders and the public. Yet the true value of a free trade agreement or its functional equivalent would come first from the trust building that occurs in the course of successful negotiations and then in the structural adjustment that agreements would trigger within the Taiwan economy. In both respects, doing a series of individual agreements in sequence may have advantages over trying to do a comprehensive free trade agreement. That approach would put less stress at any one time on the agencies responsible for the negotiations. Starting with easy issues would create a sense of achievement and momentum for more difficult ones.

There is another reason to keep a "building blocks" approach in mind. That is, the U.S. executive branch's authority to negotiate FTAs with other economies and then submit them to Congress for a no-amendments, up-or-down vote ("trade promotion authority") expires on July 1, 2021. The chances of Washington and Taipei negotiating a comprehensive FTA by then is virtually impossible, in part because of the political transition that will occur in the United States during that period. The possibility of renewal of trade promotion authority sometime after the coming expiration is uncertain.[52]

Declaratory Policy

In declaratory policy making, the most important thing is to follow the Hippocratic oath and do no harm. The various elements of U.S. declaratory policy have accumulated over time. Each element serves a purpose, but what is important is the entire package and the stress that is placed on some elements over others at a particular point in time. Dropping this or that element is usually more trouble than it is worth. For example, reiterating a commitment to the TRA but not to the three U.S.-PRC communiqués can send a signal to both Taipei and Beijing that unnecessarily alarms the latter and gives excessive hope to the former.[53]

Because it is now more than forty years since the establishment of U.S.-PRC relations and the severing of U.S.–Republic of China relations, American diplomats of the twenty-first century do not necessarily know the rationale for this or that part of the lexicon of U.S.-Taiwan relations. That is all the more reason to have an integrated policy process, to help U.S. officials stay on message. Yet when Trump was untethered from what passed for decisionmaking in his administration, and given the transactional and isolated nature of his interactions with Xi Jinping, there was a danger that Xi might induce him to talk inadvertently about U.S. Taiwan policy in ways that benefit the PRC and hurt Taiwan. For example, if, at Xi's quiet suggestion, Trump had said that it was now U.S. policy to favor unification based on the one country, two systems formula, it would have totally undercut the position of leaders in Taiwan, both Green and Blue.

Yet it is not just Taiwan's political leaders who have a stake in how U.S. leaders speak about Taiwan; it is the island's people, as well. All the more reason for the United States to place even more stress on the democracy element of the U.S. rhetorical package. This element arose during the late 1990s and was given its most authoritative rendering by Bill Clinton in a March 2000 speech: "We will continue to reject the use of force as a means to resolve the Taiwan question, making absolutely clear that the issues between Beijing and Taiwan must be resolved peacefully and with the assent of the people of Taiwan."[54] This should not be seen as a revolutionary change in American policy but rather as a statement of reality, that Taiwan's democratization had given the people of the island a significant say, and probably the final say, on how to resolve the dispute with the PRC through negotiations. If Beijing wishes to make progress toward its objective of unification, it is the island's voters whom it must convince. Moreover, as noted in a previous chapter, it will have to build broad enough support to enact constitutional amendments. American diplomats should reject the PRC's standard claims that continued U.S. arms sales to Taiwan or a purported policy of containment are what is obstructing unification. The obstacle is Beijing's own unification formula— one country, two systems—which Taiwan leaders and people have rejected since it was proffered in the early 1980s. When it comes to cross-Strait relations, Taiwan's democracy has matured in the years since Clinton made his statement, so it is all the more important that U.S. officials regularly remind their PRC counterparts that Beijing's road to Taipei does not run through Washington.

Security

In the area of security, U.S. policy should start with a recognition that there are two threats to Taiwan's security: one is military, the other is political. The purpose of both threats is the same, which is to compel the island's leaders to capitulate and accept unification on Beijing's terms. But the means are different. The first threat would take the form of a military campaign against

Taiwan that targeted the island's armed forces and its territory. It could take a fairly short period of time, depending on how determined Taiwan is to resist and the U.S. response. The second, more political threat would target the self-confidence of Taiwan's leaders and the public. Accordingly, and to achieve this psychological effect, it uses various elements of PRC power in combination: diplomatic, political, information, cyber, military, and so on (on the military front, the PLA only displays force and does not use it).

Because Taiwan faces two types of security threats, a United States that seeks to help Taiwan should do so along the same two tracks. On the military side, the Pentagon should continue to help Taiwan acquire capabilities that, once acquired and ready, would raise the cost of PLA action to such an unacceptable level that it would never be initiated. The premise of such dissuasion should be to demonstrate that Taiwan would be able to resist long enough for the U.S. military to intervene in force. The basis for U.S. support of Taiwan should start with the Ministry of National Defense's credible acceptance of the Overall Defense Concept (ODC) and adoption of procurement plans that support that concept. Taiwan should eschew acquisition of advanced systems that contribute little or nothing to the sort of deterrence that the ODC dictates. Creation of capabilities that exploit PLA weaknesses and make it think twice about a kinetic attack should receive priority from both Taiwan's defense ministry and the Pentagon. Of course, the creation of those capabilities probably requires continuing increases in the budget resources available to ministry.

How the United States should help Taiwan cope with the second threat is more complicated, because Beijing has a range of tools at its disposal and will use them to achieve a much more psychological than material effect. In some areas, such as cybersecurity, the United States has worked to improve Taiwan's resilience, work that should continue. A finalized U.S.-Taiwan free trade agreement would strengthen the island's competitiveness over the long term, but even just an announcement by Washington that it was prepared to negotiate an agreement would strengthen Taiwan psychologically, and right away. The Trump administration has warned some of Taiwan's diplomatic partners not to shift diplomatic relations to Beijing, which signals to people in Taiwan that they are not alone. So do U.S. public statements that counter PRC rhetoric on cross-Strait relations and actions by the U.S. military that respond to PLA patrolling close to Taiwan. In this regard, the sale of American F-16V aircraft to Taiwan's air force gives it a better ability to respond, in a signaling sense, to the PLA's air force patrols. What on first glance would appear to be a legacy system that does not contribute to deterrence of PLA military action (because PLA missiles and anti-aircraft systems would diminish their war-fighting value) does help in the fight to sustain the confidence of the Taiwan public by scrambling to monitor at least some PLA flights. Also, a deterrence purpose is served.

In September 2020, Richard Haass, president of the Council on Foreign Relations, and his colleague David Sacks starkly questioned whether past U.S. declaratory policy on Taiwan's security was still effective in deterring a PRC attack, given the improvements in the PLA's capabilities. They termed that policy "strategic ambiguity," that is, creating doubts in both Taipei and Beijing whether Washington would come to Taiwan's defense. They called instead for a shift to "strategic clarity." By this they meant "a presidential statement and accompanying executive order that reiterates U.S. support for its one-China policy but also unequivocally states that the United States would respond should Taiwan come under Chinese armed attack." At the same time, the statement would make clear that the United States does not support Taiwan independence.[55]

Even if strategic ambiguity had been an accurate descriptor of U.S. security policy at one time, I believe that by 1996, at the earliest, and 2004, at the latest, it had been superseded by "dual deterrence," which includes warning Beijing against any change in the cross-Strait status quo. That formulation implies that the United States would react militarily to such a change. More significantly, effective deterrence requires more than public statements, no matter how clear. In the case of Taiwan, it includes sound analysis of how Chinese leaders are reading U.S. intentions and of whether the deployment and operations of PLA assets suggest a shift to war. It entails private U.S. messaging through diplomatic and national security channels that apply the general public U.S. warning against using force to the circumstances of any potential crisis. Above all, it requires improving U.S. capabilities, which can have long lead times, to ensure that American intervention would be effective (among other things, to raise the costs and risks to the PLA of an attack). It also mandates shaping Taiwan's defense strategy and capabilities so that they are able to hold on until U.S. intervention can occur.[56] In assessing U.S. intentions, Chinese leaders who might contemplate a military campaign against Taiwan would evaluate all of these factors. In effect, they will not only listen to what U.S. leaders say but also what the Pentagon does to prepare for war. If they conclude that American declaratory policy concerning Taiwan's security is not backed up with sufficient capabilities, they will interpret rhetorical warnings as hollow. Hence, even if U.S. policymakers decide that a dual deterrence formula is not sufficiently precise, they should evaluate whether the military capabilities at their disposal give that declaratory policy credibility. If they do not, then improving them is necessary.

The degree of clarity of U.S. declaratory policy must also take into account the policies that the government in Taipei pursues, and whether those policies challenge China's interests to the point of provoking military action. Based on past experience, Washington must be careful not to give a green light to Taiwan to pursue policies that risk war and are inconsistent with U.S. objectives. Without giving Beijing its own green light to interpret Taipei's actions in a self-serving way, Washington and Taipei should not ignore the impact of PRC perceptions or misperceptions in dictating its actions.[57]

Conduct of the Relationship

At the time the United States established diplomatic relations, it said that the government of the PRC was the sole, legal government of China. That is, Washington had a one-China policy, and not a two-Chinas policy. This actually was a choice that both Beijing and Taipei imposed on the United States. A derivative of that policy was a pledge to Beijing that it would have unofficial relations with Taiwan, but successive administrations have reserved the right to define what that pledge meant practically for the conduct of relations.[58] Indeed, the ways in which U.S. and Taiwan officials interact has expanded greatly since the early 1990s, and practices that would once have been rejected out of hand have become commonplace.

A couple of factors should govern whether and how far that expansion should continue in the future. One is whether a particular action so obviously crosses the fuzzy line between official and unofficial that it cannot be justified, in part because it would quite likely trigger the PRC to suspend or break diplomatic relations with the United States. There may be Americans who would welcome such an outcome, but I suspect that the mainstream American view is that whatever the current difficulties in U.S.-PRC relations, the cost of a suspension of diplomatic relations outweighs any benefits. There is a point at which an atrophy of U.S. communication with the PRC government harms U.S interests. An example of such obvious crossing of the line would be a visit by Taiwan's president to Washington, D.C., to include a meeting with the president or the secretary of state. Another factor is the balance of substance and symbolism in a precedent-breaking action. Although U.S. officials understand that sometimes symbolic actions are substantive in their effect, the long-standing American preference has been to take actions that are clearly substantive and ignore those that are symbols for symbol's sake.

For example, there has been talk in American defense and congressional circles about having a U.S. Navy ship make a port call in Taiwan. That would clearly be symbolic and very welcomed by many in Taiwan, but it is hard to argue that deterrence is strengthened in any way. A final factor is how Taiwan's leadership is conducting its policy toward the PRC and how much that policy converges with U.S. interests. Beijing may be changing the status quo in the Taiwan Strait, which the United States should oppose, but Taipei helps itself by not making that fraught situation worse (which has been the case since 2008).

Conclusion

There are steps that Taiwan can take to help itself, such as unilaterally aligning its economic policies with what the United States would probably demand in a bilateral free trade agreement, increasing defense spending and using those funds for the right things, and so on. The balanced and cautious approach that the island's leaders have recently taken toward the PRC, even in light of Beijing's pressure tactics, are important contributions to peace and security in the Taiwan area, a key U.S. interest. But it is becoming increasingly necessary for Washington to better define its goals concerning the PRC, as well as the implications of that stance for ties with Taiwan. It is not in Taiwan's interest that U.S.-PRC relations deteriorate so badly that Taiwan is indeed the victim of friendly fire, as sometimes appeared possible during the Trump administration.[59] Washington should base Taiwan policy on its own interests, but it should not ignore Taiwan's interests as it calibrates its policy actions. Nor should people in Taiwan assume that U.S.-PRC tensions will always work to their advantage or negate the need for caution. Taiwan does face tough choices in coping with its PRC challenge. As it makes those choices, it needs a proper understanding of American interests and intentions.

15

What to Do?

Can Taiwan have both security and the good life? Or, to put the question more precisely, can it have more security and more of the good life at the same time? Taiwan is already a prosperous society whose government strives to provide the public goods that are needed to meet this stage of social and economic development. It has a vibrant democratic system that regularly registers the public will on who should lead the government and whether they are doing a good job. Also, Taiwan is fairly secure. With the aid of the United States, it has survived even after its marginalization from the international community began in the early 1970s. Indeed, one might say that Taiwan people were able to create the good life that many of them enjoy today precisely because the United States has provided a security umbrella.

If a pollster asked people in Taiwan whether they would like more security and more of the good life, they undoubtedly would say yes. If they were asked whether they would like less security and less prosperity, they certainly would say no. The more difficult question arises if it is not possible to get each of these two desirable conditions at the same time. Which, then, is more important? What are the trade-offs that people would be willing to make between the two to have some of each? If more security can only be bought through a reduction in Taiwan's standard of living, is that a price worth paying? Does preserving all or part of the current "good life" require accommodating to the People's Republic of China (PRC) to some degree? If so, how much, and at what risk?

Adding to the complexity, the current status quo is not static. Taiwan's population will continue to age. The People's Liberation Army will continue to enhance its military capabilities and do so faster than Taiwan can improve its own, despite the alliance-like commitment of the United States. The damage from greenhouse gases will occur faster than the international community, including Taiwan, can summon the ability and will to do something about it.

Polling organizations in Taiwan do not usually go into this level of detail in formulating their questions, and it is not clear that survey research is the best way to get reliable answers (in contrast to focus groups, for example). Yet the findings in previous chapters of this book provide some clues. The World Happiness Report has regularly found that Taiwan people are the happiest in East Asia. A majority believes that preserving economic growth is the top policy priority, favors the preservation of the status quo of cross-Strait relations, deems that cross-Strait relations should develop more quickly than they are now, and values a moderate approach to Beijing generally but adamantly opposes the one country, two systems formula (1C2S) for resolving the fundamental dispute with the PRC. Up through 2019, a majority thought that using the 1992 Consensus (defined in Taiwan as different interpretations of one China) was an acceptable basis for conducting cross-Strait relations. Whether it does now, after Xi Jinping's January 2109 speech on Taiwan politics and the PRC crackdown on Hong Kong, is another question. Still, various polls taken together suggest that the public at least hopes that it is possible to have both security and the good life.

The mainstream view of the Kuomintang (KMT) also holds that Taiwan can achieve both objectives as long as it provides Beijing ambiguous reassurance on the issue of one China. Yet the current KMT leadership has recognized the domestic political risk of strongly associating the party with the 1992 Consensus. The mainstream view of the Democratic Progressive Party (DPP) is that too much economic dependence on mainland China and accepting its political preconditions entail excessive risks and give Beijing leverage to compel unification. It advocates boosting Taiwan's domestic economy, diversifying its trade partners, and relying more on the United States for security. But each of these avenues is cluttered with obstacles. Each camp plays down the problems with its preferred approach.

Although some Taiwan elections indicate clear-cut public support for one detailed policy approach over another, the 2020 presidential contest was not one of them. President Tsai Ing-wen easily beat Kaohsiung mayor Han Kuo-yu by framing the contest as a referendum on whether Taiwan supported unification with China using that formula. This was an easy case for her to make, since a majority in Taiwan consistently opposes unification under the 1C2S formula. Her framing did serve an effective electoral purpose by putting Han and the KMT permanently on the defensive but did not stimulate a serious discussion on how Taiwan should reconcile competing priorities. For his part, Han tried to put Tsai on the defensive by claiming that he would do a better job at meeting the needs of the "common people," but Tsai successfully countered by reminding voters of what her administration had actually done to deal with real social and economic problems.[1]

The central question remains: Can Taiwan's political system both enhance security and ensure the good life? The conclusion of this book is that the system's performance on these questions has been suboptimal. One plausible reason is that, so far, the policy problems Taiwan faces are technically difficult to solve. When it comes to domestic issues such as energy security, Taiwan is not the only advanced economy to face these problems. And if the two sides of the Taiwan Strait could have been creative enough to have devised a mutually acceptable formula for resolving the cross-Strait dispute, they would have done so long ago.

It may be that Taiwan's democratic system itself is part of the problem, because it does a poor job of balancing competing priorities in a way that promises sustained public support. Even when technocratic solutions to problems exist, they often cannot be implemented because of political opposition, and sometimes political dynamics limit policy options. That is, the difficulties that Taiwan faces are structural in nature, not the result of the failures of individual leaders or groups. So it is not inconceivable that the combination of policy difficulty and suboptimal politics means that the current status quo is the best that Taiwan can get, which would be too bad.

Getting More of the Good Life

Several issues illustrate the numerous challenges that the Taiwan political system faces in its efforts to provide the good life for its citizens. The most significant are the government budget, energy, transitional justice, and the economy.

The Government Budget

The discussion on the budget demonstrates that in some areas, change was either automatic or responsive to the problem concerned. Payments for social insurance increased by about a third between 2009 and 2019 because the law required it. The Ma administration increased the amount to be spent in the category of economic development to counteract the depressive effects on growth of the global financial crisis, a response that was successful. It also undertook an initiative to encourage women to get married and have children and to expand preschool childcare, which sought to help women remain in the workforce. Families that have two wage earners will have higher disposable income, which, in turn, will stimulate domestic demand. But in other areas, it was difficult to use the budget adjustments to change Taiwan's domestic and external environment.

Pension reform illustrates the difficulty any administration will face in reallocating resources among budget categories. The Ma administration understood that the existing system was not sustainable and tried to carry out appropriate reforms but ultimately had to admit defeat. The Tsai administration's efforts were more successful, prolonging the system's solvency. But there was a serious political cost. Some defenders of the status quo conducted regular and sometimes violent demonstrations against any significant change in their generous benefits. Exacerbating the conflict, political history overlaid the search for a good technocratic solution. Defenders of the existing system insisted that the benefits under the old system represented a legal obligation of the government that had to be honored and that reform should not occur to their disadvantage. People in the Green camp saw the existing system as a legacy of authoritarian rule and the KMT regime's way of buying the support of the civil service, teachers, and the officer corps. In the end, pension reform did go through, but for a time the process fostered deeper political division, not broader consensus.

Another area is education. The problem here is the constitutional requirement that 15 percent of the central government budget and 35 percent of local government budgets be spent on education. Superficially, that makes sense because a good education system is one key to economic competitiveness. Yet Taiwan already has an excess of universities and a very low birth rate. Over the past decade, private universities have closed or merged, but still there is an excess of university places.[2] Objectively, does the current level of spending on education and the constitutional mandate that sets that level really fit Taiwan's needs? Is it time to repeal that mandate? Would a repeal be politically possible, since expanding education is one way that Legislative Yuan (LY) members and local government leaders demonstrate what they claim is good performance? Is it more feasible to shift the orientation of the educational system so that it better fits the needs of employers?

Spending more on defense has the potential to drain funds for domestic spending. Between 2008 and 2019, defense spending constituted around 11 percent of the total government budget. The Tsai administration has been successful in raising the actual amount of defense dollars, but continuing to do so to cope with the PRC threat may reduce domestic spending; in this way, the search for security might hurt the preservation of the good life.

The root of Taiwan's budget problem is less a misallocation of resources than the government's inability or unwillingness to extract more resources from society. From 2008 to 2018, Taiwan's GDP increased by about one-third, while tax revenues as a share of GDP remained stable at an average of 12.4 percent. Expenditures as a share of GDP fell from 17.9 percent to 16.0 percent. Increasing revenues is never popular in any democratic system. There is always a risk that increasing taxes on companies will reduce their global competitiveness. But the information available on Taiwan's distribution of wealth suggests that the government can increase revenues fairly without exceeding the public's ability and willingness to pay. To do so, political leaders—preferably the leaders of all major parties—would need to make a convincing case that Taiwan is hurting itself by taxing too little and explain why sacrifice is necessary.

The question arises whether the LY should gain more power relative to the executive branch on budget issues, and particularly relative to the technocrats in the Finance Ministry and Directorate-General of Budget, Accounting, and Statistics. The constitution prohibits LY members from increasing the amounts in various budget categories; they can only reduce them. My own judgment is that the current balance of power is proper, despite the limits it places on more democratic budget making. Members of the LY already have the option of lobbying the Executive Yuan and the president's office on behalf of their favorite programs. Giving them even more power might actually make the budget situation worse, because they would be inclined to increase spending that benefits their constituents and disinclined to make tough choices between conflicting priorities.

Energy

Taiwan is trying to balance several competing priorities: keeping the economic machine going, reducing the consumption of coal and oil (and the amount of greenhouse gases they create), increasing the share of wind and solar power in the energy mix, ending nuclear power, keeping the price of energy relatively low, and sustaining a comfortable lifestyle. Attempting to fulfill all of those goals at the same time has been a struggle, as it would be in any society with a similar mix of resources and values.

Clearly, however, the strong, anti-nuclear mindset of some parts of the DPP has reduced the flexibility of the government and other stakeholders in arriving at a sustainable, mixed strategy. As political power has moved from the DPP to the KMT and back to the DPP, energy policy has been reformulated with each change of administration. In addition, when it comes to disposal of nuclear waste and restarting reactors that have been brought down for repair, the Atomic Energy Council has ceded the final decision to the LY, even though the council has more expertise. More broadly, it might have been prudent to preserve nuclear as a backup beyond 2025 until it is certain that half of Taiwan's energy needs can be met with natural gas and that 20 percent can be met with renewables. But politics and ideology have blocked discussion of that option to the point that it has become no option at all. If nuclear power is ended in 2025 and renewables do not yield the energy share that the Tsai administration is planning, the default will be to import more coal and oil and emit even more greenhouse gases. Constraining choices even more is the public opposition to pricing electricity to its true market cost.

Transitional Justice

The need to pursue transitional justice in Taiwan is understood, and the Lee Teng-hui administration made an initial effort in the early 1990s. The question is not whether to undertake transitional justice at all, but to define the scope of the process, plus assess the present and the future consequences of whatever decision is made. On the issue of scope, it makes humanitarian sense to open the archives of cases from the early authoritarian period (when most of the cases occurred). There is probably no escaping transparency regarding incidents such as the 1979 Kaohsiung incident that occurred late in the authoritarian period, because some current, senior members of the DPP were jailed as a result. For example, Chen Chu, who served as secretary general of the Office of the President during most of Tsai Ing-wen's first term, was convicted of sedition regarding the incident. But some calls are harder to make because the KMT of today's democratic system evolved from the KMT that dominated the authoritarian regime until the early 1990s. On an issue such as party assets, for example, it is hard for those in charge of carrying out transitional justice to avoid creating the impression that their actions are motivated by a desire for revenge or political advantage. The result is not reconciliation between the KMT and DPP but deeper division. Making matters more complicated, those responsible for implementing transitional justice made mistakes and did not anticipate that the KMT would block their actions.

The Economy

Even if the PRC did not exist, Taiwan would face challenges in keeping its economy competitive. There are things that Taiwan could do to help itself meet those challenges, but they would entail political costs.

Perhaps the optimal way for Taiwan to circumvent the dilemmas inherent in its dependence on the mainland market would be to significantly upgrade economic ties with the United States and Japan. This could be done through general free trade agreements or more limited but still significant trade pacts. But there should be no illusions about the costs that Taiwan will have to bear to reap the benefits. Both Washington and Tokyo will demand significant reforms in the island's economy, including the deregulation of the financial sector. If Taipei accepts those demands, the result will be structural adjustments that produce domestic winners and losers in the short term, even though there will be a better economy in the long term.

Moreover, even beginning those discussions may be difficult for Taiwan. Japan will only consider negotiations once the ban on food products from the Fukushima area, the site of the 2011 nuclear disaster, is lifted. Even then, Japan may worry that food-safety nongovernmental organizations in Taiwan might try to reinstate the ban. Regarding the United States, Tsai Ing-wen's August 2020 decision on market access for American beef and pork removed the existing obstacle to forward-looking discussions on improving the bilateral economic relationship, including a free trade agreement. Whether the new U.S. administration will seize that opportunity remains to be seen. If it chose to move forward on an agreement, the Taiwan government would have to reduce opposition from sectors that would be negatively affected.

Although liberalization of trade and investment with countries such as the United States and Japan is desirable, agreements would not be reached overnight. As a parallel effort, Taiwan could take steps to help itself in ensuring economic competitiveness and spreading the benefits of growth widely. In short, Taiwan needs to revise the business model that was constructed after the opening of the China market in the 1980s, if only because the factors that fostered that model, such as low-cost labor, have weakened over time.

Some Taiwan sectors are stronger than others. The information technology sector remains strong, pending, of course, the future of U.S. policy on the control of sensitive technology. Taiwan also has a number of capable service industries. But in both manufacturing and services, some enterprises are inefficient and do not offer good employment opportunities. The structural adjustments that will come with high-quality free trade agreements will accelerate the decline of sunset industries as it incentivizes the emergence of new, more profitable sectors.

Taiwan does not need to wait for externally induced structural adjustments to begin moving forward. The policy steps that should be part of a domestic reform program are similar to the concessions that Taiwan would have to make in a free trade agreement with the United States or Japan and those that would be required if it became possible to join the Comprehensive and Progressive Agreement for Trans-Pacific Partnership. The temptation to defer these measures until they are raised in those trade negotiations is understandable, but there is no certainty how long it will take to achieve those agreements or even that they will ever be possible at all. These are the kinds of steps that Taiwan should start making unilaterally, in its own interests. If a U.S.-Taiwan free trade agreement or Taiwan's joining regional agreements (or both) become possible, then much of the work will already be done, and Taiwan will gain credit for having taken the initiative.

But even in the information technology sector, there are weak points that should be remedied to strengthen its capacity for innovation. Here, one priority should be to increase government funding for advanced research into the technologies of the future, in the way that fostered the semiconductor industry in the first place. A second priority area should be improving science, technology, engineering, and mathematics (STEM) education now and in the future to ensure a steady stream of capable talent. This might be done through increased funding, fostering university start-up incubators through an industry-government partnership, linking business and technical training to facilitate better understanding between people across Taiwan's sectors, and giving Taiwan-based start-ups greater international exposure.[3]

Policies are also needed to overcome the small size of Taiwan's economy, which can be an obstacle to developing a strong software sector. This can be done, writes Evan Feigenbaum, by developing Taiwan as a hub for next-generation software industry products and services and also by emphasizing data quality over data quantity. It can build a comparative advantage as a trusted supplier and conduit in the information technology sector.[4] In an era when the risks of operating in the PRC are growing, Taiwan can become a safe haven for affected companies while simultaneously aligning itself with and contributing to international industrial standards.[5] At the same time, Taiwan can help itself by making it easier for talented expatriates to work and live in Taiwan.[6]

Such a program, if properly designed, could have important employment effects by creating more and better jobs for recent university graduates to fill. That, in turn, could increase the marriage and birth rates and so ease the demands of the aging population. Of course, the government would have to give incentives to the education system to adapt itself, particularly at the university level, to the needs of employers.

Some of these steps will require money, so the budget authorities and the LY will either have to cut funding for other programs, which is difficult, or raise taxes, which is also difficult. Any trade and investment liberalization program will affect sectors that have been protected and the government agencies that regulate them. The political problem that liberalization creates for the administration that pursues it is that there is a fairly immediate negative impact on the competitiveness of sectors that are affected by market opening, while the benefits of enhanced competitiveness for the economy as a whole occurs only gradually. There are steps that the government can take to ease the transition. Still, an administration that promotes liberalization will face a tough political challenge in explaining to the public how the long-term benefits outweigh the short-term costs and that improved growth and a higher standard of living makes the inevitable sacrifices worth bearing. The Ma administration was not successful in making that case regarding the service-trade agreement, but that episode may provide lessons for the future.

The Beijing Factor

The economy, energy policy, and balancing budget choices are problems that many other advanced countries also face. Taiwan is also not unique in its struggle over transitional justice, even if the island's special history defines the nature of that struggle. What does make Taiwan unique is the challenge that the PRC poses to its economic, social, and political future. Since the 1980s, Taiwan's prosperity has depended on access to the mainland market, both for its customers and its people to work in the production and assembly plants of Taiwan companies. At the same time, the PRC government seeks to incorporate the island into its constitutional system and, if the experience in Hong Kong is any guide, would want to maintain a degree of control after unification that would be inconsistent with the island's democracy. What Beijing has yet to conclusively determine is exactly how to bring about the outcome it seeks. Persuasion has not worked. Intimidation may work but probably only over a long period of time. Even though the use of force would be risky, it remains an option. For Taiwan, therefore, the toughest policy trade-off is how to manage the relationship with the PRC while maintaining economic competitiveness and prosperity, which are crucial to preserving the good life. Since Taiwan's democratic transition, the PRC has always been not just the key security issue and economic partner (see chapter 8) but also the policy issue that most roils Taiwan politics for political parties.[7]

That divided domestic politics have impeded formulation of sensible responses to the Beijing challenge has vexed those Taiwan people with a sense of perspective. A Taiwanese acquaintance of mine, a talented woman in her thirties, exemplifies that frustration. She grew up in Taiwan in a family that was probably Green in its political leaning. She went to graduate school in the United States and then worked in Washington, D.C., in the private sector for several years, focusing on issues related to Taiwan. She then returned home in the late 2010s after a decade away in the United States. I had the opportunity to chat with her not long thereafter and was curious to hear her impressions of Taiwan after she had been exposed to domestic politics every day. What struck and worried her the most was the intensity of the conflict between the Blue and Green camps, even though the substantive policy differences between the KMT and DPP did not seem that great to her. But the modest gap did not mitigate the "I live, you die" atmosphere in which politicians interacted. Each camp saw the other as adversary, ignoring what she felt was obvious, that the real enemy was ninety miles away, on the other side of the Taiwan Strait.[8]

My friend's frustration about domestic political division does provoke the question: Is the PRC truly Taiwan's enemy? As discussed in chapter 8, the DPP generally believes that the PRC is the adversary and that it intends to use its economic power to induce Taiwan's political capitulation. Therefore, it is felt, Taiwan should remain on guard and not fall into Beijing's trap. Leaders of the KMT believe that sustaining economic growth and ensuring security simultaneously is, in fact, possible. Yet they have also believed that it is necessary and reasonable for Taipei to calm Beijing's fears about the possibility of de jure independence, specifically by accepting the 1992 Consensus.

Also, each camp believes that the other is a part of the problem. Many Greens regard the Blue camp as the PRC's stalking horse within Taiwan and the instrument of its penetration of Taiwan politics. They might point to PRC support for and guidance of the *China Times* group as evidence for that charge, as discussed in chapter 12. They can definitely cite Beijing's Hong Kong crackdown in 2019 and 2020 as clear evidence that too much engagement with the PRC will end very badly. Some in the Blue camp regard the DPP with suspicion, either because of its historical support for de jure independence or because they think Tsai, by not endorsing the 1992 Consensus explicitly, has erected unnecessary obstacles to continued and mutually beneficial cross-Strait economic relations, or both. For them, Beijing's response to her administration was foreordained. Yet there are other people in the Blue camp, native Taiwanese by family history, who worry that their mainlander Blue colleagues are going to sell out their country (that is, the country of the native Taiwanese).[9]

Clearly, if the two camps disagree on this key analytical issue—whether the PRC is the adversary—then they are likely to disagree on the answers to the two policy-relevant questions discussed in chapter 8. That is, are Beijing's intentions revisionist or supportive of the status quo? And are PRC leaders risk averse or risk accepting? Lack of clarity on those, in turn, will produce disputes over how Taiwan should respond—either with accommodation or deterrence. If the two camps regard each other as the adversary, then responses to the challenge the PRC poses will be even more suboptimal.

I would like to believe that the KMT is correct in its logic, that the PRC's attitude toward Taiwan is benign and not malign, and that acceptance of the 1992 Consensus by whoever is in power in Taipei would end the current impasse. Yet there are reasons to question such a belief. First of all, we must examine the claim that Beijing would have been friendlier to the DPP government installed in 2016 if Tsai Ing-wen, for the sake of continuity in cross-Strait relations, had decided to accept the 1992 Consensus when she took office. As noted in chapter 8, Beijing actually asked her to do more than repeat Ma Ying-jeou's way of accepting the 1992 Consensus by insisting that she explicitly state that Taiwan was included in the sovereign territory of the state China. She declined to do so, both because many in the DPP would have opposed such a statement and because she believed that accommodating Beijing in this way would have conceded a point that should be a subject of negotiations. Moreover, she had worked hard before her election to privately offer reassurance and did try to address these points ambiguously in her inaugural address. But Beijing was unwilling to take yes for an answer and engage in a trust-building exercise with her. My own interpretation is that Beijing set the bar of accommodation higher than she could reasonably clear, so that it would not have to develop a modus vivendi with her government through dialogue.

Second, the Tsai administration aside, Beijing and the KMT have different definitions of the 1992 Consensus. For Taiwan people in the Blue camp, it is "one China, different interpretations," with the Republic of China being their interpretation of that one China. The PRC view, as enunciated by Xi Jinping in January 2019, is that "the two sides of the Strait belong to one China and would work together to seek national reunification."[10] There is no indication here that Beijing is willing for Taiwan to adopt its "different interpretations" of one China, particularly if it is the Republic of China. Beijing most likely let Ma Ying-jeou perform his sleights of hand on these points not because it accepted Ma's elaborations but because it trusted his broader intentions and hoped that he would begin political talks. It is difficult to see how Beijing would now allow even a new, non-DPP administration to repeat Ma's gambit.

Third, the 1992 Consensus was deliberately designed to facilitate cross-Strait cooperation on economic and social affairs while political matters were set aside. It was never intended to be the basis of political talks. The PRC government's pressure on the Ma administration to begin those talks was intended to take cross-Strait relations to a new stage, though Ma demurred. In response, Beijing rejected pleas from the Ma administration to allow an expansion of Taiwan's international space beyond a couple of free trade agreements and Taiwan's attendance at a few meetings of international organizations. The logic of PRC officials was that any expansion of Taiwan's international space was a political issue that first had to be addressed in cross-Strait political talks. None of this should have been terribly surprising. Beijing's engagement with the Ma administration was framed as easy issues first and harder ones later, and economic issues first and political issues later. There was no mystery, then, about where the PRC wanted to go, and it is unlikely its approach would be any different if a new, non-DPP president accepted the 1992 Consensus and if Beijing trusted that person's basic intentions. It would have sufficient reason to renormalize economic relations and reaffirm past agreements on "easy" issues. Yet before long, that Taiwan administration would face both demands from the PRC for political talks and domestic resistance to any cross-Strait discussions on political issues.

Complicating the ability of any non-DPP government to strike a balance between cross-Strait policy and domestic politics is the law that the LY passed in May 2019 setting the terms for negotiating and approving agreements with Beijing that had a "major constitutional or political effect." This law sets such stringent requirements that agreements could only be negotiated and approved if both the KMT and DPP believed that the measure was in Taiwan's interests. But it is likely that sooner or later after a new, non-DPP government took power, Beijing would demand that they begin political talks, which the law would make virtually impossible. Of course, the new government could try to repeal that legislation, and Beijing might demand that it do so. Until repeal happens, Beijing would be unable to move forward on its agenda.

It might seem that the Tsai government's approach to the PRC—less accommodating to its demands than the KMT and more reliant on the support of the United States—is "good enough" in protecting Taiwan's interests. The Tsai administration has undertaken a set of policies designed to maintain economic growth and security in spite of the PRC's choice to isolate, marginalize, and punish it. These include the 5+2 Major Innovative Industries economic program, the New Southbound Policy, and sustaining close relations with the United States. The progress attained on those policies during Tsai's first term probably contributed to her reelection in January 2020, even though the Hong Kong protests were very influential. Yet despite the administration's relative success in making it through the first term, PRC policies do create problems for Taiwan.

For example, issues affecting the interests of Taiwan companies with mainland exposure that can only be addressed through interaction and agreements between the Straits Exchange Foundation and the Association for Relations across the Taiwan Straits, analogous to those concluded during the Ma period. For example, under the cross-Strait Economic Cooperation Framework Agreement signed in June 2010, the two sides were to negotiate accords on investment protection and dispute settlements, in addition to the proposed agreements on trade in goods and services. Negotiations began but were quickly stalled over an array of obstacles. Both of those agreements are less important to Beijing than they are to Taiwan companies with operations on the mainland, so Beijing has no urgency to come to closure. In addition, it probably sees no reason to provide the Tsai administration with an achievement that will improve the DPP's standing. But Beijing's suspension of contacts between the Straits Exchange Foundation and the Association for Relations across the Taiwan Straits, which it blames on Tsai, serves as a convenient excuse.

More consequential is the effect of Beijing's post-2016 campaign of coercion without violence on the self-confidence of the Taiwan public. The target of its actions in the economic, diplomatic, political, military, propaganda, and other domains is public morale, and the goal is to create division and despair. (It has also strengthened the view in the Green camp that Beijing's goals are indeed revisionist.) To counter a weakening of public confidence, the Taiwan government and the DPP must develop additional ways to strengthen the sense that Taiwan can survive despite Beijing's efforts. It has stressed the return of a number of companies to Taiwan from the mainland, the strength of the relationship with the United States, the gradual success of the New Southbound Policy, and the capacity that the government displayed in responding to COVID-19 in the first half of 2020. All of these are important, as was the affirmation of voters in the 2020 election. But they may not be sufficient to counter a sense of national despair (*wangguogan*). Taiwan's leaders certainly cannot assume that coercion without violence will not work.

In short, whether the ruling party in Taiwan is the DPP or an alternative, neither will find cross-Strait relations to be smooth sailing. Indeed, since the 1990s, the Taipei government has had to play, in Robert Putnam's seminal phrase, "a two-level game."[11] That is, successive Taiwan administrations have had to take account of domestic political forces in its dealings with Beijing. Thus the DPP's Deep Green faction and the people it represents have placed limits on what their own president can do. Similarly, Ma Ying-jeou lost the policy initiative when the DPP and youthful protesters successfully blocked passage of his cross-Strait trade agreement. Taiwan is thus caught in a more significant catch-22 than simply the stalemate caused by Beijing's response to Tsai Ing-wen's presidency (Beijing has its own politics, but its two-level game is easier to play). As much as the DPP and the KMT would like to sustain the economic benefits Taiwan and its companies enjoy from the PRC, each party in its own way faces noneconomic constraints imposed by Beijing that are difficult to circumvent and that may well entail a domestic political price.

Taiwan has tried to develop intellectual and policy defenses against PRC ambitions by redefining national and state identity. On the one hand, an exclusive Taiwanese identity or a hybrid Chinese-Taiwanese identity have been posed as contrasts to the singular Han Chinese identity, which is the basis of PRC national identity. On the other hand, the long-standing Taiwan stress on the principle that the Republic of China or Taiwan is a sovereign entity has served as a barrier to Beijing's insistence that Taiwan under 1C2S will be as a subordinate entity in a centralized unitary state (like Hong Kong) and to its rejection of alternative unification formulas that people in Taiwan might find worth exploring (such as federation or confederation). There has also been a trend in framing Taiwan's national and state identity in terms of its democratic system. Yet there is not unanimity when it comes to defining the nation and the state, and the definitions offered are sometimes meager in their content, even when agreement exists.

Taiwan leaders and the public therefore have homework to do in forging a stronger consensus regarding the nation and the state and on aligning one with the other. Because the PRC has clear views on those subjects, and because Taiwan has fashioned conflicting views as a defensive shield, it needs to advocate those views more clearly and coherently. Even if the people of the island would prefer to maintain the status quo, as polls suggest, they and their government cannot rule out the possibility that at some point they may get drawn into political talks with Beijing. In those talks, PRC officials will most likely seek to get clear and definitive commitments from Taiwan that territorially it belongs to the state called China and that unification is the goal.

If there is to be broader consensus on nation and state, it will have to be formulated by people in Taiwan. Doing this homework will not only enable Taipei to rebut Beijing about Taiwan's status. A more unified approach on the issues of nation and state can contribute to a stronger sense of security. This is not a task for foreigners, but the discussion in this book suggests several points of departure.

First of all, there needs to be a more precise and sophisticated study of the extent and content of Taiwanese identity, both exclusively Taiwanese and dual identity. Some research suggests that dual identity is actually stronger than exclusive identity. If that is in fact true, then the content of this hybrid needs to be defined. In what ways are people willing to acknowledge and accept that they are Chinese? More important, creating public support for an in-depth understanding of identity will require a broad and intensive educational effort. A shared understanding that people in Taiwan are Chinese, at least ethnically, socially, and culturally, can be reassuring to Beijing.

Second, concerning the state, a couple of issues are at play. The first is the need to strengthen the widely supported claim that Taiwan is a sovereign entity. In particular, it must work to better define what Stephen Krasner calls its Westphalian-cum-Vattelian sovereignty, which relates to how Taiwan might fit legally and politically into a unified China. If it is not to be a subordinate entity like Hong Kong, it needs to be prepared to specify how it is willing to fit. Would, for example, Taiwan's leaders and citizens be willing to accept some type of confederal relationship, assuming that Beijing were willing to entertain it?[12] To undertake such a discussion would usefully undermine the PRC view that Taiwan's claim of sovereignty is tantamount to seeking independence. This type of sovereignty is different from the question of whether Taiwan is a sovereign entity within the international community, which is what most of the island's leaders think of when they refer to sovereignty. (That will remain an important issue, but the other is crucial.) In theory, there may be aspects of Taiwan's Westphalian sovereignty that its political leadership and the people may be willing to give up if they are part of a good deal. It is imperative, therefore, that there be more study of which elements of sovereignty might be traded away, which are negotiable, and which must be defended at all costs. However this balance is struck, it seems that Taiwan can strengthen its claim of sovereignty by asserting that the Republic of China, which was founded in 1912, thirty-seven years before the PRC, still exists on Taiwan and by building support for that object of loyalty.

Finally, if democracy is going to be an additional basis of national and state identity, then efforts will be needed to make the political system more effective.

Improving Taiwan's Democracy

If neither a Blue nor a Green administration is likely to get satisfaction from Beijing on both security and economic growth, and if public morale is in question, then Taiwan can better protect itself and preserve prosperity by better managing the politics of those pressing concerns. That, in turn, will require improving how the political system operates.

Politicians and political scientists have long discussed how to make the Taiwan political system work better. Some of those ideas involve major structural changes that often require constitutional amendments, such as moving from the current semi-presidential system to either a presidential or parliamentary form of government. Precisely because such changes cannot be enacted without amendments to the constitution, they are not worth considering in the current political climate. Indeed, for any proposed amendments to clear the threshold of a three-quarters majority in the LY, they would need the support of both the KMT and the DPP, and even then, approval by referendum by a majority of eligible voters (not of people casting ballots) would also be required. Based on the experience of the amendments enacted after democratization began in the 1990s and of the one amendment passed during Chen Shui-bian's administration, constitutional amendments do not get passed unless the KMT and the DPP agree to do so. The precise process for passing those amendments was somewhat different from the one that would be used today, but the principle is the same. Unless the KMT and DPP agree to pass an amendment, and unless the initiative enjoys broad public support, the constitution cannot be changed.[13]

An alternative to changing the current political system would be for the

DPP, the KMT, or some other party to gain a dominant position for an extended period of time. In that case, this dominant party could pursue the same basic policies on a sustained basis without facing a serious challenge or having to make major structural changes. Japan is the precedent here; its Liberal Democratic Party has been in power for all but a few years since its formation in 1955. There have been adjustments from time to time, but successful opposition challenges have clearly been exceptions to the rule.

Taiwan may be moving in that direction, but it has not arrived there yet. The system has been majoritarian since 2008, with the KMT controlling the executive and legislative branches until 2016 and the DPP now positioned to do so until 2024. If the DPP can maintain control of both branches after that election, it will be a strong indicator of movement to a one-party-dominant system. But recent experience suggests that the DPP will be better positioned to achieve dominance if it continues the Tsai administration's relatively cautious approach concerning the PRC. Shifting to the Deep Green agenda of pushing the PRC envelope by appearing to challenge the current status quo might be dangerous, and it would certainly be contrary to status-quo sentiments of the population. Even if the DPP chooses continuity over change in 2024, there is no guarantee that it can keep winning elections. The island has enough independent voters to shift the electoral balance of power that neither the DPP nor KMT can take its victories for granted.

One-party dominance may be good for the party doing the dominating, but it is not good for Taiwan's democratic system. Even the possibility of a regular rotation of power gives the ruling party reason to avoid mistakes and to eschew initiatives that lack public support. An effective democratic system requires a strong opposition party. If the KMT can mount an effective challenge in 2024, the current pattern of rotating majoritarianism will continue. With it, the reasonable probability that the ruling party of the moment can lose power at the next election will continue to exist, which creates a greater level of accountability than in a one-party dominant system. But that requires the KMT to become competitive again. It survived defeat in the presidential elections of 2000 and 2004 to come back in 2008, so a future return to power cannot be ruled out. But there are several things that it will have to get right.

First of all, the party must come up with a new strategy for securing the resources it needs to compete effectively in electoral campaigns. Second, having relied historically on organizational mechanisms to mobilize voters, especially rural voters, it needs to emphasize even more methods that are appropriate to Taiwan's urban and media-intensive society. Third, and relatedly, it must foster new appeals to young people and be responsive to their concerns, to negate the impression that is a party dominated by old men. Fourth, it must develop a new mechanism for selecting its presidential candidates, one that better bridges the party's internal cleavages. The absence of such a mechanism is the main reason the KMT candidates lost so badly in 2016 and 2020.

Fifth, and more than anything, the KMT will have to formulate a new vision for cross-Strait relations that responds to current realities: the changing business environment on the mainland, greater clarity on Beijing's long-term ambitions, and trends in domestic public opinion. On the latter, Yu Ching-hsin, a political scientist with Election Study Center, clearly states the problem: "The increase in Taiwanese identity has been detrimental to the KMT's political appeal, and has made it much harder for the party to argue that active and positive engagement with the PRC would benefit Taiwan."[14] So, a new KMT vision must convincingly refute the suspicion in some quarters that the party is more interested in serving the interests of the PRC and large Taiwan companies than it is society as a whole.

By mid-2020, the leadership of the KMT had taken a few steps in these directions. In March, the party selected Johnny Chiang Chi-chen as its chairman. Born in 1972, he is a generation younger than the Ma Ying-jeou cohort and thus a symbol of outreach to the youth generation. Chiang sought to play up his multifaceted identity: Chinese by ethnicity, Taiwan born and bred, and a citizen of the Republic of China.

After taking office, Chiang established a reform committee and within it a task force on cross-Strait discourse. The rationale for the latter, Chiang said, was that the top priority for Taiwan and the KMT was to "find the key to solving the current stalemate between the two sides" of the Strait. But the task force's proposal did not satisfy all within the party. It proposed four principles for cross-Strait relations: safeguarding the sovereignty of the Republic of China, protecting democracy and human rights, prioritizing Taiwan's security, and building a win-win situation and prosperity in cross-Strait relations. None of these principles were controversial, but the absence of the 1992 Consensus in the list was notable and did cause intra-party disagreement. The task force had proposed that the formula be viewed as "a historical description of past cross-Strait interaction." Some in the party were sharply critical. Darby Liu Ta-yuan described the proposal as the "worst cross-Strait theory" he had ever seen, and has said that it left the KMT only "parroting the rhetoric of the DPP."[15] That reflected not just a division within the party over how great a domestic political liability the 1992 Consensus posed but also a growing generational divide.[16]

After extensive consultations among the various factions, the KMT Party

Congress met in early September 2020. The key product of the meeting was an eight-point compromise statement on "Cross-Strait Discourse." The first four points demonstrated that the party had not resolved the dilemmas before it:

> First, the ROC Constitution not only fosters democracy and freedom but also provides a legal basis for cross-Strait exchanges. Second, official cross-Strait dialogue must face squarely the ROC's constitutional order and respect the existence of the ROC. Third, past KMT statements on the 1992 Consensus and "one China, respective interpretations" were based on the ROC Constitution. Fourth, the 1992 Consensus based on the ROC Constitution should be used to continue cross-Strait exchanges.

Even if these rhetorical formulations were enough to satisfy different factions within the KMT, they probably were insufficient for the Taiwan public at large, and they likely contradicted Beijing's view that the ROC did not exist and so its constitution could not be the basis for cross-Strait interaction. Moreover, this "discourse" provided no guidance on how to translate its principles into policy.[17]

Clearly, the KMT has work to do if it is to close its internal divisions over policy and positions and find a way to satisfy both Taiwan voters and Beijing policymakers simultaneously. Gunter Shubert, professor of Greater China Studies at University of Tubingen, has accurately summed up the KMT's dilemma:

> To become a ruling party under the given circumstances, it must convince the voters that it is a "Taiwan first" party that is ready to take a clear-cut stance against China's "unification speak" and, in doing so, parts company with the Beijing government. It must also step up and create innovative new policies in the domestic arena. The KMT stands at a crossroads, and whatever road it takes, it is going to be extremely bumpy.[18]

Even if the KMT were to revive itself and regain control of the presidency and the legislature, or if another party emerged to replace it as an effective rival to the DPP, that would not necessarily change the majoritarian character of the system, particularly on compelling issues such as the PRC. A continuing alternation of power between parties with mutually contradictory policy packages would quite likely reinforce current political divisions rather than reduce them. It is not inconceivable, of course, that an institutional sharing of power—wherein one party controls the presidency and another party or coalition of parties controls the legislature—might promote convergence. But the one case of divided control—the Chen Shui-bian presidency, which was marked by intense interparty rivalry—does not yield much hope in that regard.

No matter what the configuration of political power going forward, it is crucial that political leaders and politicians increase public confidence in representative government. Phenomena such as mass protest, promotion of referendums, and populism occurred because citizens lost confidence in the system of indirect democracy that was created in the 1990s. They were symptoms of the problem, not the problem itself. Whereas 59.4 percent of those surveyed in the World Values Survey in 2012 had confidence in the civil service, the percentages of those who trusted the performance of the legislature was 27.6 percent and 22.4 percent for political parties.[19] Legislators may be more effective than the public realizes, working out compromises behind the scenes on issues that never come to public attention. What citizens do see in the media is polarized conflict that sometimes leads to physical clashes on the floor of the LY. Thus the negative image of legislators and political parties is unlikely to give people confidence that they are worthy of the public's trust, particularly on those issues, like policy toward Beijing, that will define Taiwan's long-term future.

Institutional reforms that place greater emphasis on seniority and expertise and that provide legislators with more staff support are overdue. Even more important is a change in the LY culture, in the direction of greater comity and a willingness to compromise, along the lines that the late U.S. senator John McCain counseled his colleagues in his last speech on the Senate floor before his passing. (An extract of the speech appears as the epigraph of this book.) Such changes will contribute to giving the public what it expects and deserves: a political system whose leaders represent their interests and values, particularly when the stakes are high.

Expanding Common Ground

On a number of issues, there is broad consensus among Taiwan people on what they oppose. Beijing's 1C2S formula is one of those. It has been more difficult for Taiwan's leaders to make authoritative decisions that define what the society is for and how it should reconcile competing objectives. The PRC challenge is at the top of the list of these difficult choices, and the stakes are too high to delay making clear choices. That will probably require competing political camps to agree that a serious external threat exits and that the society's interest and their respective political interests require collaboration to meet that common threat. This is far from easy, but it should not be impossible. There are historical cases where such agreement has happened. The first example presented here comes from Taiwan's own history. The others are drawn from other regions and political systems.

During the first two centuries of frontier Taiwan's early existence, social conflict was the norm rather than the exception. Solidarity was strong within indigenous groups but not between them. Unity existed among Han Chinese settlers, but only on the basis of where on the mainland they had come from. Regularly, and in different combinations, aborigines, Han from the Quanzhou prefecture, Han from the Zhangzhou prefecture, and Han Hakka from eastern Guangdong fought one another over land, water, women, and so on. The imperial government was unwilling to spend the resources necessary to impose order.[20] Then the Sino-Japanese war of 1894 and 1895 occurred, and the Qing dynasty government ceded Taiwan to Japan. Intergroup solidarity to meet the new, outside foe replaced intergroup conflict, at least at the north end of the island. Historian Stevan Harrell explains that "within the short span of forty years, the local elite of north Taiwan transformed itself from a fragmented series of leaders of local, ethnically-organized communities to a highly connected network organized on the basis of social class; they went from fighting each other to fighting the Japanese."[21]

Great Britain in 1947 decided that it no longer had the resources to support the security of Greece and Turkey. At that very time, there was fear in the West that the Soviet Union was working to undermine the governments of those countries as they had in the rest of Eastern Europe. The Truman administration understood the threat that this posed to Europe, and its instinct was to provide assistance to Athens and Ankara. But it was handicapped by the isolationism of the Republican Party, and even the Democratic Party was new to the idea of an activist American role in world affairs. But the administration won the support of a faction of the Republican Party led by Senator Arthur Vandenberg, who was chairman of the Senate Foreign Relations Committee from 1947 to 1949. Truman administration officials, particularly Secretary of State Dean Acheson, fashioned a mostly bipartisan foreign policy and moved crucial pieces of legislation through Congress. Vandenberg helped Acheson by reducing politically motivated Republican attacks on the administration's security policy. It was he who coined the phrase that "politics stops at the water's edge" and who urged the Truman administration to set the problems of Greece and Turkey in the context of "the larger confrontation between the Soviet Union and ourselves."[22] That is, emphasizing the danger the USSR posed fostered a broader consensus on security policy within the American political elite.[23]

The early postwar period also posed a severe challenge to Finland, the Soviet Union's immediate Scandinavian neighbor. Finland had fought against the Red Army in World War II and had aligned with Hitler's Germany but still wished to preserve its independence and avoid having to submit to the type of arrangements that Moscow imposed on Poland, East Germany, and, ultimately, all of Eastern Europe. The Finnish elite also wanted to preserve its democratic system, one in which the communist party did not play a significant role. It therefore pledged to Moscow that it would remain neutral in the emerging Cold War rivalry between East and West. Finnish leaders recognized also that preserving national independence required them to accept some restraints on political activity at home, something that the Finnish public soon came to understand. John Lukacs explains that accommodating Moscow "necessarily involved self-imposed and sometimes government-imposed restrictions on free expression in the press, in publishing and other kinds of communications in order to avoid anything that would irritate Moscow."[24] Finnish journalist Max Jacobson wrote in 1980 that "the Finns deny themselves the luxury of making emotionally satisfying gestures. They are careful to avoid arousing suspicions in Moscow or engaging the prestige of the Soviet superpower."[25]

To be clear, by offering the example of Finland, I am not indirectly proposing that Taiwan adopt a neutral position in the competition between the PRC and the United States. The circumstances are very different. At the same time, some variant of an accommodationist approach should not be dismissed at the outset of any discussion. At least one American scholar saw a Finnish echo in the policies of Ma Ying-jeou, and one Taiwan scholar and politician, Chang Ya-chung, has publicly supported the Finland example.[26] But my sole focus here—an important one—is on how an external threat can induce the target country's political leaders and people to mitigate their past conflicts in order to better meet that threat.

Recent developments in Afghanistan provide a rather extreme and negative example here on the importance of common ground within the elite. The Taliban is a serious threat to the country's peace and stability and to the survival of the established government. The Trump administration negotiated an agreement with the Taliban under which the United States will withdraw most of its military personnel from the country, which would strengthen the Taliban's internal position. Washington, however, did not use the agreement to impose a binding requirement that the Taliban negotiate seriously with the Afghan government. But that same government is deeply divided, to the point that after presidential elections in 2019, each candidate held a separate inauguration ceremony. Their respective political camps continue to regard each other as the enemy, despite the growing danger that the Taliban poses. Taiwan is in much better shape, but Afghanistan is still a cautionary lesson.[27]

Rhetorically at least, some Taiwan leaders in rival political camps understand the importance of unity. Ma Ying-jeou said the following in his second inaugural address in May 2012:

> We are a family and Taiwan is home to us all. We strongly believe that no matter what political differences there may be between the ruling and opposition parties, we are still one family. Despite the many difficulties over the past several years between the ruling and opposition parties, I believe we share a common commitment to democracy. On this foundation, we can surely seek consensus and work together to solve problems. Over the past four years, I have continually invited civic groups to engage in dialogue. I sincerely hope to open up dialogue with the opposition leaders as soon as possible. We will show the people that the ruling and opposition parties can not only compete but also cooperate. For the welfare of all our people, let us jointly set a good example for Taiwan's democracy.[28]

Tsai Ing-wen has repeatedly made similar appeals. For example, on the evening of her reelection victory in January 2020, she concluded her acceptance speech by saying, "I want to remind everyone that now that the elections are over, any conflicts that arose during the campaign process should end as well. I ask that none of my supporters attempt to provoke our opponents. We need to embrace each other and unite under the banner of democracy if we want to overcome the challenges facing our country."[29] Unity was a theme that she had been pressing for some time. She had her own interest in doing so, of course, as did Ma in 2012. Both had discovered after one term in office that governing would be easier if the opposition chose to cooperate with their administrations. But there is a fundamental truth in what they said, in that a divided society will be less able to solve the problems facing it than one in which political forces cooperate. This is true of any political system, but it is particularly true if a large, predatory neighbor is just over the horizon.

Rhetoric is one thing. Turning rhetoric into political arrangements that are both effective and enduring in addressing critical policy challenges is another. Almost by definition, democracy is a system that encourages division that reflects the differences in interests and values that exist in any society. Democracy may institutionalize the resulting competition and so mitigate its divisive consequences, but not always. For sure, greater unity in Taiwan will not occur if one camp insists that the other accept its point of view as a point of departure. Nor will it happen if one side or the other rejects the norms governing the political system's institutions, as when the DPP or KMT party caucus violates the rules governing the operation of the LY or when the minority party takes over the chamber to block action by the majority.[30]

There is one precedent for major interparty cooperation in Taiwan. This was in the 1990s when constitutional amendments were required to complete Taiwan's democratic transition. Passage of constitutional amendments almost requires the KMT and the DPP, or at least parts of each, to work together. In the 1990s case, Lee Teng-hui exploited the divisions within the KMT and DPP to put together a working coalition that combined the Light Blue faction of the KMT and Light Green faction of the DPP to pass the necessary amendments. Yet this cooperation was most likely a function of Lee's charisma and the stakes that each faction had in its success. Moreover, party discipline has been higher since Lee left office, and it is not in the interest of the leaders of the KMT and DPP party caucuses to have the president split their ranks.

Yet the ad hoc interparty cooperation that Lee Teng-hui engineered does not speak to Taiwan's current situation. What is needed, it seems, is cooperation that is based on a clear consensus among leaders of various parties on objectives and how to achieve them, mutual agreement that each party has more to gain by working together than working separately, and implementation that is sustained as long as necessary to address the problem. Such an arrangement cannot work if the Deep-Light divisions continue within the two major parties; it probably requires "Light dominance" within each. Also necessary is a way of incorporating the views of various social sectors (the business community, civil society, young people, and so on) and the U.S. government. But the goal is clear: to socialize all actors to agreement on two norms. The first, to paraphrase Senator Vandenberg, is that politics stops at the shores of the Taiwan Strait. The second is the warning attributed to Benjamin Franklin at the time he signed the Declaration of Independence: "We must, indeed, all hang together, or most assuredly we shall all hang separately."[31]

Such an arrangement will be more successful if it is based on the following: a Taiwanese-Chinese dual identity that has more definition than the ambiguity that exists today; a commitment to solving policy problems rather than contending at the level of political symbols;[32] a clear-eyed sense of the character of Beijing's objectives concerning Taiwan; an agreement on elements of the current status quo that are worth preserving at all costs and those that might be negotiable; a defense posture that genuinely enhances deterrence against People's Liberation Army attack; a shared understanding of the ways in which the PRC is interfering in Taiwan's democracy by distorting the will of the people; a consensus on the opportunities and risks of locating business operations domestically, on the mainland, and elsewhere; a recognition of the imperative of maintaining a close and strong relationship with the United States; and a clear sense of the stakes involved in successfully addressing the challenge that Beijing poses and the serious costs of failure.

To make this idea even more concrete, is it conceivable that the leaders of the KMT and the DPP could summon the will and creativity to do the following on a joint basis?

- Develop a bipartisan reform of government finance that increases revenues in a progressive way (taxing capital more than is currently the case) and put pension and healthcare programs on a sustainable basis.

- Improve governance by instituting tough restrictions against corruption by officials in all branches of government.

- Continue to expand economic relations with trading partners besides the PRC, especially Japan and the United States; regarding the United States, agree that Tsai Ing-wen's August 2020 action on beef and pork was a necessary first step toward a free trade agreement that would benefit the entire Taiwan economy.

- Agree on the acceptable degree of Taiwan's dependence on the mainland economy; depending on that assessment, consider whether to revive the cross-Strait agreement on trade in services (as well as developing revisions to deal with specific defects in the original agreement), and move to resume negotiations with Beijing on the agreement on trade in commodities.

- Agree on a defense strategy that is responsive to the current threat environment and work together to ensure that the policies of the armed forces concerning force structure, personnel, and procurement are consistent with that policy.

- Develop a "whole of government" approach to meeting the challenge of the PRC's campaign of coercion without violence.

- Develop a cross-party approach to cross-Strait relations that conveys objectively credible reassurances about Taiwan's future course (instead of letting the PRC impose the 1992 Consensus as the terms of engagement). Amend or repeal the May 2019 legislation on political agreements with the PRC to increase the possibility that such agreements might be approved if they gain reasonable public support.

- State as a matter of basic principle that any approach to resolving the fundamental cross-Strait dispute must be approved by passing a constitutional amendment.

- State their joint expectation that Beijing will remain neutral—in word and deed—in Taiwan's elections and respect the outcome thereof.

- Reject proactively any effort by pro-unification forces to instigate, along the lines of Xi Jinping's January 2019 speech, formation of a body composed of "representative individuals" that are "recommended by various political parties and various circles" on both sides, but only on "the common political basis of adhering to the '1992 Consensus' and opposing 'Taiwan independence'" (since Beijing would use that precondition to exclude the DPP).[33]

- Develop new rules of procedure for the LY that, among other things, foster a greater sense of decorum and bar takeovers of the LY chamber by a party caucus or outside group.

None of these initiatives will be easy, but undertaking them on a joint basis would put Taipei in a stronger negotiating position with Beijing and strengthen political support domestically.

How to undertake this kind of substantive cooperation in terms of process is not easy, either. Hypothetically, it could have a rather ad hoc character and might be sustainable if agreements on fundamentals hold. Probably more enduring, and appropriate for the challenge Taiwan faces, would be the creation of a formal government of national unity. Whatever the form, a convergence between the two parties will probably only occur if their top leaders take the initiative to make it happen. After all, leading is their job. To expect it to occur from the bottom up is unrealistic, even though the rank and file of various parties and people from other sectors will have to go along.

Clearly, it is easy for me to suggest these ideas from halfway around the world from Taiwan. It will be very difficult for Taiwan leaders and followers to construct and sustain the sort of structure I have in mind. I expect that it will be very difficult if the KMT is not able to reinvigorate itself to the point that the DPP takes it seriously, or if the trend within the DPP is toward a Deep Green leadership. But Taiwan's political leaders cannot afford to take Beijing's ambition lightly. They cannot expect to simply cope, hoping for the best. For the foreseeable future, navigating the proper way to counter the PRC's ambition is the most serious challenge that Taiwan's democratic system must address. To fail to do so is to break faith with voters—both Green and Blue—who have entrusted leaders with the task of preserving Taiwan's good life, its security, and its very political existence. After all, democracy is not just a system for selecting leaders through free and fair elections and for debating the issues of the day without fear. It is also a system that vests in those elected leaders the obligation of good performance for the benefit of society as a whole.

To simply try to muddle through, or to ignore the forces that can deepen national despair, is to renege on the obligation to promote the public good and meet the needs of the voters who selected them to govern in the first place. The situation is not hopeless. Taiwan's elected officials do have the ability to meet the public's expectation that they perform well. The question is whether they have the will. Formulating good policy to ensure security and the good life will certainly require choices among competing priorities and then explaining to the public why the options chosen are the best available. Therefore, because the stakes are high and the costs of failure can be profound, political leaders must meet a new standard of responsibility. The people of Taiwan deserve no less.

Notes

Chapter 1

1. For convenience, I use "the island" as a synonym for Taiwan, but that usage is not precise. Taiwan's government has jurisdiction over a number of other islands, though most of the population lives on what people usually think of when they think of Taiwan. These include the Penghu/Pescadores Archipelago to the west of the Taiwan proper and several small islands close to the southeast coast of mainland China, the most prominent of which are Jinmen/Quemoy and Mazu/Matsu.

2. See, for example, Thomas G. Mahnken and others, "Tightening the Chain: Implementing a Strategy of Maritime Pressure in the Western Pacific," Center for Strategic and Budgetary Assessments, May 23, 2019.

3. International Monetary Fund, "World Economic Outlook Database," October 2017.

4. "Taiwan Population (Live)," Worldometers; "Urban Population (% of total population)," World Bank, based on United Nations Population Division, World Urbanization Prospects: 2018 revision.

5. *Statistical Yearbook of the Republic of China* (Directorate-General Budget, Accounting and Statistics, ROC, September 2019), table 15, "Higher Education," and table 39, "General Situation of National Income" (https://eng.stat.gov.tw/public /data/dgbas03/bs2/yearbook_eng/Yearbook2018.pdf); *Taiwan Statistical Data Book, 2019* (Taipei: National Development Council, ROC [Taiwan], 2019), table 3-1, "Gross Domestic Product and Gross National Income."

6. *Statistical Yearbook of the Republic of China,* tables 7, 15 and 39.

7. *Taiwan Statistical Data Book,* table 13-6a, "Number of Students Receiving Higher Education by Discipline"; table 13-9, "Availability of Schools and Teachers"; and table 13-10, "Educational Expenditure per Student at All Levels." *The CIA World*

Factbook, 2020-2021 (New York: Skyhorse Publishing, 2020), "Taiwan," section on "People and Society," p. 917.

8. *Taiwan Statistical Data Book,* table 2-4, "Population Aged 15 and Over by Level of Education."

9. "Taiwan Likes Facebook, Has Highest Penetration," *Taipei Times,* February 28, 2014.

10. *Taiwan Statistical Data Book,* table 3-2a, "Average Annual Growth Rate of Real GDP."

11. *Statistical Yearbook of the Republic of China,* table 46, "Average Disposable Income per Household by Disposable Income Quintile."

12. *Statistical Yearbook of the Republic of China,* table 9, "Unemployment Rates by Educational Attainment and Age."

13. Lalaine C. Delmendo, "Taiwanese House Prices Continue to Fall Due to Harsh Taxes," *Global Property Guide,* August 8, 2019.

14. Syaru Shirley Lin, "Taiwan in the High Income Trap and Its Implications for Cross-Strait Relations," in *Taiwan's Economic and Diplomatic Challenges and Opportunities,* ed. Dafydd Fell (London: Routledge, forthcoming).

15. National Development Council. "Population Projections for the R.O.C. (Taiwan): 2018–2065," in Population Projections for the R.O.C. (Taiwan): 2020–2070, pt. A.

16. Central Intelligence Agency, "Taiwan"; National Development Council, "Population Projections for the R.O.C. (Taiwan): 2018–2065."

17. National Development Council. "Population Projections for the R.O.C. (Taiwan): 2018–2065."

18. *World Factbook*; Yale University, Environmental Performance Index, 2014 (http://archive.epi.yale.edu/epi/country-profile/taiwan).

19. On the definitions of hard and soft authoritarianism, see Edwin A. Winckler, "Institutionalization and Participation on Taiwan: From Hard to Soft Authoritarianism?" *China Quarterly,* no. 99 (September 1984), pp. 481–99.

20. "Remarks by AIT Chairman James Moriarty at Brookings Institution," October 12, 2017, American Institute in Taiwan (www.ait.org.tw/remarks-ait-chairman-james-moriarty-brookings-institution/).

21. Richard C. Bush, *At Cross Purposes: U.S.-Taiwan Relations Since 1942* (Armonk, N.Y.: M. E. Sharpe, 2004), pp. 179–219.

22. The Clinton administration sent me, in my capacity as chairman of the American Institute in Taiwan, to state its unhappiness with Lee's statement.

Chapter 2

1. Unless otherwise indicated, when I use "China," I am referring to the PRC government or the area of mainland China, not to China as a member of the international system.

2. The report seeks to measure the level of happiness ("subjective well-being") among people in countries around the world, drawing on variables such as GDP per capita, social support, healthy life expectancy, freedom to make life choices, gener-

osity, and perceptions of corruption. John F. Helliwell, Richard Layard, and Jeffrey D. Sachs, eds., *World Happiness Report 2018*, New York: Sustainable Development Solutions Network, figures 2.2 and 2.3. In 2020, Taiwan had risen to twenty-fifth worldwide and was still number one in East Asia. William Yen, "Taiwan Ranked Happiest Country in East, Southeast Asia: Survey," *Focus Taiwan*, March 21, 2020.

3. To complicate matters even further, what constitutes happiness in one culture may differ from how people define it in another culture. Moreover, what makes people happy at one stage of the life cycle may differ from what does at another.

4. "Taiwan Telephone and Mobile Phone Interview Survey of the Presidential Satisfaction: The Twenty-Second Wave," Taiwan's Election and Democratization Study, National Chengchi University, survey conducted December 2017 (http://teds .nccu.edu.tw/main.php).

5. André Laliberté, "Religion and Politics," in *Routledge Handbook of Contemporary Taiwan*, edited by Gunter Schubert (Abingdon, U.K.: Routledge, 2016), p. 338.

6. Central Intelligence Agency, "Taiwan," *The CIA World Factbook*, 2020–2021 (New York: Skyhorse Publishing, 2020), pp. 914–15. The native Taiwanese majority was divided into three subgroups: people from Zhangzhou and Quanzhou prefectures in southern Fujian province and those from Hakka from eastern Guangdong province.

7. Ralph N. Clough, *Island China* (Harvard University Press, 1978), p. 37.

8. T. Y. Wang, "Changing Boundaries: The Development of the Taiwan Voters' Identity," in *The Taiwan Voter*, edited by Christopher H. Achen and T. Y. Wang (University of Michigan Press, 2017).

9. "World Values Survey: Taiwan, 2012," study# 552, vol. 20180912 (www. worldvaluessurvey.org/WVSDocumentationWV6.jsp; click on "WV6_Results_ Taiwan 2012_v20180912.")

10. Stephan Haggard and Robert R. Kaufman, *Development, Democracy, and Welfare States: Latin America, East Asia, and Eastern Europe* (Princeton University Press, 2008).

11. On social movements, see Dafydd Fell, ed., *Taiwan's Social Movements under Ma Ying-jeou: From the Wild Strawberries to the Sunflowers* (New York: Routledge, 2017).

12. For a detailing of this shift of young people away from voting and toward online participation, see Min-hua Huang and Mark Weatherall, "Online Political Participation in East Asia: Replacement or a Substitute for Electoral Participation," Asian Barometer, Working Paper 112, 2016 (/www.asianbarometer.org/publications //1de82720b3151fd962872eee584d7f71.pdf).

13. Ming-sho Ho, "The Activist Legacy of Taiwan's Sunflower Movement," Carnegie Endowment for International Peace, August 2, 2018.

14. Lin Xingfei, "2017 'Tianxia' Guoqing Diaocha: 39 sui, Minyi di Duanliedian" [The 2017 Tianxia state-of-the-nation survey: 39 years old is the point of cleavage], *Tianxia*, no. 614 (January 3, 2017) (www.cw.com.tw/article/articleLogin. action?id=5080204).

15. *Statistical Yearbook of the Republic of China, 2019* (Directorate-General

Budget, Accounting and Statistics, ROC, September 2019), table 9, "Unemployment Rates by Educational Attainment and Age."

16. Ming-sho Ho, "The Activist Legacy of Taiwan's Sunflower Movement."

17. Shelley Rigger, *Taiwan's Rising Rationalism: Generations, Politics, and "Taiwanese Nationalism,"* Policy Studies 26 (Washington, D.C.: East-West Center Washington, 2006).

18. Shelley Rigger, "The China Impact on Taiwan's Generational Politics," in *Taiwan and the "China Impact": Challenges and Opportunities*, edited by Gunter Schubert (New York: Routledge, 2015), pp. 70–90.

19. Regarding generation, the WVS only differentiated among the twenty-five years and below, thirty to thirty-nine, and fifty and above age groups.

Chapter 3

1. Jessica T. Mathews, "America's Indefensible Defense Budget," *New York Review of Books*, July 18, 2019, p. 23.

2. Yeun-Wen Ku and James Cherng-Tay Hsueh, "Social Welfare," in *Routledge Handbook of Contemporary Taiwan*, edited by Gunter Schubert (New York: Routledge, 2016), pp. 342–58.

3. This discussion is based on Tsai-tsu Su, "Public Budgeting System in Taiwan: Does It Lead to Better Value for Money?," in *Value for Money: Budget and Financial Management Reform in the People's Republic of China, Taiwan, and Australia*, edited by Andrew Podger and others (Canberra: Australia National University Press, 2018), pp. 79–93.

4. The government also has connections with a number of state enterprises and nonprofit revolving funds, which are self-financing and not subject to annual action by the executive and legislative branches of the government.

5. Rebecca Lin and Pei-hua Yu, "Taiwan on the Edge of a Precipice?," *CommonWealth Magazine* 607 (October 11, 2016).

6. *Taiwan Statistical Data Book, 2018* (Taipei: National Development Council, ROC [Taiwan], 2018), table 2-5, "Population by Dependent and Working Age Groups (1)."

7. "2017 Central Government Budget Overview," Central Government General Budget Proposal, Fiscal Year 2017, updated February 17, 2017, Directorate-General for Budget, Accounting and Statistics, ROC (https://eng.dgbas.gov.tw/public/Attachment/7217104714ZX60WRZE.pdf). It is estimated that pension funds are future-facing contingent obligations that, as of June 2016, totaled over NT$17,592 billion (US$582 million at December 2019 exchange rates). The Directorate-General's report on the 2017 budget warned of the burden that this would pose: "These future contingent obligations are either statutory spendings in the future, which should be provided for by [the] annual budget for each corresponding year, or possible payments for underfunded social insurances, which could otherwise be compensated by premium adjustments or other pension reforms."

8. "It's Time to Raise NHI Premiums," editorial, *Taipei Times*, May 29, 2020.

9. "Taiwan (Republic of China)'s Constitution of 1947 with Amendments

through 2005," *Constitute* (www.constituteproject.org/constitution/Taiwan_2005 .pdf?lang=en).

10. For background on this, see Eva E. Chen and Hui Li, "Early Childhood Education in Taiwan," in *Early Childhood Education in Chinese Societies*, edited by Nirmala Rao, Jing Zhou, and Jin Sun (Dordrecht, Neth.: Springer, 2017), pp. 217–24.

11. *Taiwan Statistical Data Book, 2018,* pp. 267–68.

12. "Taiwan Telephone and Mobile Phone Survey of the Presidential Satisfaction: The Sixth Wave," Taiwan's Election and Democratization Study, National Chengchi University, survey conducted September 2019 (http://teds.nccu.edu.tw/main.php).

13. Su, "Public Budgeting System in Taiwan."

14. Ibid.

15. Central Intelligence Agency, "Taiwan," *The World Factbook*, last updated December 6, 2019 (www.cia.gov/library/publications/the-world-factbook/geos/tw. html).

16. Su, "Public Budgeting System in Taiwan," p. 82.

17. "Taiwan (Republic of China)'s Constitution of 1947 with Amendments through 2005," *Constitute.*

18. The amounts can be found at the section of the website of the Directorate-General for Budget, Accounting and Statistics that presents figures for the "Budget Proposal" and the "Legal Budget." See "Fiscal Year 2007–Fiscal Year 2017," Central Budget Information, Directorate-General for Budget, Accounting and Statistics, ROC (http://eng.dgbas.gov.tw/np.asp?ctNode=1911&mp=2).

19. The budget-making process at the local level is subject to a different set of dynamics. On one hand, local jurisdictions are subject to guidance imposed by the Directorate-General for Budget, Accounting and Statistics, which constrain their choices. On the other hand, they are not subject to tight fiscal constraints and often seek grants from the central government when spending exceeds revenue. Su, "Public Budgeting System in Taiwan," pp. 85–86.

20. "Introduction to the Special Budget," Directorate-General for Budget, Accounting and Statistics, ROC, last updated October 29, 2009 (https://eng.dgbas .gov.tw/ct.asp?xItem=25529&CtNode=5304&mp=2); Wang Yung-yu, Justin Su, and Elizabeth Hsu, "Legislature Passes Special Budget for F-16 Purchase," *Focus Taiwan*, November 22, 2019.

21. "New NT$210bn Virus Budget to be Introduced," *Taipei Times,* July 10, 2020.

22. *Taiwan Statistical Data Book, 2019* (Taipei: National Development Council, ROC [Taiwan], 2018), p. 181.

23. Central Intelligence Agency, "Taiwan."

24. Anthony Shorrocks, Jim Davies, and Rodrigo Lluberas, *Global Wealth Databook 2018* (Zurich: Credit Suisse Research Institute, October 2018), p. 156.

25. Central Intelligence Agency, "Taiwan."

26. Ministry of Finance, *Guide to ROC Taxes, 2018* (www.mof.gov.tw/file/ Attach/80779/File_106065.pdf), pp. 5-6.

27. *Taiwan Statistical Data Book,* 2019, table 9(2b), "Net Government Revenues of All Levels by Source," p. 178.

28. Chenwei Lin, "Weak Taxation and Constraints of the Welfare State in Democratized Taiwan," *Japanese Journal of Political Science* 19 (September 2018), pp. 397-416.

29. On the low amount of revenue from stock market capital gains and the property tax, see "Taiwan: 'Island of Inequity'?," *CommonWealth Magazine*, vol. 445, April 22, 2010 (https://english.cw.com.tw/magazine/magazine.action?id=175).

30. Ministry of Finance, *Guide to ROC Taxes, 2018,* p. 20.

31. Ibid., p. 9.

32. Jane Rickards, "A Taxing Problem: Taiwan's Comparatively High Personal Income Tax-Rates," *Taiwan Business Topics*, August 2018 (https://topics.amcham.com.tw/2018/08/a-taxing-problem-taiwans-comparatively-high-personal-income-tax-rates/).

33. "Central Government General Budget, Fiscal Year 2013," Directorate-General for Budget, Accounting, and Statistics, ROC (https://eng.dgbas.gov.tw/ct.asp?xItem=33683&CtNode=6002&mp=2); "The General Budget Proposal of Central Government: Summary Table for Annual Expenditures by Functions, FY 2019," Directorate-General of Budget, Accounting, and Statistics, ROC (https://eng.dgbas.gov.tw/public/Attachment/89271149T64V6LTY.pdf).

34. Thomas Piketty, *Capital in the Twenty-First Century* (Cambridge, Mass: Belknap Press, 2014).

35. On those programs, see "Taiwan (China)," Social Security Programs Throughout the World: Asia and the Pacific, 2018, U.S. Social Security Administration (https://www.ssa.gov/policy/docs/progdesc/ssptw/2018-2019/asia/taiwan.html).

36. Shih Jiunn Shi, "The Fragmentation of the Old-Age Security System: The Politics of Pension Reform in Taiwan," in *Social Cohesion in Greater China: Challenges for Social Policy and Governance*, Ka Ho Mok and Yeun-Wen Ku, eds. (Hackensack, N.J.: World Scientific, 2010), p. 365.

37. Ibid., p. 365.

38. Stephan Haggard and Robert R. Kaufman, *Development, Democracy, and Welfare States: Latin America, East Asia, and Eastern Europe* (Princeton University Press, 2008), p. 256.

39. Lin and Yu, "Taiwan on the Edge of a Precipice?," *CommonWealth Magazine.*

40. James Lin, "Pension Promises Disguise Reality," *Taipei Times,* July 1, 2019.

41. Jens Kastner, "Projected Pension Cuts Outrage Taiwan's Military," *Asia Sentinel,* July 4, 2018; J. Michael Cole, "Unprecedented Violence, Possible China Link as Anti-Pension Reform Protesters Storm Taiwan's Legislature," *Taiwan Sentinel,* April 27, 2018.

42. Lin Chang-chun, Elizabeth Hsu, and Christie Chen, "Parts of Pension Reform Laws Violate Constitution: Court," *Focus Taiwan*, August 23, 2019.

43. Feng Chien-san, "Combating Injustice with Fair Taxes," *Taipei Times*, February 18, 2019.

Chapter 4

1. Robert Wade, *Governing the Market: Economic Theory and the Role of Government in East Asian Industrialization* (Princeton University Press, 1990).

2. Gary G. Hamilton and Cheng-shu Kao, *Making Money: How Taiwanese Industrialists Embraced the Global Economy* (Stanford University Press, 2018).

3. *Taiwan Statistical Data Book, 2019* (Taipei: National Development Council, ROC [Taiwan], 2019), tables 11-9a and 11-9e, "Commodity Trade with Major Trading Partners." This figure includes two-thirds of Taiwan's exports to Hong Kong, which are high-tech items that are likely trans-shipped through Hong Kong to the mainland.

4. Ali Wyne, "Potential Downsides to U.S.-China Trade Tensions on Taiwan's Economy," *Global Taiwan Brief* 5, no. 5 (2020).

5. On developments in Ma's first term, see Richard C. Bush, *Uncharted Strait: The Future of China-Taiwan Relations* (Brookings Institution Press, 2013).

6. *Taiwan Statistical Data Book, 2019*, table 3-6, "Per Capita National Income," p. 58.

7. Central Intelligence Agency, "Taiwan," *The CIA World Factbook*, 2020–2021 (New York: Skyhorse Publishing, 2020), p. 917.

8. Directorate-General for Budget, Accounting, and Statistics, Republic of China, "2017 Nian Woguo HDI, GII Fenbie Weiju Quanqiu di 21 ming ji di 8 ming" [In 2017, Taiwan's HDI and GII ranked 21st and 8th in the world, respectively], *Guoqing Tongji Tongbao* [National statistics bulletin], October 2018, (www.dgbas. gov.tw/public/Data/81030161446GEYJEAG4.pdf). Although Taiwan is not included in the United Nations Development Program's Human Development Index (because it is not a UN member), its Directorate-General for Budget, Analysis, and Statistics used UNDP's most recent methodology to calculate the figure.

9. Klaus Schwab, ed., *The Global Competitiveness Report 2019* (Geneva: World Economic Forum, 2019). The quoted passage is at p. 2. The overall global rankings are at p. xiii. The information concerning Taiwan is at pp. 538–41 and for China at pp. 154–57.

10. Schwab, *Global Competitiveness Report 2019*, p. 7. Taiwan scores well on similar studies. In the World Bank's Doing Business survey, which focuses on the ease or difficulty of setting up and operating a business in the context of government regulatory regimes, Taiwan ranked thirteenth in 2019. See World Bank Group, *Doing Business 2019: Training for Reform* (Washington, D.C.: World Bank, 2019). The International Institute for Management Development, which uses a methodology similar to the WEF's, ranked Taiwan eleventh in 2020. See "Taiwan Up to 11th in IMD Competitiveness Rankings," *Taipei Times*, June 17, 2020. Ratings exercises such as those of the WEF are not perfect, however. The factors used to assess both rich and poor economies may not be sufficiently discriminating in evaluating only advanced ones, which compete with one another. Moreover, while some of the indicators in the WEF survey can be objectively measured, such as the number of internet users as a percentage of the population, others rely on the judgment of business executives in the country concerned, as determined in a two-stage survey. In the case of Taiwan, the

WEF's partner institution was the National Development Council, a government organization that would have an understandable interest in Taiwan having a high rating. Before 2019, the WEF gave the number of survey respondents from each economy; from Taiwan there were only 112 in 2018, which seems rather low considering the Taiwan economy's vibrant business community. After 2018, the number of respondents was not provided. See Schwab, *Global Competitiveness Report 2018*, p. 627.

11. *Taiwan Statistical Data Book, 2019,* table 3-1, "Gross Domestic Product and Gross National Income."

12. Robyn Mak, "Taiwan, Not China, Is Its Own Worst Enemy," Reuters Breakingviews, April 24, 2017.

13. George Liao, "MOI: Taiwan Officially Becomes an Aged Society with People over 65 Years Old Breaking the 14% Mark," *Taiwan News*, April 10, 2018.

14. "Taiwan," *The CIA World Factbook*, 2020–2021, p. 914.

15. "Taiwan Population 2020 (Live)," *World Population Review.*

16. Central Intelligence Agency, "Taiwan"; National Development Council, "Population Projections for the R.O.C. (Taiwan): 2018–2065," in Population Projections for the R.O.C. (Taiwan): 2020–2070, part A.

17. National Statistics, Republic of China (Taiwan), "Population."

18. "Number of Married Couples in Decline; Singles Hit 4.4m," *Taipei Times*, October 25, 2017; *Taiwan Statistical Data Book, 2019* (Taipei: National Development Council, ROC [Taiwan], 2019), tables 2-7a and 2-7b, pp. 33–34, "Percentages of Population by Age Group."

19. *Taiwan Statistical Data Book, 2019*, table 1-1e, "Indicators of the Taiwan Economy," p. 23.

20. *Statistical Yearbook of the Republic of China, 2018* (Directorate-General Budget, Accounting and Statistics, ROC, September 2018).

21. Observation from an anonymous reviewer.

22. Elizabeth Hsu, "Taiwan Has 13th Most Millionaires of Any Country," *Focus Taiwan*, November 15, 2017.

23. Bloomberg, *Bloomberg Billionaires Index*, as of October 20, 2020 (www.bloomberg.com/billionaires/?sref=ctSjKj2N).

24. Chen Cheng-wei and Evelyn Kao, "Taiwan's Average Household Net Worth Hit NT$11.23 Million in 2015," *Focus Taiwan*, April 27, 2016.

25. Tsai Yi-chu and Chang Yu-hsi, "Taiwanese Parents Save 17% of Monthly Income in Education Funds," *Focus Taiwan*, September 11, 2017.

26. Chiu Po-shen, Ko Lin, and Wang Szu-chi, "Majority of Taiwanese in Their Thirties Owe Big Debts: Survey," *Focus Taiwan*, July 12, 2018 (http://focustaiwan.tw/news/asoc/201807120024.aspx).

27. Syaru Shirley Lin, "Taiwan in the High Income Trap and Its Implications for Cross-Strait Relations," in *Taiwan's Economic and Diplomatic Challenges and Opportunities,* edited by Dafydd Fell (London: Routledge, forthcoming); citation to Ministry of Interior.

28. Jane Rickards, "What's Holding Down Salaries in Taiwan?" *Taiwan Business Topics*, March 15, 2018.

29. Category 1 includes manufacturing, construction, mining, and quarrying, with investment capital from shareholders of NT$80 million (US$2.42 million) or less and with fewer than 200 regular employees. Category 2 includes agriculture, forestry and fisheries, water, electricity and gas, commercial, transportation, warehousing and communications, finance, insurance and real estate, industrial and commercial services, and social and personal services industries with sales revenues of NT$100 million (US$3.03 million) in the last year and with fewer than 100 regular employees. See Tzong-Ru Lee and Irsan Prawira Julius Jioe, "Taiwan's Small and Medium Enterprises (SMEs)," *Education about Asia* 22, no. 1 (2017), pp. 32–34.

30. Timothy Ferry, "Taiwan Tech in Education," *Taiwan Business Topics*, August 15, 2016.

31. Timothy Ferry "Taiwan Needs Talent," *Taiwan Business Topics*, April 25, 2018; Rickards, "What's Holding Down Salaries in Taiwan?"

32. Molly Reiner, "The Search for Balance in the Taiwan IT Industry," *Taiwan Business Topics*, September 13, 2015. The following four quotations are also from this source.

33. American Chamber of Commerce in Taipei, "AmCham Taipei White Paper, 2020 edition," *Taiwan Business Topics* 50, no. 6 (June 2020), p. WP 7.

34. Timothy Ferry, "Asia·Silicon Valley—Don't Forget the Dot!" *Taiwan Business Topics*, May 8, 2017.

35. Matthew Fulco, "Taiwanese Startups: Making up for Lost Time," *Taiwan Business Topics*, March 8, 2015. See also Matthew Fulco, "Five Taiwanese Startups to Watch," *Taiwan Business Topics*, March 6, 2015, and Matthew Fulco, "Taiwan's Rising Startups," *Taiwan Business Topics*, May 23, 2018. On risk-averse investors, see Linda Lew, "Taiwan Turnaround: An Asian Tiger Catching Up in the Internet Sector," *Technode*, August 30, 2017.

36. Jason Lanier and E. Glen Wey, "How Civic Technology Can Help Stop a Pandemic," *Foreign Affairs*, March 20, 2020.

37. Linda Lew, "Taiwan Turnaround: Going Global," *Technode*, September 6, 2017.

38. Linda Lew, "Taiwan Turnaround: Are Regulators Killing Innovation?," *Technode*, October 25, 2017.

39. U.S. Taiwan Business Council, *An Assessment and Analysis of Taiwan's Private Equity Environment,* report (Arlington, Va., May 28, 2020).

40. Angelica Oung, "Tsai Vows to Liberalize Finance Rules," *Taipei Times*, August 1, 2020.

41. Matthew Fulco, "Is Taiwan Winning the U.S.-China Trade War," *Taiwan Business Topics*, August 2019, pp. 16–20.

42. Liu Shih-chung, "Taiwan Faces a Changed Economic Outlook in Asia Following COVID-19," Taiwan-U.S. Quarterly Analysis, Brookings Institution, June 29, 2020.

43. Michael Reilly, "Can Taiwan Decouple from the Chinese Economy?" *Taiwan Insight*, February 17, 2020.

44. Central Intelligence Agency, "Taiwan."

45. Naoko Munakata, *Transforming East Asia: The Evolution of Regional Economic Integration* (Brookings Institution Press, 2006).

46. World Trade Organization, "Information Technology Agreement," 2020.

47. World Trade Organization, *Report of the Working Party on the Accession of China* and *Working Party on the Accession of the Separate Customs Territory of Taiwan, Penghu, Kinmen and Matsu* (https://docs.wto.org/dol2fe/Pages/FE_Search /FE_S_S006.aspx?Query=@Symbol=%20(wt/acc/chn/49/add.1)&Language=EN GLISH&Context=FomerScriptedSearch&languageUIChanged=true#).

48. Kevin G. Cai, "The China-ASEAN Free Trade Agreement and Taiwan," *Journal of Contemporary China* 14, no. 45 (2005), pp. 585–97; William A. Reinsch, Jack Caporal, and Lydia Murray, "At Last, an RCEP Deal," Center for Strategic and International Studies, December 4, 2019.

49. "FTAs Signed with Trading Partners," Bureau of Foreign Trade, Ministry of Economic Affairs.

50. "Full Text of Ma Ying-jeou's Inaugural Address," *Focus Taiwan*, May 20, 2012.

51. Bush, *Uncharted Strait*.

52. Meeting with a senior PRC official in Washington, DC, April 12, 2012, under Chatham House rules.

53. Richard C. Bush, "Taiwan and the Trans-Pacific Partnership: the Political Dimension," Brookings Institution, February 11, 2014.

54. Presidential candidate Hillary Clinton opposed the TPP during her campaign, but it was understood that if elected she might have found a way to facilitate entry after she took office.

55. Prashanth Parameswara, "Assessing Taiwan's New Southbound Policy," *The Diplomat*, April 23, 2019.

56. David Madland, "Growth and the Middle Class," *Democracy: A Journal of Ideas*, no. 20 (Spring 2011); Jonathan D. Ostrey, Andrew Berg, and Charalambos G. Tsangarides, "Redistribution, Inequality, and Growth," International Monetary Fund Discussion Note 14/2, April 2014.

57. Rickards, "What's Holding Down Salaries in Taiwan?"

58. Matthew Fulco, "Resolving Taiwan's Talent Exodus," *Taiwan Business Topics*, August 22, 2017; Central Intelligence Agency, "Taiwan."

59. *Taiwan Statistical Data Book 2019*, tables 3-2a and 3-2b, "Average Annual Growth Rate of Real GDP," pp. 52–53.

60. Phillip Liu, "Bill to Ease Way for Foreign Professionals," *Taiwan Business Topics*, August 22, 2017.

61. Rickards, "What's Holding Down Salaries in Taiwan?"

62. Ibid.

63. Ibid.

64. Ibid.

65. Fulco, "Resolving Taiwan's Talent Exodus."

66. Ibid.

67. Ibid.

68. Ibid.

69. Rickards, "What's Holding Down Salaries in Taiwan?"

70. Ibid.

71. Oxford Economics, *Global Talent 2021: How the New Geography of Talent Will Transform Human Resource Strategies*, n.d.

72. Rickards, "What's Holding Down Salaries in Taiwan?"

73. Timothy Ferry, "Taiwan Tech in Education," *Taiwan Business Topics*, August 15, 2016.

74. Rickards, "What's Holding Down Salaries in Taiwan?"

75. William Zyzo, "What Competence Do Taiwan Talents Need for Good Jobs?" *Taiwan Business Topics*, May 16, 2017.

76. Albert O. Hirschmann, *Exit, Voice, and Loyalty: Responses to Decline in Firms, Organizations, and States* (Harvard University Press, 1970).

77. Fulco, "Resolving Taiwan's Talent Exodus."

78. Ting-feng Wu and Chia Lun Huang, "Taiwan's Dire Brain Drain," *Common-Wealth* 550, June 27, 2014.

79. Judith Norton and Edward J. Barss, "China's 31 Measures," East Asia Peace and Security Initiative, March 22, 2018.

80. Wang Xiaoqing and Han Wei, "Welcome Mat Fades for Taiwan Businesses," *Caixin*, August 26, 2016.

81. For China to provide preferential treatment to another member of the World Trade Organization, such as Taiwan, and not to anyone else is arguably a violation the WTO's fundamental principle of most-favored-nation treatment. See Ian C. Forsyth, "Analyzing China's 31 Measures for Taiwan," *China-U.S. Focus*, April 24, 2018.

82. Timothy Ferry, "Taiwan Competes for Talent and Manpower," *Taiwan Business Topics*, April 18, 2018.

83. For an example, see "MAC Announces Report on the Implementation Results of the 'Eight Strategies for a Stronger Taiwan: Responses to Mainland China's 31 Taiwan-Related Measures,'" Mainland Affairs Council, Republic of China (Taiwan), September 6, 2018.

84. Rickards, "What's Holding Down Salaries in Taiwan?"

85. André Beckershoff, "The Sunflower Movement: Origins, Structures, and Strategies of Taiwan's Resistance Against the 'Black Box,'" in *Taiwan's Social Movement under Ma Ying-jeou: From the Wild Strawberries to the Sunflower Movement*, edited by Dafydd Fell (New York: Routledge, 2017), pp. 113–33. On the Sunflower movement, see also Hsu Szu-Chien, "The China Factor and Taiwan's Civil Society Organizations in the Sunflower Movement: The Case of the Democratic Front against the Cross-Strait Service Trade Agreement," ibid., pp. 134–53; and Ming-sho Ho, "Occupy Congress in Taiwan: Political Opportunity, Threat, and the Sunflower Movement," *Journal of East Asian Studies* 15 (April 2015), pp. 69–97.

86. Pan Tzu-yu and Chiang Yi-ching, "Taiwan Cuts 2020 GDP Growth Forecast Due to COVID-19 Impact," *Focus Taiwan*, May 28, 2020.

87. The term is used differently by Sir Arthur Lewis, whose focus was the urban-rural divide in developing countries. For his seminal insight, see W. A. Lewis, "Eco-

nomic Development with Unlimited Supply of Labour," *Manchester School* 22, no. 2 (1954), pp. 139–99.

88. *Taiwan Statistical Data Book*, 2019, tables 5-3a, 5-3b, and 5-3c, "Indices of Industrial Production by Sectors," pp. 107–09. In the index, 100 was the figure for 2016.

89. American Chamber of Commerce in Taipei, "AmCham Taipei White Paper, 2019 Edition," *Taiwan Business Topics* 49, no. 6 (2019), pp. WP 6–8.

90. Evan A. Feigenbaum, "Assuring Taiwan's Innovation Future," Carnegie Endowment for International Peace, February 2020.

91. Mainland Affairs Council, "A Year after Mainland China Announced the 31 Taiwan-Related Measures, the Implementation Results Are Overstated and the So-Called 'Favor Taiwan and Encourage Integration' Intends to 'Benefit China and Promote Unification,'" February 27, 2019.

92. "Taiwan Telephone and Mobile Phone Survey of the Presidential Satisfaction: The Twenty-Second Wave," Taiwan's Election and Democratization Study, National Chengchi University, survey conducted September 2019 (http://teds.nccu.edu.tw/main.php).

Chapter 5

1. *The CIA World Factbook*, 2020–2021 (New York: Skyhorse Publishing, 2020), "Taiwan," p. 917.

2. *Statistical Yearbook of the Republic of China, 2019* (Directorate-General Budget, Accounting and Statistics, ROC, September 2019), table 26, "Emissions of Greenhouse Gases."

3. Bureau of Energy, Ministry of Economic Affairs, "Per Capita GDP and Primary Energy Consumption in Major Countries (2016)," Energy Statistical Annual Reports, Republic of China (Taiwan) (www.moeaboe.gov.tw/ECW/english/content/ContentLink.aspx?menu_id=1540).

4. Anthony Rowley, "Taipei in Push to Reduce Energy Imports," *The National*, December 26, 2017; U.S. Energy Information Administration, "U.S. Natural Gas Exports and Re-Exports by Country," Department of Energy, August 31, 2020.

5. Timothy Ferry, "Phasing Out Nuclear Power in Taiwan," *Taiwan Business Topics*, September 15, 2015.

6. As detailed later in this chapter, developing nuclear power had both an economic and security purpose.

7. "Telephone and Mobile Phone Interview Survey of the Presidential Satisfaction: The Twenty-Second Wave," Taiwan's Election and Democratization Study, National Chengchi University, survey conducted December 2017 (http://teds.nccu.edu.tw/teds_plan/list.php?g_isn=127).

8. Keoni Everington, "44% of Taiwanese Mistakenly Believe Most of Taiwan's Energy Comes from Nuclear Power," *Taiwan News*, December 5, 2018.

9. "Telephone and Mobile Phone Interview Survey of the Presidential Satisfaction: The Twenty-Second Wave," survey conducted December 2018 (http://teds.nccu.edu.tw/teds_plan/list.php?g_isn=127).

10. Bureau of Energy, Ministry of Economic Affairs, "Structure of Electricity

Generation (by Fuel) (2018)" (www.moeaboe.gov.tw/ECW/english/content/ContentLink.aspx?menu_id=1540).

11. Bureau of Energy, Ministry of Economic Affairs, "Per Capita Real GDP and Per Capita Energy Consumption" (www.moeaboe.gov.tw/ECW/english/content/ContentLink.aspx?menu_id=1540).

12. The government-set pricing structure has also caused Taipower, a state-owned enterprise, to run deficits for years. See Ferry, "Phasing Out Nuclear Power in Taiwan." I am grateful to Samantha Gross for explaining the price implications of distinctions between legacy and new facilities.

13. Timothy Ferry, "Is Renewable Energy the Way Forward for Taiwan?," *Taiwan Business Topics,* September 15, 2015; John Weaver, "Solar Price Declines Slowing, Energy Storage in the Money," *PV Magazine,* November 8, 2019.

14. Timothy Ferry, "An Early Nuclear-Free Homeland," *Taiwan Business Topics,* October 19, 2016; Timothy Ferry, "Taiwan Undertakes Power Market Reforms," *Taiwan Business Topics,* November 4, 2016.

15. Timothy Ferry, "Keeping Taiwan from Going Dark," *Taiwan Business Topics,* October 13, 2017.

16. *Taiwan Statistical Data Book, 2019* (Taipei: National Development Council, ROC [Taiwan]), table 5-5a, "Installed Capacity and Operation of the Power System (1)," and table 5-6a, "Power Generation and Consumption."

17. Central Intelligence Agency, "Taiwan"; Yale University, Environmental Performance Index, 2018; Tsai Shu-yuan, "Taichung Air Pollution 'a Crisis,'" *Taipei Times,* March 18, 2019.

18. Chao Li-yan, Su Mu-chun, and Matthew Mazzetta, "Taichung Government, Taipower Clash over Coal-Powered Generator," *Focus Taiwan,* June 26, 2020.

19. "2018: Surveys on Taiwanese People's Attitudes towards Climate Change and Energy," Taiwan Institute for Sustainable Energy, May 2018.

20. Timothy Ferry, "Taiwan's Energy Dilemma: Emission Reductions vs. Dwindling Supply," *Taiwan Business Topics,* September 15, 2015.

21. Lin Chia-nan, "White Paper Urges Drastic Plans on Greenhouse Gas," *Taipei Times,* June 7, 2019.

22. Derek J. Mitchell, "Taiwan's Hsin Chu Program: Deterrence, Abandonment, and Honor," in *The Nuclear Tipping Point: Why States Reconsider Their Nuclear Choices,* edited by Kurt M. Campbell, Robert J. Einhorn, and Mitchell B. Reiss (Brookings Institution Press, 2004), pp. 293–314; Vincent Wei-cheng Wang, "Taiwan: Conventional Deterrence, Soft Power, ant the Nuclear Option," in *The Long Shadow: Nuclear Weapons and Security in 21st Century Asia,* edited by Muthiah Alagappa (Stanford University Press, 2008), pp. 404–28.

23. James Reardon-Anderson, *Pollution, Politics, and Foreign Investment in Taiwan: Lukang Rebellion* (New York: Routledge, 1992).

24. This discussion is based on Simona Grano, "The Evolution of the Anti-Nuclear Movement in Taiwan Since 2008," in *Taiwan's Social Movements under Ma Ying-jeou: From the Wild **Strawberries to the Sunflowers,* edited by Dafydd Fell (New York: Routledge, 2018), pp. 154–76; Simona A. Grano, "Anti-Nuclear Power

Movement," in *Routledge Handbook of Contemporary Taiwan*, edited by Gunter Schubert (New York: Routledge, 2016), pp. 297–312; Ming-Sho-Ho, "The Politics of Anti-Nuclear Protest in Taiwan: A Case of Party-Dependent Movement (1980–2000)," *Modern Asian Studies* 37, no. 3 (2003), pp. 683–708.

25. Not all of the corporate sector was happy with the DPP's reversal. A growing sector of independent power producers was seeking a market niche in competition with state-owned Taipower.

26. Yu Hsiao-han and Elizabeth Hsu, "President, Ex-Premier to Attend Annual Anti-Nuclear March: Organizers," *Focus Taiwan*, April 24, 2019.

27. Decommissioning is a twenty-five-year process, so "nuclear-free" will not come quickly. Chinshan's reactor number two was officially decommissioned in July 2019, the first to gain that status. But Taipower was unable to take the next steps in the process because it was caught in a dispute with the New Taipei City government over how to dispose of the spent fuel in the cooling ponds. See Timothy Ferry, "Nuclear Decommissioning Stuck in Limbo," *Taiwan Business Topics* 50, no. 2 (February 2020).

28. Ferry, "Phasing Out Nuclear Power in Taiwan." Increasing supplies from hydropower is not an option because all the potential resources have already been exploited, and silting and droughts reduce the supply that is normally available; Everington, "44% of Taiwanese Mistakenly Believe Most of Taiwan's Energy Comes from Nuclear Power."

29. "2018: Surveys on Taiwanese People's Attitudes towards Climate Change and Energy."

30. "Climate and Weather Averages in Yaichung, Taiwan," Time and Date.com.

31. Timothy Ferry, "Taiwan's 'Energiewende': Developing Renewable Energy," *Taiwan Business Topics*, October 20, 2016; Frank Hiroshi Ling, "Recommendations for Taiwan's Energy Policy," *Taiwan Business Topics*, February 14, 2017.

32. Ferry, "Phasing Out Nuclear Power in Taiwan"; Ferry, "Taiwan's 'Energiewende.'"

33. Timothy Ferry, "Reaching Peak Energy in Taiwan," *Taiwan Business Topics*, October 19, 2016.

34. Ferry, "Taiwan's 'Energiewende.'"

35. Timothy Ferry, "Solar Power Moves Ahead in Taiwan Despite Obstacles," *Taiwan Business Topics*, October 19, 2017.

36. Ling, "Recommendations for Taiwan's Energy Policy."

37. Ferry, "Solar Power Moves Ahead in Taiwan Despite Obstacles."

38. Ibid.

39. Ferry, "Phasing Out Nuclear Power in Taiwan."

40. Ferry, "Solar Power Moves Ahead in Taiwan Despite Obstacles."

41. Ibid.

42. Angelica Oung, "New Solar Farm Rules Trigger Debate," *Taipei Times*, July 14, 2020.

43. Ibid.

44. Ibid.

45. Timothy Ferry, "Green Energy for a Nuclear-Free, Low-Carbon Future," *Taiwan Business Topics*.

46. Timothy Ferry, "Vast Potential in Taiwan for Offshore Wind Power," *Taiwan Business Topics*, October 19, 2017.

47. Ferry, "Phasing Out Nuclear Power in Taiwan."

48. Ibid.

49. Ferry, "Taiwan's 'Energiewende.'"

50. Wang Shu-fen and Evelyn Kao, "CAA Reiterates Opposition to Wind Farm Off Taoyuan Coast," *Focus Taiwan*, September 3, 2020.

51. United Daily News, "Wind Power Generation: Operators Scramble to Sign Contracts at 'NT$5.8 Per kWh,'" KMT Official Website, December 8–9, 2018.

52. Ted Chen, "Final Feed-In Tariff Set for Wind Farms," *Taipei Times*, January 31, 2019; Jerry Liu, "Politics Scaring Off Foreign Investors," *Taipei Times*, January 17, 2019.

53. Evan Feigenbaum and Jen-yi Hou, "Overcoming Taiwan's Energy Trilemma," Carnegie Endowment for International Peace, April 27, 2020.

54. Timothy Ferry, "Energy in Taiwan: Uncertainty in Liquefied Natural Gas," *Taiwan Business Topics*, November 2017.

55. Currently, Datan is supplied by a pipeline from the south.

56. Ferry, "Energy in Taiwan."

57. Ted Chiou, "EPA Move Spells the End of the Green Ideal," *Taipei Times*, October 16, 2018.

58. Lin Chia-nan, "Premier Urged to Jettison Gas Terminal Project," *Taipei Times*, January 9, 2019.

59. Nathan Batto, "The Current (Missing) Energy Crisis," *Frozen Garlic* (blog), August 30, 2019.

60. Timothy Ferry, "Harnessing the Wind," *Taiwan Business Topics* 49, September 2019, pp. 17–21; Ferry, "Despite Referendum, Nuclear Power Faces 2025 Deadline," pp. 22–24; Ferry, "Balancing Solar Energy Development and Biodiversity," pp. 24–25.

61. Ferry, "Taiwan's Energy Dilemma."

62. Ibid. Owing to the Ma administration's emissions-reduction policies, LNG has become the fuel source for over 30 percent of Taipower's total generation, even though, at NT$3.91 per kilowatt-hour, the cost of power generation at LNG-fired plants is more than the utility can charge its customers.

63. Alex Jiang, "President Revises Electricity Rate Hike Plan amid Growing Anger," *Focus Taiwan*, May 1, 2012.

64. Liao Yu-yang and Elizabeth Hsu, "Government Keeps Electricity Rates at Current Level," *Focus Taiwan*, March 18, 2019; Liao Yu-yang and Evelyn Kao, "Electricity Prices Projected to Rise to NT$3.39 Per K Wh by 2025," *Focus Taiwan*, March 4, 2019.

65. "2018 Taiwanese Referendum," Central Election Commission, November 24, 2018 (https://web.archive.org/web/20181125031636/http://referendum.2018 .nat.gov.tw/pc/en/00/00000000000000000.html).

66. "Referendum Act," Laws and Regulations Database of the Republic of China,

amended on June 21, 2019 (https://law.moj.gov.tw/ENG/LawClass/LawAll. aspx?pcode=D0020050).

67. David Spencer, "Lessons from Taiwan's Recent Referendums and Why E-Voting Is the Way Forward," *Taiwan News*, December 1, 2018.

68. Elaine Hou and Chi Jo-yao, "Cabinet Agrees to Abolish Nuclear Free Goal," *Focus Taiwan*, December 6, 2018.

69. Sean Lin, "KMT Decries 'Reinstatement' of Nuclear Policy," *Taipei Times*, February 2, 2019.

70. Wang Cheng-chung and Elizabeth Hsu, "2 Nuclear Power–Related Referendum Proposals Pass Initial Screening," *Focus Taiwan*, March 19, 2019; Wang Cheng-chung and Evelyn Kao, "Anti-Nuclear Referendum Petition Delivered," *Focus Taiwan*, April 2, 2019.

71. Nathan Batto, "Energy Policy and Referenda," *Frozen Garlic* (blog), December 1, 2018.

72. Feigenbaum and Hou, "Overcoming Taiwan's Energy Trilemma." This paper, which makes a number of useful suggestions for technical policy changes, was released after the present volume was completed.

Chapter 6

1. David Goodman, Shane White, and Lawrence W. Levine, " 'The Future Is Secure; It's Only the Past That's Uncertain': An Interview with Lawrence W. Levine," *Australasian Journal of American Studies* 7, no. 2 (1988), p. 28.

2. Later chapters detail the debates in Taiwan concerning the island's legal identity and its relationship with China.

3. United Nations Security Council, "The Rule of Law and Transitional Justice in Conflict and Post-Conflict Societies: Report of the Secretary-General," August 23, 2004; cited in Vladimir Stolojan, "Transitional Justice and Collective Memory in Taiwan: How Taiwanese Society Is Coming to Terms with its Authoritarian Past," *China Perspectives*, no. 2 (2017), p. 27.

4. Jau-Yuan Hwang, "Transitional Justice in Postwar Taiwan," in *Routledge Handbook of Contemporary Taiwan*, edited by Gunter Schubert (London: Routledge, 2016), pp. 169–83.

5. Naiteh Wu, "Transition without Justice, or Justice without History: Transitional Justice in Taiwan," *Taiwan Journal of Democracy* 1 (July 2005), pp. 77–102.

6. Neil Kritz, "The Dilemmas of Transitional Justice," in *Transitional Justice: How Emerging Democracies Reckon with Former Regimes*, vol. 1, *General Considerations*, edited by Neil Krinz (Washington, D.C.: U.S. Institute of Peace, 1997), p. xxi.

7. George H. Kerr, *Formosa Betrayed* (Irvine, Calif.: Taiwan Publishing, 1992); Steven Phillips, *Between Independence and Assimilation: The Taiwan Elite and Nationalist Chinese Rule, 1945–1950* (Stanford University Press, 2002); and Richard C. Bush, "Difficult Dilemmas: The United States and Kuomintang Repression, 1949–1979," in *At Cross Purposes: U.S.-Taiwan Relations since 1942* (Armonk, N.Y.: M. E. Sharpe, 2004), pp. 40–84.

8. Until the enactment of the Temporary Provisions, Article 9 of the Constitution barred military courts from trying civilians.

9. For fictional and nonfictional accounts of the repression, see, among others, Tehpen Tsai, *Elegy of Sweet Potatoes: Stories of Taiwan's White Terror* (Upland, Calif.: Taiwan Publishing, 2002); Peng Ming-min, *A Taste of Freedom: Memoirs of a Formosan Independence Leader* (New York: Holt, Rinehart and Winston, 1972); and Vern Sneider, *A Pail of Oysters* (Manchester, U.K.: Camphor Press, 2016).

10. Wu, "Transition without Justice, or Justice without History," p. 96.

11. Ibid., p. 90.

12. Sheena Chestnut Greitens, *Dictators and Their Secret Police: Coercive Institutions and State Violence* (Cambridge University Press, 2016), pp. 75–111.

13. Ibid., pp. 179–210. The charts from which the numerical estimates are drawn appear on p. 181. In addition, a system to control hooligans (*liumang*), analogous to the PRC's system of reeducation through labor, was gradually reformed to constrain police excesses. See Jerome A. Cohen and Margaret K. Lewis, *Challenge to China: How Taiwan Abolished Its Version of Re-education through Labor* (New York: US-Asia Law Institute, 2013).

14. Edwin A. Winckler, "Institutionalization and Participation on Taiwan: From Hard to Soft Authoritarianism?" *China Quarterly*, no. 99 (September 1984), pp. 481–99.

15. Mab Huang, *Intellectual Ferment for Political Reform in Taiwan, 1971–1973*, Monographs in Chinese Studies (University of Michigan Center for Chinese Studies, 1976).

16. While I was on the staff of the U.S. House Asian and Pacific Affairs Subcommittee at the time, I organized the February 7, 1985, hearing on the Henry Liu case. See Richard C. Bush, "Congress Gets into the Taiwan Human Rights Act," in *At Cross Purposes*, pp. 206–09.

17. U.S. Department of State, *Country Reports on Human Rights Practices for 1986* (U.S. Government Printing Office, 1987), pp. 698–708.

18. Sean Lin, "Transitional Justice Act: ANALYSIS: Judge Law in terms of Security Act: Academics," *Taipei Times*, December 10, 2017.

19. Wu, "Transition without Justice, or Justice without History," p. 11.

20. Hwang, "Transitional Justice in Postwar Taiwan," p. 177.

21. Robert E. Goodin, "Disgorging the Fruits of Historical Wrongdoing," *American Political Science Review* 107, no. 3 (2013), pp. 478–91.

22. "Key Statements from the Second Presidential Debate of the 2016 Elections," based on broadcast by *Sanlih Cable News Channel*, January 2, 2016 (U.S. government, Open Source Enterprise, CHO2016010760163614). (Access to OSE was terminated for nongovernment employees in July 2019. A copy of this item is in the author's files).

23. "KMT Pans Party Assets Bill as DPP Pushes for Quick Passage," *Taiwan News*, July 14, 2016; Central News Agency, "KMT Defends, Maps Handling of Party Assets, in New Policy Platform," *Taiwan News*, September 4, 2016.

24. C. Donovan Smith, "Save the Sinking Ship: Can the KMT Reform?," Ketagalan Media, February 3, 2020.

25. "Key Statements from the Second Presidential Debate."

26. "Full Text of Tsai Ing-wen Inaugural Address," *Focus Taiwan*, May 20, 2016.

27. David G. Brown, "Governing Taiwan Is Not Easy: President Tsai Ing-wen's First Year," Brookings Institution, May 17, 2017.

28. Yuan-Ming Chiao, "Ill Gotten Party Assets Bill Passes in LY," *China Post*, July 26, 2016.

29. Stacy Hsu, "KMT Claims Ex-Japanese Assets as Compensation," *Taipei Times*, March 24, 2017.

30. Jason Pan, "Ruling Upholds Ill-Gotten Assets Act, Committee," *Taipei Times*, August 29, 2020 (see page 112 for details).

31. "Court to Petition for Judicial Review over NWL Case / IGPASC Not to File Interlocutory Appeal," *United Daily News*, March 8, 2019, summary at KMT Official Website.

32. Stacy Hsu, "Agency Seals Off KMT Properties," *Taipei Times*, August 18, 2018.

33. Chen Yu-fu and Jonathan Chin, "Plan to Disburse KMT Ill Gotten Wealth Detailed," *Taipei Times*, June 14, 2019; Chen Yu-fu and Dennis Xie, "KMT Asset Suits Moving at Snail's Pace," *Taipei Times*, March 24, 2020.

34. "Collective Silence: An Accomplice in Unconstitutional Act of IGPASC," *United Daily News*, November 30, 2016, KMT Official Website.

35. "Ma Criticizes IGPASC as Unconstitutional, Fears Totalitarian Taiwan," *China Times*, February 13, 2017, KMT Official Website.

36. Chin Heng-wei, "An Easy Path to Transitional Justice," *Taipei Times*, November 15, 2016.

37. Chen Yu-fu and Dennis Xie, "KMT Asset Suits Moving at Snail's Pace," *Taipei Times*, March 24, 2020.

38. Jason Pan, "Ruling Upholds Ill-Gotten Assets Act, Committee," *Taipei Times*, August 29, 2020.

39. Hwang, "Transitional Justice in Postwar Taiwan," p. 180.

40. "KMT Plans to Resume System of Fundraising by Party Officials and Public Officials of KMT Affiliation," *United Daily News*, December 10, 2017, KMT Official Website.

41. Lee Hsin-fang, "Executive Yuan Approves NAA Document Collection," *Taipei Times*, February 27, 2017.

42. Lu Hsin-hui, Claudia Liu, and S. C. Chang, "Advocates Demand More Government Action on 'Transitional Justice,'" *Focus Taiwan*, February 27, 2017; Stacy Hsu, "All 228 Incident Documents Declassified," *Taipei Times*, February 27, 2017.

43. "Taiwan's Leader Tsai Vows to 'Prudently' Handle 1947 Massacre," *Kyodo World Service*, February 28, 2017, U.S. government, Open Source Enterprise (OSE), JPR2017022850262747); copy in author's files.

44. Lee Hsin-fang, "Su Urged to Act on Transitional Justice," *Taipei Times,* May 31, 2017.

45. Shih Hsiu-chuan, "Veteran Democracy Advocate to Lead Transitional Justice Work," *Focus Taiwan*, March 27, 2018.

46. Shih Hsiu-chuan, "Transitional Justice Legislation Passes Legislature," *Focus Taiwan*, December 5, 2018. By August 2020, the commission could report that gradual progress had occurred. Fifty-four institutions had either removed their symbols of authoritarian rule or had formulated plans to do so. Chen Yu-fu and Jake Chung, "Progress Made on Removal of Authoritarian-Era Statues," *Taipei Times*, August 13, 2020.

47. Chin Heng-wei, "The DPP Must Implement the Law" *Taipei Times*, December 13, 2017; Chen Yu-fu, "Inventory Identifies 1,083 Chiang Kai-Shek Monuments," *Taipei Times*, December 8, 2018.

48. That vengeance was the real motivation was no doubt confirmed for some government employees when it later emerged that the some on the Transitional Justice Commission wanted to undertake lustration—removal from office of individuals associated with the old regime—more than two decades after the transformation of that regime. See Sean Lin, "KMT Again Disrupts Premier's Report," *Taipei Times*, September 29, 2018.

49. "Liberty Times Editorial: Seeking the Truth They Want to Bury," *Taipei Times,* December 14, 2017.

50. Chang Kuo-tsai, "Admission of Guilt Is Necessary for Justice," *Taipei Times*, January 9, 2018. Shih Ming-hsiung, a former political prisoner, saw a more practical reason that the perpetrator issue would be difficult: "The perpetrators of repression . . . foresaw that there would eventually be a shift in power, leading to cases being overturned. Fearing that their roles would be investigated, the participants had all along planned to conceal their names, backgrounds and positions, and their roles in the criminal repression. They destroyed as much evidence as they could while they still had the power to do so." See Shih Ming-hsiung, "Perpetrators Must Not Be Allowed to Edit History," *Taipei Times*, December 4, 2018.

51. Lin, "Transitional Justice Act."

52. Wu Ching-chin, "Transitional Justice Vaguely Defined," *Taipei Times*, December 15, 2017.

53. "Ma: Transformational Justice Statute Violates Principles of 'Rule of Law,'" *United Daily News*, December 26, 2017, KMT Official Website (www1.kmt.org.tw/english/page.aspx?type=article&mnum=112&anum=20392).

54. Shelley Shan, "KMT Rejects Transitional Justice Commission Invite," *Taipei Times*, July 24, 2018.

55. Chen Yu-fu, "Commission Creating Justice Database," *Taipei Times*, September 23, 2018; Matt Yu and Matthew Mazzetta, "TJC Unveils Online Database of Persecutions in Martial Law Period," *Focus Taiwan*, February 26, 2020.

56. Shelley Shan, "Justice Commission Asks for the Impossible: KMT," *Taipei Times*, August 14, 2018; Chen Yu-fu, "Declassification Slowing Justice Process: Source," *Taipei Times*, December 31, 2018; Chen Yu-fu and Shery Hsiao, "Declassification of Political Cases Urged," *Taipei Times*, April 9, 2019.

57. Hsieh Chia-chen and Matthew Mazzetta, "Intelligence Reports on Kaohsiung Incident Declassified," *Focus Taiwan*, December 7, 2019; Wen Kuei-hsiang and Matthew Mazzetta, "Academia Historica to Publish Materials on Activist Chen

Wen-chen," *Focus Taiwan*, December 28, 2019; Chen Yu-fu and William Hetherington, "New Details Revealed in Activist's Death, *Taipei Times*, May 5, 2020.

58. Lu Hsin-hui and Flor Wang, "Tsai Apologies to Political Victims after Convictions Rescinded," *Focus Taiwan*, October 10, 2018; "1,505 Victims of Political Persecution Exonerated in Taiwan," *Taiwan Today*, December 10, 2018; Chen Yu-fu and Sherry Hsiao, "More than 2,000 Convictions Overturned," *Taipei Times*, May 31, 2019.

59. Elaine Hou and Y. F. Low, "Taiwan's Cabinet Announces Nominees to Transitional Justice Committee," *Focus Taiwan*, March 31, 2018.

60. Stacy Hsu, "Internal Meeting Probe Published," *Taipei Times*, September 22, 2018; Sean Lin, "Lai Apologizes over Justice Incident," *Taipei Times*, October 3, 2018.

61. Elaine Hou and Lee Hsin-Yin, "Taiwan's Transitional Justice Commission Chairman Resigns," *Focus Taiwan*, October 6, 2018; Sean Lin, "KMT Seeks to Eliminate Transitional Justice Purse," *Taipei Times*, December 9, 2018 (www.taipeitimes.com/News/front/archives/2018/12/09/2003705769); Fan Chenghsiang and Christie Chen, "Legislature Approves NT$1.998 Trillion Government Budget for 2019," *Focus Taiwan*, January 10, 2019.

62. "No Truth without Reconciliation," editorial, *Taipei Times*, February 28, 2020.

63. "President Tsai Leads 228 Incident Commemoration," *Focus Taiwan*, February 28, 2020.

64. Wu, "Transition without Justice, or Justice without History."

65. "Full Text of President Tsai's Inaugural Address," *Focus Taiwan*, May 20, 2016.

66. Chang Hsiao-ti, "Draft Bill on Transitional Justice Promotion Finalized," *Taipei Times*, March 29, 2016.

67. "The Liberty Times Editorial: Accelerating Transitional Justice," *Taipei Times*, March 14, 2020.

68. Hu Wen-chi, "Taiwan Must Face Truth to Heal," March 1, 2020.

Chapter 7

1. This and succeeding chapters deal with relations between the governments in Taipei and Beijing and distinguish between "China," the state that is a member of the international community, and the governments that have claimed to be the governments of that China—the ROC and the PRC. Because of this, although conventional usage regarding cross-Strait relations refers to "China" and "Taiwan," I use "the PRC" or "Beijing" for "China."

2. For English usage, the PRC refers to its goal as "reunification," to emphasize that Taiwan was a part of China before the Japanese colonial period. "Unification" is the English word usually used on Taiwan. But the same Chinese word is used in both places: *tongyi*.

3. This section is based on the seminal study by the late Alan M. Wachman, in his *Why Taiwan? Geostrategic Rationales for China's Territorial Integrity* (Stanford University Press, 2007), pp. 43–68.

4. Richard C. Bush, *At Cross Purposes: US-Taiwan Relations, 1942–2000* (Armonk, N.Y.: M. E. Sharpe, 2004), pp. 9–39; Wachman, *Why Taiwan?*, pp. 69–81.

5. "President Truman's Statement on the Situation in Korea," *DocsTeach*, National Archives, June 27, 1950.

6. Robert Accinelli, *Crisis and Commitment: United States Policy towards Taiwan, 1950–1955* (University of North Carolina Press, 1996), p. 33. The administration was concerned that in the future a growing number of countries would recognize the PRC as the government of China and adopt the position that Taiwan was legally a part of China, in which case, according to international law, the United States could not come to Taiwan's defense. Hence the reformulation of the Taiwan issue as one of international peace and security.

7. On U.S.-Taiwan relations in the early 1950s, see Accinelli, *Crisis and Commitment.*

8. "Working Together to Realize Rejuvenation of the Chinese Nation and Advance China's Peaceful Reunification," speech by Xi Jinping at the Meeting Marking the 40th Anniversary of the Issuance of the Message to Compatriots in Taiwan, Beijing, January 2, 2019, Taiwan Affairs Office of the State Council (www .gwytb.gov.cn/m/news/201904/t20190412_12155846.htm).

9. Ibid.

10. Hu Bo, *2049 di Zhongguo Haishang Quanli: Haiyang Qiangguo Jueqi zhi Lu* [China's maritime power in 2049: The path of an oceanic great power's rise] (Beijing: Zhongguo Fazhan Press, 2015), pp. 8–9. I am grateful to Lauren Dickey for referring me to this source.

11. Frank Dikotter, *The Tragedy of Liberation: A History of the Chinese Revolution, 1945–1957* (New York: Bloomsbury Press, 2013), pp. 21–24.

12. These were three territories that the PRC government claimed for China but over which it did not have jurisdiction or control.

13. The uncertainty arises because early statements about 1C2S for Taiwan included a promise that the military would continue to exist, but Xi Jinping did not include that in his authoritative speech on January 2, 2019, "Working Together to Realize Rejuvenation of the Chinese Nation and Advance China's Peaceful Reunification." See Richard C. Bush, "8 Key Things to Notice from Xi Jinping's New Year Speech on Taiwan," Brookings Institution, January 7, 2019.

14. Christopher H. Achen and T. Y. Wang "The Power of Identity in Taiwan," in *The Taiwan Voter*, edited by Christopher H. Achen and T. Y. Wang (University of Michigan Press, 2017), pp. 273–92.

15. Miao Zong-han and Emerson Lim, "Big Majority Reject 'One Country, Two Systems': Survey," *Focus Taiwan*, March 21, 2019.

16. Part of Beijing's effort to constrain first Lee and then Chen was to try to mobilize the United States—first the Clinton administration and then the George W. Bush administration—to constrain them.

17. Douglas Mendel, *The Politics of Formosan Nationalism* (University of California Press, 1970).

18. Peng Ming-min, *A Taste of Freedom: Memoirs of a Formosan Independence Leader* (New York: Holt, Rinehart and Winston, 1972).

19. See, for example, Yan Yu, "Thoughts on Tsai Ing-wen's Address," *China-US Focus*, May 27, 2020.

20. Bush, *At Cross Purposes*, pp. 85–123. The State Department's two-China formula was designed in the expectation that Beijing would reject it and so assume responsibility for its exclusion. But Chiang Kai-shek would not agree to it until 1971, by which time it was too late.

21. As evidence of this dual fear, there is the small case of Taiwan's small conservation NGO, the Chinese Wild Bird Federation (CWBF). The CWBF has participated in BirdLife International, an international partnership, for a number of years, but it has faced demands from BirdLife over nomenclature, demands most likely stimulated by Beijing. In 2020, BirdLife ended CWBF's participation because it would not sign a document pledging to not "promote or advocate the legitimacy of the Republic of China or the independence of Taiwan from China." See Matt Yu and Chiang Yi-ching, "MOFA Blames China for Conversation Group's Removal from Partnership," *Focus Taiwan*, September 15, 2020.

22. For my analysis of the Ma administration through 2012, see Richard C. Bush, *Uncharted Strait: The Future of China-Taiwan Relations* (Brookings Institution Press, 2013).

23. PRC official, conversation with author, April 2012, Washington, DC.

24. "Working Together to Realize Rejuvenation of the Chinese Nation and Advance China's Peaceful Reunification." Unless otherwise indicated, the quotations in this section are from Xi's speech.

25. The premise that Xi states is a reference to what China calls its "core interests," and Beijing reserves for itself the right to define how these interests are applied in specific circumstances.

26. Richard C. Bush, *Untying the Knot: Making Peace in the Taiwan Strait* (Brookings Institution Press, 2005), pp. 91–99, 230–33.

27. Xi had dropped that principle from his report to the CCP's Nineteenth Party Congress, even though it had appeared in previous reports by the general secretary of the CCP. The interpretation at the time was that Beijing had lost hope in the KMT as a partner in working toward unification. The KMT's strong performance in the 2018 local elections was probably the reason that Xi restored the principle to the PRC's policy lexicon.

28. James Townsend, "Chinese Nationalism," *Australian Journal of Chinese Affairs*, no. 27 (January 1992), pp. 97–130; and Frank Dikotter, "Racial Identities in China: Context and Meaning," *China Quarterly*, no. 138 (June 1994), pp. 404–12.

29. James A. Millward, "What Xi Jinping Hasn't Learned from China's Emperors," *New York Times*, October 1, 2019 (www.nytimes.com/2019/10/01/opinion/xi-jinping-china.html?searchResultPosition=7).

30. Richard C. Bush, *Hong Kong in the Shadow of China: Living with the Leviathan* (Brookings Institution Press, 2016).

31. "President Tsai Issues Statement on China's President Xi's 'Message to Compatriots in Taiwan,'" *Focus Taiwan*, January 2, 2019.

32. Richard C. Bush, "A Requiem for the City of Hong Kong," Brookings Institution, November 18, 2019; Donald Clarke, "Hong Kong's National Security Law: An Assessment," *China Leadership Monitor,* July 13, 2020.

33. Luo Yuan, "Major General: Exercise in Taiwan Strait is a Reunification Rehearsal," *China Military Online,* April 20, 2018; Luo Yuan, "Luo Yuan: 'Yiguo Liangzhi' di 'Yiguo' Burong Taolun" [Luo Yuan: The "one country" part of "one country, two systems" is not up for debate], *Global Times,* July 22, 2019. The passage cited appears in the *China Military Online* item.

34. Thomas Christensen applies the concept of "windows"—that decisionmakers act based on their assessment of whether gains or losses are more likely—to East Asia in his "Windows and War: Changes in the International System and China's Decision to Use Force," in *New Approaches to China's Foreign Relations: Essays in Honor of Allen S. Whiting,* edited by Alastair Iain Johnston and Robert Ross (Stanford University Press, 2006), pp. 50–85.

35. Muthiah Alagappa, "PacNet #26: China's Taiwan Dilemma; Beijing Must Rethink Its Ideas of Nation, State, and Sovereignty," March 28, 2017, Pacific Forum-CSIS.

36. Chinese scholar, conversation with author, October 2016, Beijing.

37. "Dangqian Guoji Guanxi Yenjiuzhong de Ruogan Zhongdian Wenti" [Certain major issues in studying current international relations], *Guoji Zhanwang* [International forecast], February 15, 2001, p. 7.

Chapter 8

1. "Working Together to Realize Rejuvenation of the Chinese Nation and Advance China's Peaceful Reunification," speech by Xi Jinping at the meeting marking the fortieth anniversary of the issuance of the message to compatriots in Taiwan, January 2, 2019, website of the Taiwan Affairs Office of the State Council (www.gwytb.gov.cn/m/news/201904/t20190412_12155846.htm).

2. Richard C. Bush, *Untying the Knot: Making Peace in the Taiwan Strait* (Brookings Institution Press, 2005), pp. 107–41.

3. Barry R. Posen, *Restraint: A New Foundation for U.S. Grand Strategy* (Cornell University Press, 2014), pp. 1–3. I am grateful to Rush Doshi for referring me to Posen's work.

4. David A. Baldwin, "The Concept of Security," *Review of International Studies* 23, no. 1 (1997), p. 13.

5. The examples of what is valued are from Helga Haffendorn, "The Security Puzzle: Theory-Building and Discipline-Building in International Security," *International Studies Quarterly* 35, no. 1 (1991), pp. 4–5.

6. *Taiwan Statistical Data Book, 2019* (Taipei: National Development Council, ROC [Taiwan], 2018), tables 11-9a and 11-9e, "Commodity Trade with Major Trading Partners." I estimate that two-thirds of Taiwan's exports designated as going to Hong Kong are actually transshipped through to the PRC.

7. Brian Hioe, "The Dried Mango Strips of National Doom," Popula, November 6, 2019.

8. "Working Together to Realize Rejuvenation of the Chinese Nation and Advance China's Peaceful Reunification."

9. Taiwan National Security Survey, Program in Asian Security Studies, Duke University (https://sites.duke.edu/pass/taiwan-national-security-survey/).

10. Christopher H. Achen and T. Y. Wang, "The Power of Identity in Taiwan," in *The Taiwan Voter*, edited by Christopher H. Achen and T. Y. Wang (University of Michigan Press, 2017).

11. Randall L. Schweller, "Managing the Rise of Great Powers: History and Theory," in *Engaging China: The Management of an Emerging Power*, edited by Alastair Iain Johnston and Robert S. Ross (New York: Routledge, 1999), pp.1–31.

12. Ibid., p.14. Schweller defines engagement as "the use of non-coercive means to ameliorate the non–status quo elements of a rising major power's behavior."

13. Tim Bouverie, *Appeasement, Chamberlain, Hitler, Churchill, and the Road to War* (New York: Random House, 2019).

14. Thomas Christensen, "Windows and War: Changes in the International System and China's Decision to Use Force," in *New Approaches to China's Foreign Relations: Essays in Honor of Allen S. Whiting*, edited by Alastair Iain Johnston and Robert Ross (Stanford University Press, 2006), pp. 50–85.

15. Baldwin, "The Concept of Security," pp. 14–18.

16. J. Michael Cole, "Proxy Organizations in Taiwan Align with Beijing's Push for 'One Country, Two Systems,'" *Global Taiwan Brief* 4, no. 17 (2019).

17. Paul Kennedy, "The Tradition of Appeasement in British Foreign Policy, 1865–1939," in *Strategy and Diplomacy, 1870–1945* (New York: HarperCollins, 1989), p. 16; cited in Schweller, "Managing the Rise of Great Powers," p. 14.

18. Richard C. Bush, *Uncharted Strait: The Future of China-Taiwan Relations* (Brookings Institution Press, 2013), pp. 87–91, 116–17.

19. Nathan Batto, "What Is Taiwan Independence?," *Frozen Garlic* (blog), June 1, 2019.

20. On *biaotai* in PRC statecraft, see David Shambaugh, "China's External Propaganda Work: Missions, Messengers, Mediums," *Party Watch Annual Report 2018*, October 2018.

21. "Cross-Strait Relations at a Crossroad: A View from Ma Ying-jeou, Former President of the Republic of China," speech to the Oxford Union, October 31, 2019, copy in author's files.

22. Yang Hsin-hui and Jake Chung, "China Skewed '1992 Consensus,' Ma Says," *Taipei Times*, January 19, 2020.

23. "Tsai Ing-wen at CSIS, DPP Transcript of Speech and Q&A," *The View from Taiwan* (blog), June 4, 2015.

24. The DPP leaders had read Richard H. Solomon, *Chinese Negotiating Behavior: Pursuing Interests through "Old Friends"* (Washington, D.C.: U.S. Institute of Peace, 1999), a study of Chinese negotiating behavior which stressed the danger of this trap.

25. "Full Text of President Tsai's Inaugural Address," *Focus Taiwan*, May 20, 2016.

26. Ibid.; Richard C. Bush, "Tsai's Inauguration: It Could Have Been Worse," May 23, 2016, Brookings Institution.

27. Lally Weymouth, "Taiwanese President Tsai Ing-wen: Beijing Must Respect Our Democratic Will, *Washington Post*, July 21, 2016.

28. Fu Ying, "China's Advice to Trump and Kim Jong Un," *Washington Post*, June 10, 2018.

29. "Full Text of Former Ma Ying-jeou's Video Speech at SOPA," *Focus Taiwan*, June 16, 2016.

30. Sean Lin and Chung Li-hua, "Presidential Office Rebuts Ma's '1992 Consensus' Claims," *Taipei Times*, August 23, 2020.

31. Ibid.

32. "President Tsai Delivers 2017 National Day Address," October 10, 2017, Republic of China (Taiwan), Office of the President.

33. "President Tsai delivers 2018 National Day Address," October 10, 2018, Republic of China (Taiwan), Office of the President.

34. "President Tsai delivers 2019 National Day Address," October 10, 2019, Republic of China (Taiwan)], Office of the President.

35. Bonnie Glaser and Matthew P. Funaiole, "China's Provocations around Taiwan Aren't a Crisis," *Foreign Policy*, May 15, 2020.

36. Matt Rivers, Steven Jiang, and Ben Westcott, "Taiwan Vulnerable to Chinese Invasion without US, Foreign Minister Says," CNN, July 23, 2018.

37. For views on a cross-Strait war, see chapter 9.

38. Ibid.

39. "Public's View on Current Cross-Strait Relations," 2018, Republic of China (Taiwan), Mainland Affairs Council. The surveys on Chinese hostility and the pace of cross-Strait relations are conducted about three times a year; those issues are not covered in every poll.

40. The Taiwan National Security Survey found a similar result. Those surveyed believed that cross-Strait relations were not especially hostile or friendly.

41. Election Studies Center, NCCU, "Trends in Core Political Attitudes among Taiwanese: Changes in the Unification: Independence Stances of Taiwanese as Tracked in Surveys by Elections Study Center, NCCU (1994–2017.12)," December 2017 (https://esc.nccu.edu.tw/pic.php?img=167_8a93afa2.jpg&dir=news&title=Image).

42. Election Studies Center, NCCU, "Trends in Core Political Attitudes among Taiwanese: Changes in the Unification – Independence Stances of Taiwanese as Tracked in Surveys by Elections Study Center, NCCU (1992/06~2019/06)," July 10, 2019 (https://esc.nccu.edu.tw/pic.php?img=167_bad0ecc6.jpg&dir=news&title=Image).

43. Taiwan National Security Survey, 2017. These polls are conducted by the Election Study Center.

44. Ibid.

45. Ibid.

46. "Taiwan Telephone and Mobile Phone Survey of the Presidential Satisfaction,"

Taiwan's Election and Democratization Study, National Chengchi University, surveys conducted January 2012, January 2016, and December 2017 (http://teds. nccu.edu.tw/main.php). The survey question did not use Ma's definition of "one China, different interpretations"; respondents were left to define the terms of the consensus for themselves.

47. When the survey controlled for education, there was really no difference between levels, with most hovering about the average for support overall, which was 59.7 percent.

48. Only the results of the 2016, 2017, and 2019 Taiwan National Security Survey are readily available.

49. Bush, *Uncharted Strait*, pp. 98–114.

50. This, in turn, is connected with the debate in the international community between the schools of defensive realism and of offensive realism.

51. On reassurance and deterrence in cross-Strait relations, see Thomas J. Christensen, "The Contemporary Security Dilemma: Deterring a Taiwan Conflict," *Washington Quarterly* 25, no. 4 (2002), pp. 5–21.

Chapter 9

1. *China Military Power: Modernizing a Force to Fight and Win* (U.S. Defense Intelligence Agency, 2019), p. 33. Quotations in the following two paragraphs are from this source, pp. 55–86, 33–44.

2. Ibid., pp 45–46.

3. Peter Mattis, "Counterintelligence Remains Weakness in Taiwan's Defense," *China Brief* 17, no. 11 (August 2017).

4. *China Military Power,* pp. 25–28. For an exhaustive treatment of the military reforms, see Phillip E. Sanders and others, eds., *Chairman Xi Remakes the PLA: Assessing China's Military Reforms* (Washington, D.C.: National Defense University Press, 2019).

5. "Annual Report to Congress: Military and Security Developments Involving the People's Republic of China," U.S. Department of Defense, Office of the Secretary of Defense, September 2020, p. 95.

6. *2017 Quadrennial Defense Review: Republic of China* (Republic of China, Ministry of National Defense), p. 9.

7. "The One-China Principle and the Taiwan Issue," Taiwan White Paper, Taiwan Affairs Office and the Information Office of the State Council, Embassy of the People's Republic of China in the United States, February 21, 2000; and "Anti-Secession Law (Full text)," Embassy of the People's Republic of China in the United States, March 15, 2005,

8. Zhu Weidong, "Xinshidai Zhongguo heping tongyi Jincheng mianlin di tiaozhan yu yingdui" [Challenges faced in the course of China's peaceful unification in the new period and responses], *Zhongguo Pinglun,* no. 247 (July 22, 2018) (http:/ /hk.crntt.com/doc/1051/2/1/9/105121941.html?coluid=136&kindid=4711& docid=105121941&mdate=0724132606).

9. *Annual Report to Congress: Military and Security Developments Involving the People's Republic of China*), p. 113–14.

10. Ibid.," pp. 83, 113–14.

11. *2017 Quadrennial Defense Review,* pp. 21–22, 24–25.

12. *Annual Report to Congress,* p. 83; emphasis added.

13. M. Taylor Fravel, "China's Search for Military Power," *Washington Quarterly* 31, no. 3 (2008), pp. 125–41.

14. *China Military Power,* p. 65.

15. Ibid., pp. 40, 45.

16. Eric Heginbotham and others, *The U.S.-China Military Scorecard: Forces, Geography, and the Evolving Balance of Power, 1996–2017* (Santa Monica, Calif.: Rand, 2015), p. 282.

17. Su Chi, " 'Gaicheng shishi': Taiwan anquan xinmihao" ("Fait accompli": New codeword on Taiwan security), *Lien Ho Pao (United Daily News),* June 28, 2020 (https://udn.com/news/story/7339/4663710); copy of English translation in author's files.

18. Kharis Templeman, "The Domestic Politics of Defense Spending," paper presented at seminar, "Monitoring the Cross-Strait Balance," Taiwan Democracy and Security Project, Stanford University, March 4, 2019; copy in author's files.

19. *2017 Quadrennial Defense Review,* p. 28.

20. Jessica T. Mathews, "America's Indefensible Defense Budget," *New York Review of Books,* July 18, 2019, p. 23.

21. "General Budget of Central Government Summary Table for Annual Expenditures by Agencies FY2019," Directorate-General of Budget, Accounting, and Statistics, Taiwan (https://eng.dgbas.gov.tw/public/Attachment/9226143559Q 5ISNJQV.pdf); "General Budget Proposal of Central Government Summary Table for Annual Expenditures by Agencies FY2020," Directorate-General of Budget, Accounting, and Statistics, Taiwan (https://eng.dgbas.gov.tw/public/Attachment /995162924N41Q4GNS.pdf); "General Budget of Central Government Summary Table for Annual Expenditures by Functions FY2018," Directorate-General of Budget, Accounting, and Statistics, Taiwan (https://eng.dgbas.gov.tw/public/Attach ment/83984949XUOZUPXC.pdf); Flor Wang and Yu Hsiang, "Executive Yuan Passes 2021 Central Government Budget Plan," *Focus Taiwan,* August 13, 2020.

22. Wang Yang-yu, Justin Su, and Elizabeth Hsu, "Legislature Passes Special Budget for F-16 Purchase," *Focus Taiwan,* November 22, 2019.

23. *Annual Report to Congress,* p. 90.

24. "Greater Threat Awareness Needed," editorial, *Taipei Times,* January 24, 2019.

25. Templeman, "The Domestic Politics of Defense Spending."

26. This discussion is based on Drew Thompson, "Hope on the Horizon: Taiwan's Radical New Defense Concept," *War on the Rocks,* October 2, 2018. Former Pentagon officials spoke of the need for Taiwan to "break free of the traditional focus of commanders on big-ticket weapons like tanks and fighter jets." See Steven Lee Myers

and Javier C. Hernandez, "With a Wary Eye on China, Taiwan Moves to Revamp Its Military," *New York Times*, August 30, 2020; Tanner Greer, "Why I Fear for Taiwan: Tanner Greer," *The Scholar's Stage* (blog), September 11, 2020.

27. Ibid.

28. *Annual Report to Congress,* p. 90.

29. David F. Helvey, "Keynote Remarks," delivered at US-Taiwan Defense Industry Conference, Ellicott City, Maryland, October 7, 2019 (http://us-taiwan.org /reports/2019_october07_david_helvey_dod_keynote.pdf).

30. Ibid.

31. Chang Guan Chung, "Opening Remarks: Hand in Hand for the Peace and Stability of the Indo-Pacific Region," US-Taiwan Defense Industry Conference, October 7, 2019 (http://us-taiwan.org/reports/2019_october07_vice_minister_ chang_mnd_keynote.pdf).

32. David F. Helvey, "Closing Keynote Remarks," speech, US-Taiwan Defense Industry Conference, October 6, 2019.

33. Philip Caruso, "Taiwan Needs More Than Election Victories to Fend Off China," *Foreign Policy,* January 17, 2020.

34. Taiwan National Security Survey, Program in Asian Security Studies, Duke University (https://sites.duke.edu/pass/taiwan-national-security-survey/).

Chapter 10

1. G. William Skinner, *Chinese Society in Thailand: An Analytical History* (Cornell University Press, 1957), especially pp. 253–60; and G. William Skinner, *Leadership and Power in the Chinese Community of Thailand* (Cornell University Press, 1958), pp. 148–70.

2. Clifford Geertz, "The Integrative Revolution: Primordial Sentiments and Civil Politics in New States," in *Old Societies and New States,* edited by Clifford Geertz (New York: Free Press, 1963), pp. 259–60.

3. Benedict Anderson, *Imagined Communities: Reflections on the Origin and Spread of Nationalism,* rev. ed. (New York: Verso, 2016), p. 6.

4. Margaret McMillan, *The War That Ended Peace: The Road to 1914* (New York: Random House, 2013, Kindle ed.), loc. 4157.

5. Suisheng Zhao, *Nation-State by Construction: Dynamics of Modern Chinese Nationalism* (Stanford University Press, 2004), pp. 4–5.

6. Linda Colley, *Britons: Forging the Nation, 1707–1837,* rev. ed. (Yale University Press, 2009).

7. James Townsend, "Chinese Nationalism," *Australian Journal of Chinese Affairs,* no. 27 (January 1992), pp. 97–130. Instrumentalists would not regard essentialist elements as irrelevant. But they would treat them as weapons in the struggle to define the parameters of their imagined community. Contenders use essentialist elements that support their instrumentalist version of reality and refute that of their opponents. Yet instrumentalists would reject a claim that essentialist elements are objective categories existing outside of human reality, ones that trap their people into a particular identity.

8. Charter of the United Nations and Statute of the International Court of Justice, San Francisco, 1945.

9. Francis Fukuyama, *State-Building: Governance and World Order in the 21st Century* (Cornell University Press, 2004), p. 6. The emphasis is in the original.

10. Charles Tilley, ed., *The Formation of National States in Western Europe* (Princeton University Press, 1975), p. 42.

11. Fukuyama, *State-Building*, pp. 6–14.

12. The "state" should be distinguished conceptually from "regime," which is the type of political system. Thus three different regimes ruled Taiwan in the twentieth century: Japanese colonialism, KMT authoritarianism, and democracy. I am grateful to an anonymous reviewer for noting this distinction.

13. Stephen D. Krasner, "Building Democracy after Conflict: The Case for Shared Sovereignty," *Journal of Democracy* 16, no. 1 (2005), pp. 70–71.

14. Hurst Hannum, *Autonomy, Sovereignty, and Self-Determination: The Accommodation of Conflicting Rights*, 1st ed. (University of Pennsylvania Press, 1990), p. 15.

15. Brian J. McVeigh, *Nationalisms of Japan: Managing and Mystifying Identity* (New York: Roman and Littlefield, 2004), p. 3.

16. Jill Lepore, *This America: The Case for the Nation* (New York: Liveright Publishing, 2019), p. 26–29, cited sentence on p. 29.

17. Mathew Mathews, ed., *The Singapore Ethnic Mosaic: Many Cultures, One People* (Singapore: World Scientific, 2018), pp. xi–xxxvii.

18. The best Chinese translation of *state* in the sense of governing institution is probably *shizheng jigou* (施政機構), which literally means "administrative machinery" or "administrative institution."

19. Wu Jingrong and Cheng Zhen Qiubian, eds., *Xinshidai Hanying Dacidian* [New Age Chinese-English dictionary] (Beijing: Commercial Press, 2014).

20. On this period, see John Robert Shepherd, *Statecraft and Political Economy on the Taiwan Frontier, 1600–1800* (Stanford University Press, 1993); and Melissa J. Brown, *Is Taiwan Chinese? The Impact of Culture, Power, and Migration on Changing Identities* (University of California Press, 2004).

21. On this cleavage, see Stephane Corcuff, ed., *Memories of the Future: National Identity Issues and the Search for a New Taiwan* (Armonk, N.Y.: M. E. Sharpe, 2002).

22. Denny Roy, *Taiwan: A Political History* (Cornell University Press, 2002). Hoover Institution scholar Hsiao-ting Lin called it an "accidental state." See his *Accidental State: Chiang Kai-shek, the United States, and the Making of Taiwan* (Harvard University Press, 2016).

23. Jay Taylor, *The Generalissimo's Son: Chiang Ching-kuo and the Revolutions in China and Taiwan* (Harvard University Press, 2000); Lloyd E. Eastman, "Who Lost China? Chiang Kai-shek Testifies," *China Quarterly*, no. 88 (December 1981), pp. 658–68; Ramon H. Myers and Hsiao-ting Lin, "Starting Anew on Taiwan: Chiang Kai-shek and Taiwan in 1949," *Hoover Digest*, April 2008; Peter Chen-main Wang, "A Bastion Created, A Regime Reformed, An Economy Reengineered, 1949–1970," in *Taiwan: A New History*, edited by Murray A. Rubenstein (Armonk, N.Y.: M. E. Sharpe, 1999), pp. 320–38.

24. On the shifting Taiwan political economy, see Thomas B. Gold, *State and Society in the Taiwan Miracle*, 1st ed. (Armonk, N.Y.: M. E. Sharpe, 1997).

25. To be sure, tensions surfaced among the different elements of the regime, in part because they had different tasks. The national-security establishment of the state and the economic technocracy did not always see eye to eye. Export-led growth required greater flexibility in the circulation of people and money, for example.

26. Edwin A. Winckler, "Institutionalization and Participation on Taiwan: From Hard to Soft Authoritarianism?" *China Quarterly*, no. 99 (September 1984), pp. 481–99. On the impact of even limited elections on the political system, see Shelley Rigger, *Politics in Taiwan: Voting for Democracy* (New York: Routledge, 1999).

27. Richard C. Bush, *At Cross Purposes: US-Taiwan Relations, 1942–2000* (Armonk, N.Y.: M. E. Sharpe, 2004), pp. 85–123.

28. Steven E. Phillips, *Between Assimilation and Independence: The Taiwanese Encounter Nationalist China, 1945–1950* (Stanford University Press, 2003), p. 43. On the growth of Taiwanese identity before 1945, at least among the elite, see Evan N. Dawley, "The Question of Identity in Recent Scholarship on China," *China Quarterly*, no. 198 (June 2009), pp. 442–52.

29. Christopher Hughes, "Post-Nationalist Taiwan," in *The Politics of Modern Taiwan: Critical Issues in Modern Politics*, vol. 1, *Nationalism and National Identity*, edited by Dafydd Fell (New York: Routledge, 2008) pp. 217–19.

30. Hill Gates, "Ethnicity and Social Class," in *The Anthropology of Taiwanese Society*, edited by Emily Martin Ahern and Hill Gates (Stanford University Press, 1981), pp. 241–86.

31. For the case of Peng Ming-min, who tried to make public a manifesto for independence, see Peng Ming-min, *A Taste of Freedom: Memoirs of a Formosan Independence Leader* (New York: Holt, Rinehart and Winston, 1972).

32. Joseph R. Allen, *Taipei: City of Displacements* (University of Washington Press, 2012), pp. 81–87.

33. Alan M. Wachman, *Taiwan: National Identity and Democratization* (Armonk, N.Y.: M. E. Sharpe, 1994), pp. 106, 119.

34. "Changsuo di Beiai: Sheng wei Taiwanren di beiai" ["A place of sorrow: The sorrow of being born a Taiwanese"], in Lee Teng-hui, *Jingying Da Taiwan* [*Managing Great Taiwan*] (Taipei: Yuanliu Publishing, 1995), pp. 469–83; "Son of Taiwan" is the English translation of the title of Chen Shui-bian, *Taiwan zhi Zi* (Taipei: Chenxing Publishing, 2000).

35. Hughes, "Post-Nationalist Taiwan," p. 228.

36. Richard C. Bush, *Untying the Knot: Making Peace in the Taiwan Strait* (Brookings Institution Press, 2005), pp. 45–71; Da-Chi Liao, Boyu Chen, and Chichen Huang, "The Decline of 'Chinese Identity' in Taiwan?!: An Analysis of Survey Data from 1992 to 2012," *East Asia* 30 (October 2013), pp. 273–90.

37. Richard C. Bush, *Uncharted Strait: The Future of China-Taiwan Relations* (Brookings Institution Press, 2013), pp. 80–81.

38. Hughes, "Post-Nationalist Taiwan," pp. 218–33.

39. "Taiwan Telephone and Mobile Phone Interview Survey of the Presidential Satisfaction: The Twenty-Second Wave," Taiwan's Election and Democratization Study, National Chengchi University, survey conducted December 2017 (http://teds.nccu.edu.tw/main.php).

40. Shelley Rigger, "The China Impact on Taiwan's Generational Politics," in *Taiwan and the "China Impact,"* edited by Gunter Schubert (New York: Routledge, 2016), p. 88.

41. Before democratization, this problem did not exist terminologically. The contrast was between was "*benshengren*" and "*waishengren*," not "Taiwanese" and "mainlanders" or "Chinese."

42. Alaister Iain Johnston and George Yin, "Meilidao 2018 Liangan Guanxi Mindiao (1): Daduoshu Taiwan Minzhong Shifou Zhi Rentong Taiwan, bu Rentong Zhongguo?" [Formosa 2018 Cross-Strait Relations Survey: (1) Do the majority of the Taiwan public identify with Taiwan but not with China?] *Meilidao Dianzibao* [Formosa Magazine], April 17, 2018.

43. Zheng Sufen, "Jiexi 'Taiwanren/Zhongguoren' renting de chixu yubianyi" [Analyzing continuity and change in "Taiwanese/Chinese" identity], paper presented at the "Symposium on Taiwan's Democratization and Free Elections" at the Election Study Center of National Chengchi University, May 25, 2019.

44. "Taiwan Telephone and Mobile Phone Interview Survey of the Presidential Satisfaction: The Sixth Wave," Taiwan's Election and Democratization Study, National Chengchi University, survey conducted December 2013 (http://teds.nccu.edu.tw/main.php).

45. Yang Zhong, "Explaining National Identity Shift in Taiwan," *Journal of Contemporary China* 25, no. 99 (February 2016), p. 341. Yang infers that this result means that Taiwan people "reject the notion of a separate and distinctive Taiwanese ethno-cultural identity." That is somewhat belied by the results of a different question in the survey: "In your opinion, which of the following is the closest to the meaning of being Taiwanese?" Among respondents, 7.7 percent said "people with common blood," 39.2 percent said "people who identify with Taiwanese culture and history," and 44.9 percent said "people who live and work in Taiwan."

46. Brown, *Is Taiwan Chinese?*; Chen Shu-juo, "How Han Are Taiwanese Han? Genetic Inference of Plains Indigenous Ancestry among Taiwanese Han and Its Implications for Taiwan Identity," Ph.D. diss., Stanford University, 2009. There is a similar debate in mainland China, where those who assert the predominance of Han ancestry must face up to—or ignore—DNA evidence that many "Han" people carry the genes of peoples from today's Southeast Asia and the Pacific Islands; see Yinghong Cheng, "DNA and the Globalization of Humanity," *AsiaGlobal Online*, January 17, 2019.

47. This was a question posed by a Taiwanese specialist on popular culture at a conference I attended.

48. Robert P. Weller, "Identity and Social Change in Taiwanese Religion," in *Taiwan: A New History*, edited by Murray A. Reubinstein (Armonk, N.Y.: M. E. Sharpe, 1999), pp. 358–61.

49. Grace Tsoi, "Taiwan Has Its Own Textbook Controversy," *Foreign Policy*, July 21, 2015.

50. "Only by Removing Tsai Ing-wen from Office Can We Rectify and Reinstate Guidelines for High School History Textbooks," editorial, *China Times*, August 12, 2019, excerpt at the KMT Official Website.

51. Su started his political career as an opponent of Japanese colonial rule but later was drawn to Marxism and aligned himself with the CCP. By the time Chiang Kai-shek's forces were defeated in 1949, Su had seen enough of the CPP's brutality. He moved to Taiwan but quickly soured on the KMT regime. In 1952 he joined a plot to assassinate Chiang and was fortunate to have escaped to Japan after the plot was discovered. See "Su Beng, a Father of Taiwan Independence, Dies at 100," *New York Times*, October 4, 2019.

52. Su Beng, *Taiwan's 400 Year history: The Origins and Development of the Taiwanese Society and People* (Washington, D.C.: Taiwanese Culture Grass Roots Association, 1986), p. 5. Su's Taiwan-as-colony framework has been elaborated by other scholars, most notably by the late Bruce Jacobs. See Bruce Jacobs, "Whither Taiwanization? The Colonization, Democratization, and Taiwanization of Taiwan," *Japanese Journal of Political Science* 14, no. 4 (2013), pp. 567–86.

53. "The Liberty Times Editorial: Chiang Kai-shek's Place in History," *Taipei Times*, April 11, 2017.

54. "The Liberty Times Editorial: Returning Taiwan to Taiwanese," *Taipei Times*, December 18, 2015.

55. "Guomindang zhuxi Lian Zhan zai Beijing daxue de yanjiang" [KMT Chairman Lien Chan's speech at Peking University], May 5, 2005, Radio Free Asia; emphasis added.

56. Chang Ya-chung, "A Modest Proposal for a Basic Agreement on Peaceful Cross-Strait Development," *Journal of Current Chinese Affairs* 39, no. 1 (2010), pp. 133–48.

57. "Paving the Way for a Sustainable Taiwan" (full text of Chen Shui-bian's 2004 inaugural speech), *Taipei Times*, May 21, 2004.

58. "Ma Ying-Jeou, 'Inaugural Address,' May 20, 2008," US-China Institute at the University of Southern California. Sun Yat-sen was the founder of the KMT.

59. "Full Text of President Ma Ying-jeou's Inaugural Address," *Focus Taiwan*, May 20, 2012.

60. Lin Liang-sheng, "KMT's Chiang Says He Is 'Taiwanese and Chinese,'" *Taipei Times*, March 19, 2020.

61. Shelley Rigger, "Disaggregating the Concept of National Identity," *Asia Program Special Report*, no. 114 (Washington, D.C.: Woodrow Wilson International Center for Scholars, 2003), pp. 17–21.

62. "President Tsai Addresses Copenhagen Democracy Summit Via Video," *Focus Taiwan*, June 19, 2020.

63. On Ma's negative views of Tsai's policies, see Ma Ying-jeou, "Cross-Strait Relations at a Critical Time," lecture delivered at the Taoyuan Campus of Ming Chuan University, May 23, 2020; copy in author's files.

Chapter 11

1. Richard C. Bush, *Untying the Knot: Making Peace in the Taiwan Strait* (Brookings Institution Press, 2005), pp. 39–54, on which this section is based.

2. Ko Shu-ling "'State to State' Theory Is Dead, Ma Says," *Taipei Times*, September 4, 2008.

3. "Join in a Common Struggle for Realizing the Nation's Great Rejuvenation and Promoting the Motherland's Peaceful Reunification," speech by Xi Jinping at the Rally to Commemorate the 40th Anniversary of Issuing the "Letter to Taiwan Compatriots," January 2, 2019, *Xinhua Domestic Service*, translation by Open Source Enterprise, translation in author's files.

4. Hurst Hannum, *Autonomy, Sovereignty, and Self-Determination: The Accommodation of Conflicting Rights*, 1st ed. (University of Pennsylvania Press, 1990), p. 15.

5. Bush, *Untying the Knot*, p. 85.

6. Taiwan National Security Survey, 2017, Program in Asian Security Studies, Duke University (https://sites.duke.edu/pass/taiwan-national-security-survey/).

7. The National Assembly had only limited powers: selecting the president indirectly (like the U.S. Electoral College) and considering constitutional amendments. In June 2005, it was suspended pending national unification.

8. Cited in Shelley Rigger, *From Opposition to Power: Taiwan's Democratic Progressive Party* (Boulder, Colo.: Lynne Rienner Publishers, 2001), p. 125.

9. For the PRC to concede sovereignty for Taiwan would not have ruled out unification, but it did rule out using one country, two systems as the basis.

10. "Closing Remarks to the Thirteenth Plenum of the National Unification Council," July 22, 1998, in *President Lee Teng-hui's Selected Addresses and Messages: 1998* (Taipei: Government information Office, 1999), pp. 113–20.

11. Montevideo Convention on the Rights and Duties of States, signed December 26, 1933 and entered into force on December 26, 1934.

12. "Zongtong Jieshou Deguo zhi Yin Zhuanfang" [The president receives an exclusive interview by Deutsche Velle], July 9, 1999, Office of the President website (www.president.gov.tw/NEWS/5749); "Interview of Taiwan President Lee Teng-hui with *Deutsche Welle* Radio," July 9, 1999, *New Taiwan: Ilha Formosa* (www.taiwandc.org/nws-9926.htm).

13. For historical background on the relationship between a state and its territory, see Hendrik Spruyt, *The Sovereign State and Its Competitors: An Analysis of Systems Change* (Princeton University Press, 1994).

14. For a detailed account of the process that led to the statement, see Bush, *Untying the Knot*, pp. 55–57, 218–21. The Clinton administration dispatched me, in my capacity as chairman of the American Institute in Taiwan, to convey its views about the absence of consultation on the statement and the serious situation it had created.

15. Taiwan (Republic of China)'s Constitution of 1947 with Amendments through 2005, ConstituteProject.org); Su Chi, *Taiwan's Relations with Mainland China: A Tail Wagging Two Dogs* (New York: Routledge, 2008), pp. 61–62. Su's account is the best available on this episode.

16. Statement by the President Truman on Korea, June 27, 1950, History and

Public Policy Program Digital Archive, Wilson Center. Harry S. Truman, 1945 to 1953 (see also www.trumanlibrary.gov/library/public-papers/173/statement-president-situation-korea).

17. For Japan's treaty with the ROC, see Treaty of Peace between the Republic of China and Japan, signed at Taipei, April 28, 1952, Taiwan Documents Project.

18. For the case of the Taiwan Civil Government, see Brian Hioe, "Taiwan Civil Government Proves a Peculiarly Taiwanese Example of Conspiracy Theories Found Worldwide," *New Bloom*, May 21, 2018; and Jason Pan, "Heads of Taiwan Civil Government Released on Bail," *Taipei Times*, October 5, 2018.

19. Additional Articles to the Constitution of the Republic of China (Sixth Revision, 2000), Government Information Office, Republic of China, Taiwan Documents Project. This round of amendments shifted the power of amending the constitution and altering the national territory from the National Assembly to the Legislative Yuan, because in 1999 the National Assembly had tried to extend their terms in office, which provoked a public backlash. See Shelley Rigger, "The Politics of Constitutional Revision," in *Taiwan's Democracy: Economic and Political Challenges*, edited by Robert Ash, John Garver, and Penelope Prime (New York: Routledge, 2013), pp. 37–38.

20. Based on the traditional KMT view that the ROC was the government of all of China, including the provinces on the mainland that it did not control, there needed to be a provincial government for Taiwan. Such a government existed in practice until 1998, after which all of its functions were transferred to the central government. But so far it has not been formally abolished because the position of "governor of Taiwan province" is mentioned in the ROC constitution.

21. "DPP Resolution on Taiwan's Future," TaiwanDC.org, May 8, 1999.

22. "The DPP Platform," DPP 2000, an internet resource developed by Shelley Rigger, Davidson College, copy in author's files.

23. Taiwan (Republic of China)'s Constitution of 1947 with Amendments through 2005.

24. "Ma on Cross-Strait Relations: One Republic of China, Two Areas," KMT Official Website, March 3, 2010.

25. "Full Text of President Ma Ying-Jeou's Inaugural Address," *Focus Taiwan*, May 20, 2012.

26. Sherry Hsiao, "Beijing Needs to Accept Complete 'Consensus': Ma," *Taipei Times*, July 7, 2020; emphasis added.

27. Zheng Sufen, "Jiexi 'Taiwanren/Zhongguoren' renting de chixu yubianyi" [Analyzing continuity and change in "Taiwanese/Chinese" Identity], paper presented at the "Symposium on Taiwan's Democratization and Free Elections" at the Election Study Center of National Chengchi University, May 25, 2019; copy in author's files.

28. "Ma Ying-Jeou, 'Inaugural Address,' May 20, 2008," US-China Institute, at the University of Southern California.

29. Liu Chien-kuo and others, "Language: A Tool for Messages or Identity,"

Taipei Times, January 18, 2017; Lee Min-yung, "Taiwan Needs to Develop Its Own Culture, *Taipei Times,* December 24, 2017.

30. "DPP Resolution on Taiwan's Future," *New Taiwan, Ilha Formosa.*

31. "Ma Ying-Jeou, 'Inaugural Address,' May 20, 2008," USC US-China Institute. As noted in the previous chapter, in 2020 KMT Chairman Johnny Chiang said he was "Taiwanese by birth, Chinese by ethnicity, and a citizen of the ROC." See Lin Liang-sheng, "KMT's Chiang Says He Is 'Taiwanese and Chinese,'" *Taipei Times,* March 19, 2020.

32. EDITORIAL: "Time for Taiwan (Republic of China)," *Taipei Times,* August 24, 2020.

Chapter 12

1. J. Michael Cole, "China Hardening Rhetoric toward Taiwan Foreshadows Increased Tensions," *Global Taiwan Brief* 5, no. 9 (2020); John Dotson, "Military Activity and Political Signaling in the Taiwan Strait in Early 2020," *China Brief* 20, no. 6 (2020).

2. "PLA Conducts Combat-Ready Patrols and Exercises in Taiwan Straits— Ministry of National Defense," *China Military Online,* September 18, 2020; Michael Mazza, "Signaling from Chinese Military Exercises around Taiwan," *Global Taiwan Brief* 5, no. 19 (October 7, 2020).

3. J. Michael Cole, "China Acting on 'Lebanization' Threat against Taiwan," *Taiwan Sentinel,* May 18, 2018.

4. Ian Easton, "Taiwan's Anti-Invasion Strategy: Elevating Defense Capabilities from Crisis to Wartime," Project 2049 Institute, March 7, 2017.

5. Scott L. Kastner, "Is the Taiwan Strait Still a Flash Point? Rethinking the Prospects for Armed Conflict between China and Taiwan," *International Security* 40, no. 3 (2015–2016), p. 84.

6. Bonnie Glaser and Matthew P. Funaiole, "China's Provocations around Taiwan Aren't a Crisis," *Foreign Policy,* May 15, 2020.

7. June Teufel Dreyer, "The Big Squeeze: Beijing's Anaconda Strategy to Force Taiwan to Surrender," Foreign Policy Research Institute, August 13, 2018.

8. Sean Lin, "China Ramping Up Military Threats: Yen," *Taipei Times,* November 13, 2019.

9. Keoni Everington, "China Fires Long March Rocket Directly Over Taiwan," *Taiwan News,* September 15, 2020.

10. Sun Tzu and Sun Pin, *The Complete Art of War: Sun Tzu, Sun Pin,* translated by Ralph D. Sawyer (Boulder, Colo.: Westview Press, 1996), p. 50. The full quotation is, "Attaining one hundred victories in one hundred battles is not the pinnacle of excellence. Subjugating the enemy's army without fighting is the true pinnacle of excellence." The original Chinese is "是故百戰百勝, 非善之善者也; 不戰而屈人之兵, 善之善者也."

11. Alastair Iain Johnston, *Cultural Realism: Strategic Culture and Grand Strategy in Chinese History* (Princeton University Press, 1995), pp. 107–08.

12. On the danger of accidental clashes, see Brendan Taylor, *Dangerous Decade: Taiwan's Security and Crisis Management*, International Institute for Strategic Studies (London: Routledge, 2019). See also Glaser and Funaiole, "China's Provocations around Taiwan Aren't a Crisis"; Gerry Shih, "Taiwan Says Threat of Military Clash with China Is 'on the Rise,'" *Washington Post*, July 22, 2020.

13. In my 2013 book, *Uncharted Strait*, I warn of the possibility of just such a strategy employing intimidation and pressure if China could not advance its political objectives through persuasion, as it tried and failed to do during the administration of Ma Ying-jeou. See Richard C. Bush, *Uncharted Strait: The Future of China-Taiwan Relations* (Brookings Institution Press, 2013), pp. 137–58.

14. Nathan Beauchamp-Mustafaga, "Cognitive Domain Operations: The PLA's New Holistic Concept for Influence Operations," *China Brief* 19, no. 16, September 6, 2019.

15. Vincent W. F. Chen, "Republic of China, Taiwan's Unique Status Shall Not Perish: CCP's Influence Operations against Taiwan," paper presented at the Jamestown Foundation's Ninth Annual China Defense and Security Conference, Washington, D.C., October 15, 2019; copy of speech in author's files.

16. Ibid.

17. Bush, *Uncharted Strait*, pp. 49–51.

18. "Yearly Statistics: Visitor Arrival by Residence," Tourism Statistics, Tourism Bureau, Ministry of Communication and Transportation, Republic of China, 2018.

19. "Monthly Statistics: Visitor Arrivals by Residence," Tourism Statistics, Tourism Bureau, Ministry of Communication and Transportation, Republic of China, 2018.

20. "Chinese Tourist Numbers Declined 68% Last Month," *Taipei Times*, October 19, 2019.

21. Ian C. Forsyth, "Analyzing China's 31 Measures for Taiwan," *China-US Focus*, April 24, 2018. See also Zhu Songlin, "Thirty-One Measures: From Ideas and Principles to Policies," *China-US Focus*, May 28, 2018.

22. "Opening Statement of Syaru Shirley Lin," U.S.-China Economic and Security Review Commission, Hearing on "U.S.-China Relations in 2019: A Year in Review," Washington, D.C., September 4, 2019.

23. Ku Chuan, Shen Peng-ta, and Joseph Yeh, "China's '26 Measures' Seek to Influence Elections: Taiwan Government," *Focus Taiwan*, October 4, 2019.

24. Lee Hsin-fang and Jake Chung, "New Policies to Counter China Incentives," *Taipei Times*, March 17, 2018.

25. "Taiwan Brain Drain Reaches 1 Million," *China Post*, April 28, 2019; "MAC Announces Report on the Implementation Results of the 'Eight Strategies for a Stronger Taiwan: Responses to Mainland China's 31 Taiwan-Related Measures,'" press release, Mainland Affairs Council, September 18, 2018; Kensaku Ihara, "Taiwan to Call Businesses Home from China, Says Economic Minister," *Nikkei Asian Review*, March 29, 2018.

26. Miao Zong-han and Chung Yu-chen, "67 Taiwanese Missing in China since Tsai Took Office: Agency," *Focus Taiwan*, September 19, 2019; Miao Zong-han and Matthew Mazzetta, "China Confirms Detentions of Three Taiwanese," *Focus*

Taiwan, November 13, 2019; Russell Hsiao, "Fortnightly Review: Taiwan Academic Missing in China as Broader Clamp Down of Foreign Nationals by Chinese Authorities on National Security Grounds," *Global Taiwan Brief* 4, no. 21 (2019) (http://globaltaiwan.org/2019/11/vol-4-issue-21/#RussellHsiao11062019).

27. Abraham Gerber, "Taipei Urged to Be Tough on Rights Advocate's Vanishing," *Taipei Times*, March 25, 2017; Chris Horton, "China Sentences Taiwanese Human Rights Activist in Subversion Case," *New York Times*, November 27, 2017; J. Michael Cole, "What Lee Ming-che's Show Trial Tells Us," *Taiwan Sentinel*, September 12, 2017.

28. On the law, see Donald Clarke, "Hong Kong's National Security Law: An Assessment," *China Leadership Monitor*, July 13, 2019.

29. Ibid.

30. Li Zhenguang, "Xianggang Guoanfa Jiang Yancheng 'Taidu' Luangang Xingjing" ["Hong Kong's National Security Law will severely punish 'Taiwan Independence' for acts of chaos in Hong Kong,"] *Global Times*, July 4, 2020. The law's use of the term "external forces" in this provision was a reference to Taiwan, since in the PRC view Taiwan as a part of China and not a foreign entity.

31. Peng Wan-hsin, "Taiwanese Risk Deportation to China," *Taipei Times*, July 13, 2020.

32. Kathrin Hille, "China Is Influencing Taiwan's Elections—through TV," OZY, July 26, 2019.

33. J. Michael Cole, "An Analysis of Possible Chinese Influence Operations against Taiwan: The Want-Want Case," *Prospect Foundation Newsletter* 9, May 6, 2019.

34. Ibid.

35. Stacy Hsu and Chiang Yi-ching, "China Pressured Media Outlets in Taiwan: U.S. Human Rights Report," *Focus Taiwan*, March 12, 2020.

36. Hille, "China Is Influencing Taiwan's Elections."

37. Luke Sabatier and Emerson Lim, "Chinese Official Bashes U.S. at Cross-Strait Media Gathering," *Focus Taiwan*, May 12, 2019.

38. Central Intelligence Agency, "Taiwan," *CIA World Factbook* (www.cia.gov/library/publications/resources/the-world-factbook/index.html).

39. Lin Chia-nan, "False Information on the Rise in Taiwan: Academic," *Taipei Times*, September 28, 2019.

40. Lauren Dickey, *Taiwan Security Brief: Disinformation, Cybersecurity, and Energy Security*, edited by Yuki Tatsumi, Pamela Kennedy, and Jason Li (Washington, D.C.: Henry L. Stimson Center, September 2019), pp. 11–32; cited passage on p. 16, brackets in original.

41. Paul Huang, "Chinese Cyber-Operatives Boosted Taiwan's Insurgent Candidate," *Foreign Policy*, June 26, 2019.

42. Elaine Hou and Ko Lin, "AIT Posts Chairman Moriarty's Interview on Facebook Page," *Focus Taiwan*, November 17, 2018.

43. "Gov't Is the Least Qualified to Determine What News Is True or Fake," editorial, *China Times*, December 18, 2018 (www1.kmt.org.tw/english/page.aspx?type=article&mnum=113&anum=22460).

44. Dickey, "Confronting the Challenge of Online Disinformation in Taiwan," in *Disinformation, Cybersecurity, and Energy Security,* pp. 15–17. See also, Facebook, "Defending Election Integrity in Taiwan," October 2020.

45. Jason Lanier and E. Glen Wey, "How Civic Technology Can Help Stop a Pandemic," *Foreign Affairs,* March 20, 2020.

46. Lyman P. Van Slyke, *Enemies and Friends: The United Front in Chinese Communist History* (Stanford University Press, 1967).

47. Christine Loh, *Underground Front: The Chinese Communist Party in Hong Kong* (University of Hong Kong Press, 2010).

48. State Council Information Office of the People's Republic of China, "China's National Defense in the New Era," July 24, 2019.

49. Chen, "Republic of China, Taiwan's Unique Status Shall Not Perish."

50. At the time, I worked on the staff of the Asia subcommittee of the House Committee on Foreign Affairs and organized a hearing on the Liu killing.

51. David E. Kaplan, *Fires of the Dragon* (New York: Scribner, 1992).

52. Teng Pei-ju, "Pro-China Political Party Backs Han for Taiwan President," *Taiwan News,* August 11, 2019.

53. Chen, "Republic of China, Taiwan's Unique Status Shall Not Perish"; Gary Schmitt and Mark Mazza, "Blinding the Enemy: CCP Interference in Taiwan's Democracy," Global Taiwan Institute, October 2019.

54. Emerson Lim, "KMT Pulls Out of Cross-Strait Forum over Chinese TV Comment," *Focus Taiwan,* September 14, 2020.

55. Luo Cheng-tsung, "Taiwan Can't Control Its Temples and China Knows It," Ketagalan Media, December 28, 2019.

56. Chen Yu-fu, "Chinese Troupe to Stage Unification-Themed Show," *Taipei Times,* October 28, 2019; "Dance Tour a 'United Front' Tactic," editorial, *Taipei Times,* November 1, 2019.

57. Sean Lin, "Legislature Passes Anti-Infiltration Act," *Taipei Times,* January 1, 2020.

58. Tsai Peng-min, Joe Yeh, and Frances Huang, "Business Groups Fear Chilling Effect From Anti-Infiltration Act," *Focus Taiwan,* January 1, 2020.

59. Yeh Su-ping and others, "President Reassures Public after Anti-Infiltration Act Takes Effect," *Focus Taiwan,* January 15, 2020.

60. Andy Greenberg, "Chinese Hackers Have Pillaged Taiwan's Semiconductor Industry," *Wired,* August 6, 2020.

61. Timothy Ferry, "Cybercrime Poses a Mounting Problem in Taiwan," *Taiwan Business Topics,* May 17, 2018; Philip Hsu, "Taiwan's Emerging Push for Cyber Autonomy," *China Brief* 18, no. 13 (2018); Lee Hsin-Yin, "U.S.-Taiwan Cooperation Crucial for Global Cybersecurity: AIT Head," *Focus Taiwan,* September 17, 2019.

62. Lee, "U.S.-Taiwan Cooperation Crucial: AIT Head."

63. Ibid.; Timothy Ferry, "Government Seeks to Thwart Cyber Threats," *Taiwan Business Topics,* May 17, 2018; Holmes Liao, "Mitigating China's Threat to Taiwanese Telecom Networks," *Prospect Foundation Newsletter* 3, February 19, 2019.

64. Timothy Ferry, "Taiwan Wakes Up to the Need for Stricter Cybersecurity,"

Taiwan Business Topics, May 11, 2018; Ferry, "Government Seeks to Thwart Cyber Threats;" Russell Hsiao, "Taiwan Launches National Communications Reliability and Cyber Security," *Global Taiwan Brief* 23, no. 23 (2018); Laney Zhang, "Taiwan: New Cybersecurity Law Takes Effect," Library of Congress, Global Legal Monitor, January 30, 2019; Lee Hsin-fang and Sean Lin, "Cabinet Says Ban Aimed at Boosting National Security," *Taipei Times*, January 25, 2019; Sean Lin, "Cabinet Unveils Cybersecurity Guidance," *Taipei Times,* April 20, 2019; Lee Hsin-fang, "Tighter Cybersecurity System Proposed," *Taipei Times*, May 27, 2019; Russel Hsiao, "United States and Taiwan Step Up Cybersecurity Cooperation amid Uptick in China's Cyber Offensive," *Global Taiwan Brief* 4, no. 19 (2019).

65. Lawrence Chung, "Taiwan Braced for Wave of Cyberattacks from Mainland China Ahead of Local Elections," *South China Morning Post*, September 20, 2018. On the cyber threat to Taiwan's telecommunications networks, see Liao, "Mitigating China's Threat to Taiwanese Telecom Networks."

Chapter 13

1. Kharis Templeman, "How Taiwan Stands Up to China," *Journal of Democracy* 31, no. 3 (July 2020), p. 86.

2. "Sheping: Zhongguo Lishi Juebuhui Kuanshu Tuidong Fenlie di Ren" ["Editorial: Chinese history will never forgive promoters of separatism,"] *Huanqiu Shibao*, July 31, 2020 (https://huanqiu.com/article/3zGnd9P3ng).

3. Larry Diamond, *The Spirit of Democracy: The Struggle to Build Free Societies throughout the World* (New York: Times Books, 2008), pp. 88–112; Linda Chao and Ramon Myers, *The First Chinese Democracy: Political Life in the Republic of China on Taiwan* (Johns Hopkins University Press, 1997).

4. "2018 Human Rights Report (Taiwan Part)," American Institute in Taiwan, March 15, 2019.

5. Kharis Templeman, "The Party System Before and After the 2016 Election," in *Dynamics of Democracy in Taiwan: The Ma Ying-jeou Years*, edited by Kharis Templeman, Yun-han Chu, and Larry Diamond (Boulder, CO: Lynne Reiner Publishers, 2020), p. 125.

6. Pippa Norris, *Making Democratic Governance Work: How Regimes Shape Prosperity, Welfare, and Peace* (Cambridge University Press, 2012), pp. 58–59.

7. Larry Diamond, "Facing Up to the Democratic Deficit," *Journal of Democracy* 26, no. 1 (2015), pp. 141–55, cited passage on p. 152.

8. "Corruption Perceptions Index," Transparency International, 2019.

9. See, for example, Chuck Freilich, "This Is Israel's Last Ever Zionist Election," *Haaretz*, September 12, 2019.

10. Susan Rice, "A Divided America Is a National Security Threat," *New York Times*, September 22, 2020.

11. The 1946 constitution was adopted in December 1946, promulgated on January 1, 1947, and went into effect on December 25, 1947.

12. Ch'ien Tuan-sheng, *The Government and Politics of China, 1912–1949* (Stanford University Press, 1950), pp. 317–30.

13. On this type of political transition, see James Loxton, "Authoritarian Successor Parties," *Journal of Democracy* 26, no. 3 (2015), pp. 157–70; Mikael Mattlin, *Politicized Society: The Long Shadow of Taiwan's One-Party Legacy* (Copenhagen: NIAS Press, 2011).

14. "DPP Lawmakers Want Name Change for Academia Sinica," *Focus Taiwan*, March 9, 2020.

15. Ku Chuan, Chen Chun-hua, and Lee Hsin-Yin, "Resolutions Passed to Highlight 'Taiwan' on Passport, CAL Jet," *Focus Taiwan*, July 22, 2020; "Taiwan to Change Passport, Fed Up with Confusion with China," Reuters, September 2, 2020.

16. "Taiwan Lianheguo Xiejinhui: Jianzhang" [Taiwan United Nations: Alliance General regulations], (www.taiwan-un-alliance.org.tw/document/intro.htm.

17. "If names be not rectified, then words are not appropriate. If words are not appropriate, then deeds are not accomplished," Confucius, *The Analects*, translated by Raymond Dawson (Oxford University Press, 1993), p. 49.

18. Don Shapiro, "Taiwan Shows Its Mettle in Coronavirus Crisis While the WHO Is MIA," Brookings Institution, March 19, 2020.

19. Yun-han Chu and others, "Re-assessing the Popular Foundation of Asian Democracies: Findings from Four Waves of the Asian Barometer Survey," Working Paper Series 120, Asian Barometer, 2016.

20. World Values Survey, "Taiwan, 2012," study 552, vol. 20180912 (www.worldvaluessurvey.org/WVSDocumentationWV6.jsp; click on "WV6_Results_Taiwan 2012_v20180912").

21. Yun-han Chu and Min-hua Huang, "The Meanings of Democracy: Solving an Asian Puzzle," *Journal of Democracy* 21, no. 4 (2010), pp. 114–22, results on p. 118.

22. World Values Survey, "Taiwan, 2012."

23. Corruption Perceptions Index," *Transparency International*, 2019. Information concerning Taiwan can be found at www.transparency.org/en/cpi/2019/results/twn#details, as well as access to the global data set. The CPI draws upon a number of surveys to derive a composite index that reflects the views of experts and business executives on the level of corruption of a country's public sector.

24. Jason Pan, "Five Politicians Charged with Graft," *Taipei Times*, September 22, 2020.

25. Taiwan people seem to be fairly uniform when it came to membership in secular, voluntary social groups. That is, they had a fairly high rate of nonparticipation. Only for sports and recreation organizations did more than 25 percent of those surveyed say they were "active members." Religion is the exception to this pattern of social activity. Ibid.

26. Yun-han Chu and Wen-chin Wu, "Sources of Regime Legitimacy in East Asian Societies," Asian Barometer Survey, Working Paper 135, Asian Barometer, p. 20.

27. Yu-tzung Chang and Yun-han Chu, "Assessing Support for Democracy," in *Dynamics of Democracy in Taiwan*, p. 241.

28. Thomas Carothers and Andrew O'Donohue, *Democracies Divided: The Global Challenge of Political Polarization* (Brookings Institution Press, 2019), pp.

6–8. The quoted passage is from Murat Somer and Jennifer McCoy, "Déjà vu? Polarization and Endangered Democracies in the 21st Century," *American Behavioral Scientist*, no. 62 (January 2018), pp. 3–15, from which Carothers and O'Donohue draw.

29. Larry Diamond, *Developing Democracy: Toward Consolidation* (Johns Hopkins University Press, 1999), pp. 100–101.

30. "2016 Taiwan Legislative Elections," Wikipedia, September 16, 2020.

31. Chiu Yen-ling and Sherry Hsiao, "KMT Bid to Block Legislative Votes Fails," *Taipei Times*, June 30, 2020.

32. Kuo Chien-shen and others, "Legislators Fight, Hundreds Protest as Controversial Nominees Confirmed," *Focus Taiwan*, July 17, 2020.

33. Lu Ling, "A Story of Old Overseas Taiwanese Independence Activists," Ketagalan Media, July 3, 2019.

34. I am grateful to an outside reviewer for illuminating this point.

35. "DPP's Oversight Bill Flawed, Sunflower Activist Says," *Taipei Times*, April 25, 2016.

36. Isaac Shih-hao Huang and Shing-yuan Sheng, "Legislative Politics," in *Dynamics of Democracy in Taiwan*, pp. 177–78.

37. World Values Survey, "Taiwan, 2012, Questions 96–101."

38. Richard C. Bush, "Taiwan's Local Elections, Explained," Brookings Institution, December 5, 2018.

39. Ching-hsin You, "Parties, Partisans, and Independents in Taiwan," in *The Taiwan Voter*, edited by Christopher H. Achen and T. Y. Wang (University of Michigan Press, 2017).

40. "The TPP Might Be Good for Taiwan," editorial, *Taipei Times*, October 24, 2019.

41. "Taiwan's Legislative Yuan: Oversight or Overreach?," Brookings Institution, Center for East Asia Policy Studies, June 23, 2014.

42. Matthew Strong, "Taiwan Requires Referendum for Political Agreements with China," *Taiwan News*, March 28, 2019.

43. Sean Lin, "Rules for Deals with China Beefed Up," *Taipei Times*, June 1, 2019.

44. Francis Fukuyama, *Political Order and Political Decay*, vol. 2, *From the Industrial Revolution to the Globalization of Democracy* (New York: Farrar, Straus and Giroux, 2014), pp. 39, 488–505. See also George Tsebelis, "Decision Making in Political Systems: Veto Players in Presidentialism, Parliamentarism, Multicameralism, and Multipartyism," *British Journal of Political Science* 25, no. 3 (1995), pp. 289–325.

45. This tension between participation and institutions was the theme of Samuel Huntington's classic work, *Political Order in Changing Societies* (Yale University Press, 1968).

46. Huang Min-Hua, "The Rise of the Internet and Changing Political Participation in Asia," working paper, Brookings Institution, Center for East Asia Policy Studies, June 2015, pp. 5, 25–26; copy in author's files. For a later presentation of the argument, see Huang Min-Hua and others, "How Does Rising Internet Usage Affect Political Participation in East Asia? Explaining Divergent Effects," *Asian Perspective* 41, no. 4 (2017), pp. 527–58.

47. James Reardon-Anderson, *Pollution, Politics, and Foreign Investment in Taiwan: The Lukang Rebellion* (New York: Routledge, 1992).

48. Dafydd Fell, "Social Movements in Taiwan after 2008: From the Strawberries to the Sunflowers and Beyond," in *Taiwan's Social Movements under Ma Ying-jeou: From the Wild Straberries to the Sunflowers*, edited by Dafydd Fell (New York: Routledge, 2017; Kindle ed.), loc. 372–433.

49. Ming-sho Ho, *Challenging Beijing's Mandate of Heaven: Taiwan's Sunflower Movement and Hong Kong's Umbrella Movement* (Temple University Press, 2019), pp. 63, 64, 66.

50. On the impact of social media, see Eric Chen-hua Yu and Jia-sin Yu, "Social Media and Cyber Mobilization," in *Dynamics of Democracy in Taiwan*, pp. 311–38.

51. "The Rise of People Power," editorial, *Taipei Times*, August 6, 2013.

52. For a series of case studies that demonstrate the development and learning of activist movements, see Fell, *Taiwan's Social Movement under Ma Ying-jeou.*

53. This discussion is based on Ming-sho Ho, "Occupy Congress in Taiwan: Political Opportunity, Threat, and the Sunflower Movement," *Journal of East Asian Studies* 15, no. 1 (2015), pp. 69–97.

54. Jimmy Hsiung, "2016 State of the Nation Survey: Ready to Test a New President," *CommonWealth Magazine*, January 8, 2016.

55. On this point, I am grateful to Kharis Templeman for his clarification.

56. Results of the poll are in the author's files.

57. "DPP Says Trade Accord Cannot be Forced," *Taipei Times*, March 11, 2014.

58. Ibid.

59. Ibid.

60. The relatively low level of transparency was not dissimilar from that of trade agreements negotiated by the U.S. government.

61. "Lawmakers Get Ready to Tackle Thorny Trade Pact," *Taipei Times*, March 12, 2014.

62. "Legislative Review Descends into Chaos," *Taipei Times*, March 13, 2014.

63. "DPP Renews Trade Pact Renegotiation Call," *Taipei Times*, March 13, 2014.

64. "Trade Pact Review Meeting Cut Short," *Taipei Times,* March 18, 2014.

65. "KMT Obstructs Infrastructure Bill," *Taipei Times*, May 3, 2017.

66. Liu Shih-yi, Liu Kuan-ting, and Evelyn Kao, "Acquittal Verdicts Overturned for 7 Sunflower Movement Protesters," *Focus Taiwan*, April 28, 2020; Liu Kuan-ting, Lin Chang-shun, and Matthew Mazzetta, "Former President Cleared of Using Excessive Force During Protests," *Focus Taiwan*, September 15, 2020.

67. The most useful analyses are Ho, "Occupy Congress in Taiwan"; Andre Beckershoff, "The Sunflower Movement: Origins, Structures and Strategies of Taiwan's Response against the Black Box," in Fell, *Taiwan's Social Movements under Ma Ying-jeou*, and Hsu Szu-chien, "The China Factor and Taiwan's Civil Society Organizations in the Sunflower Movement: The Case of the Democratic Front against the Cross-Strait Service Trade Agreement," in Fell, *Taiwan's Social Movements under Ma Ying-jeou.*

68. Moreover, the service-trade agreement may have been negotiated in a non-

transparent way, but that is often the case with trade agreements (it certainly is in the United States).

69. Fell, "Social Movements in Taiwan after 2008," locs. 714, 731–32.

70. William Yang, "Five Years On, the Sunflower Generation's Outlook for Taiwan," Ketagalan Media, March 19, 2019.

71. Taiwan's (Republic of China) Constitution of 1947 with Amendments through 2005, Constitute Project.

72. H.Con.Res.293, 101st Congress (1989–1990), expressing the sense of the Congress concerning the future of Taiwan.

73. Cited in Shelley Rigger, *From Opposition to Power: Taiwan's Democratic Progressive Party* (Boulder, CO: Lynne Rienner Publishers, 2001), p. 125.

74. Tsai's diagnosis of the Taiwan system at this time echoed with the reason Sun Yat-sen—a Chinese nationalist—advocated instituting mechanisms of direct democracy, that a system of indirect democracy would focus on governing and not be attentive to the views of the people.

75. Additional articles of the ROC Constitution are those that passed during the transition to democracy and subsequently.

76. "Zhonghua Minguo Xianfa Zengxiu Tiaowen" [Additional Articles of the ROC Constitution], website of the constitutional court of the Judicial Yuan (https://law.judicial.gov.tw/FLAW/dat02.aspx?lsid=FL000002&). The Chinese is "經中華民國自由地區選舉人投票複決."

77. Joseph Lee, "The Referendum Law 2003 in Taiwan: Not Yet the End of the Affair," *China Perspectives,* no. 65 (May–June 2006).

78. Ibid.

79. "2018 Human Rights Report (Taiwan Part)."

80. On the same-sex marriage issue, see C. Donovan Smith, "The DPP's Disaster: The Mishandling of Marriage Equality," Ketagalan Media, May 14, 2019.

81. "Tsai, DPP Defend Referendum Act Amendment," *Focus Taiwan,* July 7, 2019.

82. Ibid.

83. Nathan Batto, "Energy Policy and Referenda," *Frozen Garlic* (blog), December 1, 2018.

84. Nathan Batto, "Do Referendums Reflect Public Opinion?" *Frozen Garlic* (blog), November 7, 2019.

85. Marc F. Plattner, "Populism, Pluralism, and Liberal Democracy," *Journal of Democracy* 21, no. 1 (2010), pp. 81–92.

86. Jan-Werner Muller, *What Is Populism?* (University of Pennsylvania Press, 2016), p. 101.

87. Cas Mudde, "The Populist Zeitgeist," *Government and Opposition*, 29, no. 4 (2004), p. 543.

88. Huang is affiliated with the Institute of Sociology at Academia Sinica.

89. Hsin-huang Michael Hsiao, "Observations on Rising Populism in Taiwan Politics," *Ketagalan Media*, August 6, 2019; reprinted from *Global Taiwan Brief,* July 31, 2019.

90. Nathan Batto, "Populism and Han Kuo-yu," *Frozen Garlic* (blog), December 27, 2019.

91. C. Donovan Smith, "Political Power Players to Watch, Part 1: Terry Gou, Ko Wen-che, and Wang Jin-pymg," Ketagalan Media, August 29, 2019.

92. Ibid.

93. William Yang, "Five Years On, the Sunflower Generation's Outlook for Taiwan," Ketagalan Media, March 19, 2019.

94. Yi-chih Wang, "Who Are Han Kuo-yu's Hardcore Fans?," *CommonWealth Magazine,* July 17, 2019.

95. "Meilidao Mindiao: 2019 nian, 11 yue Guozheng Mindiao," [My Formosa public opinion poll: November 2019, National Politics Poll], *Meilidao Dianzibao* [My Formosa], November 2019, table 10, (http://my-formosa.com/DOC_151991 .htm).

96. Nathan F. Batto, "When Populism Can't Beat Identity Politics," *New York Times,* January 12, 2020.

97. Chu and others, "Re-assessing the Popular Foundation of Asian Democracies."

98. *Social Science Encyclopedia,* 3rd ed., *s.v.* "legitimacy."

99. Richard C. Bush, *Hong Kong under the Shadow of China: Living with the Leviathan* (Brookings Institution Press, 2016), pp. 161, 168–69.

100. Daniel Bell, a political theorist at Beijing's Tsinghua University, writes, "The basic idea of political meritocracy is that everybody should have an equal opportunity to be educated and to contribute to politics, but not everybody will emerge from this process with an equal capacity to make morally informed political judgments. Hence, the task of politics is to identify those with above average ability and to make them serve the political community. If the leaders perform well, the people will basically go along." See Daniel A. Bell, *The East Asian Challenge for Democracy: Political Meritocracy in Comparative Perspective,* edited by Daniel A. Bell and Chenyang Li (Cambridge University Press, 2013), introduction, pp. 3, and pp. 238–340.

Chapter 14

1. Matt Rivers, Steven Jiang, and Ben Westcott, "Taiwan Vulnerable to Chinese Invasion without US, Foreign Minister Says," CNN, July 23, 2018.

2. The PLA did shell the offshore island of Jinmen (Quemoy) in August 1958, and U.S. forces assisted the Republic of China military in holding its ground. It was a serious national security crisis, but any threat to the island of Taiwan was more psychological than military.

3. On why, see Richard C. Bush, "The 'Sacred Texts' of United States–China–Taiwan Relations," in *At Cross Purposes: U.S.-Taiwan Relations since 1942* (Armonk, N.Y.: M. E. Sharpe, 2004), pp. 124–78.

4. Ibid.

5. Richard C. Bush, *Untying the Knot: Making Peace in the Taiwan Strait* (Brookings Institution Press, 2005).

6. Mike Pence, "Remarks by Vice President Pence on the Administration's Policy toward China," White House, Washington, D.C., October 4, 2018.

7. Rita Cheng and Joseph Yeh, "U.S. Supports Taiwan Self-Defense Capability: Schriver," *Focus Taiwan*, February 8, 2019.

8. David Stilwell, "Statement of David Stilwell Nominee to be Assistant Secretary of State for East Asian and Pacific Affairs," Washington, D.C., March 27, 2019, Senate Committee on Foreign Relations.

9. Mike Pence, "Remarks by Vice President Pence at the Frederic V. Malek Memorial Lecture," Conrad Hotel (Washington, D.C., October 24, 2019), White House.

10. Stephen E. Biegun, "U.S. Policy toward China," testimony before the Senate Committee on Foreign Relations, July 22, 2020.

11. *Indo-Pacific Strategy Report: Preparedness, Partnerships, and Promoting a Networked Region* (U.S. Department of Defense, June 1, 2019).

12. Ibid., "Message from the Secretary of Defense," n.p.

13. Ibid, pp. 7–8.

14. Ibid., p. 31.

15. Ibid., p. 21; emphasis added. Note that the report does not state a commitment to come to Taiwan's defense if it is attacked.

16. John Bolton, "The Scandal of Trump's China Policy," *Wall Street Journal*, June 17, 2020.

17. Elaine Hou, Matt Yu, and Emerson Lim, "U.S., Taiwan Seal Arms Deals," *Focus Taiwan*, December 21, 2019.

18. Bush, *At Cross Purposes*.

19. Warren Christopher, "American Interests and the U.S.-China Relationship," address to the Asia Society, the Council on Foreign Relations, and the National Committee on U.S.-China Relations, New York, May 17, 1996; cited in Shirly Kan, *China/Taiwan: Evolution of the 'One China' Policy; Key Statements from Washington, Beijing, and Taipei* (Washington, D.C.: Congressional Research Service, October 10, 2014) , pp. 60–61.

20. James A. Kelly, "Overview of U.S. Policy toward Taiwan," testimony before the House International Relations Committee Hearing on Taiwan, Washington, D.C., April 21, 2004.

21. Thomas Wright, "The 2016 Presidential Campaign and the Crisis of American Foreign Policy," Lowy Institute, October 10, 2016.

22. Bob Woodward, *Fear: Trump in the White House* (New York: Simon and Schuster, 2019), p. 305.

23. Josh Rogin, "Trump Is Failing to Counter China's Diplomatic Assault on Taiwan," *Washington Post*, September 6, 2018.

24. Bolton, "The Scandal of Trump's China Policy."

25. *The CIA World Factbook*, 2020–2021 (New York: Skyhorse Publishing, 2020), pp. 916–17.

26. U.S. Census Bureau, "Top Trading Partners, December 2019."

27. "Number of International Students in the U.S., by Country of Origin, 2018–19," *Statista*.

28. Yeh Su-ping, Emerson Lim, and Evelyn Kao, "President Pitches Bilateral Trade Pact in Meeting with U.S. Official," *Focus Taiwan*, December 19, 2019.

29. Derek Scissors, "Prospects for US-Taiwan Economic and Trade Cooperation in 2020," remarks at panel discussion, Global Taiwan Institute, Washington, D.C., February 5, 2020.

30. Ana Swanson, "U.S. to Start Trade Talks with Kenya to Counter China's Influence," *New York Times*, February 6, 2020.

31. American Chamber of Commerce in Taipei, "AmCham Taipei White Paper, 2020 edition," *Taiwan Business Topics* 50, no. 6 (June 2019), p. 13.

32. "President Tsai Issues Remarks Regarding International Trade," Office of the President website, August 28, 2020.

33. Shelley Shan, "KMT Thwarts Premier's Policy Address," *Taipei Times*, September 23, 2020.

34. Chen Chun-hua, Yeh Su-ping, and Matthew Mazzetta, "KMT Submits Petition for Referendum on Government Pork Policy," *Focus Taiwan*, September 23, 2020.

35. Lee Hsien-feng, Wang Chen-chung, and Elizabeth Hsu, "KMT Pushes Local Governments to Set, Uphold Anti-Ractopamine Rules," *Focus Taiwan*, August 31, 2020.

36. Early in Trump's term, the United States did impose tariffs on steel imported from a number of countries, including Taiwan, on the implausible grounds that those imports posed a threat to U.S. national security.

37. Matthew Fulco, "Is Taiwan Winning the U.S.-China Trade War?," *Taiwan Business Topics* 49, no. 8 (2019), pp. 16–20.

38. Hannah Kirk, "The Geo-Technological Triangle between the US, China, and Taiwan," *The Diplomat*, February 8, 2020.

39. Ali Wyne, "Potential Downsides to U.S.-China Trade Tensions on Taiwan's Economy," *Global Taiwan Brief* 5, no. 5 (2020); Raymond Zhong, "U.S.-China Tech Feud, Taiwan Feels Heat from Both Sides," *New York Times*, October 1, 2020.

40. Ana Swanson, "U.S. Delivers Another Blow to Huawei with New Tech Restrictions," *New York Times*, May 15, 2020; Ana Swanson, Paul Mozur, and Raymond Zhong, "U.S. Is Using Taiwan as a Pressure Point in Tech Fight with China," *New York Times*, May 19, 2020.

41. "TSMC Warns China-U.S. Deleveraging Will Drive Up Costs," Reuters, September 24, 2020.

42. In January 2020, it was reported that the Trump administration had pressured TSMC to move production of the chips it provides to the U.S. military projects to the United States. See Lauly Li and Cheng Ting-fang, "Exclusive: Washington Pressures TSMC to Make Chips in US," *Nikkei Asian Review*, January 15, 2020.

43. Lindsey Ford, "Refocusing the China Debate: American Allies and the Question o US-China 'Decoupling,'" Brookings Institution, February 7, 2020.

44. U.S. Congress, Public Law 115-232, "John S. McCain National Defense Authorization Act for Fiscal Year 2019," H.R. 5515, secs. 1257 and 1258.

45. U.S. Congress, Public Law 115-135, "Taiwan Travel Act," H.R 535.

46. U.S. Congress, 116th Congress, "Taiwan Symbols of Sovereignty (SOS) Act of 2020," S. 3310.

47. Donald J. Trump, *Statement on Signing the John S. McCain National Defense Authorization Act for Fiscal Year 2019 August 13, 2018* (Government Printing Office); emphasis added.

48. Taiwan National Security Survey, Program in Asian Security Studies, Duke University (https://sites.duke.edu/pass/taiwan-national-security-survey/).

49. Su Chi, "Should Taiwan Take Sides between the U.S. and China?," *United Daily News,* June 16, 2019.

50. Parris Chang, "Taiwan Must Act on US Goodwill," *Taipei Times*, August 30, 2018.

51. Taiwan National Security Survey.

52. Barbara Weisel, "Next Steps for Enhancing US-Taiwan Trade Relations," *Global Taiwan Brief* 5, no. 19 (September 24, 2020).

53. On the rhetorical imprecision of successive American administrations, see Alan D. Romberg, *Rein In at the Brink of the Precipice: American Policy towards Taiwan and U.S.-PRC Relations* (Washington, D.C.: Henry L. Stimson Center, 2003).

54. "Full Text of Clinton's Speech on China Trade Bill" speech delivered at the Paul H. Nitze School of Advanced International Studies, Johns Hopkins University, March 9, 2000.

55. Richard Haass and David Sacks, "American Support for Taiwan Must Be Unambiguous," *Foreign Affairs*, September 2, 2020.

56. Haass and Sacks acknowledge this imperative, but only in passing.

57. Although Haass and Sacks do say that the U.S. statement should include an expression of nonsupport for Taiwan independence, in and of itself that is probably not sufficient to reassure Beijing or a revisionist government in Taipei.

58. Richard C. Bush, "A One-China Policy Primer," Brookings Institution, March 2017.

59. Ryan Hass, "This US-China Downturn May Be Difficult for Taiwan," Brookings Institution, February 24, 2020.

Chapter 15

1. Nathan F. Batto, "When Populism Can't Beat Identity Politics," *New York Times,* January 12, 2020.

2. Bethany Green, "Taiwan's Universities Are Fighting for Their Lives as Birth Rates Plummet," Ketagalan Media, January 30, 2020.

3. Evan A. Feigenbaum, "Assuring Taiwan's Innovation Future," Carnegie Endowment for International Peace, January 2020, pp. 23–25.

4. Ibid., pp. 26–28.

5. Ibid., pp. 30–31.

6. Phillip Liu, "Bill to Ease Way for Foreign Professionals," *Taiwan Business Topics*, August 22, 2017; Matthew Fulco, "Resolving Taiwan's Talent Exodus," *Taiwan Business Topics*, August 22, 2017.

7. Christopher H. Achen and T. Y. Wang "The Power of Identity in Taiwan," in *The Taiwan Voter*, edited by Christopher H. Achen and T. Y. Wang (University of Michigan Press, 2017).

8. Unnamed informant, conversation with author, June 2018. Ironically, my friend's comment recalls the first sentences of the first essay of Mao Zedong's *Selected Works*: "Who are our enemies? Who are our friends? This is a question of the first importance for the revolution. The basic reason why all previous revolutionary struggles in China achieved so little was their failure to unite with real friends in order to attack real enemies." See Mao Zedong, "Analysis of the Classes in Chinese Society" (1925), in *Selected Works of Mao Zedong* (Peking: Foreign Language Press, 1965), p. 1.

9. Native Taiwanese official, conversation with author, May 2012.

10. "Working Together to Realize Rejuvenation of the Chinese Nation and Advance China's Peaceful Reunification," speech by Xi Jinping at the Meeting Marking the 40th Anniversary of the Issuance of the Message to Compatriots in Taiwan, Beijing, January 2, 2019, Taiwan Affairs Office of the State Council, PRC (www.gwytb.gov.cn/m/news/201904/t20190412_12155846.htm).

11. Robert D. Putnam, "Diplomacy and Domestic Politics: The Logic of Two-Level Games," *International Organization* 42, no. 3 (1988), pp. 427–60.

12. Richard C. Bush, *Untying the Knot: Making Peace in the Taiwan Strait* (Brookings Institution Press, 2005), pp. 271–73.

13. Through 2005, passage of constitutional amendments was the responsibility of the now defunct National Assembly. Since then, the LY-centered process described above has been in effect.

14. Ching-hsin Yu, "Trends in Public Opinion," in *Dynamics of Democracy in Taiwan: The Ma Ying-jeou Years*, edited by Kharis Templeman, Yun-han Chu, and Larry Diamond (Boulder, CO: Lynne Reiner Publishers, 2020), p. 269.

15. Flor Wang and Yu Hsiang, "KMT Criticized for Sidestepping Consensus That Enabled Good Relations," *Focus Taiwan*, June 19, 2020; Shih Hsiao-kuang and Dennis Xie, "KMT Task Force Unveils Four Pillars for Stable, Peaceful Cross-Strait Relations," *Taipei Times*, June 20, 2020.

16. William Yang, "KMT's Proposal for Cross-Strait Policy Exposes Generational Differences in Views toward China," *Global Taiwan Brief* 5, no. 13 (2020).

17. David G. Brown, "Can the KMT Reform—and Remain Relevant," *The Diplomat*, September 11, 2020.

18. Gunter Shubert, "Quo Vadis, KMT?" *Taiwan Insight*, June 5, 2020.

19. World Values Survey: Taiwan, 2012, study 552, vol. 20180912 (www.worldvaluessurvey.org/WVSDocumentationWVV6.jsp; click on "WV6_Results_Taiwan 2012_v20180912").

20. John Robert Shepherd, *Statecraft and Political Economy on the Taiwan Frontier, 1600–1800* (Stanford University Press, 1993).

21. Stevan Harrell, "From *Xiedou* to *Yijun*: The Decline of Ethnicity in Northern Taiwan, 1885–1895," *Late Imperial China* 11, no. 1 (1990), pp. 99–127.

22. Dean Acheson, *Present at the Creation: My Years at the State Department* (New York: W. W. Norton, 1969), p. 225.

23. Bipartisanship was not possible when it came to U.S. policy toward China. Republicans strongly supported Chiang Kai-shek and the KMT regime in their fight against Mao's communists, while the Truman administration believed it was in the

United States' interest to disengage from the Chinese civil war, even to the point of accepting the fall of Taiwan.

24. John Lukacs, "Finland Vindicated," *Foreign Affairs* 71, no. 4 (1992), p. 59.

25. Max Jacobson, "Substance and Appearance: Finland," *Foreign Affairs* 18, no. 5 (1980), p. 1041.

26. Bruce Gilley, "Not So Dire Straits: How the Finlandization of Taiwan Benefits U.S. Security," *Foreign Affairs* 89, no. 1 (2010), pp. 44–-60; see also the rejoinder by Hans Mouritzen, "The Difficult Art of Finlandization," *Foreign Affairs* 89, no. 3 (2010), pp. 130–31; also Tu Ho-ting, "Examining the Security Situation," *Taipei Times*, February 20, 2019.

27. Mujib Mashal, Fatima Faizi, and Najim Rahim, "Ghani Takes the Oath of Afghan President; His Rival Does, Too," *New York Times*, March 9, 2020; Vanda Felbab-Brown, "What's in Store after the US-Taliban Deal," Brookings Institution, March 4, 2020.

28. Ma Ying-jeou, "Full Text of President Ma Ying-jeou's Inaugural Address," Taipei, May 20, 2012, *Focus Taiwan*.

29. Tsai Ing-wen, "Full Text of Taiwan President Tsai Ing-wen's Acceptance Speech," Taipei, January 11, 2020, *Focus Taiwan*.

30. As the KMT caucus did in June 2020; see chapter 13.

31. Elizabeth Knowles, ed., *Oxford Dictionary of Quotations* (Oxford University Press, 2009), p. 218.

32. David Brooks, "America Is Facing 5 Epic Crises All at Once," *New York Times*, June 25, 2020.

33. "Working Together to Realize Rejuvenation of the Chinese Nation and Advance China's Peaceful Reunification."

Index

277–278; constitutional amendments and, 333; cooperation with DPP, 341–344; corruption and, 262; democratization of Taiwan and, 108, 254–255; energy policy and, 95, 323; historical views of, 102–103; immigration to Taiwan and, 21; intraparty struggles and, 267–268; majoritarianism and, 264–265, 334; pensions and, 44, 319; during pre-democratic period, 104–107, 281; referendums and, 282–284, 301; Taiwan-China relations and, 120, 124, 128, 242–243, 276–277, 327, 335–336; Taiwanese economy and, 47; Taiwanese national identity and, 193–198, 209, 215, 335; Taiwanese sovereignty and, 211–212, 225; third parties and, 270–271; transitional justice and, 115–118, 320; vetocracy and, 272

Lai Ching-te, William, 246
Lee Ming-che, 235
Lee Teng-hui, 9, 106, 130, 214–219, 248–249, 270; interparty cooperation and, 341; Taiwan-China relations and, 10–11, 15, 49, 141, 166, 214–218, 225, 242, 297; Taiwanese independence and, 10–11, 15, 129–130, 168, 215, 293; Taiwanese national identity and, 197, 286, 293; Taiwan-US relations and, 12; transitional justice and, 108, 323
Legislative Yuan (LY) of Taiwan, 32, 106, 197, 219, 252–253, 280, 322, 343; 1946 constitution and, 253, 322; anti-nuclear movement and, 87; attitudes towards, 261; budgeting process and, 33, 37–39, 176, 257, 272, 322, 326; constitutional amendments and, 131, 221, 283–284, 333; corruption and, 262; COVID-19 pandemic and, 258; culture of, 337; disinformation and,

239; DPP and, 31, 109, 219, 246, 264, 272; economy of Taiwan and, 64–65; education policy and, 322; energy policy and, 99; free trade agreements and, 65, 67; interparty conflict and, 110, 119, 277–278, 337, 341; KMT and, 104, 254, 265; majoritarianism and, 264–265, 268; protest movements and, 27, 45, 273, 278–280, 301; referendums and, 284–285; relative power of, 323; small parties and, 271, 280; Taiwan-China relations and, 106, 268, 272–273, 277, 329; Taiwanese sovereignty and, 216; transitional justice and, 110, . 113, 2576; vetocracy and, 271–272
legitimacy, political, 209, 217, 263, 280, 282, 289–290
Lei Chen, 116
Lepore, Jill, 191
Lien Chan, 206, 207, 219
Light Blue political perspectives, 8–9, 149, 165, 266, 341; interparty cooperation and, 341; party loyalty and, 269–270, 269tt; Taiwan-China relations and, 9, 327–328. *See also* Kuomintang
Light Green political perspectives, 8–9, 149, 266–267, 341; interparty cooperation and, 341; party loyalty and, 269–270, 269tt; Taiwan-China relations and, 9, 327–328. *See also* Democratic Progressive Party
Li Mingju, 235
Lin, Jamie, 57
Lincoln, Abraham, 18
Lin Fei-fan, 280, 287
Ling Frank Hiroshi, 91
Lin Yi-hsiung, 87–89, 107, 115
Liu, Henry, 107, 241
Liu Shi-chung, 59
Liu Ta-yuan, Darby, 335
loyalty, 71

United Kingdom, 188
United Nations: China and, 194, 213;
    Taiwanese membership in, 6, 194,
    210–213, 215, 218, 220, 256, 284
United States: 2016 presidential
    elections in, 237; Afghanistan and,
    339–340; Cold War and, 123–124,
    338–339; congressional bills of,
    305–307; corruption in, 262;
    economic relations with China, 15,
    59, 302–304; electricity prices in,
    98; employment in, 71; free trade
    agreements and, 64–67; happiness
    in, 19; national identity and, 191;
    political relations with China, 6–7,
    107, 124, 292, 294–296, 312–313,
    316; Taiwan and (*See* Taiwan-US
    relations); Taiwan-China unification
    and, 125, 128; tax revenue in, 40;
    WWII and, 123
US Trade Representative (USTR) office,
    301, 307
Uruguay Round (of GATT), 60–61
US-ROC Mutual Defense Treaty,
    124–125, 156

Vandenberg, Arthur, 338, 341
vetocracy, 271–273
victimhood, 205–206, 209
Vietnam, 62
voice, 73–74

Wachman, Alan, 196
Wang Daohan, 214–216
Wang Jin-pyng, 242, 267, 268, 272,
    277–279
Wang Yang, 237
Want Want China Times Media Group,
    236–237
Weber, Max, 189
Westphalian-cum-Vattelian sovereignty,
    190, 211, 332–333

White Terror, 105–106, 108, 116–117
Wilson, Woodrow, 190
Winckler, Edwin, 106
wind power energy generation, 80–85,
    89–90, 93–96, 100, 323
Wolfers, Arnold, 145
Woodward, Bob, 298
World Happiness Report, 19, 23, 319
World Health Organization, 132
World Trade Organization (WTO), 15,
    60–61, 65
World Values Survey (WVS), 22–23,
    260–261, 268, 337
World War II, 6, 122–123, 191, 339
Wu, Joseph, 156, 230, 291
Wu Naiteh, 103, 106

Xi Jimping, 124, 227, 232; Tai-
    wan-China relations and, 133–140,
    142, 147, 243, 288, 319, 329, 343;
    Taiwanese independence and,
    144; Trump administration and,
    299–300, 308, 310, 313
Xinjiang, 122, 137

Yang Zhong, 203
Yao Chia-wen, 116
Yen De-fa, 229–230
Yin, George, 201–202
Yok Yu-min, 149
youth movements, 26–30. *See also* pro-
    test movements
Yuans of Taiwan. *See* Control Yuan;
    Examination Yuan; Executive Yuan;
    Legislative Yuan (LY)
Yu Ching-hsin, 268–270

Zheng Chenggong, 205
Zheng Sufen, 202–203
Zionism, 190–191
Zyzo, William, 71

www.ingramcontent.com/pod-product-compliance
Lightning Source LLC
Chambersburg PA
CBHW030634270326
41929CB00007B/68